# KINGFISHER
# READERS

**level 1**

# Colorful
# Coral Reefs

Thea Feldman

## KINGFISHER
NEW YORK

# KINGFISHER
## LONDON & NEW YORK

Copyright © Kingfisher 2012
Published in the United States by Kingfisher,
175 Fifth Ave., New York, NY 10010
Kingfisher is an imprint of Macmillan Children's Books, London.
All rights reserved.

Distributed in the U.S. and Canada by Macmillan,
175 Fifth Ave., New York, NY 10010

Library of Congress Cataloging-in-Publication data
has been applied for.

Series editor: Thea Feldman
Literacy consultant: Ellie Costa, Bank Street College, New York

ISBN: 978-0-7534-6750-3 (HB)
ISBN: 978-0-7534-6751-0 (PB)

Kingfisher books are available for special promotions
and premiums. For details contact: Special Markets
Department, Macmillan, 175 Fifth Ave.,
New York, NY 10010.

For more information, please visit
www.kingfisherbooks.com

Printed in China
9 8 7 6 5 4 3 2
2TR/1012/WKT/UNTD/105MA

Picture credits
The Publisher would like to thank the following for permission to reproduce their material.
Every care has been taken to trace copyright holders. However, if there have been unintentional
omissions or failure to trace copyright holders, we apologize and will, if informed, endeavor to make
corrections in any future edition.
Top = t; Bottom = b; Center = c; Left = l; Right = r
Cover Shutterstock/tubuceo & bernd.neeser; Pages 3 Frank Lane Picture Agency (FLPA)/R. Dirscherl;
4–5 Photolibrary/Peter Arnold Images; 5 FLPA/Norbert Wu/Minden; 6t FLPA/Chris Newbert/Minden;
6b Corbis/Brandon Cole; 7t Getty/Science Faction; 7b Alamy/Cristiano Burmester; 8t Corbis/Robert
Yin; 8b Getty/Science Faction; 9t Getty/Ken Lucas; 9b Photolibrary/Waterframe Underwater Images;
10 Shutterstock/bunpot; 11 Alamy/Steve Bloom Images; 12t Alamy/Jane Gould; 12b Getty/Comstock
Images; 13t Shutterstock/Vlad61; 13b Shutterstock/marro31; 14t Photolibrary/Imagebroker;
14b Alamy/Amar & Isabelle Guillen; 15t Photolibrary/Ross Armstrong; 15b Photolibrary/Waterframe
Underwater Images; 16 FLPA/Norbert Probst; 17 Shutterstock/Ian Scott; 18 Photolibrary/OSF;
19 Alamy/Satish Arikkath; 20 Photolibrary/Pacific Stock; 21t Photolibrary/Datacraft; 21c Photolibrary/
Bios; 21b Photolibrary/Animals Animals; 22 Shutterstock/Brian Lasenby; 23 Shutterstock/R Gombarik;
24 Shutterstock/John A. Anderson; 25 Photolibrary/Waterframe Underwater Images; 26 Alamy/Bruce
Coleman Inc; 27 Corbis/Carole Valkenier/All Canada Photos; 28–29 Shutterstock/cbpix;
30–31 Photolibrary/OSF.

Welcome to a coral **reef**!

It is the most colorful place in the sea.

Look at all the **coral**!

Coral grows in many sizes, shapes, and colors.

It can look like a rock.

It can look like a plant.

But it is made of many tiny animals that grow connected to one another.

Some coral is called hard coral.

There are many kinds
of hard coral.

Some coral is called soft coral.

There are many kinds
of soft coral.

Look at all the coral reef fish!

There are thousands
of different kinds.

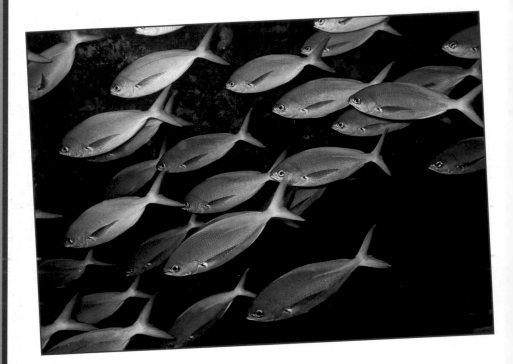

Some fish are one bright color.

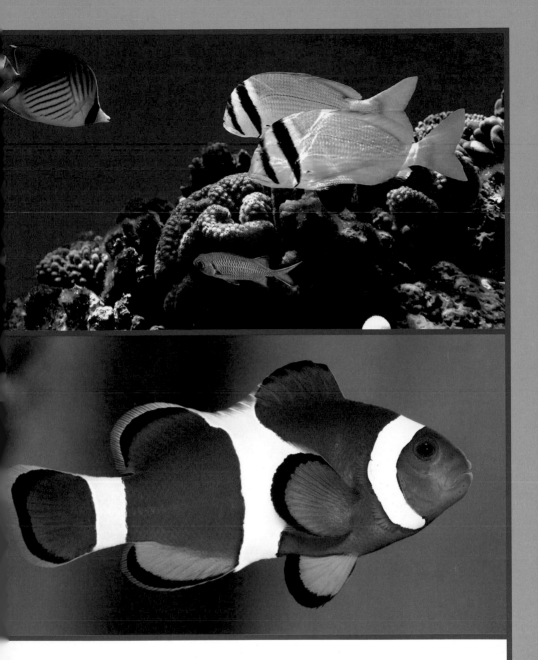

Some fish are more than
one color.

Some fish have stripes.

Some fish have spots.

Did you know that some sharks live in coral reefs?

Sharks are fish too!

**Sea horses** are coral
reef fish too.

So are **sea dragons**!

Many other animals live in coral reefs.

In the daytime,
green turtles swim.

**Sea cucumbers** crawl.

Sea stars
move
on the reef.

Giant clams
stay still.

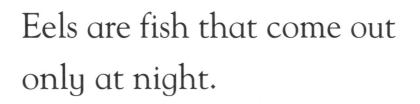

Eels are fish that come out only at night.

Some kinds of crabs come out
at night too.

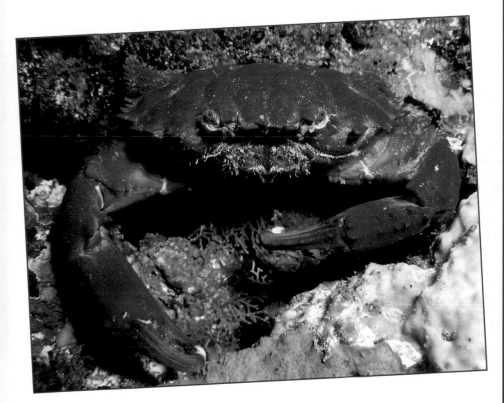

**Sponges** are animals that look like plants.

Sea grass is a coral reef plant.

**Sea anemones** are animals that look like flowers.

They sting fish with poison. Then they eat the fish.

Is this **clown fish** in danger?

No. The sea anemone's poison cannot hurt the clown fish.

In fact, a clown fish can live
in a sea anemone!

So many amazing animals live in colorful coral reefs.

Let's keep coral reefs safe.

The animals are counting on us!

# Glossary

**clown fish**  a colorful coral reef fish that can live in a sea anemone

**coral**  many tiny sea animals that grow together as one animal at a reef

**reef**  a structure under the sea that can be made of coral

**sea anemones**  coral reef animals that look like flowers

**sea cucumbers**  animals that crawl in a coral reef in the daytime

**sea dragons**  coral reef fish that look like dragons

**sea horse**  coral reef fish that look a bit like horses

**sponges**  coral reef animals that look like plants

THIRD EDITION

# Java™ Threads

*Scott Oaks and Henry Wong*

O'REILLY®

Beijing · Cambridge · Farnham · Köln · Paris · Sebastopol · Taipei · Tokyo

**Java™ Threads, Third Edition**
by Scott Oaks and Henry Wong

Copyright © 2004, 1999, 1997 O'Reilly Media, Inc. All rights reserved.
Printed in the United States of America.

Published by O'Reilly Media, Inc., 1005 Gravenstein Highway North, Sebastopol, CA 95472.

O'Reilly books may be purchased for educational, business, or sales promotional use. Online editions are also available for most titles (*safari.oreilly.com*). For more information, contact our corporate/institutional sales department: (800) 998-9938 or *corporate@oreilly.com*.

| | |
|---|---|
| **Editors:** | Mike Loukides and Debra Cameron |
| **Production Editor:** | Matt Hutchinson |
| **Production Services:** | Octal Publishing, Inc. |
| **Cover Designer:** | Emma Colby |
| **Interior Designer:** | David Futato |

**Printing History:**

| | |
|---|---|
| January 1997: | First Edition. |
| January 1999: | Second Edition. |
| September 2004: | Third Edition. |

 This book uses RepKover™, a durable and flexible lay-flat binding.

ISBN: 0-596-00782-5
[M]

# Table of Contents

# Preface

When Sun Microsystems released the alpha version of Java™ in the winter of 1995, developers all over the world took notice. There were many features of Java that attracted these developers, not the least of which were the set of buzzwords Sun used to promote the language. Java was, among other things, robust, safe, architecture-neutral, portable, object-oriented, simple, and multithreaded. For many developers, these last two buzzwords seemed contradictory: how could a language that is multithreaded be simple?

It turns out that Java's threading system is simple, at least relative to other threading systems. This simplicity makes Java's threading system easy to learn so that even developers who are unfamiliar with threads can pick up the basics of thread programming with relative ease.

In early versions of Java, this simplicity came with tradeoffs; some of the advanced features that are found in other threading systems were not available in Java. Java 2 Standard Edition Version 5.0 (J2SE 5.0) changes all of that; it provides a large number of new thread-related classes that make the task of writing multithreaded programs that much easier.

Still, programming with threads remains a complex task. This book shows you how to use the threading tools in Java to perform the basic tasks of threaded programming and how to extend them to perform more advanced tasks for more complex programs.

## Who Should Read This Book?

This book is intended for programmers of all levels who need to learn to use threads within Java programs. This includes developers who have previously used Java and written threaded programs; J2SE 5.0 includes a wealth of new thread-related classes and features. Therefore, even if you've written a threaded program in Java, this book can help you to exploit new features of Java to write even more effective programs.

The first few chapters of the book deal with the issues of threaded programming in Java, starting at a basic level; no assumption is made that the developer has had any experience in threaded programming. As the chapters progress, the material becomes more advanced, in terms of both the information presented and the experience of the developer that the material assumes. For developers who are new to threaded programming, this sequence should provide a natural progression of the topic.

This book is ideally suited to developers targeting the second wave of Java programs—more complex programs that fully exploit the power of Java's threading system. We make the assumption that readers of the book are familiar with Java's syntax and features. In a few areas, we present complex programs that depend on knowledge of other Java features: AWT, Swing, NIO, and so on. However, the basic principles we present should be understandable by anyone with a basic knowledge of Java. We've found that books that deal with these other APIs tend to give short shrift to how multiple threads can fully utilize these features of Java (though doubtless the reverse is true; we make no attempt to explain nonthread-related Java APIs).

Though the material presented in this book does not assume any prior knowledge of threads, it does assume that the reader has knowledge of other areas of the Java API and can write simple Java programs.

## Versions Used in This Book

Writing a book on Java in the age of Internet time is hard—the sand on which we're standing is constantly shifting. But we've drawn a line in that sand, and the line we've drawn is at the Java 2 Standard Edition (J2SE) Version 5.0 from Sun Microsystems. This software was previously known as J2SE Version 1.5.

It's likely that versions of Java that postdate this version will contain some changes to the threading system not discussed in this edition of the book. We will also point out the differences between J2SE 5.0 and previous versions of Java as we go so that developers using earlier releases of Java will also be able to use this book.

Most of the new threading features in J2SE 5.0 are available (with different APIs) from third-parties for earlier versions of Java (including classes we developed in earlier editions of this book). Therefore, even if you're not using J2SE 5.0, you'll get full benefit from the topics covered in this book.

## What's New in This Edition?

This edition includes information about J2SE 5.0. One of the most significant changes in J2SE 5.0 is the inclusion of Java Specification Request (JSR) 166, often referred to as the "concurrency utilities." JSR-166 specifies a number of thread-related enhancements to existing APIs as well as providing a large package of new APIs.

These new APIs include:

*Atomic variables*
> A set of classes that provide threadsafe operations without synchronization

*Explicit locks*
> Synchronization locks that can be acquired and released programmatically

*Condition variables*
> Variables that can be the subject of a targeted notification when certain conditions exist

*Queues*
> Collection classes that are thread-aware

*Synchronization primitives*
> New classes that perform complex types of synchronization

*Thread pools*
> Classes that can manage a pool of threads to run certain tasks

*Thread schedulers*
> Classes that can execute tasks at a particular point in time

We've fully integrated the new features of J2SE 5.0 throughout the text of this edition. The new features can be split into three categories:

*New implementations of existing features*
> The Java language has always had the capability to perform data synchronization and thread notification. However, implementation of these features was somewhat limited; you could, for example, synchronize blocks of code or entire methods but synchronizing across methods and classes required extra programming. In J2SE 5.0, explicit locks and condition variables allow you more flexibility when using these features.
>
> These new implementations do not introduce new concepts for a developer. A developer who wants to write a threadsafe program must ensure that her data is correctly synchronized, whether she uses J2SE 5.0's explicit locks or the more basic synchronized keyword. Therefore, both are presented together when we talk about data synchronization. The same is true of condition variables, which provide thread notification and are discussed alongside Java's wait( ) and notify( ) methods, and of queues, which are discussed along with Java's other collection classes.

*Important thread utilities*
> At some point in time, virtually all developers who write threaded programs will need to use basic thread utilities such as a pool or a scheduler; many of them will also need to use advanced synchronization primitives. A recognition of this fact is one thing that drove JSR-166—it was certainly possible in previous versions of Java to develop your own thread pools and schedulers. But given the importance

of threading in the Java platform, adding these basic utilities greatly increases programmer productivity.

*Minimal synchronization utilities*

Java's new atomic classes provide a means by which developers can, when necessary, write applications that avoid synchronization. This can lead to programs that are highly concurrent.

If you've read previous editions of this book, the concepts presented in the first two categories will be familiar. In previous editions, we developed our own data synchronization classes, thread pools, and so on. In those editions, we explained in detail how our implementations worked and then used them in several examples. In this edition, we focus solely on how to use these classes effectively.

The information that falls into the third category is completely new to this edition. The classes that perform minimal synchronization require new support from the virtual machine itself and could not be developed independent of those changes.

# Organization of This Book

Here's an outline of the book, which includes 15 chapters and 1 appendix:

Chapter 1, *Introduction to Threads*

This chapter forms a basic introduction to the topic of threads: why they are useful and our approach to discussing them.

Chapter 2, *Thread Creation and Management*

This chapter shows you how to create threads and runnable objects while explaining the basic principles of how threads work.

Chapter 3, *Data Synchronization*

This chapter discusses the basic level at which threads share data safely—coordinating which thread is allowed to access data at any time. Sharing data between threads is the underlying topic of our next four chapters.

Chapter 4, *Thread Notification*

This chapter discusses the basic technique threads use to communicate with each other when they have changed data. This allows threads to respond to data changes instead of polling for such changes.

Chapter 5, *Minimal Synchronization Techniques*

This chapter discusses classes and programming methods that achieve data safety while using a minimal amount of synchronization.

Chapter 6, *Advanced Synchronization Topics*

In this chapter, we complete our examination of data sharing and synchronization with an examination of deadlock, starvation, and miscellaneous locking classes.

Chapter 7, *Threads and Swing*

Swing classes are not threadsafe. This chapter discusses how multithreaded programs can take full advantage of Swing.

Chapter 8, *Threads and Collection Classes*

Java collection classes are written for a variety of circumstances. Some are threadsafe and some are not, and J2SE 5.0 introduces new collection classes for use specifically with thread utilities. We sort all that out in this chapter.

Chapter 9, *Thread Scheduling*

Scheduling is the process whereby a single CPU selects a thread to run. Thread scheduling is more a property of an operating system (OS) than a Java program, and this chapter discusses the relationship between the virtual machine and the OS in this area.

Chapter 10, *Thread Pools*

This chapter discusses thread pools—a collection of threads that can be used to run arbitrary tasks. We use the thread pool implementation of J2SE 5.0 for discussion of the general principles of using thread pools.

Chapter 11, *Task Scheduling*

Task schedulers execute a task one or more times at some point in the future. This set of classes includes timers (Java has had timer classes since JDK 1.3) and a general task scheduler available in J2SE 5.0.

Chapter 12, *Threads and I/O*

Dealing with I/O is one of the primary reasons why developers use threads in Java. In this chapter, we use all of Java's threading features to show you how to handle I/O effectively in multithreaded programs.

Chapter 13, *Miscellaneous Thread Topics*

In this chapter, we complete our examination of thread-related features of Java by examining thread security, thread groups, thread stacks, and other topics.

Chapter 14, *Thread Performance*

Performance of thread-related features—and particularly synchronization constructs—is key to writing multithreaded programs. In this chapter, we test various low-level programming features and explore some truths and myths about thread performance.

Chapter 15, *Parallelizing Loops for Multiprocessor Machines*

In this chapter, we show a process for exploiting the power of multiprocessor machines to calculate CPU-intensive loops in parallel.

Appendix, *Superseded Threading Utilities*

J2SE 5.0 introduces a number of thread-related classes. Many of these classes are similar to classes developed in previous editions of this book; we list those classes in this appendix as an aid to developers who cannot yet upgrade to J2SE 5.0.

# Conventions Used in This Book

The following typographical conventions are used in this book:

*Italic*

Indicates URLs and filenames, and is used to introduce new terms. Sometimes we explain thread features using a question-and-answer format. Questions posed by the reader are rendered in italic.

`Constant width`

Indicates code examples, methods, variables, parameters, and keywords within the text.

**`Constant width bold`**

Indicates user input, such as commands that you type on the command line.

# Code Examples

All examples presented in the book are complete, running applications. However, many of the program listings are shortened because of space and readability considerations. The full examples may be retrieved online from *http://www.oreilly.com/catalog/jthreads3*.

This book is here to help you get your job done. In general, you may use the code in this book in your programs and documentation. You do not need to contact us for permission unless you're reproducing a significant portion of the code. For example, writing a program that uses several chunks of code from this book does not require permission. Selling or distributing a CD-ROM of examples from O'Reilly books *does* require permission. Answering a question by citing this book and quoting example code does not require permission. Incorporating a significant amount of example code from this book into your product's documentation *does* require permission.

We appreciate, but do not require, attribution. An attribution usually includes the title, author, publisher, and ISBN. For example: "*Java Threads*, Third Edition, by Scott Oaks and Henry Wong. Copyright 2004 O'Reilly Media, 0-596-00782-5."

If you feel your use of code examples falls outside fair use or the permission given above, feel free to contact us at *permissions@oreilly.com*.

# How to Contact Us

Please address comments and questions concerning this book to the publisher:

O'Reilly Media, Inc.
1005 Gravenstein Highway North
Sebastopol, CA 95472

(800) 998-9938 (in the United States or Canada)
(707) 829-0515 (international or local)
(707) 829-0104 (fax)

O'Reilly maintains a web page for this book, where we list errata, examples, and any additional information. You can access this page at:

*http://www.oreilly.com/catalog/jthreads3*

To comment or ask technical questions about this book, send email to:

*bookquestions@oreilly.com*

For more information about O'Reilly books, conferences, Resource Centers, and the O'Reilly Network, see our web site at:

*http://www.oreilly.com*

## Safari Enabled

 When you see the Safari® Enabled icon on the back cover of your favorite technology book, that means the book is available online through the O'Reilly Network Safari Bookshelf.

Safari offers a solution that's better than e-books. It's a virtual library that lets you easily search thousands of top technology books, cut and paste code samples, download chapters, and find quick answers when you need the most accurate, current information.

Try it for free at *http://safari.oreilly.com*.

## Acknowledgments

As readers of prefaces are well aware, writing a book is never an effort undertaken solely by the authors who get all the credit on the cover. We are deeply indebted to the following people for their help and encouragement: Michael Loukides, who believed us when we said that this was an important topic and who shepherded us through the creative process; David Flanagan, for valuable feedback on the drafts; Deb Cameron, for editing sometimes rambling text into coherency; Hong Zhang, for helping us with Windows threading issues; and Reynold Jabbour, Wendy Talmont, Steve Wilson, and Tim Cramer for supporting us in our work over the past six years.

Mostly, we must thank our respective families. To James, who gave Scott the support and encouragement necessary to see this book through (and to cope with his continual state of distraction), and to Nini, who knew to leave Henry alone for the ten percent of the time when he was creative, and encouraged him the rest of the time—thank you for everything!

Finally, we must thank the many readers of the earlier editions of this book who sent us invaluable feedback. We have tried our best to answer every concern that they have raised. Keep those cards and letters coming!

# CHAPTER 1

# Introduction to Threads

This is a book about using threads in the Java programming language and the Java virtual machine. The topic of threads is very important in Java—so important that many features of the threading system are built into the Java language itself while other features of the threading system are required by the Java virtual machine. Threading is an integral part of using Java.

The concept of threads is not a new one: for some time, many operating systems have had libraries that provide the C programmer a mechanism to create threads. Other languages, such as Ada, have support for threads embedded into the language, much as support for threads is built into the Java language. Nonetheless, until Java came along, the topic of threads was usually considered a peripheral programming topic, one that was only needed in special programming cases.

With Java, things are different: it is impossible to write any but the simplest Java program without introducing the topic of threads. And the popularity of Java ensures that many developers, who might never have considered learning about threading possibilities in a language such as C or C++, need to become fluent in threaded programming.

Futhermore, the Java platform has matured throughout the years. In Java 2 Standard Edition Version 5.0 (J2SE 5.0), the classes available for thread-related programming rival many professional threading packages, mitigating the need to use any commercial library (as was somewhat common in previous releases of Java). So Java developers not only need to become knowledgeable in threaded programming to write basic applications but will want to learn the complete, rich set of classes available for writing complex, commercial-grade applications.

# Java Terms

Let's start by defining some terms used throughout this book. Many Java-related terms are used inconsistently in various sources; we endeavor to be consistent in our usage of these terms throughout the book.

*Java*

First, is the term Java itself. As you know, Java started out as a programming language, and many people today still think of Java as being simply a programming language. But Java is much more than just a programming language: it's also an API specification and a virtual machine specification. So when we say Java, we mean the entire Java platform: the programming language, its APIs, and a virtual machine specification that, taken together, define an entire programming and runtime environment. Often when we say Java, it's clear from the context that we're talking specifically about the programming language, or parts of the Java API, or the virtual machine. The point to remember is that the threading features we discuss in this book derive their properties from all the components of the Java platform taken as a whole. While it's possible to take the Java programming language, directly compile it into assembly code, and run it outside of the virtual machine, such an executable may not necessarily behave the same as the programs we describe in this book.

*Virtual machine, interpreters, and browsers*

The Java virtual machine is the code that actually runs a Java program. Its purpose is to interpret the intermediate bytecodes that Java programs are compiled into; the virtual machine is sometimes called the Java interpreter. However, modern virtual machines usually compile the majority of the code they run into native instructions as the program is executing; the result is that the virtual machine does little actual interpretation of code.

Browsers such as Mozilla, Netscape Navigator, Opera, and Internet Explorer all have the capability to run certain Java programs (applets). Historically, these browsers had an embedded virtual machine; today, the standard Java virtual machine runs as a plug-in to these browsers. That means that the threading details of Java-capable browsers are essentially identical to those of a standard Java virtual machine. The one significant area of difference lies in some of the default thread security settings for browsers (see Chapter 13).

Virtual machine implementations are available from many different vendors and for many different operating systems. For the most part, virtual machines are indistinguishable—at least in theory. However, because threads are tied to the operating system on which they run, platform-specific differences in thread behavior do crop up. These differences are important in relatively few circumstances, and we discuss them in Chapter 9.

*Programs, applications, applets, and other code*

This leads us to the terms that we use for things written in the Java language. Like traditional programming models, Java supports the idea of a standalone application, which in the case of Java is run from the command line (or through a desktop chooser or icon). The popularity of Java has led to the creation of many new types of Java-enabled containers that run pieces of Java code called *components*. Web server containers allow you to write components (servlets and Java Server Page or JSP classes) that run inside the web server. Java-enabled browsers allow you to write applets: classes that run inside the Java plug-in. Java 2 Enterprise Edition (J2EE) application servers execute Enterprise Java Beans (EJBs), servlets, JSPs, and so on. Even databases now provide the ability to use server-side Java components.

As far as Java threads are concerned, the distinction between the different types of containers is usually only the location of the objects to be executed. Certain containers place restrictions on threaded operations (which we discuss in Chapter 13), and in that case, we discuss specific components. Apart from the rare case where we specifically mention a type of component, we just use the term program since the concepts discussed apply to all of the Java code you might write.

*Concurrency and threads*

J2SE 5.0 includes a package known as the "concurrency utilities," or JSR-166. Concurrency is a broad term. It includes the ability to perform multiple tasks at the same time; we generally refer to that ability as parallelism. As we'll see throughout this book, threaded programming is about more than parallelism: it's also about simpler program design and coping with certain implementation features of the Java platform. The features of Java (including those of JSR-166) help us with these tasks as well.

Concurrency also includes the ability to access data at the same time in two or more threads. These are issues of data synchronization, which is the term we use when discussing those aspects of concurrency.

## Java Versions, Tools, and Code

We also need to be concerned with specific versions of Java itself. This is an artifact of the popularity of Java, which has led to several major enhancements in the platform. Each version supplements the thread-related classes available to developers, allowing them to work with new features or no longer to rely on externally developed classes.

We focus in this book on J2SE 5.0.* This version contains a wealth of new thread-related classes and features. These classes greatly simplify much of the work in developing threaded applications since they provide basic implementations of common threading paradigms.

The new features of J2SE 5.0 are integrated throughout the Java platform; we've integrated the new features throughout our discussion as well. When we discuss J2SE 5.0, we clearly identify the new features as such. If you're unable to use those features because you cannot yet upgrade the version of Java you're using, you'll find similar functionality to almost all J2SE 5.0 features in the classes provided in the Appendix, which contains implementations of common threading utilities that were developed in previous versions of this book; these utilities use an earlier version of Java.

---

### All Things Just Keep Getting Better

It's interesting to note the differences between this edition of *Java Threads* and the previous editions. In earlier editions of this book, we developed classes to perform explicit locks, condition variables, thread pooling, task scheduling, and so on. All that functionality and more is now included in the core J2SE 5.0 platform. In Chapter 14, we look at thread performance; the performance of basic thread-related operations (and especially uncontended lock acquisition) has greatly improved since we first looked at this in JDK 1.1. And in order to obtain meaningful, long-running results for our parallelism tests in Chapter 15, we had to increase the number of calculations by a significant factor.

---

## About the Examples

Full code to run all the examples in this book can be downloaded from *http://www.oreilly.com/catalog/jthreads3*.

Code is organized by packages in terms of chapter number and example number. Within a chapter, certain classes apply to all examples and are in the chapter-related package (e.g., package javathreads.examples.ch02). The remaining classes are in an example-specific package (e.g., package javathreads.examples.ch02.example1). Package names are shown within the text for all classes.

Examples within a chapter (and often between chapters) tend to be iterative, each one building on the classes of previous examples. Within the text, we use ellipses in

---

* Note the version number change or perhaps we should say leap. The predecessor to J2SE 5.0 was J2SE 1.4. In beta, J2SE 5.0 was also known as J2SE 1.5. In this book, we refer to earlier versions using the more commonly used phrase JDK 1.x rather than J2SE 1.x.

code samples to indicate that the code is unchanged from previous examples. For instance, consider this partial example from Chapter 2:

```
package javathreads.examples.ch02.example2;
...
public class SwingTypeTester extends JFrame {
    ...
    private JButton stopButton;
    ...
    private void initComponents( ) {
        ...
        stopButton = new JButton( );
```

The package name tells us that this is the second example in Chapter 2. Following the ellipses, we see that there is a new instance variable (stopButton) and some new code added to the initComponents( ) method.

For reference purposes, we list the examples and their main class at the end of each chapter.

## Compiling and Running the Examples

The code examples are written to be compiled and run on J2SE 5.0. We use several new classes of J2SE 5.0 throughout the examples and occasionally use new language features of J2SE 5.0 as well. This means that classes must be compiled with a -source argument:

```
piccolo% java -source 1.5 javathreads/examples/ch02/example1/*.java
```

While the -source argument is not needed for a great many of our examples, we always use it for consistency.

Running the examples requires using the entire package name for the main class:

```
piccolo% java javathreads.examples.ch02.example1.SwingTypeTester
```

It is always possible to run each example in this fashion: first compile all the files in the example directory and then run the specific class. This can lead to a lot of typing. To make this easier, we've also supplied an Ant build file that can be used to compile and run all examples.

The ant build file we supply has a target for each example that you can run; these targets are named by chapter and example number. For instance, to run the first example from Chapter 2, you can execute this command:

```
piccolo% ant ch2-ex1
```

The ant target for each example is also listed at the end of each chapter. Some examples require a command-line argument. When using ant, these arguments have a default value (specified in the *build.xml* file) and can be overridden on the command line. For example, to specify the number of threads for a particular example in Chapter 5, you can run the example like this:

```
piccolo% ant -DCalcThreadCount=5 ch5-ex4
```

---

### Ant

On its home page, *http://ant.apache.org*, the authors describe Ant as "a Java-based build tool. In theory, it is kind of like Make, but without Make's wrinkles." Because it's written in Java, it is portable; its design makes it extensible as well.

To use Ant, you must download it from *http://ant.apache.org/*. Unzip the downloaded archive, and add the ant binary directory to your path.

You don't need to know anything about how ant works in order to use it for our examples, but if you're planning on doing serious Java development, learning about ant is well worth the (rather minimal) effort.

---

The properties and their defaults are listed at the end of the chapter, like this:

```
<property name="CalcThreadCount" value="10"/>
```

# Why Threads?

The notion of threading is so ingrained in Java that it's almost impossible to write even the simplest programs in Java without creating and using threads. And many of the classes in the Java API are already threaded, so often you are using multiple threads without realizing it.

Historically, threading was first exploited to make certain programs easier to write: if a program can be split into separate tasks, it's often easier to program the algorithm as separate tasks or threads. Programs that fall into this category are typically specialized and deal with multiple independent tasks. The relative rareness of these types of programs makes threading in this category a specialized skill. Often, these programs were written as separate processes using operating system–dependent communication tools such as signals and shared memory spaces to communicate between processes. This approach increased system complexity.

The popularity of threading increased when graphical interfaces became the standard for desktop computers because the threading system allowed the user to perceive better program performance. The introduction of threads into these platforms didn't make the programs any faster, but it created an illusion of faster performance for the user, who now had a dedicated thread to service input or display output.

In the 1990s, threaded programs began to exploit the growing number of computers with multiple processors. Programs that require a lot of CPU processing are natural candidates for this category since a calculation that requires one hour on a single-processor machine could (at least theoretically) run in half an hour on a two-processor machine or 15 minutes on a four-processor machine. All that is required is that the program be written to use multiple threads to perform the calculation.

Although computers with multiple processors have been around for a long time, we're now seeing these machines become cheap enough to be very widely available. The advent of less expensive machines with multiple processors, and of operating systems that provide programmers with thread libraries to exploit those processors, has made threaded programming a hot topic as developers move to extract every benefit from these machines. Until Java, much of the interest in threading centered on using threads to take advantage of multiple processors on a single machine.

However, threading in Java often has nothing at all to do with multiprocessor machines and their capabilities; in fact, the first Java virtual machines were unable to take advantage of multiple processors on a machine. Modern Java virtual machines no longer suffer from this limitation, and a multithreaded Java program takes advantage of all the CPUs available on its host machine. However, even if your Java program is destined to be run on a machine with a single CPU, threading is still very important.

One reason that threading is important in Java is that, until JDK 1.4, Java had no concept of asynchronous behavior for I/O. This meant that many of the programming techniques you've become accustomed to using in typical programs were not applicable in Java; instead, until recently, Java programmers had to use threading techniques to handle asynchronous behavior. Another reason is the graphical nature of Java; since the beginning, Java was intended to be used in browsers, and it is used widely in environments with graphical user interfaces. Programmers need to understand threads merely to be able to use the asynchronous nature of the GUI library.

This is not to say there aren't other times when threads are a handy programming technique in Java; certainly it's easy to use Java for a program that implements an algorithm that naturally lends itself to threading. And many Java programs implement multiple independent behaviors. The next few sections cover some of the circumstances in which Java threads are a needed component of the program—either directly using threads or using Java libraries that make heavy use of threads. Many of these circumstances are due to the need for asynchronous behavior or the elegance that threading lends to the program.

## Nonblocking I/O

In Java, as in most programming languages, when you try to get input from the user, you execute a read( ) method specifying the user's terminal (System.in in Java). When the program executes the read( ) method, the program typically waits until the user types at least one character before it continues and executes the next statement. This type of I/O is called *blocking I/O*: the program blocks until some data is available to satisfy the read( ) method.

This type of behavior is often undesirable. If you're reading data from a network socket, that data is often not available when you want to read it: the data may have been delayed in transit over the network, or you may be reading from a network server that sends data only periodically. If the program blocks when it tries to read from the socket, it's unable to do anything else until the data is actually available. If the program has a user interface that contains a button and the user presses the button while the program is executing the read( ) method, nothing happens: the program is unable to handle the mouse events and execute the event processing method associated with the button. This can be very frustrating for the user, who thinks the program has hung.

Traditionally, three techniques are available to handle this situation:

*I/O Multiplexing*

Developers often take all input sources and use a system call like select( ) to notify them when data is available from a particular source. This allows input to be handled much like an event from the user (in fact, many graphical toolkits use this method transparently to the developer, who simply registers a callback function that is called whenever data is available from a particular source).

Beginning with JDK 1.4, this feature is provided with the NIO library—a library that allows a programmer to deal with I/O in an asynchronous manner.

*Polling*

Polling allows a developer to test if data is available from a particular source. If data is available, the data can be read and processed: if it is not, the program can perform another task. Polling can be done either explicitly—with a system call like poll( )—or, in some systems, by making the read( ) function return an indication that no data is immediately available.

Polling is also supported by the NIO library of JDK 1.4. In the traditional I/O library, there is only limited support for polling via the available( ) method of the FilterInputStream class. Unfortunately, this method does not have the rich semantics that polling typically has in most operating systems and is not recommended as a reliable technique to determine whether data is actually available.

*Signals*

A file descriptor representing the input source can often be set so that an asynchronous signal is delivered to the program when data is available on that input source. This signal interrupts the program, which processes the data and then returns to whatever task it had been doing. Java does not support this technique.

While the issue of blocking I/O can conceivably occur with any data source, it occurs most frequently with network sockets. If you're used to programming sockets, you've probably used one of these techniques to read from a socket, but perhaps not to write to one. Many developers, used to programming on a local area network (LAN), are vaguely aware that writing to a socket may also block, but it's a possibility that many of them ignore because it happens only under certain circumstances, such as a backlog in getting data onto the network. This backlog rarely happens on a fast LAN, but if you're using Java to program sockets over the Internet, the chances of this backlog happening are greatly increased, thus increasing the chance of blocking while attempting to write data onto the network. In Java, you may need two threads to handle the socket: one to read from the socket and one to write to it.

As a result, writing a program that uses I/O means either using multiple threads to handle traditional (blocking) I/O or using the NIO library (or both). The NIO library itself is very complex—much more complex than the thread library. Consequently, it is still often easier to set up a separate thread to read the data (using traditional I/O) from a blocking data source. This separate thread can block when data isn't available, and the other thread(s) in the Java program can process events from the user or perform other tasks.

On the other hand, there are many times when the added complexity of the NIO library is worthwhile and where the proliferation of threads required to process thousands of data sources would be untenable. But using the NIO library doesn't remove all threading complexities; that library has its own thread-related issues.

We examine the threading issues related to I/O in depth in Chapter 12.

## Alarms and Timers

Traditional operating systems typically provide some sort of timer or alarm call: the program sets the timer and continues processing. When the timer expires, the program receives some sort of asynchronous signal that notifies the program of the timer's expiration.

In early versions of Java, the programmer had to set up a separate thread to simulate a timer. That thread slept for the duration of a specified time interval and then notified other threads when the timer expired. As Java matured, multiple new classes that provide this functionality were added. These new classes use the exact same technique to provide the functionality, but they hide (at least some of) the threading details from the developer. For complete details on these timers, see Chapter 11.

## Independent Tasks

A Java program is often called on to perform independent tasks. In the simplest case, a single applet may perform two independent animations for a web page. A more complex program would be a calculation server that performs calculations on behalf of several clients simultaneously. In either case, while it is possible to write a single-threaded program to perform multiple tasks, it's easier and more elegant to place each task in its own thread.

The complete answer to the question "Why threads?" really lies in this category. As programmers, we're trained to think linearly and often fail to see simultaneous paths that our program might take. But there's no reason why processes that we've conventionally thought of in a single-threaded fashion need necessarily remain so: when the Save button in a word processor is pressed, we typically have to wait a few seconds until we can continue. Worse yet, the word processor may periodically perform an autosave, which invariably interrupts the flow of typing and disrupts the thought process. In a threaded word processor, the save operation would be in a separate thread so that it didn't interfere with the work flow. As you become accustomed to writing programs with multiple threads, you'll discover many circumstances in which adding a separate thread makes your algorithms more elegant and your programs more responsive.

## Parallelizable Algorithms

With the advent of virtual machines that can use multiple CPUs simultaneously, Java has become a useful platform for developing programs that use algorithms that can be parallelized; that is, running one iteration of the loop on one CPU while another iteration of the loop is simultaneously running on another CPU. Dependencies between the data that each iteration of the loop needs may prohibit a particular loop from being parallelized, and there may be other reasons why a loop should not be parallelized. But for many programs with CPU-intensive loops, parallelizing the loop greatly speeds up the execution of the program when it is run on a machine with multiple processors.

Many languages have compilers that support automatic parallelization of loops, but as yet, Java does not. However, as we'll see in Chapter 15, parallelizing a loop by hand is often not a difficult task.

# Summary

In this chapter, we've provided a basic overview of where we're going in our exploration of threaded programs. Threading is a basic feature of Java, and we've seen some of the reasons why it's more important to Java than to other programming platforms.

In the next few chapters, we look into the basics of thread programming. We start by looking at how threads are created and used in an application.

# CHAPTER 2

# Thread Creation and Management

In this chapter, we cover all the basics about threads: what a thread is, how threads are created, and some details about the lifecycle of a thread. If you're new to threading, this chapter gives you all the information you need to create some basic threads. Be aware, however, that we take some shortcuts with our examples in this chapter: it's impossible to write a good threaded program without taking into account the data synchronization issues that we discuss in Chapter 3. This chapter gets you started on understanding how threads work; coupled with the next chapter, you'll have the ability to start using threads in your own Java applications.

## What Is a Thread?

Let's start by discussing what a thread actually is. A thread is an application task that is executed by a host computer. The notion of a task should be familiar to you even if the terminology is not. Suppose you have a Java program to compute the factorial of a given number:

```
package javathreads.examples.ch02.example1;

public class Factorial {
    public static void main(String[] args) {
        int n = Integer.parseInt(args[0]);
        System.out.print(n + "! is ");
        int fact = 1;
        while (n > 1)
            fact *= n--;
        System.out.println(fact);
    }
}
```

When your computer runs this application, it executes a sequence of commands. At an abstract level, that list of commands looks like this:

- Convert args[0] to an integer.
- Store that integer in a location called *n*.

- Print some text.
- Store 1 in a location called fact.
- Test if *n* is greater than 1.
- If it is, multiply the value stored in fact by the value stored in *n* and decrement *n* by 1.
- If it isn't, print out the value stored in fact.

Behind the scenes, what happens is somewhat more complicated since the instructions that are executed are actually machine-level assembly instructions; each of our logical steps requires many machine instructions to execute. But the principle is the same: an application is executed as a series of instructions. The execution path of these instructions is a thread.*

Consequently, every computer program has at least one thread: the thread that executes the body of the application. In a Java application, that thread is called the main thread, and it begins executing statements with the first statement of the main( ) method of your class. In other programming languages, the starting point may be different, and the terminology may be different, but the basic idea is the same.

## Starting a Program

For Java applications, execution begins with the main( ) method of the class being run. What about other Java programs?

In applets, servlets, and other J2EE programs, execution still begins with the main( ) method of the program, but in this case, the main( ) method belongs to the Java plug-in or J2EE container. Those containers then call your code through predetermined, well-known locations. An applet is called via its init( ) and start( ) methods; a servlet is called through its doGet( ) and doPost( ) methods, and so on.

In any case, the procedure is the same: execution of your code begins with the first statements and proceeds by a single thread sequentially.

In a Java program, it turns out that every program has more than one thread. Many of these are threads that developers are unaware of, such as threads that perform garbage collection and compile Java bytecodes into machine-level instructions. In a graphical application, other threads handle input from the mouse and keyboard and play audio. Your Java application is highly threaded, whether you program additional threads into it or not.

---

* Don't get hung up on the strict sequential ordering of the list. As a concept, thinking of a thread as an ordered list of instructions makes a lot of sense, but the ordering can change under certain circumstances (see Chapter 5).

Returning to our example, let's suppose that we wrote a program that performed two tasks: one calculated the factorial of a number and one calculated the square root of that number. These are two separate tasks, and so you could choose to write them as two separate threads. Now how would your application run?

The answer to that depends on the conditions under which the application is run. The Java virtual machine now has two distinct lists of instructions to execute. One list calculates the factorial of a number (as we outlined earlier), and the other list calculates the square root of the number. The Java virtual machine executes both of these lists almost simultaneously.

Although you may not have thought about it in these terms, this situation should also be familiar to you from the computer on which you normally do your work. The program you use to read your email is a list of instructions that the computer executes. So too is the program that you use to listen to music. You're able to read email and listen to music at the same time because the computer executes both lists of instructions at about the same time.

In fact, what happens is that the computer executes a handful of instructions from the email application and then executes a handful of instructions from the music program. It continues this procedure, switching back and forth between lists of instructions, and it does that quickly enough so that both programs appear to be executing at the same time. Quickly enough, in fact, that there are no gaps in the music.

If you happen to have more than one CPU on your computer, the lists of instructions can execute at *exactly* the same time: one list can execute on each CPU. But multiple CPUs aren't necessary to give the appearance of simultaneous execution or to exploit the power of threading. A single CPU can appear to execute both lists of instructions in parallel, letting you read your email and listen to music simultaneously.

Threads behave exactly the same way. In our case, the Java virtual machine executes a handful of the instructions to calculate the factorial and then executes a handful of instructions to calculate the square root, and so on.

So threads are simply tasks that you want to execute at roughly the same time. Why, then, write an application with multiple threads? Why not just write multiple applications? The answer lies in the fact that because threads are running in the same application, they share the same memory space in the computer. This allows them to share information seamlessly. Your email program and your music application don't communicate very well. At best, you can copy and paste some data (like the name of a file) between the two. That allows you to double-click on an MP3 attachment in your email and play it in your music application, but the only information that is shared between the two is the name of the MP3 file. This type of cooperation is shown in Figure 2-1.

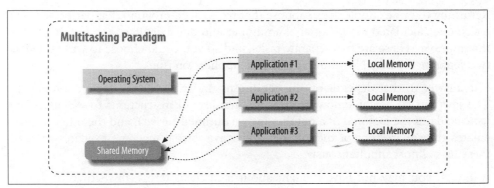

*Figure 2-1. Processes in a multitasking environment*

In a multitasking environment, data in the programs is separated by default: each has its own stack for local variables, and each has its own area for objects and other data. All the programs can access various types of shared memory (including the name of the MP3 file that you clicked on in your email program). The shared memory is restricted to information put there by other programs, and the APIs to access it are usually quite different than the APIs used to access other data in the program.

This type of data sharing is fine for dissimilar programs, but it is inadequate for other programs. Consider a network server that sends stock quotes to multiple clients. Sending a quote to a client is a discrete task and may be done in a separate thread. In fact, if the client must acknowledge the quote, then sending the data in separate threads is highly recommended: you don't want all clients to wait for a particularly slow client to respond. Here the data to be sent to the clients is the same; you don't want each client to require a separate server process which must then replicate all the data held by every other server process. Instead, you want multiple threads in one program so that they may share data and each perform discrete tasks on that data. That type of sharing is shown in Figure 2-2.

Conceptually, the threads seem to be the same as programs. The key difference here is that the global memory is the entire Java heap: threads can transparently share access between any object in the heap. Each thread still has its own space for local variables (variables specific to the method the thread is executing). But objects are shared automatically and transparently.

A thread, then, is a discrete task that operates on data shared with other threads.

# Creating a Thread

Threads can be created in two ways: using the Thread class and using the Runnable interface. The Runnable interface (generally) requires an instance of a thread, so we begin with the Thread class.

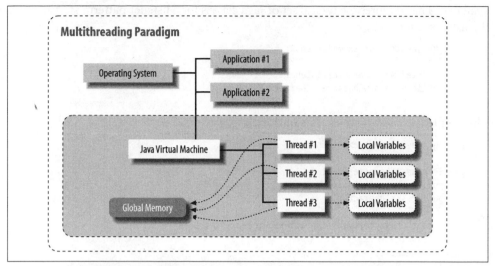

*Figure 2-2. Threads in a multithreaded environment*

In this section, we start developing a typing game. The idea of this game is that characters are displayed and the user must type the key corresponding to the character. Through the next few chapters, we add enough logic to score the user's accuracy and timing and provide enough feedback so that the user can improve her typing skills.

For now, we are content to display a random character and display the character the user types in response. This application has two tasks: one task must continually display a random character and then pause for some random period of time. The second task must display characters typed on the keyboard.

## The Example Architecture

Before we delve into the threading aspects of our code, let's look at a few utility classes used in this and subsequent examples. The typing game has two sources for characters: characters that the user types at the keyboard and characters that are randomly generated. Both sources of characters are represented by this interface:

```
package javathreads.examples.ch02;

public interface CharacterSource {
    public void addCharacterListener(CharacterListener cl);
    public void removeCharacterListener(CharacterListener cl);
    public void nextCharacter();
}
```

We want to use the standard Java pattern of event listeners to handle these characters: a listener can register with a particular source and be notified when a new character is available. That requires the typical set of Java classes for a listener pattern, starting with the listener interface:

```
package javathreads.examples.ch02;

public interface CharacterListener {
    public void newCharacter(CharacterEvent ce);
}
```

The events themselves are objects of this class:

```
package javathreads.examples.ch02;

public class CharacterEvent {
    public CharacterSource source;
    public int character;

    public CharacterEvent(CharacterSource cs, int c) {
        source = cs;
        character = c;
    }
}
```

And finally, we need a helper class that fires the events when appropriate:

```
package javathreads.examples.ch02;

import java.util.*;

public class CharacterEventHandler {
    private Vector listeners = new Vector();

    public void addCharacterListener(CharacterListener cl) {
        listeners.add(cl);
    }

    public void removeCharacterListener(CharacterListener cl) {
        listeners.remove(cl);
    }

    public void fireNewCharacter(CharacterSource source, int c) {
        CharacterEvent ce = new CharacterEvent(source, c);
        CharacterListener[] cl = (CharacterListener[] )
                        listeners.toArray(new CharacterListener[0]);
        for (int i = 0; i < cl.length; i++)
            cl[i].newCharacter(ce);
    }
}
```

In our graphical display, one canvas registers to be notified when the user types a character; that canvas displays the character. A second canvas registers to be notified when a random character is generated; it displays the new characters as they are generated. We've chosen this design pattern since, in later examples, multiple objects will be interested in knowing when new characters are generated.

Here's a utility class that can display a given character:

```
package javathreads.examples.ch02;

import java.awt.*;
import javax.swing.*;

public class CharacterDisplayCanvas extends JComponent implements CharacterListener {
    protected FontMetrics fm;
    protected char[] tmpChar = new char[1];
    protected int fontHeight;

    public CharacterDisplayCanvas() {
        setFont(new Font("Monospaced", Font.BOLD, 18));
        fm = Toolkit.getDefaultToolkit().getFontMetrics(getFont());
        fontHeight = fm.getHeight();
    }

    public CharacterDisplayCanvas(CharacterSource cs) {
        this();
        setCharacterSource(cs);
    }

    public void setCharacterSource(CharacterSource cs) {
        cs.addCharacterListener(this);
    }

    public Dimension preferredSize() {
        return new Dimension(fm.getMaxAscent() + 10,
                             fm.getMaxAdvance() + 10);
    }

    public synchronized void newCharacter(CharacterEvent ce) {
        tmpChar[0] = (char) ce.character;
        repaint();
    }

    protected synchronized void paintComponent(Graphics gc) {
        Dimension d = getSize();
        gc.clearRect(0, 0, d.width, d.height);
        if (tmpChar[0] == 0)
            return;
        int charWidth = fm.charWidth((int) tmpChar[0]);
        gc.drawChars(tmpChar, 0, 1,
                     (d.width - charWidth) / 2, fontHeight);
    }
}
```

Although this class has no references to threads, it still has thread-related issues: namely, we had to use the synchronized keyword for some of the methods. This is because of something known as a *race condition* (see Chapter 3).

## The Thread Class

Now we can program our first task (and our first thread): a thread that periodically generates a random character. In Java, threads are represented by instances of the java.lang.Thread class. They are created just like any other Java object, but they contain a special method that tells the virtual machine to begin executing the code of the thread as a separate "list." Here's a partial API of the Thread class, showing its constructors and its execution-related methods:

```java
package java.lang;
public class Thread implements Runnable {
    public Thread();
    public Thread(Runnable target);
    public Thread(ThreadGroup group, Runnable target);
    public Thread(String name);
    public Thread(ThreadGroup group, String name);
    public Thread(Runnable target, String name);
    public Thread(ThreadGroup group, Runnable target, String name);
    public Thread(ThreadGroup group, Runnable target, String name,
                  long stackSize);
    public void start();
    public void run();
}
```

As you see, threads are created with four pieces of information:

*Thread name*

> The name of a thread is part of the information shown when a thread object is printed. Otherwise, it has no significance, so give your threads names that make sense to you when you see them printed. The default name for a thread is Thread-*N*, where *N* is a unique number.

*Runnable target*

We discuss runnables in depth later in this chapter. A runnable object is the list of instructions that the thread executes. By default, this is the information in the run( ) method of the thread itself. Note that the Thread class itself implements the Runnable interface.

*Thread group*

Thread groups are an advanced topic (see Chapter 13). For the vast majority of applications, thread groups are unimportant. By default, a thread is assigned to the same thread group as the thread that calls the constructor.

*Stack size*

Every thread has a stack where it stores temporary variables as it executes methods. Everything related to the stack size of a thread is platform-dependent: its default stack size, the range of legal values for the stack size, the optimal value for the stack size, and so on. Use of the stack size in portable programs is highly discouraged. For more information, see Chapter 13.

We can use these methods of the Thread class to create our first thread:

```
package javathreads.examples.ch02.example2;

import java.util.*;
import javathreads.examples.ch02.*;

public class RandomCharacterGenerator extends Thread implements CharacterSource {
    static char[] chars;
    static String charArray = "abcdefghijklmnopqrstuvwxyz0123456789";
    static {
        chars = charArray.toCharArray( );
    }

    Random random;
    CharacterEventHandler handler;

    public RandomCharacterGenerator( ) {
        random = new Random( );
        handler = new CharacterEventHandler( );
    }

    public int getPauseTime( ) {
        return (int) (Math.max(1000, 5000 * random.nextDouble( )));
    }

    public void addCharacterListener(CharacterListener cl) {
        handler.addCharacterListener(cl);
    }

    public void removeCharacterListener(CharacterListener cl) {
        handler.removeCharacterListener(cl);
    }
```

```
public void nextCharacter( ) {
    handler.fireNewCharacter(this,
                            (int) chars[random.nextInt(chars.length)]);
}

public void run( ) {
    for (;;) {
        nextCharacter( );
        try {
            Thread.sleep(getPauseTime( ));
        } catch (InterruptedException ie) {
            return;
        }
    }
}
}
```

The first thing to note about this example is that it extends the Thread class. The class itself is constructed simply by calling its (only) constructor, and the actual list of instructions we want to execute is in the run( ) method. The run( ) method is a standard method of the Thread class; it is the place where the thread begins its execution.

In a sense, the run( ) method is similar to the main( ) method of a standalone Java application: the main( ) method is where your first thread starts executing. Subsequent threads start executing with the run( ) method of the thread. Though some subtle differences between run( ) and main( ) exist, this is the best way to think of the relationship between them.

So when the run( ) method of this class is eventually called, it fires off a new character to its listeners, sleeps for a random period of time between 1 and 5 seconds, and then repeats the process (forever, as the loop never terminates).

The second task of our application is responsible for displaying the characters typed at the keyboard. It is also responsible for creating and starting our second thread. That code looks like this:

```
package javathreads.examples.ch02.example2;

import java.awt.*;
import java.awt.event.*;
import javax.swing.*;
import javathreads.examples.ch02.*;

public class SwingTypeTester extends JFrame implements CharacterSource {

    protected RandomCharacterGenerator producer;
    private CharacterDisplayCanvas displayCanvas;
    private CharacterDisplayCanvas feedbackCanvas;
    private JButton quitButton;
    private JButton startButton;
    private CharacterEventHandler handler;
```

```java
public SwingTypeTester() {
    initComponents();
}

private void initComponents() {
    handler = new CharacterEventHandler();
    displayCanvas = new CharacterDisplayCanvas();
    feedbackCanvas = new CharacterDisplayCanvas(this);
    quitButton = new JButton();
    startButton = new JButton();
    add(displayCanvas, BorderLayout.NORTH);
    add(feedbackCanvas, BorderLayout.CENTER);
    JPanel p = new JPanel();
    startButton.setLabel("Start");
    quitButton.setLabel("Quit");
    p.add(startButton);
    p.add(quitButton);
    add(p, BorderLayout.SOUTH);

    addWindowListener(new WindowAdapter() {
        public void windowClosing(WindowEvent evt) {
            quit();
        }
    });

    feedbackCanvas.addKeyListener(new KeyAdapter() {
        public void keyPressed(KeyEvent ke) {
            char c = ke.getKeyChar();
            if (c != KeyEvent.CHAR_UNDEFINED)
                newCharacter((int) c);
        }
    });
    startButton.addActionListener(new ActionListener() {
        public void actionPerformed(ActionEvent evt) {
            producer = new RandomCharacterGenerator();
            displayCanvas.setCharacterSource(producer);
            producer.start();
            startButton.setEnabled(false);
            feedbackCanvas.setEnabled(true);
            feedbackCanvas.requestFocus();
        }
    });
    quitButton.addActionListener(new ActionListener() {
        public void actionPerformed(ActionEvent evt) {
            quit();
        }
    });
    pack();
}

private void quit() {
    System.exit(0);
}
```

```
public void addCharacterListener(CharacterListener cl) {
    handler.addCharacterListener(cl);
}

public void removeCharacterListener(CharacterListener cl) {
    handler.removeCharacterListener(cl);
}

public void newCharacter(int c) {
    handler.fireNewCharacter(this, c);
}

public void nextCharacter() {
    throw new IllegalStateException("We don't produce on demand");
}

public static void main(String args[]) {
    new SwingTypeTester().show();
}
}
```

Most of this code is, of course, GUI code. The lines to note with respect to the Thread class are in the actionPerformed( ) method associated with the Start button. In the event callback, we construct a thread object (i.e., the instance of the RandomCharacterGenerator class) like any other Java object, and then we call the start( ) method on that object. Note that we did *not* call the RandomCharacterGenerator object's run( ) method. The start( ) method of the Thread class calls the run( ) method (see the section "The Lifecycle of a Thread").

Other threads are involved in this example, even though you don't see references to them. First, there is the main thread of the application. This thread starts when you begin execution of the program (i.e., when you type the java command). That thread calls the main( ) method of your application.

The second thread of the application is the instance of the RandomCharacterGenerator class. It is created the first time the Start button is pressed.

A third thread in the application is the event-processing thread. That thread is started by the Swing toolkit when the first GUI element of the application is created. That thread is significant to us because that's the thread that executes the actionPerformed( ) and keyPressed( ) methods of the application. There are many other threads in the virtual machine that we don't interact with; for now, we're concerned about the three threads we've just discussed.

At this point, you can compile and run the application. Using our master ant script, execute this command:

```
piccolo% ant ch2-ex2
```

The GUI window shown in Figure 2-3 appears. After you press the Start button, characters appear at random intervals in the top half of the window; as you type characters, they appear in the bottom half of the window.

*Figure 2-3. The SwingTypeTester window*

At this point, we can't do much about scoring what the user types. That would require communication between the two threads of the program, which is the topic of the next chapter. However, we can clear up a few things in the display as we discuss how the RandomCharacterGenerator thread runs.

# The Lifecycle of a Thread

In our example, we gloss over some of the details of how the thread is actually started. We'll discuss that in more depth now and also give details on other lifecycle events of a thread. The lifecycle itself is shown in Figure 2-4. The methods of the Thread class that affect the thread's lifecycle are:

```
package java.lang;
public class Thread implements Runnable {
    public void start();
    public void run();
    public void stop();        // Deprecated, do not use
    public void resume();      // Deprecated, do not use
    public void suspend();      // Deprecated, do not use
    public static void sleep(long millis);
    public static void sleep(long millis, int nanos);
    public boolean isAlive();
    public void interrupt();
    public boolean isInterrupted();
    public static boolean interrupted();
    public void join() throws InterruptedException;
}
```

## Creating a Thread

The first phase in this lifecycle is thread creation. Threads are represented by instances of the Thread class, so creating a thread is done by calling a constructor of

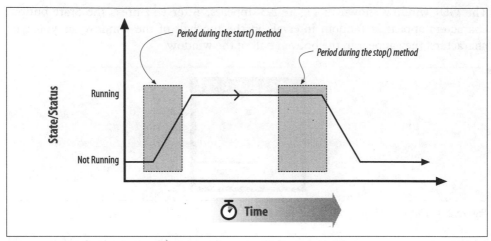

*Figure 2-4. Lifecycle of a thread*

that class. In our example, we use the simplest constructor available to us. Additional constructors of the Thread class allow you to specify the thread's name or a Runnable object to serve as the thread's target.

All threads have names that serve to identify them in the virtual machine. By default, that name consists of information about the thread: its priority, its thread group, and other thread information we discuss in later chapters. If you like, you can give a thread a different name, perhaps one that will have meaning to you if you print it out.

We discuss the Runnable interface later in this chapter.

## Starting a Thread

A thread exists once it has been constructed, but at that point it is not executing any code. The thread is in a waiting state.

In this waiting state, other threads can interact with the existing thread object. Various attributes of the waiting thread can be set: its priority, its name, its daemon status, and so on. We'll see examples of these throughout the book, but each of these attributes is set simply by calling a method on the waiting thread. Therefore, even though the thread is waiting, its state may be changed by other threads.

When you're ready for the thread to begin executing code, you call its start() method. This method performs some internal housekeeping and calls the thread's run( ) method. When the start( ) method returns, two threads are now executing in parallel: the original thread (which has returned from calling the start( ) method) and the newly started thread (which is now executing its run( ) method).

After its start( ) method has been called, the new thread is said to be alive. In fact, the Thread class has an isAlive( ) method that tells you the state of the thread: if the isAlive( ) method returns true, the thread has been started and is executing its run( ) method. If the isAlive( ) method returns false, however, the thread may not be started yet or may be terminated.

## Terminating a Thread

Once started, a thread executes only one method: the run( ) method. The run( ) method may be very complicated, it may execute forever, and it may call millions of other methods. Regardless, once the run( ) method finishes executing, the thread has completed its execution. Like all Java methods, the run( ) method finishes when it executes a return statement, when it executes the last statement in its method body, or when it throws an exception (or fails to catch an exception thrown to it).

As a result, the only way to terminate a thread is to arrange for its run( ) method to complete. If you look at the documentation of the Thread class, you notice that the class contains a stop( ) method which seems like it might be used to terminate a thread. It turns out that the stop( ) method has an inherent problem (an internal race condition, see Chapter 3). As a result, the stop( ) method is deprecated and should not be used. Some Java implementations prohibit its use directly, and the security manager can also be used to prohibit programs from calling it.

There are many threads that you don't need to stop. Often, threads are performing a fixed task, and you always want the task to run to completion. In other cases, such as our example, the thread can run until the application exits (e.g., when we call the System.exit( ) method in response to the user pressing the Quit button).

Often, however, you want a thread to continue to execute until some other condition is met. In our typing game, we might want one RandomCharacterGenerator thread to terminate so that we can start a different one (perhaps one with a different set of characters available to it). We explore some basic ways to arrange for a thread to stop later in this chapter.

The run( ) method cannot throw a checked exception, but like all Java methods, it can throw an unchecked exception. Throwing an unchecked exception (an exception that extends the RuntimeException class)—or failing to catch a runtime exception thrown by something the run( ) method has called—also causes a thread to stop. Threads can arrange for special exception processing in their termination; for details, see Chapter 13.

## Pausing, Suspending, and Resuming Threads

Once a thread begins executing its run( ) method, it continues execution until the run( ) method completes. If you're familiar with other thread models, you may know of a concept called *thread suspension*, where a thread is told to pause its execution. Later, the thread is resumed, which is to say that it is told to continue its execution.

The Thread class contains suspend( ) and resume( ) methods, but they suffer from the same race condition problem as the stop( ) method, and they, too, are deprecated.

It is possible for a thread to suspend its own execution for a specific period of time by calling the sleep( ) method. We use that method in our RandomCharacterGenerator thread. When a thread executes the sleep( ) method, it pauses for a given number of milliseconds (or milliseconds plus nanoseconds), during which it is said to be asleep. When the pause time has elapsed, the thread wakes up and continues execution with the statements immediately following the sleep( ) method.

---

### Sleep Time Resolution

The Thread class provides a version of the sleep( ) method that allows the developer to specify the time in nanoseconds. Most Java virtual machines do not support this sort of precise timing. When the sleep( ) method executes, it rounds the nanosecond argument to the nearest millisecond. In fact, most operating systems then further adjust the millisecond argument so that it is a multiple of some number: e.g., 20 or 50 milliseconds. Consequently, the least amount of time that you can sleep on most Java implementations is 20 or 50 milliseconds.

Note that this is true even in J2SE 5.0, which introduces other nanosecond time functionality (e.g., the System.nanoTime( ) method). The resolution of the sleep( ) method is still only good to a few milliseconds.

Ongoing projects within the Java Community Process are working on a real-time Java implementation; on such an implementation, the precise resolution specified in the sleep( ) method may eventually be realized. For most platforms, developers cannot design applications that require support of nanoseconds (or even exact milliseconds).

---

Strictly speaking, sleeping is not the same thing as thread suspension. One important difference is that with true thread suspension, one thread would suspend (and later resume) another thread. Conversely, the sleep( ) method affects only the thread that executes it; it's not possible to tell another thread to go to sleep.

Threads can use the wait and notify mechanism discussed in Chapter 4 to achieve the functionality of thread suspension and resumption. The difference is that the threads must be coded to use that technique (rather than a generic suspend/resume mechanism that could be imposed from other threads).

## Thread Cleanup

A thread that has completed its run( ) method has terminated. It is no longer active (the isAlive( ) method returns false). However, the thread object itself may be holding interesting information. As long as some other active object holds a reference to the terminated thread object, other threads can execute methods on the terminated thread and retrieve that information. If the thread object representing the terminated thread goes out of scope, the thread object is garbage collected. On some platforms, this also has the effect of cleaning up system resources associated with the thread.

In general, then, you should not hold onto thread references so that they may be collected when the thread terminates.

One reason to hold onto a thread reference is to determine when it has completed its work. That can be accomplished with the join( ) method. The join( ) method is often used when you have started threads to perform discrete tasks and want to know when the tasks have completed. You'll see that technique in use in the examples in Chapter 15.

The join( ) method blocks until the thread has completed its run( ) method. If the thread has already completed its run( ) method, the join( ) method returns immediately. This means that you may call the join( ) method any number of times to see whether a thread has terminated. Be aware, though, that the first time you call the join( ) method, it blocks until the thread has actually completed. You cannot use the join( ) method to poll a thread to see if it's running (instead, use the isAlive( ) method just discussed).

# Two Approaches to Stopping a Thread

When you want a thread to terminate based on some condition (e.g., the user has quit the game), you have several approaches available. Here we offer the two most common.

## Setting a Flag

The most common way of stopping a thread is to set some internal flag to signal that the thread should stop. The thread can then periodically query that flag to determine if it should exit.

We can rewrite our RandomCharacterGenerator thread to follow this approach:

```
package javathreads.examples.ch02.example3;
...
public class RandomCharacterGenerator extends Thread implements CharacterSource {
    ...
    private volatile boolean done = false;
    ...
    public void run() {
        while (!done) {
            ...
        }
    }
}
```

```
    public void setDone( ) {
        done = true;
    }
}
```

Here we've created the boolean flag done to signal the thread that it should quit. Now instead of looping forever, the run( ) method examines the state of that variable on every loop and returns when the done flag has been set. That terminates the thread.*

We must now modify our application to set this flag:

```
package javathreads.examples.ch02.example3;
...
public class SwingTypeTester extends JFrame implements CharacterSource {
    ...
    private JButton stopButton;
    ...
    private void initComponents( ) {
        ...
        stopButton = new JButton( );
        stopButton.setLabel("Stop");
        p.add(stopButton);
        ...
        stopButton.addActionListener(new ActionListener( ) {
            public void actionPerformed(ActionEvent evt) {
                startButton.setEnabled(true);
                stopButton.setEnabled(false);
                producer.setDone( );
                feedbackCanvas.setEnabled(false);
            }
        });
        ...
    }
    ...
}
```

Now we have two buttons: a Start and a Stop button. When the Stop button is pressed, the setDone( ) method is called, and the next time the RandomCharacterGenerator thread executes the top of its loop, that thread exits. This process also reenables the Start button: we can start a new thread at any time.

This raises an interesting design question: is it better to create a new thread like this, or would it be better somehow to suspend the existing thread and resume it when we're ready? Of course, we don't yet have the tools necessary to program the suspension and resumption of the thread, so that's the reason we've done it this way. It would be more natural simply to suspend and resume the thread, as we do in Chapter 4.

---

* We've also introduced the use of the Java keyword volatile for that variable. Like the synchronized keyword, it is intrinsically related to thread programming (see Chapter 3).

However, in a case like this, it actually does not matter. In our experience, developers become too hung up on the perceived performance penalties they attribute to creating a thread. If you're writing a program and it is easier to abandon a thread and create a new one rather than reusing an existing one, in most cases that's what you should do. We revisit this topic in more depth when we discuss thread pools in Chapter 10 and thread performance in Chapter 14.

Calling the setDone( ) method is a simple way for threads to communicate with each other. Threads must use special rules for communication like this (see Chapter 3). In general, though, threads can call methods on each other, as well as accessing the same objects, to pass information between themselves.

## Interrupting a Thread

The last example has a delay between when the actionPerformed( ) method called the setDone( ) method and the RandomCharacterGenerator thread exited. Delays of some sort when arranging for a thread to terminate are inevitable, but sometimes the delay needs to be minimized.

In our example, the delay occurs because the RandomCharacterGenerator thread executes some number of statements after the setDone( ) method is called and before it checks the value of the done variable. In the worst case, the event thread executing the actionPerformed( ) method calls the setDone( ) method just after the RandomCharacterGenerator thread checks the value of the done variable. Then, even though it's done, the loop gets a new character out of the array, prints it to the screen, and goes to sleep for some amount of time. Finally it wakes up, returns to the top of the loop, sees that the done variable has been set to true, and returns.

The delay in this case is minimal, but it's likely to be close to the amount of time that the RandomCharacterGenerator thread is sleeping (since the other operations are very short). If we originally specify a 15-second delay, we probably won't want to wait the entire 15 seconds before the thread terminates.

In other cases, the delay can be worse: if the thread is executing a read( ) method to obtain data from a socket, the data may never come. Or the thread may be executing the wait( ) method (see Chapter 4) and waiting for an event that may never come. Methods like these are called blocking methods because they block execution of the thread until something happens (e.g., the expiration of the sleep( ) method).

When you arrange for a thread to terminate, you often want it to complete its blocking method immediately: you don't want to wait for the data (or whatever) anymore because the thread is going to exit anyway. You can use the interrupt( ) method of the Thread class to interrupt any blocking method.

The interrupt( ) method has two effects. First, it causes any blocked method to throw an InterruptedException. In our example, the sleep( ) method is a blocking method. If the event-processing thread interrupts the RandomCharacterGenerator thread while that thread is executing the sleep( ) method, the sleep method immediately wakes up and throws an InterruptedException. Other methods that behave this way include the wait( ) method, the join( ) method, and methods that read I/O (though there are complications when handling I/O, as we discuss Chapter 12).

The second effect is to set a flag inside the thread object that indicates the thread has been interrupted. To query this flag, use the isInterrupted( ) method. That method returns true if the thread has been interrupted (even if it was not blocked).

Here's how a thread uses this information to determine whether or not it should terminate:

```
package javathreads.examples.ch02.example4;

...
public class RandomCharacterGenerator extends Thread {
    ...
    // Note: the done instance variable and setDone( ) method are removed from
    // example 2

    public void run( ) {
        while (!isInterrupted( )) {
            ...
        }
    }
}
```

This example is almost exactly the same as the one in which we use a done flag to signal that the thread should return. In this case, we use the interrupted flag instead. That means we no longer need the setDone( ) method. Instead of calling the setDone( ) method, the actionPerformed( ) method associated with the Stop button in our application now does this:

```
producer.interrupt( );
```

If the main thread executes this statement while the RandomCharacterGenerator thread is sleeping, the RandomCharacterGenerator thread gets the interrupted exception and immediately returns from the run( ) method. Otherwise, when the character-feeding thread next gets to the top of its loop, it sees that the interrupted flag has been set and returns from its run( ) method then. Either way, the random character generator thread completes its task.

Note that this technique does not completely eliminate the possibility that we sleep for some amount of time after the thread is asked to stop. It's possible for the main thread to call the interrupt( ) method just after the RandomCharacterGenerator has called the isInterrupted( ) method. The character-reading thread still executes the sleep( ) method, which won't be interrupted (since the main thread has already completed the interrupt( ) method). This is another example of a race condition that we solve in the next chapter. Since the race condition in this case is benign (it just means we sleep one more time than we'd like), this is sufficient for our purposes.

# The Runnable Interface

When we talked about creating a thread, we mentioned the Runnable interface (java. lang.Runnable). The Thread class implements this interface, which contains a single method:

```
package java.lang;
public interface Runnable {
    public void run( );
}
```

The Runnable interface allows you to separate the implementation of a task from the thread used to run the task. For example, instead of extending the Thread class, our RandomCharacterGenerator class might have implemented the Runnable interface:

```
package javathreads.examples.ch02.example5;
...
// Note: Use Example 3 as the basis for comparison
public class RandomCharacterGenerator implements Runnable {
    ...
}
```

This changes the way in which the thread that runs the RandomCharacterGenerator object must be constructed:

```
package javathreads.examples.ch02.example5;
...
public class SwingTypeTester extends JFrame implements CharacterSource {
    ...
    private void initComponents( ) {
        ...
        startButton.addActionListener(new ActionListener( ) {
            public void actionPerformed(ActionEvent evt) {
                producer = new RandomCharacterGenerator( );
                displayCanvas.setCharacterSource(producer);
                Thread t = new Thread(producer);
                t.start( );
                startButton.setEnabled(false);
                stopButton.setEnabled(true);
                feedbackCanvas.setEnabled(true);
                feedbackCanvas.requestFocus( );
            }
        });
        ...
    }
    ...
}
```

Now we must construct the thread directly and pass the runnable object (producer) to the thread's constructor. Then we start the thread (instead of starting the runnable object).

This leads to the question of whether you should use the Runnable interface or the Thread class when designing your own application. The answer is yes.

The truth is that sometimes it makes sense to use the Runnable interface and sometimes it makes sense to use the Thread class. The answer depends on whether you would like your new class to inherit behavior from the Thread class or if your class needs to inherit from other classes.

If you extend the Thread class as we do in our first examples, then you inherit the behavior and methods of the Thread class. That is very important in example 4, where we used the interrupt( ) method to signal that the RandomCharacterGenerator should cease operations. The interrupt( ) method is part of the Thread class, and the reason why we are able to interrupt the RandomCharacterGenerator thread is because it extends the Thread class.

In fact, we should point out that the full source code for example 5 is based on example 3, not example 4. We have to use the setDone( ) method to signal that the random character generator's run( ) method should terminate because that class no longer has an interrupt( ) method. If we still want to interrupt the sleep( ) method of the RandomCharacterGenerator class, then we must write the SwingTypeTester class like this:

```
package javathreads.examples.ch02.example6;
...
public class SwingTypeTester extends JFrame implements CharacterSource {
    ...
    private void initComponents() {
        ...
        stopButton.addActionListener(new ActionListener() {
            public void actionPerformed(ActionEvent evt) {
                ...
                displayThread.interrupt();
            }
        });
        ...
    }
}
```

A similar example can be used to show why it is sometimes preferable to use the Runnable interface. Let's suppose that we want the character in our display canvas to move across the screen until the user types in the matching character. This requires another thread, one that controls the animation of the character. Every few milliseconds, the character needs to be redisplayed on the canvas just slightly to the right of where it was previously displayed. This makes the character appear to be moving.

We could develop a brand new class to do this, but it shares most of the logic of the existing CharacterDisplayCanvas class. The newChar( ) method is somewhat different and there's now some animation logic to deal with, but clearly it's better in this example if we extend CharacterDisplayCanvas (and inherit the methods that set up the canvas size and font) than if we extend the Thread class. This is a case that calls for the Runnable interface:

```
package javathreads.examples.ch02.example7;

import java.awt.*;
import javax.swing.*;
import javathreads.examples.ch02.*;

public class AnimatedCharacterDisplayCanvas extends CharacterDisplayCanvas
                    implements CharacterListener, Runnable {

    private volatile boolean done = false;
    private int curX = 0;

    public AnimatedCharacterDisplayCanvas() {
    }

    public AnimatedCharacterDisplayCanvas(CharacterSource cs) {
        super(cs);
    }

    public synchronized void newCharacter(CharacterEvent ce) {
        curX = 0;
        tmpChar[0] = (char) ce.character;
        repaint();
    }

    protected synchronized void paintComponent(Graphics gc) {
        Dimension d = getSize();
        gc.clearRect(0, 0, d.width, d.height);
        if (tmpChar[0] == 0)
            return;
        int charWidth = fm.charWidth(tmpChar[0]);
        gc.drawChars(tmpChar, 0, 1,
                    curX++, fontHeight);
    }

    public void run() {
        while (!done) {
            repaint();
            try {
                Thread.sleep(100);
            } catch (InterruptedException ie) {
                return;
            }
        }
    }

    public void setDone(boolean b) {
        done = b;
    }
}
```

This class demonstrates the canonical technique to handle animation in Java: a thread makes successive calls to the repaint( ) method, which in turn calls the paintComponent( ) method. Every time the paintComponent( ) method is called, we display the character with a new X coordinate that is slightly shifted to the right.

The thread that controls the animation in this canvas is created just as before: the actionPerformed( ) method of the Start button needs to create a new thread, passing in the AnimatedCharacterCanvas as its runnable target. It also needs to start that thread. The stop( ) method, on the other hand, calls the setDone( ) method to terminate the animation. Here's how it looks:

```
package javathreads.examples.ch02.example7;
...
public class SwingTypeTester extends JFrame implements CharacterSource {
    ...
    private void initComponents( ) {
        ...
        startButton.addActionListener(new ActionListener( ) {
            public void actionPerformed(ActionEvent evt) {
                ...
                displayCanvas.setDone(false);
                Thread t = new Thread(displayCanvas);
                t.start( );
                ...
            }
        });
        stopButton.addActionListener(new ActionListener( ) {
            public void actionPerformed(ActionEvent evt) {
                displayCanvas.setDone(true);
                ...
            }
        });
        ...
    }
    ...
}
```

We began this section by wondering whether it was preferable to program a task using the Runnable interface or the Thread class. We've seen examples of why you would need each. There's an additional advantage to the Runnable interface, however. With Runnable, Java provides a number of classes that handle threading issues for you. These classes handle thread pooling, task scheduling, or timing issues. If you're going to use such a class, your task must be a Runnable object (or, in some cases, an object that has an embedded Runnable object).

If you do a thorough program design and Unified Modeling Language (UML) model of your application, the resulting object hierarchy tells you pretty clearly whether your task needs to subclass another class (in which case you must use the Runnable interface) or whether you need to use the methods of the Thread class within your task. But if your object hierarchy is silent on the parent class for your task, or if you do a lot of prototyping or extreme programming, then what? Then the choice is yours: you can use the Runnable interface, which gives you a little more flexibility at the cost of the overhead of keeping track of the thread objects separately, or you can trade that flexibility for simplicity and subclass the Thread class.

## Threads and Objects

Let's talk a little more about how threads interact. Consider the RandomCharacterGenerator thread. We saw how another class (the SwingTypeTester class) kept a reference to that thread and how it continued to call methods on that object.

Although those methods are defined in the RandomCharacterGenerator class, they are not executed by that thread. Instead, methods like the setDone( ) method are executed by the Swing event-dispatching thread as it executes the actionPerformed( ) method within the SwingTypeTester class. As far as the virtual machine is concerned, the setDone( ) method is just a series of statements; those statements do not "belong" to any particular thread. Therefore, the event-dispatching thread executes the setDone( ) method in exactly the same way in which it executes any other method.

This point is often confusing to developers who are new to threads; it can be confusing as well to developers who understand threads but are new to object-oriented programming. In Java, an instance of the Thread class is just an object: it may be passed to other methods, and any thread that has a reference to another thread can execute any method of that other thread's Thread object. The Thread object is not the thread itself; it is instead a set of methods and data that encapsulates information about the thread. And that method and data can be accessed by any other thread.

For a more complex example, examine the AnimatedCharacterCanvas class and determine how many threads execute some of its methods. You should be comfortable with the fact that *four* different threads use this object. The RandomCharacterGenerator thread invokes the newChar( ) method on that object. The timing thread invokes the run( ) method. The setDone( ) method is invoked by the Swing event-dispatching thread. And the constructor of the class (i.e., the default constructor) is invoked by the main method of the application as it constructs the GUI.

The upshot of this is that you cannot look at any object source code and know which thread is executing its methods or examining its data. You may be tempted to look at a class or an object and wonder which thread is running the code. The answer— even if the code is with a class that extends the Thread class—is that any of potentially thousands of threads could be executing the code.

## Determining the Current Thread

Sometimes, you need to find out what the current thread is. In the most common case, code that belongs to an arbitrary object may need to invoke a method of the thread class. In other circumstances, code within a thread object may want to see if the code is being executed by the thread represented by the object or by a completely different thread.

You can retrieve a reference to the current thread by calling the currentThread() method (a static method of the Thread class). Therefore, to see if code is being executed by an arbitrary thread (as opposed to the thread represented by the object), you can use this pattern:

```
public class MyThread extends Thread {
    public void run() {
        if (Thread.currentThread() != this)
            throw new IllegalStateException(
                            "Run method called by incorrect thread");
        ... main logic ...
    }
}
```

Similarly, within an arbitrary object, you can use the currentThread() method to obtain a reference to a current thread. This technique can be used by a Runnable object to see whether it has been interrupted:

```
public class MyRunnable implements Runnable {
    public void run() {
        while (!Thread.currentThread().isInterrupted()) {
            ... main logic ...
        }
    }
}
```

In fact, the Thread class includes a static method interrupted() that simply returns the value of Thread.currentThread().isInterrupted(), but you'll often see both uses within threaded programs. In examples in later chapters, we use the currentThread() method to obtain a thread reference in order to invoke other methods of the Thread class that we haven't yet examined.

# Summary

In this chapter, we've had our first taste of threads. We've learned that threads are separate tasks executed by a single program. This is the key to thinking about how to design a good multithreaded program: what logical tasks make up your program? How can these tasks be separated to make the program logic easier, or benefit your program by running in parallel? In our case, we have two simple tasks: display a random character and display the key that a user types in response. In later chapters, we add more tasks (and more threads) to this list.

At a programming level, we've learned how to construct, start, pause, and stop threads. We've also learned about the Runnable interface and how that interface allows us a great degree of flexibility in how we develop the class hierarchy for our objects. Tasks can be either Thread objects or Runnable objects associated with a thread. Using the Runnable interface allows more flexibility in how you define your tasks, but both approaches have merit in different situations.

We've also touched on how threads interoperate by calling methods on the same object. The ability of threads to interoperate in this manner includes the ability for them to share data as well as code. That data sharing is key to the benefits of a multi-threaded program, but it carries with it some pitfalls. This is covered in the next chapter.

## Example Classes

Here are the class names and Ant targets for the examples in this chapter:

| Description | Main Java class | Ant target |
|---|---|---|
| Factorial Example | javathreads.examples.ch02.example1.Factorial number | ch2-ex1 |
| First Swing Type Tester | javathreads.examples.ch02.example2.SwingTypeTester | ch2-ex2 |
| Type Tester (with Stop button) | javathreads.examples.ch02.example3.SwingTypeTester | ch2-ex3 |
| Type Tester (uses interrupt( ) method) | javathreads.examples.ch02.example4.SwingTypeTester | ch2-ex4 |
| Type Tester (uses Runnable interface) | javathreads.examples.ch02.example5.SwingTypeTester | ch2-ex5 |
| Type Tester (Runnable and interrupt( )) | javathreads.examples.ch02.example6.SwingTypeTester | ch2-ex6 |
| Type Tester (animated display) | javathreads.examples.ch02.example7.SwingTypeTester | ch2-ex7 |

The factorial program accepts a command-line argument to indicate the integer whose factorial should be calculated; that can be set with this Ant property:

```
<property name="FactorialArg" value="10"/>
```

# CHAPTER 3

# Data Synchronization

In the previous chapter, we covered a lot of ground: we examined how to create and start threads, how to arrange for them to terminate, how to name them, how to monitor their lifecycles, and so on. In the examples of that chapter, however, the threads that we examined were more or less independent: they did not need to share data between them.

There were some exceptions to that last point. In some examples, we needed the ability for one thread to determine whether another was finished with its task (i.e., the done flag). In others, we needed to change a character variable that was used in the animation canvas; this was done by a thread different than the Swing thread that redraws the canvas. We glossed over the details at the time, which may have given the implication that they are minor issues. However, we must understand that when two threads share data, complexities arise. These complexities must be taken into consideration whether we're implementing a large shared database or simply sharing a done flag.

In this chapter, we look at the issue of sharing data between threads. Sharing data between threads can be problematic due to what is known as a *race condition* between threads that attempt to access the same data more or less simultaneously (i.e., concurrently). In this chapter, we examine the concept of a race condition and mechanisms that solve the race condition. We will see how these mechanisms can be used to coordinate access to data as well as solve some other problems in thread communication.

## The Synchronized Keyword

Let's revisit our AnimatedDisplayCanvas class from the previous chapter:

```
package javathreads.examples.ch02.example7;
    private volatile boolean done = false;
    private int curX = 0;
```

```
public class AnimatedCharacterDisplayCanvas extends CharacterDisplayCanvas
                implements CharacterListener, Runnable {
    ...
    public synchronized void newCharacter(CharacterEvent ce) {
        curX = 0;
        tmpChar[0] = (char) ce.character;
        repaint();
    }

    protected synchronized void paintComponent(Graphics gc) {
        Dimension d = getSize();
        gc.clearRect(0, 0, d.width, d.height);
        if (tmpChar[0] == 0)
            return;
        int charWidth = fm.charWidth(tmpChar[0]);
        gc.drawChars(tmpChar, 0, 1,
                    curX++, fontHeight);
    }

    public void run() {
        while (!done) {
            repaint();
            try {
                Thread.sleep(100);
            } catch (InterruptedException ie) {
                return;
            }
        }
    }

    public void setDone(boolean b) {
        done = b;
    }
}
```

This example has multiple threads. The most obvious is the one that we created and which executes the run( ) method. That thread is specifically created to wake up every 0.1 seconds to send a repaint request to the system. To fulfill the repaint request, the system—at a later time and in a different thread (the event-dispatching thread, to be precise)—calls the paintComponent( ) method to adjust and redraw the canvas. This constant adjustment and redrawing is what is seen as animation by the user.

There is no race condition between these threads since no data in this object is shared between them. However, as we mentioned at the end of the last chapter, other threads invoke methods of this object. For example, the newCharacter( ) method is called from the random character–generating thread (a character source) whenever the character to be typed changes.

In this case, there is a race condition. The thread that calls the newCharacter( ) method is accessing the same data as the thread that calls the paintComponent( )

method. The random character–generating thread may change the character while the event-dispatching thread is using it. Both threads are also changing the X location that specifies where the character is to be drawn.

A race condition exists because the paintComponent( ) and newCharacter( ) methods are not *atomic*. It is possible for the newCharacter( ) method to change the values of the tmpChar and curX variables while the paintComponent( ) method is using them. Or for the newCharacter( ) and paintComponent( ) methods to leave the curX variable in a state that depends on which individual instructions of the two threads are executed first. We examine race conditions in more detail later; for now, we just have to understand that race conditions can generate different results, including unexpected results, that are dependent on execution order.

---

### Definition: Atomic

The term atomic is related to the atom, once considered the smallest possible unit of matter, unable to be broken into separate parts. When computer code is considered atomic, it cannot be interrupted during its execution. This can either be accomplished in hardware or simulated in software. Generally, atomic instructions are provided in hardware and are used to implement atomic methods in software.

In our case, we define atomic code as code that can't be found in an intermediate state. In our animated canvas example, if the acts of "resetting the variable" and "redrawing one frame of the animation" were atomic, it would not be possible to set the variable at the very moment that the character is being animated. The animation thread also couldn't find the variables in an intermediate state.

---

The Java specification provides certain mechanisms that deal specifically with this problem. The Java language provides the synchronized keyword; in comparison with other threading systems, this keyword allows the programmer access to a resource that is very similar to a mutex lock. For our purposes, it simply prevents two or more threads from calling the methods of the same object at the same time.

By declaring the newCharacter( ) and paintComponent( ) methods synchronized, we eliminate the race condition. If one thread wants to call one of these methods while another thread is already executing one of them, the second thread must wait: the first thread gets to complete execution of its method before the second thread can execute its method. Since only one thread gets to call either method at a time, only one thread at a time accesses the data.

Under the covers, the concept of synchronization is simple: when a method is declared synchronized, the thread that wants to execute the method must acquire a token, which we call a lock. Once the method has acquired (or checked out or grabbed) this lock, it executes the method and releases (or returns) the lock. No matter how the

> ### Definition: Mutex Lock
>
> A mutex lock is also known as a mutually exclusive lock. This type of lock is provided by many threading systems as a means of synchronization. Only one thread can grab a mutex at a time: if two threads try to grab a mutex, only one succeeds. The other thread has to wait until the first thread releases the lock before it can grab the lock and continue operation.
>
> In Java, every object has an associated lock. When a method is declared synchronized, the executing thread must grab the lock associated with the object before it can continue. Upon completion of the method, the lock is automatically released.

method returns—including via an exception—the lock is released. There is only one lock per object, so if two separate threads try to call synchronized methods of the same object, only one can execute the method immediately; the other has to wait until the first thread releases the lock before it can execute the method.

# The Volatile Keyword

There is still one more threading issue in this example, and it has to do with the setDone( ) method. This method is called from the event-dispatching thread when the Stop button is pressed; it is called by an event handler (an actionPerformed( ) method) that is defined as an inner class to the SwingTypeTester class. The issue here is that this method is executed by the event-dispatching thread and changes data that is being used by another thread: the done flag, which is accessed by the thread of the AnimatedDisplayCanvas class.

So, can't we just synchronize the two methods, just as we did previously? Yes and no. Yes, Java's synchronized keyword allows this problem to be fixed. But no, the techniques that we have learned so far will not work. The reason has to do with the run( ) method. If we synchronized both the run( ) and setDone( ) methods, how would the setDone( ) method ever execute? The run( ) method does not exit until the done flag is set, but the done flag can't be set because the setDone( ) method can't execute until the run( ) method completes.

The problem at this point relates to the scope of the lock: the scope of the run( ) method is too large. By synchronizing the run( ) method, the lock is grabbed and never released. There is a way to shrink the scope of a lock by synchronizing only the portion of the run( ) method that protects the done flag (which we examine later in this chapter). However, there is a more elegant solution in this case.

The setDone( ) method performs only one operation with the done flag: it stores a value into the flag. The run( ) method also performs one operation with the done flag: it reads the value during each iteration of the loop. Furthermore, it does not matter if

## Definition: Scope of a Lock

The scope of a lock is defined as the period of time between when the lock is grabbed and released. In our examples so far, we have used only synchronized methods; this means that the scope of these locks is the period of time it takes to execute the methods. This is referred to as method scope.

Later in this chapter, we'll examine locks that apply to any block of code inside a method or that can be explicitly grabbed and released; these locks have a different scope. We'll examine this concept of scope as locks of various types are introduced.

the value changes during the iteration of these methods, as each loop must complete anyway.

The issue here is that we potentially have a race condition because one piece of data is being shared between two different threads. In our first example, the race condition came about because the threads were accessing multiple pieces of data and there was no way to update all of them atomically without using the synchronized keyword. When only a single piece of data is involved, there is a different solution.

Java specifies that basic loading and storing of variables (except for long and double variables) is atomic. That means the value of the variable can't be found in an interim state during the store, nor can it be changed in the middle of loading the variable to a register. The setDone( ) method has only one store operation; therefore, it is atomic. The run( ) method has only one read operation. Since the rest of the run( ) method does not depend on the value of the variable remaining constant, the race condition should not exist in this case.

Unfortunately, Java's memory model is a bit more complex. Threads are allowed to hold the values of variables in local memory (e.g., in a machine register). In that case, when one thread changes the value of the variable, another thread may not see the changed variable. This is particularly true in loops that are controlled by a variable (like the done flag that we are using to terminate the thread): the looping thread may have already loaded the value of the variable into a register and does not necessarily notice when another thread changes the variable.

One way to solve this problem is to provide setter and getter methods for the variable. We can then simply synchronize access by using the synchronized keyword on these methods. This works because acquiring a synchronization lock means that all temporary values stored in registers are flushed to main memory. However, Java provides a more elegant solution: the volatile keyword. If a variable is marked as volatile, every time the variable is used it must be read from main memory. Similarly, every time the variable is written, the value must be stored in main memory. Since these operations are atomic, we can avoid the race condition in our example by marking our done flag as volatile.

In most releases of the virtual machine prior to JDK 1.2, the actual implementation of Java's memory model made using volatile variables a moot point: variables were always read from main memory. In subsequent iterations of Java, up to and including J2SE 5.0, implementations of virtual machines became more sophisticated and introduced new memory models and optimizations: this trend is expected to continue in future versions of Java. With all modern virtual machine implementations, developers can not assume that variables will be accessed directly from main memory.

So why is `volatile` necessary? Or even useful? Volatile variables solve only the problem introduced by Java's memory model. They can be used only when the operations that use the variable are atomic, meaning the methods that access the variable must use only a single load or store. If the method has other code, that code may not depend on the variable changing its value during its operation. For example, operations like increment and decrement (e.g., ++ and --) can't be used on a volatile variable because these operations are syntactic sugar for a load, change, and a store.

As we mentioned, we could have solved this problem by using synchronized setter and getter methods to access the variable. However, that would be fairly complex. We must invoke another method, including setting up parameters and the return variable. We must grab and release the lock necessary to invoke the method. And all for a single line of code, with one atomic operation, that is called many times within a loop. The concept of using a done flag is common enough that we can make a very strong case for the `volatile` keyword.

*The requirements of using volatile variables seem overly restrictive. Are they really important?* This question can lead to an unending debate. For now, it is better to think of the `volatile` keyword as a way to force the virtual machine not to make temporary copies of a variable. While we can agree that you might not use these types of variables in many cases, they are an option during program design. In Chapter 5, we examine similar variables (atomic variables) that are less restrictive: variables that are not only atomic but can be built on using programming techniques. This allows us to build complex atomic functionality.

*How does* `volatile` *work with arrays?* Declaring an array `volatile` makes the array reference itself volatile. The elements within the array are not volatile; the virtual machine may still store copies of individual elements in local registers. There is no way to specify that the elements of an array should be treated as volatile. Consequently, if multiple threads are going to access array elements, they must use synchronization in order to protect the data. Atomic variables can also help in this situation.

# More on Race Conditions

Let's examine a more complex example; so far, we have looked at simple data interaction used either for loop control or for redrawing. In this next iteration of our typing game, we share useful data between the threads in order to calculate additional
data needed by the application.

Our application has a display component that presents random numbers and letters
and a component that shows what the user typed. While there are data synchronization issues between the threads of this example, there is little interaction between
these two actions: the act of typing a letter does not depend on the animation letter
that is shown. But now we will develop a scoring system. Users see feedback on
whether they correctly typed what was presented. Our new code must make this
comparison, and it must make sure that no race condition exists when comparing
the data.

To accomplish this, we will introduce a new component, one that displays the user's
score, which is based on the number of correct and incorrect responses:

```java
package javathreads.examples.ch03.example1;

import javax.swing.*;
import java.awt.event.*;
import javathreads.examples.ch03.*;

public class ScoreLabel extends JLabel implements CharacterListener {

    private volatile int score = 0;
    private int char2type = -1;
    private CharacterSource generator = null, typist = null;

    public ScoreLabel (CharacterSource generator, CharacterSource typist) {
        this.generator = generator;
        this.typist = typist;

        if (generator != null)
            generator.addCharacterListener(this);
        if (typist != null)
            typist.addCharacterListener(this);
    }

    public ScoreLabel () {
        this(null, null);
    }

    public synchronized void resetGenerator(CharacterSource newGenerator) {
        if (generator != null)
            generator.removeCharacterListener(this);
        generator = newGenerator;
        if (generator != null)
            generator.addCharacterListener(this);
    }
```

```
    public synchronized void resetTypist(CharacterSource newTypist) {
        if (typist != null)
            typist.removeCharacterListener(this);
        typist = newTypist;
        if (typist != null)
            typist.addCharacterListener(this);
    }

    public synchronized void resetScore() {
        score = 0;
        char2type = -1;
        setScore();
    }

    private synchronized void setScore() {
        // This method will be explained later in chapter 7
        SwingUtilities.invokeLater(new Runnable() {
            public void run() {
                setText(Integer.toString(score));
            }
        });
    }

    public synchronized void newCharacter(CharacterEvent ce) {
        // Previous character not typed correctly: 1-point penalty
        if (ce.source == generator) {
            if (char2type != -1) {
                score--;
                setScore();
            }
            char2type = ce.character;
        }

        // If character is extraneous: 1-point penalty
        // If character does not match: 1-point penalty
        else {
            if (char2type != ce.character) {
                score--;
            } else {
                score++;
                char2type = -1;
            }
            setScore();
        }
    }
}
```

The heart of this class is the newCharacter( ) method, which is called from multiple character sources. It is called, at random times, by the source (and thread) that generates random characters. It is also called by a character source every time the user types a character (from the event dispatching thread). In our simple scoring system, we increment the score every time a character is entered correctly and decrement the score every time a character is entered incorrectly. We also penalize the user for entering the same correct character more than once or for not entering the correct character in time.

Interestingly, we don't actually need to know which threads call this method (or the other methods that access the same data). The conditional check in the method is used to find out which source sent the character—not which thread. In terms of threads, we just need to understand that this and other methods may be called by different threads, potentially at the same time. We need to understand what is being shared between the different methods—or even the same method if they are called by different threads. For this class, the actual score, the character that needs to be typed, and a few variables that hold the character sources for registration purposes comprise the shared data. Solving the race conditions means synchronizing this data at the correct scope.

In this case, synchronizing at the method level solves the problem, and making the variables volatile would not solve the problem. Since it is easier to understand the problem by examining a failure case, let's quickly examine one such case: what could happen if the newCharacter( ) method were not synchronized. Note that this is only one case of many in which incorrect synchronization would lead to incorrect behavior in this class.

- The user types a character, which happens to be correct. The event-dispatching thread calls the newCharacter( ) method, which routes to the else statement because the source is the typist. The character is determined to be correct and the score is incremented. However, before the char2type variable can be set to −1, indicating that the correct character has been typed, another thread starts to run.

- The random character source calls the newCharacter( ) method, which routes to the if statement. Since the char2type variable is not set to −1, the score is decremented as a penalty for failure to type the character correctly.

- The random character thread stores the new character in the char2type variable, the score is updated (via the setScore( ) method), and the method returns.

- The first thread sets the char2type variable to −1, updates the score, and returns from the method.

This case is dependent on a scheduling change occurring at an unfortunate time. The key to understanding this behavior is to realize that when multiple threads are executing their own list of instructions, the operating system may switch from one list of statements (i.e., one thread) to another list of statements (i.e., a different thread) at any arbitrary point in time. In reality, a scheduling change may occur at more complicated locations, such as in the middle of an instruction that is not atomic. In that case, the symptoms may be very complicated. Even with this simple failure case, we have many symptoms of failure:

- Since the score is both incremented and decremented, the user is not given credit for typing the character correctly.
- The new character from the random character generator is lost. It is actually set correctly, but the event-dispatching thread incorrectly deletes it as soon as that thread is allowed to execute.
- The character is lost only to the scoring component, not to the animation component. The user is correctly informed of the new character to be typed but is penalized again when the new character is typed correctly.

The resetScore( ) method also accesses the same common data and therefore also needs to be synchronized. You may think this is not necessary since the method is called only when the game is restarted: the other threads are not running then. The resetScore( ), resetGenerator( ), and resetTypist( ) methods are all administrative methods: they are all probably called only once and only during initialization. In this case, they are being synchronized to make the class threadsafe—allowing the methods to be called at any time—should the programmer decide to use these methods later in an unexpected manner.

This is an important point in designing classes for use in a multithreaded environment. Even if you believe that a race condition cannot occur based on the current use of the class, defensive programming principles would argue that you make the entire class safe for execution by multiple threads.

The setScore( ) method illustrates a few interesting points. First, the implemenation of the setScore( ) method uses a utility method (the invokeLater( ) method) because of threading issues related to Swing. Second, the setScore( ) method requires that the score variable be declared volatile (again because of Swing-related threading issues). The implementation of this method is explained in Chapter 7, but for now, we'll just point out that the method allows Swing code (e.g., setting the value of the label in this example) to be executed in a threadsafe manner.

At this point, we may have introduced more questions than answers. So before we continue, let's try to answer some of those questions.

*How can synchronizing two different methods prevent multiple threads calling those methods from stepping on each other?* As stated earlier, synchronizing a method has the effect of serializing access to the method. This means that it is not possible to execute the same method in one thread while the method is already running in another thread. The implementation of this mechanism is done by a lock that is assigned to the object itself. The reason another thread cannot execute the same method at the same time is that the method requires the lock that is already held by the first thread. If two different synchronized methods of the same object are called, they also behave in the same fashion because they both require the lock of the same object, and it is not possible for both methods to grab the lock at the same time. In other words, even if two or more methods are involved, they are never run in parallel in separate threads.

## When Is a Race Condition a Problem?

A race condition occurs when the order of execution of two or more threads may affect some variable or outcome in the program. It may turn out that all the different possible orders of thread execution have the same final effect on the program: the effect caused by the race condition may be insignificant and may not even be relevant. For example, if the animation thread draws the previous character instead of the new character, it is not a problem if the character has already been typed since the new character is drawn in the next repaint iteration. Alternatively, the timing of the threading system may be such that the race condition never manifests itself, despite the fact that it exists in the code.

Race conditions can be considered harmless (or benign) if you can prove that the result of the race condition is always the same. This is a common technique in some of Java's core classes (most commonly, the atomic classes discussed in Chapter 5); we'll see a few examples of it in this book. But in general, a race condition is a problem that is waiting to happen. Simple changes in the algorithm can cause race conditions to manifest themselves in problematic ways. Since different virtual machines have different ordering of thread execution, the developer should never let a race condition exist even if it is currently not causing a problem on the development system.

This is illustrated in Figure 3-1. When thread 1 and thread 2 attempt to acquire the same lock (L1), thread 2 must wait until thread 1 releases the lock before it can continue to execute.

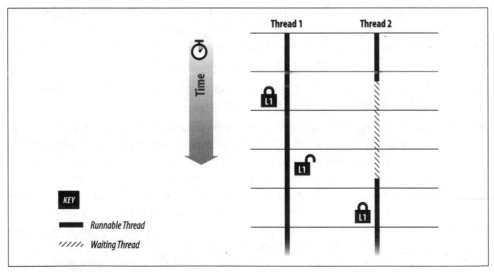

*Figure 3-1. Acquiring and releasing a lock*

The point to remember here is that the lock is based on a specific instance of an object and not on any particular method or class. Assume that we have two different scoring components that score based on different formulas; we'll call these two `ScoreLabel` objects called `objectA` and `objectB`. One thread can execute the `objectA.newCharacter()` method while another thread executes the `objectB.resetGenerator()` method. These two methods can execute in parallel because the call to the `objectA.newCharacter()` method grabs the lock associated with instance variable `objectA`, and the call to the `objectB.resetGenerator()` method grabs the object lock associated with instance variable `objectB`. Since the two objects are different objects, two different locks are grabbed by the two threads: neither thread has to wait for the other.

*How does a synchronized method behave in conjunction with an unsynchronized method?* To understand this, we must remember that all synchronizing does is to grab an object lock. This, in turn, provides the means of allowing only one synchronized method to run at a time, which in turn provides the data protection that solves the race condition. Simply put, a synchronized method tries to grab the object lock, and an unsynchronized method doesn't. This means that unsynchronized methods can execute at any time, by any thread, regardless of whether a synchronized method is currently running. At any given moment on any given object, any number of unsynchronized methods can be executing, but only one synchronized method can be executing.

*What does synchronizing static methods do? And how does it work?* Throughout this discussion, we keep talking about "obtaining the object lock." But what about static methods? When a synchronized static method is called, which object are we referring to? A static method does not have a concept of the `this` reference. It is not possible to obtain the object lock of an object that does not exist. So how does synchronization of static methods work? To answer this question, we will introduce the concept of a *class lock*. Just as there is an object lock that can be obtained for each instance of a class (i.e., each object), there is a lock that can be obtained for each class. We refer to this as the class lock. In terms of implementation, there is no such thing as a class lock, but it is a useful concept to help us understand how all this works.

When a static synchronized method is called, the program obtains the class lock before calling the method. This mechanism is identical to the case in which the method is not static; it is just a different lock. And this lock is used solely for static methods. Apart from the functional relationship between the two locks, they are not operationally related at all. These are two distinct locks. The class lock can be grabbed and released independently of the object lock. If a nonstatic synchronized method calls a static synchronized method, it acquires both locks.

As we mentioned, a class lock does not actually exist. The class lock is the object lock of the `Class` object that models the class. Since there is only one `Class` object per class, using this object achieves the synchronization for static methods. For the developer, it is best envisioned as follows. Only one thread can execute a synchronized static method per class. Only one thread per instance of the class can execute a nonstatic synchronized method. Any number of threads can execute nonsynchronized methods—static or otherwise.

We have introduced the concept of "lock scope" but only touched on avoiding a scope that is too large by locking only specific methods. What if we need to lock specific blocks of code? What if we need to lock only a few lines of code? Do we have to create private methods that can contain as little as one line of code, just to keep one line of code atomic? What if we want to do other tasks if we can't obtain the lock? What if we only want to wait for a specific period of time for a lock? What if we want locks issued in a fashion that is fair? What does it mean to be fair? We answer these questions in the remainder of this chapter.

# Explicit Locking

The purpose of the synchronized keyword is to provide the ability to allow serialized entrance to synchronized methods in an object. Although almost all the needs of data protection can be accomplished with this keyword, it is too primitive when the need for complex synchronization arises. More complex cases can be handled by using classes that achieve similar functionality as the synchronized keyword. These classes are available beginning in J2SE 5.0, but alternatives for use with earlier versions of Java are shown in the Appendix.

The synchronization tools in J2SE 5.0 implement a common interface: the Lock interface. For now, the two methods of this interface that are important to us are lock( ) and unlock( ). Using the Lock interface is similar to using the synchronized keyword: we call the lock( ) method at the start of the method and call the unlock( ) method at the end of the method, and we've effectively synchronized the method.

The lock( ) method grabs the lock. The difference is that the lock can now be more easily envisioned: we now have an actual object that represents the lock. This object can be stored, passed around, and even discarded. As before, if another thread owns the lock, a thread that attempts to acquire the lock waits until the other thread calls the unlock( ) method of the lock. Once that happens, the waiting thread grabs the lock and returns from the lock( ) method. If another thread then wants the lock, it has to wait until the current thread calls the unlock( ) method. Let's implement our scoring example using this new tool:

```
package javathreads.examples.ch03.example2;
...
import java.util.concurrent.*;
import java.util.concurrent.locks.*;

public class ScoreLabel extends JLabel implements CharacterListener {
    ...
    private Lock scoreLock = new ReentrantLock( );
    ...
```

```java
public void resetGenerator(CharacterSource newGenerator) {
    try {
        scoreLock.lock( );
        if (generator != null)
            generator.removeCharacterListener(this);

        generator = newGenerator;
        if (generator != null)
            generator.addCharacterListener(this);
    } finally {
        scoreLock.unlock( );
    }
}

public void resetTypist(CharacterSource newTypist) {
    try {
        scoreLock.lock( );
        if (typist != null)
            typist.removeCharacterListener(this);

        typist = newTypist;
        if (typist != null)
            typist.addCharacterListener(this);
    } finally {
        scoreLock.unlock( );
    }
}

public void resetScore() {
    try {
        scoreLock.lock( );
        score = 0;
        char2type = -1;
        setScore( );
    } finally {
        scoreLock.unlock( );
    }
}

private void setScore() {
    // This method will be explained later in chapter 7
    SwingUtilities.invokeLater(new Runnable( ) {
        public void run( ) {
            setText(Integer.toString(score));
        }
    });
}

public void newCharacter(CharacterEvent ce) {
    try {
        scoreLock.lock( );
        // Previous character not typed correctly: 1-point penalty
        if (ce.source == generator) {
            if (char2type != -1) {
```

```
                score--;
                setScore();
            }
            char2type = ce.character;
        }

        // If character is extraneous: 1-point penalty
        // If character does not match: 1-point penalty
        else {
            if (char2type != ce.character) {
                score--;
            } else {
                score++;
                char2type = -1;
            }
            setScore();
        }
    } finally {
        scoreLock.unlock();
    }
}
```

This new version of the ScoreLabel class is very similar to the previous version. The implementation now declares an object that implements the Lock interface: the scoreLock object which we'll now use to synchronize the methods. We instantiate an instance of the ReentrantLock class, a class that implements the Lock interface. Instead of declaring methods as synchronized, those methods now call the lock() method on entry and the unlock() method on exit. Finally, the method bodies are now placed in try/finally clauses to handle possible runtime exceptions. With the synchronized keyword, locks are automatically released when the method exits. Using locks, we need to call the unlock() method: by placing the unlock() method call in a finally clause, we guarantee the method is called when the method exits, even if an unexpected runtime exception is thrown.

In terms of functionality, this example is exactly the same as the previous example. In terms of possible enhancements, there is a difference. The difference is that by using a lock class, we can now utilize other functionality—functionality, as we shall see, that can't be accomplished by just using the synchronized keyword.

Using a lock class, we can now grab and release a lock whenever desired. We can test conditions before grabbing or releasing the lock. And since the lock is no longer attached to the object whose method is being called, it is now possible for two objects to share the same lock. It is also possible for one object to have multiple locks. Locks can be attached to data, groups of data, or anything else, instead of just the objects that contain the executing methods.

# Lock Scope

Since we now have the lock-related classes available in our arsenal, many of our earlier questions can now be addressed. Let's begin looking at the issue of lock scope by modifying our ScoreLabel class:

```java
package javathreads.examples.ch03.example3;
...
public class ScoreLabel extends JLabel implements CharacterListener {
    ...
    public void newCharacter(CharacterEvent ce) {
        if (ce.source == generator) {
            try {
                scoreLock.lock();
                // Previous character not typed correctly: 1-point penalty
                if (char2type != -1) {
                    score--;
                    setScore();
                }
                char2type = ce.character;
            } finally {
                scoreLock.unlock();
            }
        }
        // If character is extraneous: 1-point penalty
        // If character does not match: 1-point penalty
        else {
            try {
                scoreLock.lock();
                if (char2type != ce.character) {
                    score--;
                } else {
                    score++;
                    char2type = -1;
                }
                setScore();
            } finally {
                scoreLock.unlock();
            }
        }
    }
}
```

Since the lock() and unlock() method calls are explicit, we can move them anywhere, establishing any lock scope, from a single line of code to a scope that spans multiple methods and objects. By providing the means of specifying the scope of the lock, we can now move time-consuming and threadsafe code outside of the lock scope. And we can now lock at a scope that is specific to the program design instead of the object layout. In this example, we moved the source check outside of the lock, and we also split the lock in two, one for each of the conditions.

# Synchronized Blocks

It is possible for the synchronized keyword to lock a block of code within a method. It is also possible for the synchronized keyword to specify the object whose lock is grabbed instead of using the lock of the object that contains the method. Much of what we accomplish with the Lock interface can still be done with the synchronized keyword. It is possible to lock at a scope that is smaller than a method, and it is possible to create an object just so that it can be used as an synchronization object. We can implement our last example just by using the synchronized keyword:

```
package javathreads.examples.ch03.example4;
...
public class ScoreLabel extends JLabel implements CharacterListener {
    ...
    // Definition for score lock deleted
    ...
    public synchronized void resetGenerator(CharacterSource newGenerator) {
        ...
    }
    public synchronized void resetTypist(CharacterSource newTypist) {
        ...
    }
    public synchronized void resetScore() {
        ...
    }
    private synchronized void setScore() {
        ...
    }
    public void newCharacter(CharacterEvent ce) {
        // Previous character not typed correctly: 1-point penalty
        if (ce.source == generator) {
            synchronized(this) {
                if (char2type != -1) {
                    score--;
                    setScore();
                }
                char2type = ce.character;
            }
        }

        // If character is extraneous: 1-point penalty
        // If character does not match: 1-point penalty
        else {
            synchronized(this) {
                if (char2type != ce.character) {
                    score--;
                } else {
                    score++;
                    char2type = -1;
```

```
        }
        setScore( );
      }
    }
  }
}
```

This syntax of the synchronized keyword requires an object whose lock is obtained. This is similar to our scoreLock object in the previous example. For this example, we are locking with the same object that was used for the synchronization of the method: the this object. Using this syntax, we can now lock individual lines of code instead of the whole method. We can also share data across multiple objects by locking on other objects instead, such as the data object to be shared.

---

### Synchronized Methods Versus Synchronized Blocks

It is possible to use only the synchronized block mechanism even when we need to synchronize the whole method. For clarity in this book, we synchronize the whole method with the synchronized method mechanism and use the synchronized block mechanism otherwise. It is the programmer's personal preference to decide when to synchronize on a block of code and when to synchronize the whole method—with the caveat that it's always better to establish as small a lock scope as possible.

---

## Choosing a Locking Mechanism

If we compare our first implementation of the ScoreLabel class (using synchronized methods) to our second (using an explicit lock), it's easy to conclude that using the explicit lock is not as easy as using the synchronized keyword. With the keyword, we didn't need to create the lock object, we didn't need to call the lock object to grab and release the lock, and we didn't need to worry about exceptions (therefore, we didn't need the try/finally clause). So, which technique should you use? That is up to you as a developer. It is possible to use explicit locking for everything. It is possible to code to just use the synchronized keyword. And it is possible to use a combination of both. For more complex thread programming, however, relying solely on the synchronized keyword becomes very difficult, as we will see.

How are the lock classes related to static methods? For static methods, the explicit locks are actually simpler to understand than the synchronized keyword. Lock objects are independent of the objects (and consequently, methods) that use them. As far as lock objects are concerned, it doesn't matter if the method being executed is static or not. As long as the method has a reference to the lock object, it can acquire the lock. For complex synchronization that involves both static and nonstatic methods, it may be easier to use a lock object instead of the synchronized keyword.

Synchronizing entire methods is the simplest technique, but as we have already mentioned, it is possible that doing so creates a lock whose scope is too large. This can cause many problems, including creating a deadlock situation (which we examine later in this chapter). It may also be inefficient to hold a lock for the section of code where it is not actually needed.

Using the synchronized block mechanism may also be a problem if too many objects are involved. As we shall see, it is also possible to have a deadlock condition if we require too many locks to be acquired. There is also a slight overhead in grabbing and releasing the lock, so it may be inefficient to free a lock just to grab it again a few lines of code later. Synchronized blocks also cannot establish a lock scope that spans multiple methods.

In the end, which technique to use is often a matter of personal preference. In this book, we use both techniques. We tend to favor using explicit locks in the later sections of this book, mainly because we use functionality that the Lock interface provides.

## The Lock Interface

Let's look a little deeper into the Lock interface:

```
public interface Lock {
    void lock();
    void lockInterruptibly() throws InterruptedException;
    boolean tryLock();
    boolean tryLock(long time, TimeUnit unit)
                            throws InterruptedException;
    void unlock();
    Condition newCondition();
}
```

*What if we want to do other tasks if we can't obtain the lock?* The Lock interface provides an option to try to obtain the lock: the tryLock() method. It is similar to the lock() method in that if it is successful, it grabs the lock. Unlike the lock() method, if the lock is not available, it does not wait. Instead, it returns with a boolean value of false. If the lock is obtained, the return value is a boolean value of true. By inspecting the return value, we can route the thread to separate tasks: if the value returned is false, for instance, we can route the thread to perform alternative tasks that do not require obtaining the lock.

*What if we want to wait only for a specific period of time for a lock?* The tryLock() method is overloaded with a version that lets you specify the maximum time to wait. This method takes two parameters: one that specifies the number of time units and a TimeUnit object that specifies how the first parameter should be interpreted. For example, to specify 50 milliseconds, the long value is set to 50 and the TimeUnit value is set to TimeUnit.MILLISECONDS. New in J2SE 5.0, the TimeUnit class specifies time in units that are easier to understand. In previous versions of Java, most time-based functionality is either specified in nanoseconds or milliseconds (depending on the method).

This method is similar to the lock( ) method in that it waits for the lock, but only for a specified amount of time. It is similar to the tryLock( ) method in that it may return without acquiring the lock: it returns with a value of true if the lock is acquired and false if not.

*What are the other methods of the* Lock *interface used for?* We address them later in this book, starting in Chapter 4. For now, we can already see that the functionality offered by the Lock interface exceeds the functionality offered by the synchronized keyword. By using explicit locks, the developer is free to address issues specific to his program instead of being swamped with concurrency issues.

## Nested Locks

Our implementation of the newCharacter( ) method could be refactored into multiple methods. This isolates the generator and typist logic into separate methods, making the code easier to maintain.

```
package javathreads.examples.ch03.example5;
    ...
    private synchronized void newGeneratorCharacter(int c) {
        if (char2type != -1) {
            score--;
            setScore( );
        }
        char2type = c;
    }

    private synchronized void newTypistCharacter(int c) {
        if (char2type != c) {
            score--;
        } else {
            score++;
            char2type = -1;
        }
        setScore( );
    }

    public synchronized void newCharacter(CharacterEvent ce) {
        // Previous character not typed correctly: 1-point penalty
        if (ce.source == generator) {
            newGeneratorCharacter(ce.character);
        }

        // If character is extraneous: 1-point penalty
        // If character does not match: 1-point penalty
```

```
        else {
            newTypistCharacter(ce.character);
        }
    }
}
```

The two new methods (`newGeneratorCharacter()` and `newTypistCharacter()`) are synchronized because they access the shared state of the object. However, in this case, synchronizing the methods is not technically necessary. Unlike the other methods that access the shared data, these methods are private; they can be called only from other methods of the class. Within the class, they are called only from synchronized methods. So, there is no reason for these methods to acquire the lock because all calls to the method already own the lock. Yet it's still a good idea to synchronize methods like this. Developers who modify this class may not realize that their new code needs to obtain the object lock before calling one of these new methods.

The reason this works is that Java does not blindly grab the lock when it enters synchronized code. If the current thread owns the lock, there is no reason to wait for the lock to be freed or even to grab the lock. Instead, the code in the synchronized section just executes. Furthermore, the system is smart enough to not free the lock if it did not initially grab it upon entering the synchronized section of code. This works because the system keeps track of the number of recursive acquisitions of the lock, finally freeing the lock upon exiting the first method (or block) that acquired the lock. This functionality is called *nested locking*.

Nested locks are also supported by the `ReentrantLock` class—the class that implements the `Lock` interface that we have been using so far. If a lock request is made by the thread that currently owns the lock, the `ReentrantLock` object just increments an internal count of the number of nested lock requests. Calls to the `unlock()` method decrement the count. The lock is not freed until the lock count reaches zero. This implementation allows these locks to behave exactly like the `synchronized` keyword. Note, however, that this is a specific property of the `ReentrantLock` class and not a general property of classes that implement the `Lock` interface.

*Why is Java's support of nested locks important?* This was a simple example. A more complex—and very common—example is that of cross-calling methods. It is possible for a method of one class to call methods of another class, which in turn may call methods of the original class. If Java did not support nested locks—and the methods of both classes were synchronized—we could deadlock the program.

The deadlock occurs because the final method tries to grab a lock that the current thread has already grabbed. This lock can't be freed until the original method unlocks it, but it can't unlock it until it completes the execution of the original method. And the original method can't complete its execution because the final method does not return: it is still waiting to grab the lock.

Cross-calling methods are common and can be so complex that it may not be possible to even detect them, making fixing potential deadlocks very difficult. And there are more complex cases as well. Our example uses a callback mechanism by using character sources and listeners. In this case, character sources and listeners are connected independently of either class: it can become very complex if the listeners are being changed constantly during operation.

Cross-calling methods and callbacks are very prevalent in Java's core library—particularly the windowing system, with its dependency on event handlers and listeners. Developing threaded applications—or even just using Java's standard classes—would be very difficult if nested locks were not supported.

Is it possible to detect how many times a lock has been recursively acquired? It is not possible to tell with the synchronized keyword, and the Lock interface does not provide a means to detect the number of nested acquisitions. However, that functionality is implemented by the ReentrantLock class:

```java
public class ReentrantLock implements Lock {
    public int getHoldCount();
    public boolean isLocked();
    public boolean isHeldByCurrentThread();
    public int getQueueLength();
}
```

The getHoldCount() method returns the number of acquisitions that the current thread has made on the lock. A return value of zero means that the current thread does *not* own the lock: it does *not* mean that the lock is free. To determine if the lock is free—not acquired by any thread—the isLocked() method may be used.

Two other methods of the ReentrantLock class are also important to this discussion. The isHeldByCurrentThread() method is used to determine if the thread is owned by the current thread, and the getQueueLength() method can be used to get an estimate of the number of threads waiting to acquire the lock. This value that is returned is only an estimate due to the race condition that exists between the time that the value is calculated and the time that the value is used after it has been returned.

# Deadlock

We have mentioned deadlock a few times in this chapter, and we'll examine the concept in detail in Chapter 6. For now, we just need to understand what it is and why it is a problem.

Simplistically, deadlock occurs when two or more threads are waiting for two or more locks to be freed and the circumstances in the program are such that the locks are never freed. Interestingly, it is possible to deadlock even if no synchronization locks are involved. A deadlock situation involves threads waiting for conditions; this includes waiting to acquire a lock and also waiting for variables to be in a particular state. On the other hand, it is not possible to deadlock if only one thread is involved, as Java allows nested lock acquisition. If a single user thread deadlocks, a system thread must also be involved.

Let's examine a simple example. To do this, we revisit and break one of our classes—the AnimatedCharacterDisplayCanvas class. This class uses a done flag to determine whether the animation should be stopped. The previous example of this class declares the done flag as volatile. This step was necessary to allow atomic access to the variable to function correctly. In this example, we incorrectly synchronize the methods.

```
package javathreads.examples.ch03.example6;
...
public class AnimatedCharacterDisplayCanvas extends CharacterDisplayCanvas
                implements CharacterListener, Runnable {
    private boolean done = false;
    ...
    protected synchronized void paintComponent(Graphics gc) {
        ...
    }

    public synchronized void run() {
        while (!done) {
            repaint();
            try {
                Thread.sleep(100);
            } catch (InterruptedException ie) {
                return;
            }
        }
    }

    public synchronized void setDone(boolean b) {
        done = b;
    }
}
```

Two threads are involved here: the thread created by this class and the event-dispatching thread that eventually calls the setDone( ) method. Only one lock is shared between these threads: the lock attached to the object (the instance of the AnimatedCharacterDisplayCanvas class) that is being synchronized. The done flag is more interesting. It is a data variable that the run( ) method uses to determine whether it should exit. In essence, the run( ) method is waiting for the done flag to be set to true.

When the animation thread is started, the object lock is grabbed by the run( ) method. The method does not release the object lock until it has completed—which is determined by the done flag. Later, the user presses the Stop button; this generates a call to the setDone( ) method. The setDone( ) method now tries to acquire the object lock. The object lock can't be acquired until the run( ) methods exits. The run( ) method does not exit until the done flag is set. And the done flag can't be set until the setDone( ) method executes. This is obviously a catch-22 situation: a deadlock is created.

This example has other problems as well. When the system needs to draw the canvas, it calls the paintComponent( ) method from the event-dispatching thread. That thread must acquire the lock on the canvas in order to execute the paintComponent( ) method. Since that lock is already held by the animation thread itself, the paintComponent( ) method never has the opportunity to execute. When you press the Start button on the application, nothing happens (other than the application becoming totally unresponsive—you'll have to press Ctrl-C to quit).

To fix this problem, we reduce the scope of the lock used by the run( ) method. One way to do that is by introducing a new synchronized method that accesses the done flag:

```
package javathreads.examples.ch03.example7;
...
public class AnimatedCharacterDisplayCanvas extends CharacterDisplayCanvas
                implements CharacterListener, Runnable {
    ...
    public void run() {
        while (!getDone()) {
            ...
        }
    }
    public synchronized boolean getDone() {
        return done;
    }
    ...
}
```

Now that the run( ) method is synchronized only while it is executing the getDone( ) method, the other methods have the opportunity to grab the object lock, and the program executes as desired.

This is a simple example, but, as you can see, a deadlock can occur even with simple examples. The reason that a deadlock is a problem is obvious—it prevents the application from executing correctly. Unfortunately, there is another issue; deadlocks can be very difficult to detect, particularly as a program gets more complex. Making the example even slightly more complex can obscure the deadlock. To demonstrate, we break our application further by using explicit locks within the ScoreLabel class.

```
package javathreads.examples.ch03.example8;
...
public class ScoreLabel extends JLabel implements CharacterListener {
    ...
    private Lock adminLock = new ReentrantLock();
    private Lock charLock = new ReentrantLock();
    private Lock scoreLock = new ReentrantLock();
    ...
```

```
public void resetGenerator(CharacterSource newGenerator) {
    try {
        adminLock.lock( );
        if (generator != null)
            generator.removeCharacterListener(this);

        generator = newGenerator;
        if (generator != null)
            generator.addCharacterListener(this);
    } finally {
        adminLock.unlock( );
    }
}

public void resetTypist(CharacterSource newTypist) {
    try {
        adminLock.lock( );
        if (typist != null)
            typist.removeCharacterListener(this);

        typist = newTypist;
        if (typist != null)
            typist.addCharacterListener(this);
    } finally {
        adminLock.unlock( );
    }
}
...
public void newCharacter(CharacterEvent ce) {
    try {
        scoreLock.lock( );
        charLock.lock( );
        // Previous character not typed correctly: 1-point penalty
        if (ce.source == generator) {
            if (char2type != -1) {
                score--;
                setScore( );
            }
            char2type = ce.character;
        }

        // If character is extraneous: 1-point penalty
        // If character does not match: 1-point penalty
        else {
            if (char2type != ce.character) {
                score--;
            } else {
                score++;
                char2type = -1;
            }
            setScore( );
        }
    } finally {
```

```
            scoreLock.unlock();
            charLock.unlock();
        }
    }

    public void resetScore() {
        try {
            charLock.lock();
            scoreLock.lock();
            score = 0;
            char2type = -1;
            setScore();
        } finally {
            charLock.unlock();
            scoreLock.unlock();
        }
    }
}
```

Upon examining our ScoreLabel class, we got a very good idea. We noticed that the resetGenerator() and resetTypist() methods don't change the score or the character to be typed. In order to be more efficient, we create a lock just for these two methods—a lock that is used only by the administration methods. We further create a separate lock to distinguish the score and the character; this is just in case we need to modify one variable without the other at a later date. This is a good idea because it reduces contention for the locks, which can increase the efficiency of our program.

Unfortunately, during implementation we created a problem. Like our previous example, there is now a deadlock present in the code. Unlike the previous example, it may not be detected in testing. In fact, it may not be detected at all, as the resetScore() method is not called frequently enough for the problem to show up in testing. In our previous example, the problem manifested itself as soon as the application was started. In this example, the program can run correctly for millions of iterations, only to fail in production when the user presses the Stop or Start buttons in a certain way. Since this deadlock is dependent on the timing of the threads, it may never fail on the testing system due to the timing of the test scripts and other features of the underlying implementation. Our more complex example has a deadlock that is not consistent, making detection incredibly difficult.

*So, where is the deadlock?* It is related to the differences in lock acquisition between the resetScore() and newCharacter() methods. The newCharacter() method grabs the score lock first while the resetScore() method grabs the character lock first. It is now possible for one method to be called which grabs one lock, but, before it can grab the other lock, the other method is called which grabs the other lock. Both methods are waiting to grab the other lock while holding one of the locks.

Let's look at a possible run of this implementation as outlined in Figure 3-2. The thread (thread 1) that generates the random characters calls the newCharacter()

method. This method first grabs the score lock (L1) and then is about to grab the character lock. At the same time, the user presses the Start button, generating a call to the resetScore( ) method. The event-dispatching thread (thread 2) that handles the buttons calls the resetScore( ) method. Thread 2 grabs the character lock (L2) successfully but fails to grab the score lock (L1)—it then waits for the score lock to be released. After thread 1 grabs the score lock, it then tries to grab the character lock (L2). Since the character lock is already held, it waits for it to be released. The first thread is waiting for the second thread to release the second lock while the second thread is waiting for the first thread to release the first lock. Neither can release their respective locks until they are able to acquire the other lock. This generates a catch-22 situation: a deadlock has occurred.

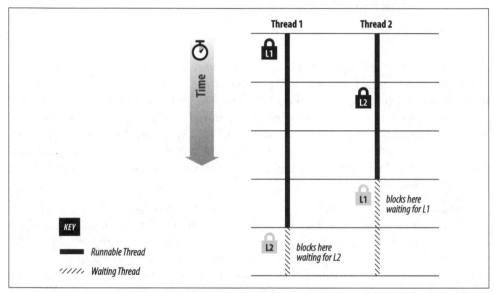

*Figure 3-2. Deadlock in the ScoreLabel class*

*Can the system somehow resolve this deadlock, just as it is able to avoid the potential deadlock when a thread tries to grab the same lock again?* Unfortunately, this problem is different. Unlike the case of the nested locks, where a single thread is trying to grab a single lock multiple times, this case involves two separate threads trying to grab two different locks. Since a thread owns one of the locks involved, it may have already made changes that make it impossible for it to free the lock. To be able to fix this problem at the system level, Java would need a system where the first lock can't be grabbed until it is safe from deadlock or provide a way for the deadlock to be resolved once it occurs. Either case is very complex and may be more complex than just having the developer design the program correctly.

In general, deadlocks can be very difficult to resolve. It is possible to have a deadlock that developers can't fix without a complete design overhaul. Given this complexity, it is not possible, or fair, to expect the underlying system to resolve deadlocks automatically. As for the developer, we look at the design issues related to deadlock prevention and even develop a tool that can be used to detect a deadlock in Chapter 6.

The technique used to fix the problem in Chapter 6 is to make sure that the resetScore( ) method acquires the locks in the same order as the newCharacter( ) method:

```
package javathreads.examples.ch03.example9;
...
public class ScoreLabel extends JLabel implements CharacterListener {
    ...
    public void resetScore( ) {
        try {
            scoreLock.lock( );
            charLock.lock( );
            score = 0;
            char2type = -1;
            setScore( );
        } finally {
            charLock.unlock( );
            scoreLock.unlock( );
        }
    }
}
```

# Lock Fairness

The last question we need to address is the question of lock fairness. What if we want locks to be issued in a fair fashion? What does it mean to be fair? The ReentrantLock class allows the developer to request that locks be granted fairly. This just means that locks are granted in as close to arrival order as possible. While this is fair for the majority of programs, the definition of "fair" can be much more complex.

Whether locks are granted fairly is subjective (i.e., it is measured by the user's perceptions or other relative means) and can be dependent on particular needs of the program. This means that fairness is based on the algorithm of the program and only minimally based on the synchronization construct that the program uses. In other words, achieving total fairness is dependent on the needs of the program. The best that the threading library can accomplish is to grant locks in a fashion that is specified and consistent.

How should locks be granted with explicit locks? One possibility is that locks should be granted on a first-come-first-served basis. Another is they should be granted in an order that permits servicing the maximum number of requests. For example, if we have multiple requests to make a withdrawal from a bank account, perhaps the smaller withdrawal requests should be accepted first or perhaps deposits should have priority over withdrawals. A third view is that locks should be granted in a fashion that is best for the platform—regardless of whether it is for a banking application, a golfing application, or our typing application.

The behavior of synchronization (using the synchronized keyword or explicit locks) is closest to the last view. Java synchronization primitives are not designed to grant locks for a particular situation—they are part of a general purpose threads library. So, there is no reason that the locks should be granted based on arrival order. Locks are granted based on implementation-specific behavior of the underlying threading system, but it is possible to base the lock acquisitions of the ReentrantLock class on arrival order.

Let's examine a slight variation to our examples. Typically, we've declared the lock as follows:

```
private Lock scoreLock = new ReentrantLock();
```

We can declare the lock like this instead:

```
private Lock scoreLock = new ReentrantLock(true);
```

The ReentrantLock class provides an option in its constructor to specify whether to issue locks in a "fair" fashion. In this case, the definition of "fair" is first-in-first-out. This means that when many lock requests are made at the same time, they are granted very close to the order in which they are made. At a minimum, this prevents lock starvation from occurring.

This change is not actually needed for our example. We have only two threads that access this lock. One thread is executed only once every second or so while the other thread is dependent on the user typing characters. Since the operation of both methods is short, the chances of any thread waiting for a lock is small and the chances of lock starvation is zero. It is up to the developer to decide whether or not to use this option—the need to provide a consistent order in granting locks must be balanced with the overhead of the extra code required to use this option.

*What if your program has a different notion of fairness?* In that case, it's up to you to develop a locking class that meets the needs of your application. Such a class needs more features of the threading library than we've discussed so far; a good model for the class would be the ReentrantReadWriteLock examined in Chapter 6.

# Summary

In this chapter, we've introduced the synchronized keyword of the Java language. This keyword allows us to synchronize methods and blocks of code. We've also examined the basic synchronization classes provided by the Java class library—the ReentrantLock class and the Lock interface. These classes allow us to lock objects across methods and to acquire and release the lock at will based on external events. They also provide features such as testing to see if the lock is available, placing time-outs on obtaining the lock, or controlling the order on granting locks.

We've also looked at a common way of handling synchronization of a single variable: the volatile keyword. Using the volatile keyword is typically easier than setting up needed synchronization around a single variable.

This concludes our first look at synchronization. As you can tell, it is one of the most important aspects of threaded programming. Without these techniques, we would not be able to share data correctly between the threads that we create. However, we've just begun to look at how threads can share data. The simple synchronization techniques of this chapter are a good start; in the next chapter, we look at how threads can notify each other that data has been changed.

## Example Classes

Here are the class names and Ant targets for the examples in this chapter:

| Description | Main Java class | Ant target |
| --- | --- | --- |
| Swing Type Tester with ScoreLabel | javathreads.examples.ch03.example1. SwingTypeTester | ch3-ex1 |
| ScoreLabel with explicit lock | javathreads.examples.ch03.example2. SwingTypeTester | ch3-ex2 |
| ScoreLabel with explicit locking at a small scope | javathreads.examples.ch03.example3. SwingTypeTester | ch3-ex3 |
| ScoreLabel with synchronized block locking | javathreads.examples.ch03.example4. SwingTypeTester | ch3-ex4 |
| ScoreLabel with nested locks | javathreads.examples.ch03.example5. SwingTypeTester | ch3-ex5 |
| Deadlocking Animation Canvas | javathreads.examples.ch03.example6. SwingTypeTester | ch3-ex6 |
| Deadlocking Animation Canvas (scope corrected) | javathreads.examples.ch03.example7. SwingTypeTester | ch3-ex7 |
| Deadlocking ScoreLabel | javathreads.examples.ch03.example8. SwingTypeTester | ch3-ex8 |
| Deadlocking ScoreLabel (deadlock corrected) | javathreads.examples.ch03.example9. SwingTypeTester | ch3-ex9 |

# CHAPTER 4

# Thread Notification

In the previous chapter, we discussed data synchronization. Using synchronization and explicit locks, threads can interoperate and safely share data without any race conditions that might corrupt the state of the data. However, as we shall see, synchronization is more than avoiding race conditions: it includes a thread-based notification system that we examine in this chapter.

Thread notification addresses a number of issues in our sample application. Two of these relate to the random character generator and the animation canvas. The random character generator is created when the user presses the Start button; it is destroyed when the user presses the Stop button. Therefore, the listeners to the random character generator are reconnected each time the Start button is pressed. In fact, the entire initialization process is repeated every time that the Start button is pressed.

A similar problem exists for the animation component. Although the component itself is not destroyed every time the user restarts, the thread object that is used for the animation is discarded and recreated. The component provides a mechanism that allows the developer to set the done flag, but the component doesn't use that data to restart the animation: once the done flag is set to true, the run( ) method of the animation canvas exits. The reason for this has to do with efficiency. The alternative is to loop forever, waiting for the done flag to be set to false. This consumes a lot of CPU cycles. Fortunately, the mechanisms we explore in this chapter can solve all these problems.

## Wait and Notify

We've seen that every Java object has a lock. In addition, every object also provides a mechanism that allows it to be a waiting area; this mechanism aids communication between threads.* The idea behind the mechanism is simple: one thread needs a certain condition to exist and assumes that another thread will create that condition. When another thread creates the condition, it notifies the first thread that has been waiting for the condition. This is accomplished with the following methods of the `Object` class:

`void wait( )`
> Waits for a condition to occur. This method must be called from within a synchronized method or block.

`void wait(long timeout)`
> Waits for a condition to occur. However, if the notification has not occurred in `timeout` milliseconds, it returns anyway. This method must be called from a synchronized method or block.

`void wait(long timeout, int nanos)`
> Waits for a condition to occur. However, if the notification has not occurred in `timeout` milliseconds and `nanos` nanoseconds, it returns anyway. This method must be called from a synchronized method or block. Note that, just like the `sleep( )` method, implementations of this method do not actually support nanosecond resolution.

`void notify( )`
> Notifies a thread that is waiting that the condition has occurred. This method must be called from within a synchronized method or block.

---

### wait( ), notify( ), and the Object Class

Just like the synchronized method, the wait-and-notify mechanism is available from every object in the Java system. However, this mechanism is accomplished by method invocations whereas the synchronized mechanism is handled by adding a keyword.

The `wait( )` and `notify( )` mechanism works because these are methods of the `Object` class. Since all objects in the Java system inherit directly or indirectly from the `Object` class, all objects are also instances of the `Object` class and therefore have support for this mechanism.

---

*What is the purpose of the wait-and-notify mechanism, and how does it work?* The wait-and-notify mechanism is a synchronization mechanism. However, it is more of a communication mechanism: it allows one thread to communicate to another

---

* With Solaris or POSIX threads, these are often referred to as condition variables; with Windows, they are referred to as event variables.

thread that a particular condition has occurred. The wait-and-notify mechanism does not specify what the specific condition is.

*Can the wait-and-notify mechanism be used to replace the synchronized mechanism?* Actually, the answer is no; wait-and-notify does not solve the race condition problem that the synchronized mechanism solves. As a matter of fact, wait-and-notify must be used in conjunction with the synchronized lock to prevent a race condition in the wait-and-notify mechanism itself.

Let's use this technique to solve the efficiency problem in our animation component. In this fixed version, the animation thread does not exit when the done flag is set. Instead, it simply waits for the done flag to be reset.

```
package javathreads.examples.ch04.example1;
...
public class AnimatedCharacterDisplayCanvas extends CharacterDisplayCanvas
                    implements CharacterListener, Runnable {
    private boolean done = true;
    ...
    public synchronized void run() {
        while (true) {
            try {
                if (done) {
                    wait();
                } else {
                    repaint();
                    wait(100);
                }
            } catch (InterruptedException ie) {
                return;
            }
        }
    }

    public synchronized void setDone(boolean b) {
        done = b;

        if (timer == null) {
            timer = new Thread(this);
            timer.start();
        }
        if (!done)
            notify();
    }
}
```

In this new version, the done flag is no longer volatile. This is because we are doing more than just setting the flag; we also need to send a notification atomically while setting the flag. Therefore, access to the done flag is now protected by a synchronized lock.

The run( ) method now no longer exits when the done flag is set to false. Instead, it calls the wait( ) method (with no arguments). The thread waits (or blocks) in that method until another thread calls the notify method, at which point it restarts the animation.

Also notice that instead of calling the sleep( ) method, the animation is achieved by calling the wait( ) method with a 100 millisecond timeout. This is due to the differences between the wait( ) and sleep( ) methods. Unlike the sleep( ) method, the wait( ) method requires that the thread own the synchronization lock of the object. When the wait( ) method executes, the synchronization lock is released (internally by the virtual machine itself). Upon receiving the notification, the thread needs to reacquire the synchronization lock before returning from the wait( ) method.

This technique is needed due to a race condition that would otherwise exist between setting and sending the notification and testing and getting the notification. If the wait( ) and notify( ) mechanism were not invoked while holding the synchronization lock, there would be no way to guarantee that the notification would be received. And if the wait( ) method did not release the lock prior to waiting, it would be impossible for the notify( ) method to be called (as it would be unable to obtain the lock). This is also why we had to use the wait( ) method instead of the sleep( ) method; if the sleep( ) method were used, the lock would never be released, the setDone( ) method would never run, and notification could never be sent.

In the online examples, the random character generator's restarting issue has also been fixed. We'll leave it up to you to examine the code at your leisure.

## The Wait-and-Notify Mechanism and Synchronization

As we just mentioned, the wait-and-notify mechanism has a race condition that needs to be solved with the synchronization lock. It is not possible to solve the race condition without integrating the lock into the wait-and-notify mechanism. This is why it is mandatory for the wait( ) and notify( ) methods to hold the locks for the object on which they are operating.

The wait( ) method releases the lock prior to waiting and reacquires the lock prior to returning from the wait( ) method. This is done so that no race condition exists. As you recall, there is no concept of releasing and reacquiring a lock in the Java API. The wait( ) method is actually tightly integrated with the synchronization lock, using a feature not available directly from the synchronization mechanism. In other words, it is not possible for us to implement the wait( ) method purely in Java: it is a native method.

This integration of the wait-and-notify mechanism and the synchronization lock is typical. In other systems, such as Solaris or POSIX threads, condition variables also require that a mutex lock be held for the mechanism to work.

In our example, both the run( ) and the setDone( ) methods are synchronized. In the previous chapter, this was not a recommended technique since the run( ) method never completes—in fact, some of our examples showed how the application broke as a result of synchronizing the run( ) method. However, because of the way the wait( ) method works, there is no longer a danger of deadlock in the example we've just shown. The wait( ) method releases the lock, which allows other threads to execute, including the thread that eventually executes the setDone( ) method. Before the wait( ) method returns, it reacquires the lock. To the developer, it appears as if the lock has been held the entire time.

*What happens when* notify( ) *is called and no thread is waiting?* This cannot happen in our animation component. Since the run( ) method does not exit, it is not possible for the lock to be freed without the thread being in a wait( ) method call. However, in general this is not the case: it is not required that some thread be executing the wait( ) method when another thread calls the notify( ) method. Since the wait-and-notify mechanism does not know the condition about which it is sending notification, it assumes that a notification goes unheard if no thread is waiting. In other words, if the notify( ) method is called when no other thread is waiting, notify( ) simply returns and the notification is lost. A thread that later executes the wait( ) method has to wait for another notification to occur.

*What are the details of the race condition that exists in the wait-and-notify mechanism?* In general, a thread that uses the wait( ) method confirms that a condition does not exist (typically by checking a variable) and then calls the wait( ) method. When another thread establishes the condition (typically by setting the same variable), it calls the notify( ) method. A race condition occurs when:

1. The first thread tests the condition and confirms that it must wait.
2. The second thread sets the condition.
3. The second thread calls the notify( ) method; this goes unheard since the first thread is not yet waiting.
4. The first thread calls the wait( ) method.

*How does this potential race condition get resolved?* This race condition is resolved by the synchronization lock discussed earlier. In order to call the wait( ) or notify( ) methods, we must have obtained the lock for the object on which we're calling the method. This is mandatory; the methods do not work properly and generate an exception condition if the lock is not held. Furthermore, the wait( ) method also releases the lock prior to waiting and reacquires the lock prior to returning from the wait( ) method. The developer must use this lock to ensure that checking the condition and setting the condition is atomic, which typically means that the check or set must be within the lock scope.

*Is there a race condition during the period that the* wait( ) *method releases and reacquires the lock?* The wait( ) method is tightly integrated with the lock mechanism.

The object lock is not actually freed until the waiting thread is already in a state in which it can receive notifications. This would have been difficult, if not impossible, to accomplish if we had needed to implement the wait( ) and notify( ) methods ourselves. The system prevents any race conditions from occurring in this mechanism.

*If a thread receives a notification, is it guaranteed that the condition is set correctly?* Simply, no. Prior to calling the wait( ) method, a thread should always test the condition while holding the synchronization lock. Upon returning from the wait( ) method, the thread should always retest the condition to determine if it should wait again. This is because another thread can also test the condition and determine that a wait is not necessary—processing the valid data that was set by the notification thread.

Let's look into how that can happen. Our animated canvas example is very simple; only one thread is actually waiting. In most programs, many threads are waiting and sending notifications. A race condition exists when multiple threads are waiting for notification. The race condition that is solved internally to the wait-and-notify mechanism prevents the loss of notifications, but it does not solve the following scenario when multiple threads are waiting:

1. Thread 1 calls a method that acquires the synchronization lock.
2. Thread 1 examines a state flag and determines that the data is not in the desired state.
3. Thread 1 calls the wait( ) method, which frees the lock.
4. Thread 2 calls a method that acquires the same synchronization lock.
5. Thread 3 calls a method that blocks waiting for the lock.
6. Thread 2 sets the state flag and calls the notify( ) method.
7. Thread 2 finishes its method and frees the lock.
8. Thread 3 acquires the lock and proceeds to process the data; it sees that the data is in the desired state, so it processes the data and resets the state flag.
9. Thread 3 exits without needing to wait.
10. Thread 1 receives the notification and wakes up.

This is a common case when multiple threads are involved in the notifications. More particularly, the threads that are processing the data can be thought of as consumers; they consume the data produced by other threads. There is no guarantee that when a consumer receives a notification that it has not been processed by another consumer. As such, when a consumer wakes up, it cannot assume that the state it was waiting for is still valid. It may have been valid in the past, but the state may have been changed after the notify( ) method was called and before the consumer thread woke up. Waiting threads must provide the option to check the state and to return back to a waiting state in case the notification has already been handled. This is why we always put calls to the wait( ) method in a loop.

Remember too that the wait( ) method can return early if its thread is interrupted. In that case, processing is application-specific, depending on how the algorithm needs to handle the interruption.

## wait( ), notify( ), and notifyAll( )

*What happens when more than one thread is waiting for notification? Which threads actually get the notification when the* notify( ) *method is called?* It depends: the Java specification doesn't define which thread gets notified. Which thread actually receives the notification varies based on several factors, including the implementation of the Java virtual machine and scheduling and timing issues during the execution of the program. There is no way to determine, even on a single processor platform, which of multiple threads receives the notification.

Another method of the Object class assists us when multiple threads are waiting for a condition:

void notifyAll( )
> Notifies all the threads waiting on the object that the condition has occurred. This method must be called from within a synchronized method or block.

The notifyAll( ) method is similar to the notify( ) method except that *all* of the threads that are waiting on the object are notified instead of a single arbitrary thread. Just like the notify( ) method, the notifyAll( ) method does not allow us to decide which thread gets the notification: they all get notified. When all the threads receive the notification, it is possible to work out a mechanism for the threads to choose among themselves which thread should continue and which thread(s) should call the wait( ) method again.

*Does the* notifyAll( ) *method really wake up all the threads?* Yes and no. All of the waiting threads wake up, but they still have to reacquire the object lock. So the threads do not run in parallel: they must each wait for the object lock to be freed. Thus, only one thread can run at a time, and only after the thread that called the notifyAll( ) method releases its lock.

*Why would you want to wake up all of the threads?* There are a few reasons. For example, there might be more than one condition to wait for. Since we cannot control which thread gets the notification, it is entirely possible that a notification wakes up a thread that is waiting for an entirely different condition. By waking up all the threads, we can design the program so that the threads decide among themselves which thread should execute next.[*]

---

[*] Later in this chapter, we discuss options to allow multiple condition variables to coexist. This allows different threads to wait for different conditions efficiently.

Another option could be when producers generate data that can satisfy more than one consumer. Since it may be difficult to determine how many consumers can be satisfied with the notification, an option is to notify them all, allowing the consumers to sort it out among themselves.

## Wait-and-Notify Mechanism with Synchronized Blocks

In our example, we showed how the wait( ) and notify( ) methods are called within a synchronized method. In that case, the lock that interacts with the wait( ) and notify( ) methods is the object lock of the this object.

It is possible to use the wait( ) and notify( ) methods with a synchronized block. In that case, the lock that the code holds is probably not the object lock of the code: it is most likely the lock of some object explicitly specified in the synchronized block. Therefore, you must invoke the wait( ) or notify( ) method on that same object, like this:

```
package javathreads.examples.ch04.example2;
...
public class AnimatedCharacterDisplayCanvas extends CharacterDisplayCanvas
                implements CharacterListener, Runnable {
    ...
    private Object doneLock = new Object();

    public synchronized void newCharacter(CharacterEvent ce) {
        ...
    }

    protected synchronized void paintComponent(Graphics gc) {
        ...
    }

    public void run( ) {
        synchronized(doneLock) {
            while (true) {
                try {
                    if (done) {
                        doneLock.wait( );
                    } else {
                        repaint( );
                        doneLock.wait(100);
                    }
                } catch (InterruptedException ie) {
                    return;
                }
            }
        }
    }

    public void setDone(boolean b) {
        synchronized(doneLock) {
            done = b;
```

```
        if (timer == null) {
            timer = new Thread(this);
            timer.start();
        }
        if (!done)
            doneLock.notify();
    }
  }
}
```

In this example, we've separated the synchronization that protects the animation (the tmpChar[] and curX variables) from the synchronization that protects the thread state (the timer and done variables). In programs with a lot of contention for object locks, this technique is useful since it allows more threads to access different methods at the same time (e.g., two threads can now simultaneously access the paintComponent( ) and run( ) methods).

Now when the wait( ) and notify( ) methods are called, we're holding the object lock of the doneLock object. Consequently, we explicitly call the doneLock.wait( ) and doneLock.notify( ) methods. That follows the same logic we outlined earlier; it's simply a different lock now.

It may help to remind yourself how Java objects work in this regard. In our first example, we had this statement:

```
wait( );
```

which is equivalent to this statement:

```
this.wait( );
```

So the wait( ) and notify( ) methods are consistent: they are always called with an object reference, even if that reference is the implied this object. The object reference must always be one that you hold the object lock for—and again, the synchronized method grabs the object lock of the this object.

## Condition Variables

Condition variables are a type of synchronization provided by many other threading systems. A condition variable is very similar to Java's wait-and-notify mechanism—in fact, in most cases it is functionally identical. The four basic functions of a POSIX condition variable—wait( ), timed_wait( ), signal( ), and broadcast( )—map directly to the methods provided by Java (wait( ), wait(long), notify( ), and notifyAll( ), respectively). The implementations are also logically identical. The wait( ) operation of a condition variable requires that a mutex lock be held. It releases the lock while waiting and reacquires the lock prior to returning to the caller. The signal( ) function wakes up one thread whereas the broadcast( ) function wakes up all the waiting threads. These functions also require that the mutex be held during the call. The race conditions of a condition variable are solved in the same way as those of Java's wait-and-notify mechanism.

There is one subtle difference, however. The wait-and-notify mechanism is highly integrated with its associated lock. This makes the mechanism easier to use than its condition variable counterpart. Calling the wait( ) and notify( ) methods from synchronized sections of code is just a natural part of their use. Using condition variables, however, requires that you create a separate mutex lock, store that mutex, and eventually destroy the mutex when it is no longer necessary.

Unfortunately, that convenience comes at a small price. A POSIX condition variable and its associated mutex lock are separate synchronization entities. It is possible to use the same mutex with two different condition variables, or even to mix and match mutexes and condition variables in any scope. While the wait-and-notify mechanism is much easier to use and is usable for most cases of signal-based synchronization, it is not capable of assigning any synchronization lock to any notification object. When you need to signal two different notification objects while requiring the same synchronization lock to protect common data, a condition variable is more efficient.

J2SE 5.0 adds a class that provides the functionality of condition variables. This class is used in conjunction with the Lock interface. Since this new interface (and, therefore, object) is separate from the calling object and the lock object, its usage is just as flexible as the condition variables in other threading systems. In Java, condition variables are objects that implement the Condition interface. The Condition interface is tied to the Lock interface, just as the wait-and-notify mechanism is tied to the synchronization lock.

To create a Condition object from the Lock object, you call a method available on the Lock object:

```
Lock lockvar = new ReentrantLock( );
Condition condvar = lockvar.newCondition( );
```

Using the Condition object is similar to using the wait-and-notify mechanism, with the Condition object's await( ) and signal( ) method calls replacing the wait( ) and notify( ) methods. We'll modify our typing program to use the condition variable instead of the wait-and-notify methods. This time, we'll show the implementation of the random character generator; the code for the animation character class is similar and can be found online.

```
package javathreads.examples.ch04.example3;
...
public class RandomCharacterGenerator extends Thread implements CharacterSource {
    ...
    private Lock lock = new ReentrantLock( );
    private Condition cv = lock.newCondition( );
    ...
    public void run( ) {
        try {
```

```
        lock.lock();
        while (true) {
            try {
                if (done) {
                    cv.await();
                } else {
                    nextCharacter();
                    cv.await(getPauseTime(), TimeUnit.MILLISECONDS);
                }
            } catch (InterruptedException ie) {
                return;
            }
        }
    } finally {
        lock.unlock();
    }
}

public void setDone(boolean b) {
    try {
        lock.lock();
        done = b;

        if (!done) cv.signal();
    } finally {
        lock.unlock();
    }
}
}
```

As we mentioned, a new Condition object is created by calling the newCondition() method provided by the Lock interface. This new Condition object is bound to the Lock instance whose method is called. This means that the lock of the Lock instance must be held in order to use the Condition object; it also means that the Condition object releases and reacquires the lock similar to the way Java's wait-and-notify mechanism works with synchronization locks.

Therefore, our new random character generator now uses a Lock object as its synchronization lock. We instantiate a Condition object, cv, which is set to the value returned by the newCondition() method of the lock object. Furthermore, calls to the wait() and notify() method are replaced by the condition object's await() and signal() method.

In this example, it doesn't look like we accomplished anything: all we do is use different methods to accomplish what we were previously able to accomplish using the wait-and-notify mechanism. In general, condition variables are necessary for several reasons.

First, condition variables are needed when you use Lock objects. Using the wait() and notify() methods of the Lock object will not work since these methods are already used internally to implement the Lock object. More importantly, just because you hold the Lock object doesn't mean you hold the synchronization lock of that object. In other words, the lock represented by the Lock object and the synchronization lock associated with the object are distinct. We need a condition variable mechanism that understands the locking mechanism provided by the Lock object. This condition variable mechanism is provided by the Condition object.

The second reason is the creation of the Condition object. Unlike the Java wait-and-notify mechanism, Condition objects are created as separate objects. It is possible to create more than one Condition object per lock object. That means we can target individual threads or groups of threads independently. With the standard Java mechanism, all waiting threads that are synchronizing on the same object are also waiting on the same condition.

Here are all the methods of the Condition interface. These methods must be called while holding the lock of the object to which the Condition object is tied:

void await( )
> Waits for a condition to occur.

void awaitUninterruptibly( )
> Waits for a condition to occur. Unlike the await( ) method, it is not possible to interrupt this call.

long awaitNanos(long nanosTimeout)
> Waits for a condition to occur. However, if the notification has not occurred in nanosTimeout nanoseconds, it returns anyway. The return value is an estimate of the timeout remaining; a return value equal or less than zero indicates that the method is returning due to the timeout. As usual, the actual resolution of this method is platform-specific and usually takes milliseconds in practice.

boolean await(long time, TimeUnit unit)
> Waits for a condition to occur. However, if the notification has not occurred in the timeout specified by the time and unit pair, it returns with a value of false.

boolean awaitUntil(Date deadline)
> Waits for a condition to occur. However, if the notification has not occurred by the absolute time specified, it returns with a value of false.

void signal( )
> Notifies a thread that is waiting using the Condition object that the condition has occurred.

void signalAll( )
> Notifies all the threads waiting using the Condition object that the condition has occurred.

Basically, the methods of the Condition interface duplicate the functionality of the wait-and-notify mechanism. A few convenience methods allow the developer to avoid being interrupted or to specify a timeout based on relative or absolute times.

# Summary

In this chapter, we introduced the methods of the wait-and-notify mechanism. We also examined the Condition interface, which provides a notification counterpart for the Lock interface.

With these methods of the Object class and Condition interface, threads are able to interoperate efficiently. Instead of just providing protection against race conditions, we now have ways for threads to inform each other about events or conditions without resorting to polling and timeouts.

In later chapters, we examine classes and techniques that provide even higher level support for data synchronization and thread communication.

# Example Classes

Here are the class names and Ant targets for the examples in this chapter:

| Description | Main Java class | Ant target |
| --- | --- | --- |
| Swing Type Tester with wait-and-notify mechanism | javathreads.examples.ch04.example1.<br>SwingTypeTester | ch4-ex1 |
| Swing Type Tester with wait-and-notify mechanism in synchronized blocks | javathreads.examples.ch04.example2.<br>SwingTypeTester | ch4-ex2 |
| Swing Type Tester with condition variables | javathreads.examples.ch04.example3.<br>SwingTypeTester | ch4-ex3 |

# CHAPTER 5

# Minimal Synchronization Techniques

In the previous two chapters, we discussed ways of making objects threadsafe, allowing them to be used by two or more threads at the same time. Thread safety is the most important aspect of good thread programming; race conditions are extremely difficult to reproduce and fix.

In this chapter, we complete our discussion of data synchronization and thread safety by examining two related topics. We begin with a discussion of the Java memory model, which defines how variables are actually accessed by threads. This model has some surprising ramifications; one of the issues that we'll clear up from our previous chapters is just what it means for a thread to be modeled as a list of instructions. After explaining the memory model, we discuss how volatile variables fit into it and why they can be used safely among multiple threads. This topic is all about avoiding synchronization.

We then examine another approach to data synchronization: the use of atomic classes. This set of classes, introduced in J2SE 5.0, allows certain operations on certain types of data to be defined atomically. These classes provide a nice data abstraction for the operations while preventing the race conditions that would otherwise be associated with the operation. These classes are also interesting because they take a different approach to synchronization: rather than explicitly synchronizing access to the data, they use an approach that allows race conditions to occur but ensures that the race conditions are all benign. Therefore, these classes automatically avoid explicit synchronization.

## Can You Avoid Synchronization?

Developers of threaded programs are often paranoid about synchronization. There are many horror stories about programs that performed poorly because of excessive or incorrect synchronization. If there is a lot of contention for a particular lock, acquiring the lock becomes an expensive operation for two reasons:

- The code path in many virtual machine implementations is different for acquiring contended and uncontended locks. Acquiring a contended lock requires executing more code at the virtual machine level. The converse of this statement is also true, however: acquiring an uncontended lock is a fairly inexpensive operation.

- Before a contended lock can by acquired, its current holder must release it. A thread that wants to acquire a contended lock must always wait for the lock to be released.

---

## Contended and Uncontended Locks

The terms contended and uncontended refer to how many threads are operating on a particular lock. A lock that is not held by any thread is an uncontended lock: the first thread that attempts to acquire it immediately succeeds.

When a thread attempts to acquire a lock that is already held by another thread, the lock becomes a contended lock. A contended lock has at least one thread waiting for it; it may have many more. Note that a contended lock becomes an uncontended one when threads are no longer waiting to acquire it.

---

In practical terms, the second point here is the most salient: if someone else holds the lock, you have to wait for it, which can greatly decrease the performance of your program. We discuss the performance of thread-related operations in Chapter 14.

This situation leads programmers to attempt to limit synchronization in their programs. This is a good idea; you certainly don't want to have unneeded synchronization in your program any more than you want to have unneeded calculations. But are there times when you can avoid synchronization altogether?

We've already seen that in one case the answer is yes: you can use the volatile keyword for an instance variable (other than a double or long). Those variables cannot be partially stored, so when you read them, you know that you're reading a valid value: the last value that was stored into the variable. Later in this chapter, we'll see another case where allowing unsynchronized access to data is acceptable by certain classes.

But these are really the only cases in which you can avoid synchronization. In all other cases, if multiple threads access the same set of data, you must explicitly synchronize *all* access to that data in order to prevent various race conditions.

The reasons for this have to do with the way in which computers optimize programs. Computers perform two primary optimizations: creating registers to hold data and reordering statements.

## The Effect of Registers

Your computer has a certain amount of main memory in which it stores the data associated with your program. When you declare a variable (such as the done flag used in several of our classes), the computer sets aside a particular memory location that holds the value of that variable.

Most CPUs are able to operate directly on the data that's held in main memory. Other CPUs can only read and write to main memory locations; these computers must read the data from main memory into a register, operate on that register, and then store the data to main memory. Yet even CPUs that can operate on data directly in main memory usually have a set of registers that can hold data, and operating on the data in the register is usually much faster than operating on the data in main memory. Consequently, register use is pervasive when the computer executes your code.

From a logical perspective, every thread has its own set of registers. When the operating system assigns a particular thread to a CPU, it loads the CPU registers with information specific to that thread; it saves the register information before it assigns a different thread to the CPU. So, threads never share data that is held in registers.

Let's see how this applies to a Java program. When we want to terminate a thread, we typically use a done flag. The thread (or runnable object) contains code, such as:

```
public void run( ) {
    while (!done) {
        foo( );
    }
}
public void setDone( ) {
    done = true;
}
```

Suppose we declare done as:

```
private boolean done = false;
```

This associates a particular memory location (e.g., 0xff12345) with the variable done and sets the value of that memory location to 0 (the machine representation of the value false).

The run( ) method is then compiled into a set of instructions:

```
Begin method run
Load register r1 with memory location OXff12345
Label L1:
Test if register r1 == 1
```

```
    If true branch to L2
    Call method foo
    Branch to L1
    Label L2:
    End method run
```

Meanwhile, the setDone( ) method looks something like this:

```
Begin method setDone
Store 1 into memory location 0xff12345
End method setDone
```

You can see the problem: the run( ) method never reloads register r1 with the contents of memory location 0xff12345. Therefore, the run( ) method never terminates.

However, suppose we define done as:

```
private volatile boolean done = false;
```

Now the run( ) method logically looks like this:

```
Begin method run
Label L1:
Test if memory location 0xff12345 == 1
If true branch to L2
Call method foo
Branch to L1
Label L2:
End method
```

Using the volatile keyword ensures that the variable is never kept in a register. This guarantees that the variable is truly shared between threads.*

Remember that we might have implemented this code by synchronizing around access to the done flag (rather than making the done flag volatile). This works because synchronization boundaries signal to the virtual machine that it must invalidate its registers. When the virtual machine enters a synchronized method or block, it must reload data it has cached in its local registers. Before the virtual machine exits a synchronization method or block, it must store its local registers to main memory.

## The Effect of Reordering Statements

Developers often hope that they can avoid synchronization by depending on the order of execution of statements. Suppose that we decide to keep track of the total score among a number of runs of our typing game. We might then write the resetScore( ) method like this:

```
public int currentScore, totalScore, finalScore
public void resetScore(boolean done) {
```

---

* The virtual machine can use registers for volatile variables as long as it obeys the semantics we've outlined. It's the principle that must be obeyed, not the actual implementation.

```
        totalScore += currentScore;
        if (done) {
            finalScore = totalScore;
            currentScore = 0;
        }
    }

    public int getFinalScore( ) {
        if (currentScore == 0)
            return finalScore;
        return -1;
    }
```

A race condition exists because we can have this order of execution by threads t1 and t2:

```
Thread1: Update total score
Thread2: See if currentScore == 0
Thread2: Return -1
Thread1: Update finalScore
Thread1: Set currentScore == 0
```

That's not necessarily fatal to our program logic. If we're periodically checking the score, we'll get −1 this time, but we'll get the correct answer next time. Depending on our program, that may be perfectly acceptable.

However, you cannot depend on the ordered execution of statements like this. The virtual machine may decide that it's more efficient to store 0 in currentScore before it assigns the final score. This decision is made at runtime based on the particular hardware running the program. In that case, we're left with this sequence:

```
Thread1: Update total score
Thread1: Set currentScore == 0
Thread2: See if currentScore == 0
Thread2: Return finalScore
Thread1: Update finalScore
```

Now the race condition has caused a problem: we've returned the wrong final score. Note that it doesn't make any difference whether the variables are defined as volatile: statements that include volatile variables can be reordered just like any other statements.

The only thing that can help us here is synchronization. If the resetScore( ) and getFinalScore( ) methods are synchronized, it doesn't matter whether the statements within methods are reordered since the synchronization prevents us from interleaving the thread execution of the methods.

Synchronized blocks also prevent the reordering of statements. The virtual machine cannot move a statement from inside a synchronized block to outside a synchronized block. Note, however, that the converse is not true: a statement before a synchronized block may be moved into the block, and a statement after a synchronized block may be moved into the block.

## Double-Checked Locking

This design pattern gained a fair amount of attention when it was first proposed, but it has been pretty thoroughly discredited by now. Still, it pops up every now and then, so here are the details for the curious.

One case where developers are tempted to avoid synchronization deals with lazy initialization. In this paradigm, an object contains a reference that is time-consuming to construct, so the developer delays construction of the object:

```
Foo foo;
public void useFoo() {
    if (foo == null) {
        synchronized(this) {
            if (foo == null)
                foo = new Foo();
        }
    }
    foo.invoke();
}
```

The developer's goal here is to prevent synchronization once the foo object has been initialized. Unfortunately, this pattern is broken because of the reasons we've just examined. In particular, the value for foo can be stored before the constructor for foo is called; a second thread entering the useFoo() method would then call foo.invoke() before the constructor for foo has completed. If foo is a volatile primitive (but not a volatile object), this can be made to work if you don't mind the case where foo is initialized more than once (and where multiple initializations of foo are guaranteed to produce the same value).

For more information on the double-checked locking pattern as well as an extensive treatement of the Java memory model, see *http://www.cs.umd.edu/~pugh/java/memoryModel/*.

# Atomic Variables

The purpose of synchronization is to prevent the race conditions that can cause data to be found in either an inconsistent or intermediate state. Multiple threads are not allowed to race during the sections of code that are protected by synchronization. This does not mean that the outcome or order of execution of the threads is deterministic: threads may be racing prior to the synchronized section of code. And if the threads are waiting on the same synchronization lock, the order in which the threads execute the synchronized code is determined by the order in which the lock is granted (which, in general, is platform-specific and nondeterministic).

This is a subtle but important point: not all race conditions should be avoided. Only the race conditions within thread-unsafe sections of code are considered a problem. We can fix the problem in one of two ways. We can synchronize the code to prevent the race condition from occurring, or we can design the code so that it is threadsafe without the need for synchronization (or with only minimal synchronization).

We are sure that you have tried both techniques. In the second case, it is a matter of shrinking the synchronization scope to be as small as possible and reorganizing code so that threadsafe sections can be moved outside of the synchronized block. Using volatile variables is another case of this; if enough code can be moved outside of the synchronized section of code, there is no need for synchronization at all.

This means that there is a balance between synchronization and volatile variables. It is not a matter of deciding which of two techniques can be used based on the algorithm of the program; it is actually possible to design programs to use both techniques. Of course, the balance is very one sided; volatile variables can be safely used only for a single load or store operation and can't be applied to long or double variables. These restrictions make the use of volatile variables uncommon.

J2SE 5.0 provides a set of atomic classes to handle more complex cases. Instead of allowing a single atomic operation (like load or store), these atomic classes allow multiple operations to be treated atomically. This may sound like an insignificant enhancement, but a simple compare-and-set operation that is atomic makes it possible for a thread to "grab a flag." In turn, this makes it possible to implement a locking mechanism: in fact, the ReentrantLock class implements much of its functionality with only atomic classes. In theory, it is possible to implement everything we have done so far without Java synchronization at all.

In this section, we examine these atomic classes. The atomic classes have two uses. Their first, and simpler, use is to provide classes that can perform atomic operations on single pieces of data. A volatile integer, for example, cannot be used with the ++ operator because the ++ operator contains multiple instructions. The AtomicInteger class, however, has a method that allows the integer it holds to be incremented atomically (yet still without using synchronization).

The second, and more complex, use of the atomic classes is to build complex code that requires no synchronization at all. Code that needs to access two or more atomic variables (or perform two or more operations on a single atomic variable) would normally need to be synchronized in order for both operations to be considered an atomic unit. However, using the same sort of coding techniques as the atomic classes themselves, you can design algorithms that perform these multiple operations and still avoid synchronization.

## Overview of the Atomic Classes

Four basic atomic types, implemented by the AtomicInteger, AtomicLong, AtomicBoolean, and AtomicReference classes, handle integers, longs, booleans, and objects, respectively. All these classes provide two constructors. The default constructor initializes the object with a value of zero, false, or null, depending on the data type. The other constructor creates the variable with an initial value that is specified by the programmer. The set( ) and get( ) methods provide functionality that is already available with volatile variables: the ability to atomically set or get the value. The get( ) and set( ) methods also ensure that the data is read from or written to main memory.

The getAndSet( ) method of these classes provides new functionality. This method atomically sets the variable to a new value while returning the previous value, all without acquiring any synchronization locks. Understand that it is not possible to simulate this functionality atomically using only get and set operators at the Java level without the use of synchronization. If it is not possible, then how is it implemented? This functionality is accomplished through the use of native methods not accessible to user-level Java programs. You could write your own native methods to accomplish this, but the platform-specific issues are fairly daunting. Furthermore, since the atomic classes are core classes in Java, they don't have the security issues related to user-defined native methods.

The compareAndSet( ) and weakCompareAndSet( ) methods are conditional modifier methods. Both of these methods take two arguments—the value the data is expected to have when the method starts, and a new value to set the data to. The methods set the variable to the new value only if the variable has the expected value. If the current value is not equal to the expected value, the variable is not changed and the method returns false. A boolean value of true is returned if the current value is equal to the expected value, in which case, the value is also set to the new value. The weak form of this method is basically the same, but with one less guarantee: if the value returned by this method is false, the variable has not been updated, but that does not mean that the existing value is not the expected value. This method can fail to update the value regardless of whether the initial value is the expected value.

The AtomicInteger and AtomicLong classes provide additional methods to support integer and long data types. Interestingly, these methods are all convenience methods implemented internally using the compare-and-set functionality provided. However, these methods are important and frequently used.

The incrementAndGet( ), decrementAndGet( ), getAndIncrement( ), and getAndDecrement( ) methods provide the functionality of the pre-increment, pre-decrement, post-increment, and post-decrement operators. They are needed because Java's increment and decrement operators are syntactic sugar for multiple load and store operations; these operations are not atomic with volatile variables. Using an atomic class allows you to treat the operations atomically.

The addAndGet( ) and getAndAdd( ) methods provide the pre- and post-operators for the addition of a specific value (the delta value). These methods allow the program to increment or decrement a variable by an arbitrary value—including a negative value, making a subtraction counterpart to these methods unnecessary.

*Does the atomic package support more complex variable types?* Yes and no. There is currently no implementation of atomic character or floating-point variables. You can use an AtomicInteger to hold a character, but using atomic floating-point numbers requires atomically managed objects with read-only floating-point values. We examine that case later in this chapter.

Some classes support arrays and variables that are already part of other objects. However, no extra functionality is provided by these classes, so support of complex types is minimal. For arrays, only one indexed variable can be modified at a time; there is no functionality to modify the whole array atomically. Atomic arrays are modelled using the AtomicIntegerArray, AtomicLongArray, and AtomicReferenceArray classes. These classes behave as arrays of their constituent data type, but an array size must be specified during construction and an index must be provided during operation. No class implements an array of booleans. This is only a minor inconvenience, as such an array can be simulated using the AtomicIntegerArray class.

Volatile variables (of certain types) that are already defined in other classes can be updated by using the AtomicIntegerFieldUpdater, AtomicLongFieldUpdater, and AtomicReferenceFieldUpdater classes. These classes are abstract. To use a field updater, you call the static newUpdater( ) method of the class, passing it the class and field names of the volatile instance variable within the class you wish to update. You can then perform the same atomic operations on the volatile field (e.g., post-increment via the getAndIncrement( ) method) as you can perform on other atomic variables.

Two classes complete our overview of the atomic classes. The AtomicMarkableReference class and the AtomicStampedReference class allow a mark or stamp to be attached to any object reference. To be exact, the AtomicMarkableReference class provides a data structure that includes an object reference bundled with a boolean, and the AtomicStampedReference class provides a data structure that includes an object reference bundled with an integer.

The basic methods of these classes are essentially the same, with slight modifications to allow for the two values (the reference and the stamp or mark). The get( ) method now requires an array to be passed as an argument; the stamp or mark is stored as the first element of the array and the reference is returned as normal. Other get methods return just the reference, mark, or stamp. The set( ) and compareAndSet( ) methods require additional parameters representing the mark or stamp. And finally, these classes contain an attemptMark( ) or attemptStamp( ) method, used to set the mark or stamp based on an expected reference.

## Using the Atomic Classes

As we mentioned, it is possible (in theory) to implement every program or class that we have implemented so far using only atomic variables. In truth, it is not that simple. The atomic classes are not a direct replacement of the synchronization tools—using them may require a complex redesign of the program, even in some simple classes. To understand this better, let's modify our ScoreLabel class* to use only atomic variables:

```java
package javathreads.examples.ch05.example1;

import javax.swing.*;
import java.awt.event.*;
import java.util.concurrent.*;
import java.util.concurrent.atomic.*;
import javathreads.examples.ch05.*;

public class ScoreLabel extends JLabel implements CharacterListener {
    private AtomicInteger score = new AtomicInteger(0);
    private AtomicInteger char2type = new AtomicInteger(-1);
    private AtomicReference<CharacterSource> generator = null;
    private AtomicReference<CharacterSource> typist = null;

    public ScoreLabel (CharacterSource generator, CharacterSource typist) {
        this.generator = new AtomicReference(generator);
        this.typist = new AtomicReference(typist);

        if (generator != null)
            generator.addCharacterListener(this);
        if (typist != null)
            typist.addCharacterListener(this);
    }

    public ScoreLabel () {
        this(null, null);
    }

    public void resetGenerator(CharacterSource newGenerator) {
        CharacterSource oldGenerator;

        if (newGenerator != null)
            newGenerator.addCharacterListener(this);

        oldGenerator = generator.getAndSet(newGenerator);
        if (oldGenerator != null)
            oldGenerator.removeCharacterListener(this);
    }

    public void resetTypist(CharacterSource newTypist) {
        CharacterSource oldTypist;

        if (newTypist != null)
            newTypist.addCharacterListener(this);
```

---

\* The ScoreLabel class also marks our first example using the J2SE 5.0 generics feature. You'll begin to see parameterized code in angle brackets; in this class <CharacterSource> is a generic reference. For more details, see *Java 1.5 Tiger: A Developer's Notebook* by David Flanagan and Brett McLaughlin (O'Reilly).

---

```
            oldTypist = typist.getAndSet(newTypist);
            if (oldTypist != null)
                oldTypist.removeCharacterListener(this);
        }

        public void resetScore() {
            score.set(0);
            char2type.set(-1);
            setScore();
        }

        private void setScore() {
            // This method will be explained in Chapter 7
            SwingUtilities.invokeLater(new Runnable() {
                public void run() {
                    setText(Integer.toString(score.get()));
                }
            });
        }

        public void newCharacter(CharacterEvent ce) {
            int oldChar2type;

            // Previous character not typed correctly: 1-point penalty
            if (ce.source == generator.get()) {
                oldChar2type = char2type.getAndSet(ce.character);

                if (oldChar2type != -1) {
                    score.decrementAndGet();
                    setScore();
                }
            }
            // If character is extraneous: 1-point penalty
            // If character does not match: 1-point penalty
            else if (ce.source == typist.get()) {
                while (true) {
                    oldChar2type = char2type.get();

                    if (oldChar2type != ce.character) {
                        score.decrementAndGet();
                        break;
                    } else if (char2type.compareAndSet(oldChar2type, -1)) {
                        score.incrementAndGet();
                        break;
                    }
                }

                setScore();
            }
        }
    }
```

When you compare this class to previous implementations, you'll see that we've made more changes here than simply substituting atomic variables for variables that were previously protected by synchronization. Removing the synchronization has affected our algorithms in different ways. We've made three kinds of modifications: simple variable substitution, changing algorithms, and retrying operations.

The point of each modification is to preserve the full semantics of the synchronized version of the class. The semantics of synchronized code are dependent upon realizing all the effects of the code. It isn't enough to make sure that the variables used by the code are updated atomically: you must ensure that the end effect of the code is the same as the synchronized version. We'll look at the different kinds of modifications we made to see the implication of this requirement.

## Variable substitution

The simplest kind of modification you may have to make is simply substituting atomic variables for the variables used in a previously synchronized method. That's what happens in our new implementation of the resetScore( ) method: The score and char2type variables have been changed to atomic variables, and this method just reinitializes them.

Interestingly, changing both variables together is not done atomically: it is possible for the score to be changed before the change to the char2type variable is completed. This may sound like a problem, but it actually isn't because we've preserved the semantics of the synchronized version of the class. Our previous implementations of the ScoreLabel class had a similar race condition that could cause the score to be slightly off if the resetScore( ) method is called while the listeners are still attached to the source.

In previous implementations, the resetScore( ) and newCharacter( ) methods are synchronized, but that only means they do not run simultaneously. A pending call to the newCharacter( ) method can still run out of order (with respect to the resetScore( ) method) due to arrival order or lock acquisition ordering. So a typist event may wait to be delivered until the resetScore( ) method completes, but when it is delivered it will be for an event that is now out of date. That's the same issue we'll see with this implementation of the class, where changing both variables in the resetScore( ) method is not handled atomically.

Remember that the purpose of synchronization is not to prevent all race conditions; it is to prevent problem race conditions. The race condition with this implementation of the resetScore( ) method is not considered a problem. In any case, we create a version of this typing game that atomically changes both the score and character later in this chapter.

## Changing algorithms

The second type of change is embodied within our new implementation of the resetGenerator( ) and resetTypist( ) methods. Our earlier attempt at having a separate synchronization lock for the resetGenerator( ) and resetTypist( ) methods was actually a good idea. Neither method changed the score or the char2type variables. In fact, they don't even change variables that are shared with each other—the synchronization lock for the resetGenerator( ) method is used only to protect the method from being called simultaneously by multiple threads. This is also true for the resetTypist( ) method; in fact, the issues for both methods are the same, so we discuss only the resetGenerator( ) method. Unfortunately, making the generator variable an AtomicReference has introduced multiple potential problems that we've had to address.

These problems arise because the state encapsulated by the resetGenerator( ) method is more than just the value of the generator variable. Making the generator variable an AtomicReference means that we know operations on that variable will occur atomically. But when we remove the synchronization from the resetGenerator( ) method completely, we must be sure that the entire state encapsulated by that method is still consistent.

In this case, the state includes the registration of the ScoreLabel object (the this object) with the character source generators. After the method completes, we want to ensure that the this object is registered with only one and only one generator (the one assigned to the generator instance variable).

Consider what would happen when two threads simultaneously call the resetGenerator( ) method. In this discussion, the existing generator is generatorA; one thread is calling the resetGenerator( ) method with a generator of generatorB; and another thread is calling the method with a generator called generatorC.

Our previous example looked like this:

```
if (generator != null)
    generator.removeCharacterListener(this);
generator = newGenerator;
if (newGenerator != null)
    newGenerator.addCharacterListener(this);
```

In this code, the two threads simultaneously ask generatorA to remove the this object: in effect, it would be removed twice. The ScoreLabel object would also be added to both generatorB and generatorC. Both of those effects are errors.

Because our previous example was synchronized, these errors were prevented. In our unsynchronized code, we must do this:

```
if (newGenerator != null)
    newGenerator.addCharacterListener(this);
oldGenerator = generator.getAndSet(newGenerator);
if (oldGenerator != null)
    oldGenerator.removeCharacterListener(this);
```

The effects of this code must be carefully considered. When called by our two threads simultaneously, the ScoreLabel object is registered with both generatorB and generatorC. The threads then set the current generator atomically. Because they're executing at the same time, different outcomes are possible. Suppose that the first thread executes first: it gets generatorA back from the getAndSet( ) method and then removes the ScoreLabel object from the listeners of generatorA. The second thread gets generatorB back from the getAndSet( ) method and removes the ScoreLabel from the listeners to generatorB. If the second thread executes first, the variables are slightly different, but the outcome is always the same: whichever object is assigned to the generator instance variable is the one (and only one) object that the ScoreLabel object is listening to.

There is one side effect here that affects another method. Since the listener is removed from the old data source after the exchange, and the listener is added to the new data source before the exchange, it is now possible to receive a character event that is neither from the current generator or typist source. The newCharacter( ) method previously checked to see whether the source is the generator source, and if not, assumes it is the typist source. This is no longer valid. The newCharacter( ) method now needs to confirm the source of the character before processing it; it must also ignore characters from spurious listeners.

## Retrying operations

The newCharacter( ) method contains the most extensive changes in this example. As we mentioned, the first change is to separate events based on the different character sources. This method can no longer assume that the source is the typist if the source is not the generator: it must also throw away any event that is from neither of the attached sources.

The handling of the generator event has only minor changes. First, the getAndSet( ) method is used to exchange the character with the new value atomically. Second, the user can't be penalized until after the exchange. This is because there is no way to be sure what the previous character was until after the exchange of the getAndSet( ) method completes. Furthermore, the score must also be decremented atomically since it could be changed simultaneously by multiple arriving events. Updates to the character and score are not handled atomically: a race condition still exists. However, once again it is not a problem. We need to update the score to credit or penalize the user correctly. It is not a problem if the user sees a very short delay before the score is updated.

The handling of the typist event is more complicated. We need to check to see if the character is typed correctly. If it isn't, the user is penalized. This is accomplished by decrementing the score atomically. If the character is typed correctly, the user can't be given credit immediately. Instead, the char2type variable has to be updated first. The score is updated only if char2type has been updated correctly. If the update operation fails, it means that another event has been processed (in another thread) while we were processing this event—and that the other operation was successful.

*What does it mean that the other thread was successful in processing another event?* It means that we must start our event processing over from the beginning. We made certain assumptions as we went along: assumptions that the value of variables we were using wouldn't change and that when our code was completed, all the variables we had set to have a particular value would indeed have that value. Because of the conflict with the other thread, those assumptions are violated. By retrying the event processing from the beginning, it's as if we never ran in the first place.

That's why this section of code is wrapped in an endless loop: the program does not leave the loop until the event is processed successfully. Obviously, there is a race condition between multiple events; the loop ensures that none of the events are missed or processed more than once. As long as we process all valid events exactly once, the order in which the events are processed doesn't matter: after processing each event, the data is left in a consistent state. Note that even when we use synchronization, the same situation applies: multiple events are not processed in a specific order; they are processed in the order that the locks are granted.

The purpose of atomic variables is to avoid synchronization for the sake of performance. However, how can atomic variables be faster if we have to place the code in an endless loop? The answer, of course, is that technically it is not an endless loop. Extra iterations of the loop occur only if the atomic operation fails, which in turn is due to a conflict with another thread. For the loop to be truly endless, we would need an endless number of conflicts. That would also be a problem if we used synchronization: an endless number of threads accessing the lock would also prevent the program from operating correctly. On the other hand, as discussed in Chapter 14, the difference in performance between atomic classes and synchronization is often not that large to begin with.

As we can tell from this example, it's necessary to balance the usage of synchronization and atomic variables. When we use synchronization, threads are blocked from running until they acquire a lock. This allows the code to execute atomically since other threads are barred from running that code. When we use atomic variables, threads are allowed to execute the same code in parallel. The purpose of atomic variables is not to remove race conditions that are not threadsafe; their purpose is to make the code threadsafe so that the race condition does not have to be prevented.

## Notifications and Atomic Variables

*Is it possible to use atomic variables if we also need the functionality of condition variables?* Implementing condition variable functionality using atomic variables is possible but not necessarily efficient. Synchronization—and the wait and notify mechanism—is implemented by controlling the thread states. Threads are blocked from running if they are unable to acquire the lock, and they are placed into a wait state until a particular condition occurs. Atomic variables do not block threads from running. In fact, code executed by unsynchronized threads may have to be placed into a loop for more complex operations in order to retry attempts that fail. In other words, it is possible to implement the condition variable functionality using atomic variables, but threads will be spinning as they wait for the desired condition.

This does not mean that you should avoid atomic variables if you need condition variable functionality. Once again, a balance must be found. It is possible to use atomic variables for portions of a program that do not entail notifications and to use synchronization elsewhere. It is possible to implement all of a program with atomic variables and use a separate library to send such notifications—a library that is internally using condition variables. Of course, in some situations, it is not a problem to allow the threads to spin while waiting.

This last alternative is the case with our typing game. First, only two threads—the animation component thread and the character generator thread—need to wait for a condition. Second, the waiting process occurs only when the game is stopped. The program is already waiting between frames of the animation; using this same loop and interval to wait for the user to restart the game does not add a significant performance penalty. Third, waiting for about 100 milliseconds (the interval period between frames of the animation) should not be noticeable to the user when the Start button is pressed; any user who notices that delay will also notice the delays in the animation itself.

Here is an implementation of our animation component using only atomic variables; it spins while the user has stopped the game. A similar implementation of the random-character generator is available in the online examples.

```
package javathreads.examples.ch05.example2;

import java.awt.*;
import javax.swing.*;
import java.util.concurrent.*;
import java.util.concurrent.atomic.*;
import javathreads.examples.ch05.*;

public class AnimatedCharacterDisplayCanvas extends CharacterDisplayCanvas
                    implements CharacterListener, Runnable {

    private AtomicBoolean done = new AtomicBoolean(true);
    private AtomicInteger curX = new AtomicInteger(0);
    private AtomicInteger tempChar = new AtomicInteger(0);
    private Thread timer = null;

    public AnimatedCharacterDisplayCanvas() {
        startAnimationThread();
    }

    public AnimatedCharacterDisplayCanvas(CharacterSource cs) {
        super(cs);
        startAnimationThread();
    }
```

```
        private void startAnimationThread( ) {
            if (timer == null) {
                timer = new Thread(this);
                timer.start( );
            }
        }

        public void newCharacter(CharacterEvent ce) {
            curX.set(0);
            tempChar.set(ce.character);
            repaint( );
        }

        protected void paintComponent(Graphics gc) {
            char[] localTmpChar = new char[1];
            localTmpChar[0] = (char) tempChar.get( );
            int localCurX = curX.get( );

            Dimension d = getSize( );
            int charWidth = fm.charWidth(localTmpChar[0]);
            gc.clearRect(0, 0, d.width, d.height);
            if (localTmpChar[0] == 0)
                return;

            gc.drawChars(localTmpChar, 0, 1,
                         localCurX, fontHeight);
            curX.getAndIncrement( );
        }

        public void run( ) {
            while (true) {
                try {
                    Thread.sleep(100);
                    if (!done.get( )) {
                        repaint( );
                    }
                } catch (InterruptedException ie) {
                    return;
                }
            }
        }

        public void setDone(boolean b) {
            done.set(b);
        }
    }
```

As with our previous example, using atomic variables is not simply a matter of replacing the variables protected by synchronization with atomic variables: the algorithm also needs to be adjusted in a fashion that allows any race conditions to be threadsafe. In our animation component, this is especially true for the code that creates the animation thread. Our previous examples created this thread when the setDone( ) method was called. We could have left the code in that method and used an atomic reference variable to store the thread object; only the thread that success-fully stored the atomic reference would actually call the start method of the new thread. However, it's much easier to implement this functionality by creating and starting the thread in a private method that is called only by the constructor of the object (since the constructor can never be called by multiple threads).

The newCharacter( ) method is only partially atomic. The individual variable opera-tions, assignments of curX and tempChar, are atomic since they are using atomic vari-ables. However, both assignments together are not atomic. This is not a problem if another thread simultaneously calls the newCharacter( ) method; both method calls set the curX variable to zero, and the character variable is assigned to the character requested by the second thread to execute the method. There is also a race condition between this method and the paintComponent( ) method, but it is probably not even noticeable. The race condition here results in a spurious increment by the paintComponent( ) method. This means that the new character is drawn starting with the second animation frame—the first animation frame is skipped—an effect that is unlikely to be noticed by the user.

The paintComponent( ) method is also not completely atomic, but as with the newCharacter( ) method, all its race conditions are acceptable. It is not possible for the paintComponent( ) method to have a conflict with itself, as the paintComponent( ) method is called only by the windowing system and only then from a single thread. So, there is no reason to protect the variables that are used only by the paintComponent( ) method. The paintComponent( ) method loads into temporary vari-ables data that it has in common with the newCharacter( ) method. If those variables happen to change during the paintComponent( ) method call, it is not a problem since another repaint( ) request will also be sent by the newCharacter( ) method. The result again is just a spurious animation frame.

The run( ) method is similar to our previous versions in that it calls the repaint( ) method every 100 milliseconds while the done flag is false. However, if the done flag is set to true, the thread still wakes up every 100 milliseconds. This means that the pro-gram does a "nothing" task every 100 milliseconds. This thread always executes every 100 milliseconds when the animation is running; it now still executes when the game is stopped. On the other hand, resuming the animation is no longer instanta-neous: the user could wait as much as 100 milliseconds to see a restart of the anima-tion. This could be solved by calling the repaint( ) method from the setDone( ) method, but that is not necessary for this example. The delay between the frames of the animation is 100 milliseconds. If a 100-millisecond delay to start the animation is noticeable, the 100-millisecond delay between the frames will be just as noticeable.

The implementation of the setDone( ) method is now much simpler. It no longer needs to create the animation thread since that is now done during construction of the component. And it no longer needs to inform the animation thread that the done flag has changed.

The major benefit of this implementation is that there is no longer any synchronization in this component. There is a slight threading overhead when the game is not running, but it is still less than when the game is running. Other programs may have a different profile. As we mentioned, developers do not just face a choice of using synchronization techniques or atomic variables; they must strike a balance between the two. In order to understand the balance, it is beneficial to use both techniques for many cases.

## Summary of Atomic Variable Usage

These examples show a number of canonical uses of atomic variables; we've used many techniques to extend the atomic operations provided by atomic variables. Here is a summary of those techniques.

---

### Optimistic Synchronization

What's happening in our examples with atomic variables is that there is no free lunch: the code avoids synchronization, but it pays a potential penalty in the amount of work it performs. You can think of this as "optimistic synchronization" (to modify a term from database management): the code grabs the value of the protected variable assuming that no one else is modifying it at the moment. The code then calculates a new value for the variable and attempts to update the variable. If another thread modified the variable in the meantime, the update fails and the code must restart its procedure (using the newly modified value of the variable).

The atomic classes use this technique internally in their implementation, and we use this technique in our examples when we have multiple operations on an atomic variable.

---

### Data exchange

Data exchange is the ability to set a value atomically while obtaining the previous value. This is accomplished with the getAndSet( ) method. Using this method guarantees that only a single thread obtains and uses a value.

*What if the data exchange is more complex? What if the value to be set is dependent on the previous value?* This is handled by placing the get( ) and the compareAndSet( ) methods in a loop. The get( ) method is used to get the previous value, which is used to calculate the new value. The variable is set to the new value using the compareAndSet( ) method—which sets the new value only if the value of the variable has not changed. If the compareAndSet( ) method fails, the entire operation can be retried because the current thread has not changed any data up to the time of the failure. Although the get( ) method call, the calculation of the new value, and the exchange of data may not be individually atomic, the sequence is considered atomic if the exchange is successful since it can succeed only if no other thread has changed the value.

### Compare and set

Comparing and setting is the ability to set a value atomically only if the current value is an expected value. The compareAndSet( ) method handles this case. This important method provides the ability to have conditional support at an atomic level. This basic functionality can even be used to implement the synchronization ability provided by mutexes.

*What if the comparison is more complex? What if the comparison is dependent on the previous or external values?* This case can be handled as before by placing the get( ) and the compareAndSet( ) methods in a loop. The get( ) method is used to get the previous value, which can be used either for comparison or just to allow an atomic exchange. The complex comparison is used to see if the operation should proceed. The compareAndSet( ) method is then used to set the value if the current value has not changed. The whole operation is retried if the operation fails. As before, the whole operation is considered atomic because the data is changed atomically and changed only if it matches the value at the start of the operation.

### Advanced atomic data types

Although the list of data types for which atomic classes are available is pretty extensive, it is not complete. The atomic package doesn't support character and floating-point types. While it does support generic object types, it doesn't support the operations needed for more complex types of objects, such as strings. However, we can implement atomic support for any new type by simply encapsulating the data type into a read-only data object. The data object can then be changed atomically by changing the atomic reference to a new data object. This works only if the values embedded within the data object are not changed in any way. Any change to the data object must be accomplished only by changing the reference to a different object— the previous object's values are not changed. All values encapsulated by the data object, directly and indirectly, must be read-only for this technique to work.

As a result, it may not be possible to change a floating-point value atomically, but it is possible to change an object reference atomically to a different floating-point value. As long as the floating-point values are read-only, this technique is threadsafe. With this in mind, we can implement an atomic class for floating-point values:

```
package javathreads.examples.ch05;

import java.lang.*;
import java.util.concurrent.atomic.*;

public class AtomicDouble extends Number {
    private AtomicReference<Double> value;
```

```java
public AtomicDouble( ) {
    this(0.0);
}

public AtomicDouble(double initVal) {
    value = new AtomicReference<Double>(new Double(initVal));
}

public double get( ) {
    return value.get().doubleValue( );
}

public void set(double newVal) {
    value.set(new Double(newVal));
}

public boolean compareAndSet(double expect, double update) {
    Double origVal, newVal;

    newVal = new Double(update);
    while (true) {
        origVal = value.get( );

        if (Double.compare(origVal.doubleValue( ), expect) == 0) {
            if (value.compareAndSet(origVal, newVal))
                return true;
        } else {
            return false;
        }
    }
}

public boolean weakCompareAndSet(double expect, double update) {
    return compareAndSet(expect, update);
}

public double getAndSet(double setVal) {
    Double origVal, newVal;

    newVal = new Double(setVal);
    while (true) {
        origVal = value.get( );

        if (value.compareAndSet(origVal, newVal))
            return origVal.doubleValue( );
    }
}

public double getAndAdd(double delta) {
    Double origVal, newVal;

    while (true) {
        origVal = value.get( );
        newVal = new Double(origVal.doubleValue( ) + delta);
```

```java
            if (value.compareAndSet(origVal, newVal))
                return origVal.doubleValue( );
        }
    }

    public double addAndGet(double delta) {
        Double origVal, newVal;

        while (true) {
            origVal = value.get( );
            newVal = new Double(origVal.doubleValue( ) + delta);
            if (value.compareAndSet(origVal, newVal))
                return newVal.doubleValue( );
        }
    }

    public double getAndIncrement( ) {
        return getAndAdd((double) 1.0);
    }

    public double getAndDecrement( ) {
        return getAndAdd((double) -1.0);
    }

    public double incrementAndGet( ) {
        return addAndGet((double) 1.0);
    }

    public double decrementAndGet( ) {
        return addAndGet((double) -1.0);
    }

    public double getAndMultiply(double multiple) {
        Double origVal, newVal;

        while (true) {
            origVal = value.get( );
            newVal = new Double(origVal.doubleValue( ) * multiple);
            if (value.compareAndSet(origVal, newVal))
                return origVal.doubleValue( );
        }
    }

    public double multiplyAndGet(double multiple) {
        Double origVal, newVal;

        while (true) {
            origVal = value.get( );
            newVal = new Double(origVal.doubleValue( ) * multiple);
            if (value.compareAndSet(origVal, newVal))
                return newVal.doubleValue( );
        }
    }
}
```

In our new `AtomicDouble` class, we use an atomic reference object to encapsulate a double floating-point value. Since the `Double` class already encapsulates a double value, there is no need to create a new class; the `Double` class is used to hold the double value.

The get( ) method now has to use two method calls to get the double value—it must now get the `Double` object, which in turn is used to get the double floating-point value. Getting the `Double` object type is obviously atomic because we are using an atomic reference object to hold the object. However, the overall technique works because the data is read-only: it can't be changed. If the data were not read-only, retrieval of the data would not be atomic, and the two methods when used together would also not be considered atomic.

The set( ) method is used to change the value. Since the encapsulated value is read-only, we must create a new `Double` object instead of changing the previous value. As for the atomic reference itself, it is atomic because we are using an atomic reference object to change the value of the reference.

The `compareAndSet( )` method is implemented using the complex compare-and-set technique already mentioned. The `getAndSet( )` method is implemented using the complex data exchange technique already mentioned. And as for all the other methods—the methods that add, multiply, etc.—they too, are implemented using the complex data exchange technique. We don't explicitly show an example in this chapter for this class, but we'll use it in Chapter 15. For now, this class is a great framework for implementing atomic support for new and complex data types.

### Bulk data modification

In our previous examples, we have set only individual variables atomically; we haven't set groups of variables atomically. In those cases where we set more than one variable, we were not concerned that they be set atomically as a group. However, atomically setting a group of variables can be done by creating an object that encapsulates the values that can be changed; the values can then be changed simultaneously by atomically changing the atomic reference to the values. This works exactly like the `AtomicDouble` class.

Once again, this works only if the values are not directly changed in any way. Any change to the data object is accomplished by changing the reference to a different object—the previous object's values must not be changed. All values, encapsulated either directly and indirectly, must be read-only for this technique to work.

Here is an atomic class that protects two variables: a score and a character variable. Using this class, we are able to develop a typing game that modifies both the score and character variables atomically:

```
package javathreads.examples.ch05.example3;

import java.util.concurrent.atomic.*;
```

```java
public class AtomicScoreAndCharacter {
    public class ScoreAndCharacter {
        private int score, char2type;

        public ScoreAndCharacter(int score, int char2type) {
            this.score = score;
            this.char2type = char2type;
        }

        public int getScore() {
            return score;
        }

        public int getCharacter() {
            return char2type;
        }
    }

    private AtomicReference<ScoreAndCharacter> value;

    public AtomicScoreAndCharacter() {
        this(0, -1);
    }

    public AtomicScoreAndCharacter(int initScore, int initChar) {
        value = new AtomicReference<ScoreAndCharacter>
                    (new ScoreAndCharacter(initScore, initChar));
    }

    public int getScore() {
        return value.get().getScore();
    }

    public int getCharacter() {
        return value.get().getCharacter();
    }

    public void set(int newScore, int newChar) {
        value.set(new ScoreAndCharacter(newScore, newChar));
    }

    public void setScore(int newScore) {
        ScoreAndCharacter origVal, newVal;

        while (true) {
            origVal = value.get();
            newVal = new ScoreAndCharacter
                        (newScore, origVal.getCharacter());
            if (value.compareAndSet(origVal, newVal)) break;
        }
    }

    public void setCharacter(int newCharacter) {
        ScoreAndCharacter origVal, newVal;
```

```
        while (true) {
            origVal = value.get();
            newVal = new ScoreAndCharacter
                        (origVal.getScore(), newCharacter);
            if (value.compareAndSet(origVal, newVal)) break;
        }
    }

    public void setCharacterUpdateScore(int newCharacter) {
        ScoreAndCharacter origVal, newVal;
        int score;

        while (true) {
            origVal = value.get();
            score = origVal.getScore();
            score = (origVal.getCharacter() == -1) ? score : score-1;

            newVal = new ScoreAndCharacter (score, newCharacter);
            if (value.compareAndSet(origVal, newVal)) break;
        }
    }

    public boolean processCharacter(int typedChar) {
        ScoreAndCharacter origVal, newVal;
        int origScore, origCharacter;
        boolean retValue;

        while (true) {
            origVal = value.get();
            origScore = origVal.getScore();
            origCharacter = origVal.getCharacter();

            if (typedChar == origCharacter) {
                origCharacter = -1;
                origScore++;
                retValue = true;
            } else {
                origScore--;
                retValue = false;
            }

            newVal = new ScoreAndCharacter(origScore, origCharacter);
            if (value.compareAndSet(origVal, newVal)) break;
        }
        return retValue;
    }
}
```

As in our AtomicDouble class, the getScore() and getCharacter() methods work because the encapsulated values are treated as read-only. The set() method has to create a new object to encapsulate the new values to be stored.

The `setScore()` and `setCharacter()` methods are implemented using the advance data exchange technique. This is because the implementation is technically exchanging data, not just setting the data. Even though we are changing only one part of the encapsulated data, we still have to read the data that is not supposed to change (in order to make sure that, in fact, it hasn't). And since we have to change the whole set of data atomically—guaranteeing that the data that isn't supposed to change did not change—we have to implement the code as a data exchange.

The `setCharacterUpdateScore()` and `processCharacter()` methods implement the core of the scoring system. The first method sets the new character to be typed while penalizing the user if the previous character has not been typed correctly. The second method compares the typed character with the current generated character. If they match, the character is set to a noncharacter value, and the score is incremented. If they do not match, the score is simply decremented. Interestingly, as complex as these two methods are, they are still atomic, because all calculations are done with temporary variables and all of the values are atomically changed using a data exchange.

Performing bulk data modification, as well as using an advanced atomic data type, may use a large number of objects. A new object needs to be created for every transaction, regardless of how many variables need to be modified. A new object also needs to be created for each atomic compare-and-set operation that fails and has to be retried. Once again, using atomic variables has to be balanced with using synchronization. Is the creation of all the temporary objects acceptable? Is this technique better than synchronization? Or is there a compromise? The answer depends on your particular program.

As these techniques demonstrate, using atomic variables is sometimes complex. The complexity occurs when you use multiple atomic variables, multiple operations on a single atomic variable, or both techniques within a section of code that must be atomic. In many cases, atomic variables are simple to use because you just want to use them for a single operation, such as updating a score.

In many cases, using this kind of minimal synchronization is not a good idea. It can get very complex, making it difficult for the code to be maintained or transferred between developers. With a high volume of method calls where synchronization can be a problem, the benefit to minimal synchronization is still debatable. For those readers that find a class or subsystem where they believe synchronization is causing a problem, it may be a good idea to revisit this topic—if just to get a better comfort level in using minimal synchronization.

## Thread Local Variables

Any thread can, at any time, define a thread local variable that is private to that particular thread. Other threads that define the same variable create their own copy of the variable. This means that thread local variables cannot be used to share state between threads; changes to the variable in one thread are private to that thread and not reflected in the copies held by other threads. But it also means that access to the variable need never be synchronized since it's impossible for multiple threads to access the variable. Thread local variables have other uses, of course, but their most common use is to allow multiple threads to cache their own data rather than contend for synchronization locks around shared data.

A thread local variable is modeled by the java.lang.ThreadLocal class:

```java
public class ThreadLocal<T> {
    protected T initialValue();
    public T get();
    public void set(T value);
    public void remove();
}
```

In typical usage, you subclass the ThreadLocal class and override the initialValue() method to return the value that should be returned the first time a thread accesses the variable. The subclass rarely needs to override the other methods of the ThreadLocal class; instead, those methods are used as a getter/setter pattern for the thread-specific value.

One case where you might use a thread local variable to avoid synchronization is in a thread-specific cache. Consider the following class:

```java
package javathreads.examples.ch05.example4;

import java.util.*;

public abstract class Calculator {

    private static ThreadLocal<HashMap> results = new ThreadLocal<HashMap>() {
        protected HashMap initialValue() {
            return new HashMap();
        }
    };

    public Object calculate(Object param) {
        HashMap hm = results.get();
        Object o = hm.get(param);
        if (o != null)
                return o;
        o = doLocalCalculate(param);
        hm.put(param, o);
        return o;
    }

    protected abstract Object doLocalCalculate(Object param);
}
```

Thread local objects are declared static so that the object itself (that is, the results variable in this example) is shared among all threads. When the get( ) method of the thread local variable is called, the internal mechanism of the thread local class returns the specific object assigned to the specific thread. The initial value of that object is returned from the initialValue( ) method of the class extending ThreadLocal; when you create a thread local variable, you are responsible for implementing that method to return the appropriate (thread-specific) object.

When the calculate( ) method in our example is called, the thread local hash map is consulted to see if the value has previously been calculated. If so, that value is returned; otherwise, the calculation is performed and the new value stored in the hash map. Since access to the map is from only a single thread, we're able to use a HashMap object rather than a Hashtable object (or otherwise synchronizing the hash map).

This approach is worthwhile only if the calculation is very expensive since obtaining the hash map itself requires synchronizing on all the threads. If the reference returned from the thread-local get() method is held a long time, it may be worth exploring this type of design since otherwise that reference would need to be synchronized for a long time. Otherwise, you're just trading one synchronization call for another. And in general, the performance of the ThreadLocal class has been fairly dismal, though this situation improved in JDK 1.4 and even more in J2SE 5.0.

Another case where this technique is useful is dealing with thread-unsafe classes. If each thread instantiates the necessary object in a thread local variable, it has its own copy that it can safely access.

## Inheritable Thread Local Variables

Values stored by threads in thread local variables are unrelated. When a new thread is created, it gets a new copy of the thread local variable, and the value of that variable is what's returned by the initialValue( ) method of the thread local subclass.

An alternative to this idea is the InheritableThreadLocal class:

```
package java.lang;
public class InheritableThreadLocal extends ThreadLocal {
    protected Object childValue(Object parentValue);
}
```

This class allows a child thread to inherit the value of the thread local variable from its parent; that is, when the get( ) method of the thread local variable is called by the child thread, it returns the same value as when that method is called by the parent thread.

If you like, you can use the childValue( ) method to further augment this behavior. When the child thread calls the get( ) method of the thread local variable, the get( ) method looks up the value associated with the parent thread. It then passes that value to the `childValue()` method and returns that result. By default, the `childValue()` method simply returns its argument, so no transformation occurs.

# Summary

In this chapter, we've examined some advanced techniques for synchronization. We've learned about the Java memory model and why it inhibits some synchronization techniques from working as expected. This has led to a better understanding of volatile variables as well as an understanding of why it's hard to change the synchronization rules imposed by Java.

We've also examined the atomic package that comes with J2SE 5.0. This is one way in which synchronization can be avoided, but it comes with a price: the nature of the classes in the atomic package is such that algorithms that use them often have to change (particularly when multiple atomic variables are used at once). Creating a method that loops until the desired outcome is achieved is a common way to implement atomic variables.

## Example Classes

Here are the class names and Ant targets for the examples in this chapter:

| Description | Main Java class | Ant target |
|---|---|---|
| Swing Type Tester using atomic ScoreLabel | `javathreads.examples.ch05.example1.SwingTypeTester` | ch5-ex1 |
| Swing Type Tester using atomic animation canvas | `javathreads.examples.ch05.example2.SwingTypeTester` | ch5-ex2 |
| Swing Type Tester using atomic score and character class | `javathreads.examples.ch05.example3.SwingTypeTester` | ch5-ex3 |
| Calculation test using thread local variables | `javathreads.examples.ch05.example4.CalculatorTest` | ch5-ex4 |

The calculator test requires a command-line argument that sets the number of threads that run simultaneously. In the Ant script, it is defined by this property:

```
<property name="CalcThreadCount" value="10"/>
```

# CHAPTER 6

# Advanced Synchronization Topics

In this chapter, we look at some of the more advanced issues related to data synchronization—specifically, timing issues related to data synchronization. When you write a Java program that makes use of several threads, issues related to data synchronization are those most likely to create difficulties in the design of the program, and errors in data synchronization are often the most difficult to detect since they depend on events happening in a specific order. Often an error in data synchronization can be masked in the code by timing dependencies. You may notice some sort of data corruption in a normal run of your program, but when you run the program in a debugger or add some debugging statements to the code, the timing of the program is completely changed, and the data synchronization error no longer occurs.

These issues can't be simply solved. Instead, developers need to design their programs with these issues in mind. Developers need to understand what the different threading issues are: what are the causes, what they should look for, and the techniques they should use to avoid and mitigate them. Developers should also consider using higher-level synchronization tools—tools that provide the type of synchronization needed by the program and that are known to be threadsafe. We examine both of these ideas in this chapter.

## Synchronization Terms

Programmers with a background in a particular threading system generally tend to use terms specific to that system to refer to some of the concepts we discuss in this chapter, and programmers without a background in certain threading systems may not necessarily understand the terms we use. So here's a comparison of particular terms you may be familiar with and how they relate to the terms in this chapter:

*Barrier*
    A barrier is a rendezvous point for multiple threads: all threads must arrive at the barrier before any of them are permitted to proceed past the barrier. J2SE 5.0

supplies a barrier class, and a barrier class for previous versions of Java can be found in the Appendix.

*Condition variable*

A condition variable is not actually a lock; it is a variable associated with a lock. Condition variables are often used in the context of data synchronization. Condition variables generally have an API that achieves the same functionality as Java's wait-and-notify mechanism; in that mechanism, the condition variable is actually the object lock it is protecting. J2SE 5.0 also supplies explicit condition variables, and a condition variable implementation for previous versions of Java can be found in the Appendix. Both kinds of condition variables are discussed in Chapter 4.

*Critical section*

A critical section is a synchronized method or block. Critical sections do not nest like synchronized methods or blocks.

*Event variable*

Event variable is another term for a condition variable.

*Lock*

This term refers to the access granted to a particular thread that has entered a synchronized method or block. We say that a thread that has entered such a method or block has acquired the lock. As we discussed in Chapter 3, a lock is associated with either a particular instance of an object or a particular class.

*Monitor*

A generic synchronization term used inconsistently between threading systems. In some systems, a monitor is simply a lock; in others, a monitor is similar to the wait-and-notify mechanism.

*Mutex*

Another term for a lock. Mutexes do not nest like synchronization methods or blocks and generally can be used across processes at the operating system level.

*Reader/writer locks*

A lock that can be acquired by multiple threads simultaneously as long as the threads agree to only read from the shared data or that can be acquired by a single thread that wants to write to the shared data. J2SE 5.0 supplies a reader-writer lock class, and a similar class for previous versions of Java can be found in the Appendix.

*Semaphores*

Semaphores are used inconsistently in computer systems. Many developers use semaphores to lock objects in the same way Java locks are used; this usage makes them equivalent to mutexes. A more sophisticated use of semaphores is to take advantage of a counter associated with them to nest acquisitions to the critical sections of code; Java locks are exactly equivalent to semaphores in this usage. Semaphores are also used to gain access to resources other than code. Semaphore classes that implement most of these features are available in J2SE 5.0.

# Synchronization Classes Added in J2SE 5.0

You probably noticed a strong pattern while reading this list of terms: beginning with J2SE 5.0, almost all these things are included in the core Java libraries. We'll take a brief look into these J2SE 5.0 classes.

## Semaphore

In Java, a semaphore is basically a lock with an attached counter. It is similar to the Lock interface as it can also be used to prevent access if the lock is granted; the difference is the counter. In those terms, a semaphore with a counter of one is the same thing as a lock (except that the semaphore would not nest, whereas the lock—depending on its implementation—might).

The Semaphore class keeps tracks of the number of permits it can issue. It allows multiple threads to grab one or more permits; the actual usage of the permits is up to the developer. Therefore, a semaphore can be used to represent the number of locks that can be granted. It could also be used to throttle the number of threads working in parallel, due to resource limitations such as network connections or disk space.

Let's take a look at the Semaphore interface:

```
public class Semaphore {
    public Semaphore(long permits);
    public Semaphore(long permits, boolean fair);
    public void acquire() throws InterruptedException;
    public void acquireUninterruptibly();
    public void acquire(long permits) throws InterruptedException;
    public void acquireUninterruptibly(long permits);
    public boolean tryAcquire();
    public boolean tryAcquire(long timeout, TimeUnit unit);
    public boolean tryAcquire(long permits);
    public boolean tryAcquire(long permits,
                              long timeout, TimeUnit unit);
    public void release(long permits);
    public void release();
    public long availablePermits();
}
```

The Semaphore interface is very similar to the Lock interface. The acquire() and release() methods are similar to the lock() and unlock() methods of the Lock interface—they are used to grab and release permits, respectively. The tryAcquire() methods are similar to the tryLock() methods in that they allow the developer to try to grab the lock or permits. These methods also allow the developer to specify the time to wait if the permits are not immediately available and the number of permits to acquire or release (the default number of permits is one).

Semaphores have a few differences from locks. First, the constructor requires the specification of the number of permits to be granted. There are also methods that return the number of total and free permits. This class implements only a grant and release algorithm; unlike the Lock interface, no attached condition variables are available with semaphores. There is no concept of nesting; multiple acquisitions by the same thread acquire multiple permits from the semaphore.

If a semaphore is constructed with its fair flag set to true, the semaphore tries to allocate the permits in the order that the requests are made—as close to first-come-first-serve as possible. The downside to this option is speed: it takes more time for the virtual machine to order the acquisition of the permits than to allow an arbitrary thread to acquire a permit.

## Barrier

Of all the different types of thread synchronization tools, the barrier is probably the easiest to understand and the least used. When we think of synchronization, our first thought is of a group of threads executing part of an overall task followed by a point at which they must synchronize their results. The barrier is simply a waiting point where all the threads can sync up either to merge results or to safely move on to the next part of the task. This is generally used when an application operates in phases. For example, many compilers make multiple passes between loading the source and generating the executable, with many interim files. A barrier, when used in this regard, can make sure that all of the threads are in the same phase.

*Given its simplicity, why is the barrier not more commonly used?* The functionality is simple enough that it can be accomplished with the low-level tools provided by Java. We can solve the coordination problem in two ways, without using a barrier. First, we can simply have the threads wait on a condition variable. The last thread releases the barrier by notifying all of the other threads. A second option is to simply await termination of the threads by using the join( ) method. Once all threads have been joined, we can start new threads for the next phase of the program.

However, in some cases it is preferable to use barriers. When using the join( ) method, threads are exiting and we're starting new ones. Therefore, the threads lose any state that they have stored in their previous thread object; they need to store that state prior to terminating. Furthermore, if we must always create new threads, logical operations cannot be placed together; since new threads have to be created for each subtask, the code for each subtask must be placed in separate run( ) methods. It may be easier to code all of the logic as one method, particularly if the subtasks are very small.

Let's examine the interface to the barrier class:

```
public class CyclicBarrier {
    public CyclicBarrier(int parties);
    public CyclicBarrier(int parties, Runnable barrierAction);
    public int await() throws InterruptedException, BrokenBarrierException;
    public int await(long timeout, TimeUnit unit) throws InterruptedException,
                     BrokenBarrierException, TimeoutException;
    public void reset();
    public boolean isBroken();
    public int getParties();
    public int getNumberWaiting();
}
```

The core of the barrier is the await( ) method. This method basically behaves like the conditional variable's await( ) method. There is an option to either wait until the barrier releases the thread or for a timeout condition. There is no need to have a signal( ) method because notification is accomplished by the barrier when the correct number of parties are waiting.

When the barrier is constructed, the developer must specify the number of parties (threads) using the barrier. This number is used to trigger the barrier: the threads are all released when the number of threads waiting on the barrier is equal to the number of parties specified. There is also an option to specify an action—an object that implements the run( ) method. When the trigger occurs, the run( ) method on the barrierAction object is called prior to releasing the threads. This allows code that is not threadsafe to execute; generally, it calls the cleanup code for the previous phase and/or setup code for the next phase. The last thread that reaches the barrier—the triggering thread—is the thread that executes the action.

Each thread that calls the await( ) method gets back a unique return value. This value is related to the arrival order of the thread at the barrier. This value is needed for cases when the individual threads need to negotiate how to divide up work during the next phase of the process. The first thread to arrive is one less than the number of parties; the last thread to arrive will have a value of zero.

In normal usage, the barrier is very simple. All the threads wait until the number of required parties arrive. Upon arrival of the last thread, the action is executed, the threads are released, and the barrier can be reused. However, exception conditions can occur and cause the barrier to fail. When the barrier fails, the CyclicBarrier class breaks the barrier and releases all of the threads waiting on the await( ) method with a BrokenBarrierException. The barrier can be broken for a number of reasons. The waiting threads can be interrupted, a thread may break through the barrier due to a timeout condition, or an exception could be thrown by the barrier action.

In every exception condition, the barrier simply breaks, thus requiring that the individual threads resolve the matter. Furthermore, the barrier can no longer be reused until it is reinitialized. That is, part of the complex (and application-specific) algorithm to resolve the situation includes the need to reinitialize the barrier. To reinitialize the barrier, you use the reset() method. However, if there are threads already waiting on the barrier, the barrier will not initialize; in fact, it will break. Reinitialization of the barrier is complex enough that it may be safer to create a new barrier.

Finally, the CyclicBarrier class provides a few operational support methods. These methods provide informational data on the number of threads already waiting on the barrier, or whether the barrier is already broken.

## Countdown Latch

The countdown latch implements a synchronization tool that is very similar to a barrier. In fact, it can be used instead of a barrier. It also can be used to implement a functionality that some threading systems (but not Java) support with semaphores. Like the barrier class, methods are provided that allow threads to wait for a condition. The difference is that the release condition is not the number of threads that are waiting. Instead, the threads are released when the specified count reaches zero.

The CountDownLatch class provides a method to decrement the count. It can be called many times by the same thread. It can also be called by a thread that is not waiting. When the count reaches zero, all waiting threads are released. It may be that no threads are waiting. It may be that more threads than the specified count are waiting. And any thread that attempts to wait after the latch has triggered is immediately released. The latch does not reset. Furthermore, later attempts to lower the count will not work.

Here's the interface of the countdown latch:

```
public class CountDownLatch {
    public CountDownLatch(int count);
    public void await() throws InterruptedException;
    public boolean await(long timeout, TimeUnit unit)
                    throws InterruptedException;
    public void countDown();
    public long getCount();
}
```

This interface is pretty simple. The initial count is specified in the constructor. A couple of overloaded methods are provided for threads to wait for the count to reach zero. And a couple of methods are provided to control the count—one to decrement and one to retrieve the count. The boolean return value for the timeout variant of the await() method indicates whether the latch was triggered—it returns true if it is returning because the latch was released.

## Exchanger

The exchanger implements a synchronization tool that does not really have equivalents in any other threading system. The easiest description of this tool is that it is a combination of a barrier with data passing. It is a barrier in that it allows pairs of threads to rendezvous with each other; upon meeting in pairs, it then allow the pairs to exchange one set of data with each other before separating.

This class is closer to a collection class than a synchronization tool—it is mainly used to pass data between threads. It is also very specific in that threads have to be paired up, and a specific data type must be exchanged. But this class does have its advantages. Here is its interface:

```
public class Exchanger<V> {
    public Exchanger();
    public V exchange(V x) throws InterruptedException;
    public V exchange(V x, long timeout, TimeUnit unit)
            throws InterruptedException, TimeoutException;
}
```

The exchange( ) method is called with the data object to be exchanged with another thread. If another thread is already waiting, the exchange( ) method returns with the other thread's data. If no other thread is waiting, the exchange( ) method waits for one. A timeout option can control how long the calling thread waits.

Unlike the barrier class, this class is very safe to use: it will not break. It does not matter how many parties are using this class; they are paired up as the threads come in. Timeouts and interrupts also do not break the exchanger as they do in the barrier class; they simply generate an exception condition. The exchanger continues to pair threads around the exception condition.

## Reader/Writer Locks

Sometimes you need to read information from an object in an operation that may take a fairly long time. You need to lock the object so that the information you read is consistent, but you don't necessarily need to prevent another thread from also reading data from the object at the same time. As long as all the threads are only reading the data, there's no reason why they shouldn't read the data in parallel since this doesn't affect the data each thread is reading.

In fact, the only time we need data locking is when data is being changed, that is, when it is being written. Changing the data introduces the possibility that a thread reading the data sees the data in an inconsistent state. Until now, we've been content to have a lock that allows only a single thread to access the data whether the thread is reading or writing, based on the theory that the lock is held for a short time.

If the lock needs to be held for a long time, it makes sense to consider allowing multiple threads to read the data simultaneously so that these threads don't need to compete against each other to acquire the lock. Of course, we must still allow only a single thread to write the data, and we must make sure that none of the threads that were reading the data are still active while our single writer thread is changing the internal state of the data.

Here are the classes and interfaces in J2SE 5.0 that implement this type of locking:

```
public interface ReadWriteLock {
    Lock readLock();
    Lock writeLock();
}

public class ReentrantReadWriteLock implements ReadWriteLock {
    public ReentrantReadWriteLock();
    public ReentrantReadWriteLock(boolean fair);
    public Lock writeLock();
    public Lock readLock();
}
```

You create a reader-writer lock by instantiating an object using the ReentrantReadWriteLock class. Like the ReentrantLock class, an option allows the locks to be distributed in a fair fashion. By "fair," this class means that the lock is granted on very close to a first-come-first-serve basis. When the lock is released, the next set of readers/writer is granted the lock based on arrival time.

Usage of the lock is predictable. Readers should obtain the read lock while writers should obtain the write lock. Both of these locks are objects of the Lock class—their interface is discussed in Chapter 3. There is one major difference, however: reader-writer locks have different support for condition variables. You can obtain a condition variable related to the write lock by calling the newCondition() method; calling that method on a read lock generates an UnsupportedOperationException.

These locks also nest, which means that owners of the lock can repeatedly acquire the locks as necessary. This allows for callbacks or other complex algorithms to execute safely. Furthermore, threads that own the write lock can also acquire the read lock. The reverse is not true. Threads that own the read lock cannot acquire the write lock; upgrading the lock is not allowed. However, downgrading the lock is allowed. This is accomplished by acquiring the read lock before releasing the write lock.

Later in this chapter, we examine the topic of lock starvation in depth. Reader-writer locks have special issues in this regard.

In this section, we've examined higher-level synchronization tools provided by J2SE 5.0. These tools all provide functionality that in the past could have been implemented by the base tools provided by Java—either through an implementation by the developer or by the use of third-party libraries. These classes don't provide new functionality that couldn't be accomplished in the past; these tools are written totally in Java. In a sense, they can be considered convenience classes; that is, they are designed to make development easier and to allow application development at a higher level.

There is also a lot of overlap between these classes. A Semaphore can be used to partially simulate a Lock simply by declaring a semaphore with one permit. The write lock of a reader-writer lock is practically the same as a mutually exclusive lock. A semaphore can be used to simulate a reader-writer lock, with a limited set of readers, simply by having the reader thread acquire one permit while the writer thread acquires all the permits. A countdown latch can be used as a barrier simply by having each thread decrement the count prior to waiting.

The major advantage in using these classes is that they offload threading and data synchronization issues. Developers should design their programs at as high a level as possible and not have to worry about low-level threading issues. The possibility of deadlock, lock and CPU starvation, and other very complex issues is mitigated somewhat. Using these libraries, however, does not remove the responsibility for these problems from the developer.

# Preventing Deadlock

Deadlock between threads competing for the same set of locks is the hardest problem to solve in any threaded program. It's a hard enough problem, in fact, that it cannot be solved in the general case. Instead, we try to offer a good understanding of deadlock and some guidelines on how to prevent it. Preventing deadlock is completely the responsibility of the developer—the Java virtual machine does not do deadlock prevention or deadlock detection on your behalf.

Let's revisit the simple deadlock example from Chapter 3.

```
package javathreads.examples.ch03.example8;
...
public class ScoreLabel extends JLabel implements CharacterListener {
    ...
    private Lock adminLock = new ReentrantLock();
    private Lock charLock = new ReentrantLock();
    private Lock scoreLock = new ReentrantLock();
    ...
    public void resetScore() {
        try {
            charLock.lock();
            scoreLock.lock();
            score = 0;
            char2type = -1;
            setScore();
        } finally {
            charLock.unlock();
            scoreLock.unlock();
        }
    }

    public void newCharacter(CharacterEvent ce) {
        try {
            scoreLock.lock();
            charLock.lock();
            // Previous character not typed correctly: 1-point penalty
            if (ce.source == generator) {
```

```
            if (char2type != -1) {
                score--;
                setScore();
            }
            char2type = ce.character;
        }

        // If character is extraneous: 1-point penalty
        // If character does not match: 1-point penalty
        else {
            if (char2type != ce.character) {
                score--;
            } else {
                score++;
                char2type = -1;
            }
            setScore();
        }
    } finally {
        scoreLock.unlock();
        charLock.unlock();
    }
    }
}
```

To review, deadlock occurs if two threads execute the newCharacter() and resetScore() methods in a fashion that each can grab only one lock. If the newCharacter() method grabs the score lock while the resetScore() method grabs the character lock, they both eventually wait for each other to release the locks. The locks, of course, are not released until they can finish execution of the methods. And neither thread can continue because each is waiting for the other thread's lock. This deadlock condition cannot be resolved automatically.

As we mentioned at the time, this example is simple, but more complicated conditions of deadlock follow the same principles outlined here: they're harder to detect, but nothing more is involved than two or more threads attempting to acquire each other's locks (or, more correctly, waiting for conflicting conditions).

Deadlock is difficult to detect because it can involve many classes that call each other's synchronized sections (that is, synchronized methods or synchronized blocks) in an order that isn't apparently obvious. Suppose we have 26 classes, A to Z, and that the synchronized methods of class A call those of class B, those of class B call those of class C, and so on, until those of class Z call those of class A. If two threads call any of these classes, this could lead us into the same sort of deadlock situation that we had between the newCharacter() and resetScore() methods, but it's unlikely that a programmer examining the source code would detect that deadlock.

Nonetheless, a close examination of the source code is the only option presently available to determine whether deadlock is a possibility. Java virtual machines do not detect deadlock at runtime, and while it is possible to develop tools that examine source code to detect potential deadlock situations, no such tools exist yet for Java.

---

## Virtual Machine–Level Deadlock Detection

In certain cases, the virtual machine can detect that two threads are deadlocked. It's possible to obtain a stack trace for all active threads in the virtual machine through a platform-specific operation. On Solaris, Linux, and other Unix systems, sending the virtual machine a –3 signal (via the kill command) produces that output. On Windows systems, entering Ctrl-Break produces the stack output.

If two or more threads are waiting for each other's locks, the virtual machine detects this and prints out that information in the thread dump. However, even though the virtual machine has detected the deadlock, it does not take any steps to resolve it.

The virtual machine cannot detect other kinds of deadlock, such as the first case we examined in Chapter 3. In that example, the deadlock occurred because the run( ) method never allowed any other method to grab the synchronization lock. That kind of application-level deadlock is impossible for the virtual machine to detect.

---

The simplest way to avoid deadlock is to follow this rule. When a lock is held, never call any methods that need other locks—i.e., never call a synchronized method of another class from a synchronized method. This is a good rule that is often advocated, but it's not the ideal rule for two reasons:

- It's impractical: many useful Java methods are synchronized, and you'll want to call them from your synchronized method. As an example, many of the collection classes discussed in Chapter 8 have synchronized methods. To avoid the usage of collection classes from synchronized methods would prevent data from being moved or results from being saved.

- It's overkill: if the synchronized method you're going to call does not in turn call another synchronized method, there's no way that deadlock can occur. Furthermore, if the class or library is accessed only through its class interface—with no cross-calling—placing extra restrictions on using the library is silly.

Nonetheless, if you can manage to obey this rule, there will be no deadlocks in your program.

Another frequently used technique to avoid deadlock is to lock some higher-order object that is related to the many lower-order objects we need to use. In our example, that means removing the efficiency that causes this deadlock: to use only one lock to protect the score and the character assignments.

Of course, this is only a simple example: we don't need to lock everything. If we can isolate the location of the deadlock, we can use a slightly higher order lock only to protect the methods that are having problems. Or we can make a rule that adds the requirement that an additional lock be held prior to acquiring the problem locks. All these variations of locking multiple objects suffer from the same lock granularity problem that we're about to discuss.

The problem with this technique is that it often leads to situations where the lock granularity is not ideal. By synchronizing with only one lock, we are preventing access to variables we may not be changing or even using. The purpose of threaded programming is to accomplish tasks simultaneously—not to have these threads waiting on some global lock. Furthermore, if we've done our program design correctly, there was probably a reason why we attempted to acquire multiple locks rather than a single global lock. Solving deadlock issues by violating this design becomes somewhat counterproductive.

The most practical rule to avoid deadlock is to make sure that the locks are always acquired in the same order. In our example, it means that either the score or character lock must be acquired first—it doesn't matter which as long as we are consistent. This implies the need for a lock hierarchy—meaning that locks are not only protecting their individual items but are also keeping an order to the items. The score lock protects not only the values of the score, but the character lock as well. This is the technique that we used to fix the deadlock in Chapter 3:

```
package javathreads.examples.ch03.example9;
...
public class ScoreLabel extends JLabel implements CharacterListener {
    ...
    public void resetScore() {
        try {
            scoreLock.lock();
            charLock.lock();
            score = 0;
            char2type = -1;
            setScore();
        } finally {
            charLock.unlock();
            scoreLock.unlock();
        }
    }
    ...
}
```

Since the resetScore() method now also grabs the score lock first, it is not possible for any thread to be waiting for the score lock while holding the character lock. This means that the character lock may eventually be grabbed and released, followed by the eventual release of the score lock. A deadlock does not occur.

Again, this is a very simple example. For much more complex situations, we may have to do all of the following:

- Use only locking objects—things that implement the Lock interface—and avoid use of the synchronized keyword. This allows the separation of the locks from the objects in the application. We do this even with our simple example.

- Understand which locks are assigned to which subsystems and understand the relationships between the subsystems. We define a subsystem as a class, group of classes, or library that performs a relatively independent service. The subsystem must have a documented interface that we can test or debug in our search for deadlocks. This allows us to form groups of locks and map out potential deadlocks.

- Form a locking hierarchy within each subsystem. Unlike the other two steps, this can actually hurt the efficiency of the application. The subsystem needs to be studied. The relationship of the locks must be understood in order to be able to form a hierarchy that will have minimal impact on the efficiency of the application.

If you are developing a very complex Java program, it's a good idea to develop a lock hierarchy when the application is being designed. It may be very difficult to enforce a lock hierarchy after much of the program has been developed. Finally, since there is no mechanism to enforce a lock hierarchy, it is up to your good programming practices to make sure that the lock hierarchy is followed. Following a lock acquisition hierarchy is the best way to guarantee that deadlock does not occur in your Java program due to synchronization.

## Deadlock and Automatic Lock Releases

There are a few more concerns about deadlock when using the Lock interface (or any locking mechanism that is not the Java synchronized keyword). The first is illustrated by how we have used the Lock class in every example up to this point. Our resetScore( ) method can be easier written (and understood) as follows:

```
public void resetScore( ) {
    scoreLock.lock( );
    charLock.lock( );
    score = 0;
    char2type = -1;
    setScore( );
    charLock.unlock( );
    scoreLock.unlock( );
}
```

However, what happens if the thread that calls the resetScore( ) method encounters a runtime exception and terminates? Under many threading systems, this leads to a type of deadlock because the thread that terminates does not automatically release the locks it held. Under those systems, another thread could wait forever when it tries to change the score. In Java, however, locks associated with the synchronized keyword are always released when the thread leaves the scope of the synchronized block, even if it leaves that scope due to an exception. So in Java when using the synchronized keyword, this type of deadlock never occurs.

But we are using the Lock interface instead of the synchronized keyword. It is not possible for Java to figure out the scope of the explicit lock—the developer's intent may be to hold the lock even on an exception condition. Consequently, in this new version of the resetScore( ) method, if the setScore( ) method throws a runtime exception, the lock is never freed since the unlock( ) methods are never called.

There is a simple way around this: we can use Java's finally clause to make sure that the locks are freed upon completion, regardless of how the method exits. This is what we've done in all our examples.

By the way, this antideadlock behavior of the synchronized keyword is not necessarily a good thing. When a thread encounters a runtime exception while it is holding a lock, there's the possibility—indeed, the expectation—that it will leave the data it was manipulating in an inconsistent state. If another thread is then able to acquire the lock, it may encounter this inconsistent data and proceed erroneously.

When using explicit locks, you should not only use the finally clause to free the lock, but you should also test for, and clean up after, the runtime exception condition. Unfortunately, given Java's semantics, this problem is impossible to solve completely when using the synchronized keyword or by using the finally clause. In fact, it's exactly this problem that led to the deprecation of the stop( ) method: the stop( ) method works by throwing an exception, which has the potential to leave key resources in the Java virtual machine in an inconsistent state.

Since we cannot solve this problem completely, it may sometimes be better to use explicit locks and risk deadlock if a thread exits unexpectedly. It may be better to have a deadlocked system than to have a corrupted system.

## Preventing Deadlock with Timeouts

Since the Lock interface provides options for when a lock can't be grabbed; can we use those options to prevent deadlock? Absolutely. Another way to prevent deadlock is not to wait for the lock—or at least, to place restrictions on the waiting period. By using the tryLock( ) method to provide alternatives in the algorithm, the chances of deadlock can be greatly mitigated. For example, if we need a resource but have an alternate (maybe slower) resource available, using the alternate resource allows us to complete the operation and ultimately free any other locks we may be holding. Alternatively, if we are unable to obtain the lock within a time limit, perhaps we can clean up our state—including releasing the locks we are currently holding—and allow other conflicting threads to finish up and free their locks.

Unfortunately, using explicit locks in this fashion is more complex than using a lock hierarchy. To develop a lock hierarchy, we simply have to figure out the order in which the locks must be obtained. To use timeouts, we need to design the application to allow alternative paths to completion, or the capability to "undo" operations for a later "redo." The advantage to timeouts is that there can be a greater degree of parallelism. We are actually designing multiple pathways to completion to avoid deadlock instead of placing restrictions on the algorithm in order to avoid deadlock.

You must decide whether these types of benefits outweigh the added complexity of the code when you design your Java program. If you start by creating a lock hierarchy, you'll have simpler code at the possible expense of the loss of some parallelism. We think it is easier to write the simpler code first and then address the parallelism problems if they become a performance bottleneck.

# Deadlock Detection

The problem with deadlock is that it causes the program to hang indefinitely. Obviously, if a program hangs, deadlock may be the cause. But is deadlock always the cause? In programs that wait for users, wait for external systems, or have complex interactions, it can be very difficult to tell a deadlock situation from the normal operation of the program. Furthermore, what if the deadlock is localized? A small group of threads in the program may deadlock with each other while other threads continue running, masking the deadlock from the user (or the program itself). While it is very difficult to prevent deadlock, can we at least detect it? To understand how to detect deadlock, we must first understand its cause.

Figure 6-1 shows two cases of threads and locks waiting for each other. The first case is of locks waiting for the owner thread to free them. The locks are owned by the thread so they can't be used by any other thread. Any thread that tries to obtain these locks is placed into a wait state. This also means that if the thread deadlocks, it can make many locks unavailable to other threads.

The second case is of threads waiting to obtain a lock. If the lock is owned by another thread, the thread must wait for it to be free. Technically, the lock does not own the thread, but the effect is the same—the thread can't accomplish any other task until the lock is freed. Furthermore, a lock can have many threads waiting for it to be free. This means that if a lock deadlocks, it can block many waiting threads.

We have introduced many new terms here—we'll explain them before we move on. We define a deadlocked lock as a lock that is owned by a thread that has deadlocked. We define a deadlocked thread as a thread that is waiting for a deadlocked lock. These two definitions are admittedly circular, but that is how deadlocks are

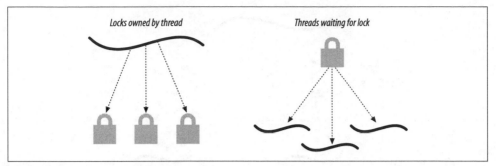

*Figure 6-1. Lock trees*

caused. A thread owns a lock that has waiting threads that own a lock that has waiting threads that own a lock, and so on. A deadlock occurs if the original thread needs to wait for any of these locks. In effect, a loop has been created. We have locks waiting for threads to free them, and threads waiting for locks to be freed. Neither can happen because indirectly they are waiting for each other.

We define a hard wait as a thread trying to acquire a lock by waiting indefinitely. We call it a soft wait if a timeout is assigned to the lock acquisition. The timeout is the exit strategy if a deadlock occurs. Therefore, for deadlock detection situations, we need only be concerned with hard waits. Interrupted waits are interesting in this regard. If the wait can be interrupted, is it a hard wait or a soft wait? The answer is not simple because there is no way to tell if the thread that is implemented to call the interrupt( ) method at a later time is also involved in the deadlock. For now, we will simply not allow the wait for the lock·to be interrupted. We will revisit the issue of the delineation between soft and hard waits later in this chapter. However, in our opinion, interruptible waits should be considered hard waits since using interrupts is not common in most programs.

Assuming that we can keep track of all of the locks that are owned by a thread and keep track of all the threads that are performing a hard wait on a lock, is detecting a potential deadlock possible? Yes. Figure 6-2 shows a potential tree that is formed by locks that are owned and formed by hard waiting threads. Given a thread, this figure shows all the locks that are owned by it, all the threads that are hard waiting on those locks in turn, and so on. In effect, each lock in the diagram is already waiting, whether directly or indirectly, for the root thread to eventually allow it to be free. If this thread needs to perform a hard wait on a lock, it can't be one that is in this tree. Doing so creates a loop, which is an indication of a deadlock situation. In summary, we can detect a deadlock by simply traversing this tree. If the lock is already in this tree, a loop is formed, and a deadlock condition occurs.

Using this algorithm, here is an implementation of a deadlock-detecting lock:

```
package javathreads.examples.ch06;

public class DeadlockDetectedException extends RuntimeException {
    public DeadlockDetectedException(String s) {
```

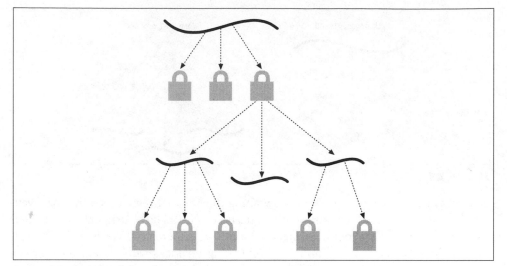

*Figure 6-2. Completed thread wait tree*

```
        super(s);
    }
}

package javathreads.examples.ch06;

import java.util.*;
import java.util.concurrent.*;
import java.util.concurrent.locks.*;

public class DeadlockDetectingLock extends ReentrantLock {
    private static List deadlockLocksRegistry = new ArrayList();

    private static synchronized void registerLock(DeadlockDetectingLock ddl) {
        if (!deadlockLocksRegistry.contains(ddl))
            deadlockLocksRegistry.add(ddl);
    }

    private static synchronized void unregisterLock(DeadlockDetectingLock ddl) {
        if (deadlockLocksRegistry.contains(ddl))
            deadlockLocksRegistry.remove(ddl);
    }

    private List hardwaitingThreads = new ArrayList();

    private static synchronized void markAsHardwait(List l, Thread t) {
        if (!l.contains(t)) l.add(t);
    }

    private static synchronized void freeIfHardwait(List l, Thread t) {
        if (l.contains(t)) l.remove(t);
    }
```

```java
private static Iterator getAllLocksOwned(Thread t) {
    DeadlockDetectingLock current;
    ArrayList results = new ArrayList();

    Iterator itr = deadlockLocksRegistry.iterator();
    while (itr.hasNext()) {
        current = (DeadlockDetectingLock) itr.next();
        if (current.getOwner() == t) results.add(current);
    }
    return results.iterator();
}

private static Iterator getAllThreadsHardwaiting(DeadlockDetectingLock l) {
    return l.hardwaitingThreads.iterator();
}

private static synchronized
        boolean canThreadWaitOnLock(Thread t, DeadlockDetectingLock l) {
    Iterator locksOwned = getAllLocksOwned(t);
    while (locksOwned.hasNext()) {
        DeadlockDetectingLock current =
                (DeadlockDetectingLock) locksOwned.next();

        if (current == l) return false;

        Iterator waitingThreads = getAllThreadsHardwaiting(current);
        while (waitingThreads.hasNext()) {
            Thread otherthread = (Thread) waitingThreads.next();

            if (!canThreadWaitOnLock(otherthread, l)) {
                return false;
            }
        }
    }
    return true;
}

public DeadlockDetectingLock() {
    this(false, false);
}

public DeadlockDetectingLock(boolean fair) {
    this(fair, false);
}

private boolean debugging;
public DeadlockDetectingLock(boolean fair, boolean debug) {
    super(fair);
    debugging = debug;
    registerLock(this);
}

public void lock() {
    if (isHeldByCurrentThread()) {
```

```java
        if (debugging) System.out.println("Already Own Lock");
        super.lock();
        freeIfHardwait(hardwaitingThreads, Thread.currentThread());
        return;
    }

    markAsHardwait(hardwaitingThreads, Thread.currentThread());
    if (canThreadWaitOnLock(Thread.currentThread(), this)) {
        if (debugging) System.out.println("Waiting For Lock");
        super.lock();
        freeIfHardwait(hardwaitingThreads, Thread.currentThread());
        if (debugging) System.out.println("Got New Lock");
    } else {
        throw new DeadlockDetectedException("DEADLOCK");
    }
}

public void lockInterruptibly() throws InterruptedException {
    lock();
}

public class DeadlockDetectingCondition implements Condition {
    Condition embedded;
    protected DeadlockDetectingCondition(ReentrantLock lock, Condition e) {
        embedded = e;
    }

    public void await() throws InterruptedException {
        try {
            markAsHardwait(hardwaitingThreads, Thread.currentThread());
            embedded.await();
        } finally {
            freeIfHardwait(hardwaitingThreads, Thread.currentThread());
        }
    }

    public void awaitUninterruptibly() {
        markAsHardwait(hardwaitingThreads, Thread.currentThread());
        embedded.awaitUninterruptibly();
        freeIfHardwait(hardwaitingThreads, Thread.currentThread());
    }

    public long awaitNanos(long nanosTimeout) throws InterruptedException {
        try {
            markAsHardwait(hardwaitingThreads, Thread.currentThread());
            return embedded.awaitNanos(nanosTimeout);
        } finally {
            freeIfHardwait(hardwaitingThreads, Thread.currentThread());
        }
    }

    public boolean await(long time, TimeUnit unit)
                                    throws InterruptedException {
        try {
```

```
            markAsHardwait(hardwaitingThreads, Thread.currentThread( ));
            return embedded.await(time, unit);
        } finally {
            freeIfHardwait(hardwaitingThreads, Thread.currentThread( ));
        }
    }

    public boolean awaitUntil(Date deadline) throws InterruptedException {
        try {
            markAsHardwait(hardwaitingThreads, Thread.currentThread( ));
            return embedded.awaitUntil(deadline);
        } finally {
            freeIfHardwait(hardwaitingThreads, Thread.currentThread( ));
        }
    }

    public void signal( ) {
        embedded.signal( );
    }

    public void signalAll( ) {
        embedded.signalAll( );
    }
}

    public Condition newCondition( ) {
        return new DeadlockDetectingCondition(this);
    }
}
```

Before we go into detail on this deadlock-detecting lock, it must be noted that this listing has been cut down for this book. For the latest, fully commented version, including testing tools, please see the online examples, which include (as example 1) a class that can be used to test this implementation.

In terms of implementation, this class inherits from the Lock interface, so it may be used anywhere that a Lock object is required. Furthermore, deadlock detection requires the registration of all locks involved in the deadlock. Therefore, to detect a deadlock, replace all the locks with this class, even the locks provided by the synchronized keyword. It may not be possible to detect a loop if any of the locks are unregistered.

To use this class, replace all instances of ReentrantLock with DeadlockDetectingLock. This slows down your program, but when a deadlock is detected, a DeadlockDetectedException is immediately thrown. Because of the performance implications of this class, we do not recommend using it in a production environment: use it only to diagnose occurrences of deadlock. The advantage of using this class is that it detects the deadlock immediately when it occurs instead of waiting for a symptom of the deadlock to occur and diagnosing the problem then.

The DeadlockDetectingLock class maintains two lists—a deadlockLocksRegistry and a hardwaitingThreads list. Both of these lists are stored in thread-unsafe lists because external synchronization will be used to access them. In this case, the external synchronization is the class lock; all accesses to these lists come from synchronized static methods. A single deadlockLocksRegistry list holds all deadlock-detecting locks that have been created. One hardwaitingThreads list exists for each deadlock-detecting lock. This list is not static; it holds all the thread objects that are performing a hard wait on the particular lock.

The deadlock locks are added and removed from the registry by using the registerLock() and unregisterLock() methods. Threads are added and removed from the hard waiting list using the markAsHardwait() and freeIfHardwait() methods respectively. Since these methods are static—while the list is not—the list must be passed as one of the parameters to these methods. In terms of implementation, they are simple; the objects are added and removed from a list container.

The getAllLocksOwned() and getAllThreadsHardwaiting() methods are used to get the two types of waiting subtrees we mentioned earlier. Using these subtrees, we can build the complete wait tree that needs to be traversed. The getAllThreadsHardwaiting() method simply returns the list of hard waiting threads already maintained by the deadlock-detecting lock. The list of owned locks is slightly more difficult. The getAllLocksOwned() method has to traverse all registered deadlock-detecting locks, looking for locks that are owned by the target thread. In terms of synchronization, both of these methods are called from a method that owns the class lock; as a result, there is no need for these private methods to be synchronized.

The canThreadWaitOnLock() method is used to traverse the wait tree, looking to see if a particular lock is already in the tree. This is the primary method that is used to detect potential deadlocks. When a thread is about to perform a hard wait on a lock, it calls this method. A deadlock is detected if the lock is already in the wait tree. Note that the implementation is recursive. The method examines all of the locks owned to see if the lock is in the first level of the tree. It also traverses each owned lock to get the hard waiting threads; each hard waiting thread is further examined recursively. This method uses the class lock for synchronization.

With the ability to detect deadlocks, we can now override the lock() method of the ReentrantLock class. This new implementation is actually not that simple. The ReentrantLock class is incredibly optimized—meaning it uses minimal synchronization. In that regard, our new lock() method is also minimally synchronized.

The first part of the lock() method is for nested locks. If the lock is already owned by this thread, there is no reason to check for deadlocks. Instead, we can just call the original lock() method. There is no race condition for this case: only the owner thread can succeed in the test for nested locks and call the original lock() method. And since there is no chance that the owner of the lock will change if the owner is the currently executing thread, there is no need to worry about the potential race condition between the isHeldByCurrentThread( ) and super.lock( ) method calls.

The second part of the lock( ) method is used to obtain new locks. It first checks for deadlocks by calling the canThreadWaitOnLock( ) method. If a deadlock is detected, a runtime exception is thrown. Otherwise, the thread is placed on the hard wait list for the lock, and the original lock( ) method is called. Obviously, a race condition exists here since the lock( ) method is not synchronized. To solve this, the thread is placed on the hard wait list before the deadlock check is done. By simply reversing the tasks, it is no longer possible for a deadlock to go undetected. In fact, a deadlock may be actually detected before it happens due to the race condition.

There is no reason to override the lock methods that accept a timeout since these are soft locks. The interruptible lock request is disabled by routing it to the uninterruptible version of the lock( ) method.

Unfortunately, we are not done yet. Condition variables can also free and reacquire the lock and do so in a fashion that makes our deadlock-detecting class much more complex. The reacquisition of the lock is a hard wait since the await( ) method can't return until the lock is acquired. This means that the await( ) method needs to release the lock, wait for the notification from the signal( ) method to arrive, check for a potential deadlock, perform a hard wait for the lock, and eventually reacquire the lock.

If you've already examined the code, you'll notice that the implementation of the await( ) method is simpler than we just discussed. It doesn't even check for the deadlock. Instead, it simply performs a hard wait prior to waiting for the signal. By performing a hard wait before releasing the lock, we keep the thread and lock connected. This means that if a later lock attempt is made, a loop can still be detected, albeit by a different route. Furthermore, since it is not possible to cause a deadlock simply by using condition variables, there is no need to check for deadlock on the condition variable side. The condition variable just needs to allow the deadlock to be detected from the lock( ) method side. The condition variable also must place the thread on the hard wait list prior to releasing the lock due to a race condition with the lock( ) method—it is possible to miss detection of the deadlock if the lock is released first.

At this point, we are sure many readers have huge diagrams on their desk—or maybe on the floor—with thread and lock scenarios drawn in pencil. Deadlock detection is a very complex subject. We have tried to present it as simply as possible, but we are sure many readers will not be convinced that this class actually works without a few hours of playing out different scenarios. To help with this, the latest online copy of this class contains many simple test case scenarios (which can easily be extended).

To help further, here are answers to some possible questions. If you are not concerned with these questions, feel free to skip or skim the next section as desired. As a warning, some of these questions are very obscure, so obscure that some questions may not even be understood without a few hours of paper and pencil work. The goal is to work out the scenarios to understand the questions, which can hopefully be answered here.

*We have stated that a deadlock condition is detected when a loop in the wait tree is detected. Is it really a loop?* The answer is yes. This means that we have to be careful in our search or we can recursively search forever. Let's examine how the loop is formed from another point of view. Any waiting thread node can have only one parent lock node. That's because a thread can't perform a hard wait on more than one lock at a time. Any owned lock node can have only one parent thread node. That's because a lock can't be owned by more than one thread at a time. In this direction, only nodes connected to the top node can form the loop. As long as none of the owned lock nodes are connected to the top thread node, we don't have a loop. It is slightly more complicated than this, but we will address it with the next question.

*Why are we using only the thread tree? What about the lock tree?* These questions introduce a couple of definitions, so let's back up a few steps. To begin, we are trying to determine whether a thread can perform a hard wait on a particular lock. We then build a wait tree using this thread object as the top node; that's what we mean by the thread tree. However, the lock isn't independent. It is also possible to build a wait tree using the lock object as the top node, which we define as the lock tree. There may be other locks in the lock tree that could be in the thread tree, possibly forming a deadlock condition.

Fortunately, we don't have to traverse the lock tree because the thread tree is guaranteed to contain a root node as the top node. The top node of the thread tree is the currently running thread. It is not possible for this thread to be currently waiting on a lock since it wouldn't be executing the lock request. The top node of the lock tree is only the root node if the lock is not owned. For a loop to form, either the lock tree or the thread tree must be a subtree of the other. Since we know that the thread tree definitely contains the root node, only the lock node can be the subtree. To test for a subtree, we just need to test the top node.

*Isn't marking the hard wait prior to checking for the deadlock condition a problem? Can it cause spurious deadlock exceptions?* The answer is no. The deadlock condition will definitely occur since the thread will eventually perform the hard wait. It is just being detected slightly before it actually happens. On the other hand, our class may throw more than one deadlock exception once the deadlock has been detected. It must be noted that the purpose of this class is not to recover from the deadlock. In fact, once a deadlock exception is thrown, the class does not clean up after it. A retry attempt throws the same exception.

*Can marking the hard wait first interfere with the deadlock check?* By marking first, we are making a connection between the thread and the lock. In theory, this connection should be detected as a deadlock condition by the deadlock check. To determine if we're interfering with the deadlock check, we have to examine where the connection is made. We are connecting the lock node to the top thread node—the connection is actually above the top thread node. Since the search starts from the top thread node, it isn't able to detect the deadlock unless the lock node can be reached first. This connection is seen from the lock tree but is not a problem because that tree is not traversed. Traversals by other threads will be detected early as a deadlock condition since the hard wait will eventually be performed.

*Can marking the hard wait first cause an error condition in other threads? Will it cause a loop in the trees?* We need to avoid a loop in the wait trees for two reasons. First, and obviously, is because it is an indication of a deadlock condition. The second reason is because we will be searching through the wait trees. Recursively searching through a tree that has a loop causes an infinite search (if the lock being sought is not within the loop).

The answer to this question is no, it can't cause an error condition. First, there is no way to enter the loop from a thread node that is not within the loop. All thread nodes within the loop are performing a hard wait on locks within the loop. And all lock nodes within the loop are owned by thread nodes within the loop. Second, it is not possible to start from a thread node that is within the loop. With the exception of the top thread node, all the thread nodes are performing a hard wait. To be able to perform the deadlock check, a thread cannot be in a wait state and therefore can't be in the wait tree. If a loop is formed, only the thread represented by the top thread node can detect the deadlock.

This answer assumes that a deadlock-detected exception has never been thrown; this class is not designed to work once such an exception is thrown. For that functionality, consider using the alternate deadlock-detecting class that is available online.

*How can the simple solution of switching the "thread owns the lock" to the "thread hard waiting for lock" work for condition variables?* Admittedly, we did a bit of hand waving in the explanation. A better way to envision it is to treat the operations as being separate entities—as if the condition variable is releasing and reacquiring the lock. Since the reacquisition is mandatory (i.e., it will eventually occur), we mark the thread for reacquisition before we release the lock. We can argue that switching the ownership state to a hard wait state removes the connection from the thread tree, making detection impossible. This is just an artifact of examining the wait tree from the condition variable's perspective. When the lock( ) method is called at a later time, we will be using a different thread object as the top node, forming a different wait tree. From that perspective, we can use either the ownership state or hard wait state for the detection of the deadlock.

*Why don't we have to check for potential deadlocks on the condition variable side?* It is not necessary. Marking for the wait operation prior to unlocking works in a pseudo atomic manner, meaning that it is not possible for another thread to miss the detection of the deadlock when using the lock( ) method. Since it is not possible to create a new deadlock just by using condition variables, we don't need to check on this end. Another explanation is that there is no need to check because we already know the answer: the thread is capable of performing a hard wait because it has previously owned the lock and has not had a chance to request additional locks.

*Isn't marking for the hard wait prior to performing the* await( ) *operation a problem? Can it cause spurious deadlock exceptions? Can it cause an error condition in other threads?* Two of these questions are very similar to the questions for the lock( ) method side. The extra question here addresses the issue of interfering with the deadlock check. That question doesn't apply on the lock( ) method side because we do not perform a deadlock check on the condition variable side.

However, the answers to the other questions are not exactly the same as before. In this case, the thread is performing a hard wait on the lock before the thread releases ownership of the lock. We are creating a temporary loop—a loop that is created even though the deadlock condition does not exist. This is not a case of detecting the deadlock early—if the loop were detected, the deadlock detected would be incorrect.

These three questions can be answered together. As with the error question on the lock( ) method side, it is not possible to enter the loop from a thread node outside of the loop. Second, the one thread node that is within this small loop is not performing a deadlock check. And finally, any deadlock check does not traverse the lock tree. This means that an error condition can't occur in another thread and that detecting a false deadlock condition also can't occur in another thread. Of course, eventually it would be possible to get to the lock node externally, but by then, the loop would have been broken. It is not possible for another thread to own the lock unless the condition variable thread releases it first.

*To review, we are traversing the thread tree to check whether the lock tree is a subtree. Instead of recursively traversing from the thread tree, isn't it easier to traverse upward from the lock tree?* Our answer is maybe. We simply list the pluses and minuses and let the reader decide. Two good points can be made for traversing from the lock tree. First, the search is not recursive. Each node of the lock tree has only one parent, so going upward can be done iteratively. Second, moving upward from lock node to parent thread node does not need any iterations—the owner thread object is already referenced by the lock object. On the other hand, moving downward from the thread node to the lock node requires iteration through the registered locks list.

Unfortunately, there are two bad points to traversing upward from the lock tree. First, moving upward from the thread node to the lock node on which it is performing the hard wait is incredibly time-consuming. We need to iterate through the registered locks list to find the hard wait lists, which we must, in turn, iterate through to find the lock node. In comparison, moving downward from the lock node to the thread node is done by iterating through one hard wait list. And it gets worse. We need to iterate through all of the hard wait lists. By comparison, we need to iterate only through the hard wait lists in the wait tree in our existing implementation. This one point alone may outweigh the good points.

The second bad point stems from the techniques that we use to solve the race conditions in the lock class. The class allows loops to occur—even temporarily creating them when a deadlock condition does not exist. Searching from a lock node that is within a loop—whether recursively downward or iteratively upward—does not terminate if the top thread node is not within the loop. Fortunately, this problem can be easily solved. We just need to terminate the search if the top lock node is found. Also note that finding the top lock node is not an indication of a deadlock condition since some temporary loops are formed even without a deadlock condition.

*To review, we are traversing the thread tree instead of the lock tree because the top thread node is definitely the root node. The top lock node may not be the root node. However, what if the top lock node is also the root node? Isn't this a shortcut in the search for a deadlock?* Yes. It is not possible for the lock tree to be a subtree of the thread tree if the top lock node is a root node. This means we can remove some calls to the deadlock check by first checking to see if the lock is already owned. This is an important improvement since the deadlock check is very time-consuming.

However, a race condition exists when a lock has no owner. If the lock is unowned, there is no guarantee that the lock will remain unowned during the deadlock check. This race condition is not a problem since it is not possible for any lock in the wait tree to be unowned at any time during the deadlock check; the deadlock check may be skipped whether or not the lock remains unowned.

This shortcut is mostly for locks that are infrequently used. For frequently used locks, this shortcut is highly dependent on the thread finding the lock to be free, which is based on the timing of the application.

The modification with some deadlock checking removed is available online in our alternate deadlock-detecting lock.

*The deadlock-detecting lock disallows interruptible locking requests. What if we do not agree with this compromise?* There are only a few options. Disallowing the interrupt was the easiest compromise that works for the majority of the cases. For those readers who believe an interruptible lock should be considered a soft lock, the change is simple—just don't override the lockInterruptibly( ) method. And for those readers who believe that an interruptible lock should be considered a hard lock while still not compromising interrupt capability, here is a modified version of the method:

```
public void lockInterruptibly( ) throws InterruptedException {
    if (isHeldByCurrentThread( )) {
        if (debugging) System.out.println("Already Own Lock");
        try {
            super.lockInterruptibly( );
        } finally {
            freeIfHardwait(hardwaitingThreads,
                            Thread.currentThread( ));
```

```
        }
        return;
    }

    markAsHardwait(hardwaitingThreads, Thread.currentThread());
    if (canThreadWaitOnLock(Thread.currentThread(), this)) {
        if (debugging) System.out.println("Waiting For Lock");
        try {
            super.lockInterruptibly();
        } finally {
            freeIfHardwait(hardwaitingThreads,
                        Thread.currentThread());
        }
        if (debugging) System.out.println("Got New Lock");
    } else {
        throw new DeadlockDetectedException("DEADLOCK");
    }
}
```

This change is also provided online in our alternate deadlock-detecting lock class. In terms of implementation, it is practically identical to that of the lock( ) method. The difference is that we now place all lock requests within a try-finally clause. This allows the method to clean up after the request, regardless of whether it exits normally or by exception.

*The deadlock-detecting lock regards all lock requests with a timeout as soft locks. What if we do not agree with this premise?* This topic is open to debate. While an application that uses timeouts should have an exit strategy when the timeout occurs, what if the exit strategy is to inform the user and then simply retry? In this case, deadlock could occur. Furthermore, at what point is retrying no longer tolerable? When the timeout period is more than an hour? A day? A month? Obviously, these issues are design-specific.

Here is an implementation of the tryLock( ) method that treats the request as a soft wait—but only if it is less than a minute:

```
public boolean tryLock(long time, TimeUnit unit)
                        throws InterruptedException {
    // Perform operation as a soft wait
    if (unit.toSeconds(time) < 60) {
        return super.tryLock(time, unit);
    }

    if (isHeldByCurrentThread()) {
        if (debugging) System.out.println("Already Own Lock");
        try {
            return super.tryLock(time, unit);
        } finally {
            freeIfHardwait(hardwaitingThreads,
                        Thread.currentThread());
        }
    }
```

```
        markAsHardwait(hardwaitingThreads, Thread.currentThread());
        if (canThreadWaitOnLock(Thread.currentThread(), this)) {
            if (debugging) System.out.println("Waiting For Lock");
            try {
                return super.tryLock(time, unit);
            } finally {
                freeIfHardwait(hardwaitingThreads,
                                Thread.currentThread());
                if (debugging) System.out.println("Got New Lock");
            }
        } else {
            throw new DeadlockDetectedException("DEADLOCK");
        }
    }
```

This change is also provided in the online examples as an alternative to the deadlock-detecting lock class (including a testing program, which is example 2 in this chapter). Its implementation is practically identical to that of the lock( ) method. Again, the difference is that we now place all lock requests within a try-finally clause. This allows the method to clean up after the request, regardless if it exits normally or by exception. This example treats the operation as a soft wait for requests that are under a minute. The request is treated as a hard wait otherwise. We leave it up to you to modify the code to suit your needs. One alternate solution could be to use a different time period to separate soft and hard wait lock operations; this time period could also be calculated depending on conditions in the program. Another alternate solution could be for the trylock( ) method to return false instead of throwing the deadlock-detected exception.

*While the deadlock-detecting lock is well-designed for detecting the deadlock condition, the design for reporting the condition is pretty weak. Are there better options?* This is actually intentional. This class is not designed to be used in a production environment. Searching for deadlocks can be very inefficient—this class should be used only during development. In fact, most readers will probably not use this class at all. The main purpose of this class is so that we can understand deadlocks—how to detect them and, eventually, how to prevent them.

For those who insist on using the deadlock-detecting lock in a production environment, there are a few options. The class can be designed to fail fast—meaning that if a deadlock is detected, the class could throw the exception for every invocation, regardless of whether the request is involved in the deadlock or not. Another option is for the class to report the condition in a manner that allows the program to shut down properly. A third, and not recommended, option is to allow the class to continue functioning. The first and third options are provided as conditional code in the alternate online example.

*This topic of deadlock detection seems to be incredibly complex. In fact, the discussion on the theory and implementation is more than twice as long as the code itself. Is this topic really that complex?* The concept of deadlock detection is complex, but there is another reason why this class is even more complex. The implementation of this class is accomplished by minimal synchronization. This is mainly because the ReentrantLock class is implemented with minimal synchronization, making the class implementation more complex.

# Lock Starvation

Whenever multiple threads compete for a scarce resource, there is the danger of starvation, a situation in which the thread never gets the resource. In Chapter 9, we discuss the concept in the context of CPU starvation: with a bad choice of scheduling options, some threads never have the opportunity to become the currently running thread and suffer from CPU starvation.

Lock starvation is similar to CPU starvation in that the thread is unable to execute. It is different from CPU starvation in that the thread is given the opportunity to execute; it is just not able to because it is unable to obtain the lock. Lock starvation is similar to a deadlock in that the thread waits indefinitely for a lock. It is different in that it is not caused by a loop in the wait tree. Its occurrence is somewhat rare and is caused by a very complex set of circumstances.

Lock starvation occurs when a particular thread attempts to acquire a lock and never succeeds because another thread is already holding the lock. Clearly, this can occur on a simple basis if one thread acquires the lock and never releases it: all other threads that attempt to acquire the lock never succeed and starve. Lock starvation can also be more subtle; if six threads are competing for the same lock, it's possible that five threads will hold the lock for 20% of the time, thus starving the sixth thread.

Lock starvation is not something most threaded Java programs need to consider. If our Java program is producing a result in a finite period of time, eventually all threads in the program will acquire the lock, if only because all the other threads in the program have exited. Lock starvation also involves the question of fairness: at certain times we want to make sure that threads acquire the locks in a reasonable order so that one thread won't have to wait for all other threads to exit before it has its chance to acquire the lock.

Consider the case of two threads competing for a lock. Assume that thread A acquires the object lock on a fairly periodic basis, as shown in Figure 6-3.

Here's what happens at various points on the graph:

T0   At time T0, both thread A and thread B are able to run, and thread A is the currently running thread.

T1   Thread A is still the currently running thread, and it acquires the object lock when it enters the synchronized block.

T2   A timeslice occurs; this causes thread B to become the currently running thread.

---

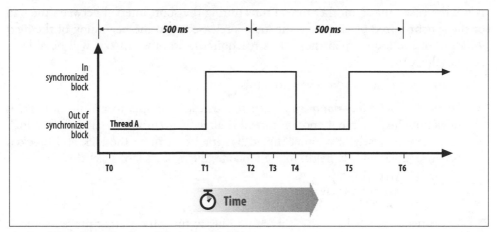

*Figure 6-3. Call graph of synchronized methods*

*T3*  Very soon after becoming the currently running thread, thread B attempts to enter the synchronized block. This causes thread B to block. That allows thread A to continue to run; thread A continues executing in the synchronized block.

*T4*  Thread A exits the synchronized block. Thread B could obtain the lock now, but it is still not running on any CPU.

*T5*  Thread A once again enters the synchronized block and acquires the lock.

*T6*  Thread B once again is assigned to a CPU. It immediately tries to enter the synchronized block, but the lock for the synchronized block is once again held by thread A. So, thread B blocks again. Thread A then gets the CPU, and we're now in the same state as we were at time T3.

It's possible for this cycle to continue forever such that thread B can never acquire the lock and actually do useful work.

Clearly, this example is a pathological case: CPU scheduling must occur only during those time periods when thread A holds the lock for the synchronized block. With two threads, that's extremely unlikely and generally indicates that thread A is holding the lock almost continuously. With several threads, however, it's not out of the question that one thread may find that every time it is scheduled, another thread holds the lock it wants.

Synchronized blocks within loops often have this problem:

```
while (true) {
    synchronized (this) {
        // execute some code
    }
}
```

At first glance, we might expect this not to be a problem; other threads can't starve because the lock is freed often, with each iteration of the loop. But as we've seen, this is not the case: unless another thread runs during the short interval between the end of the synchronized block (when the lock is released) and the beginning of the next iteration of the loop (when the lock is reacquired), no other thread will be able to acquire the lock.

There are two points to take away from this:

*Acquisition of locks does not queue.* When a thread attempts to acquire a lock, it does not check to see if another thread is already attempting to acquire the lock (or, more precisely, if another thread has tried to acquire the lock and blocked because it was already held). In pseudocode, the process looks like this:

```
while (lock is held)
        wait for a while
acquire lock
```

For threads of equal priority, there's nothing in this process that prevents a lock from being granted to one thread even if another thread is waiting.

*Releasing a lock does not affect thread scheduling.* When a lock is released, any threads that were blocked waiting for that lock could run. However, no actual scheduling occurs, so none of the threads that have just moved into the runnable state are assigned to the CPU; the thread that has just released the lock keeps access to the CPU. This can be different if the threads have different priorities or are on a multiprocessor machine (where a different CPU might be idle).

Nonetheless, lock starvation remains, as might be guessed from our example, something that occurs only in rare circumstances. In fact, each of the following circumstances must be present for lock starvation to occur:

*Multiple threads are competing for the same lock.* This lock becomes the scarce resource for which some threads may starve.

*The results that occur during this period of contention must be interesting to us.* If, for example, we're calculating a big matrix, there's probably a point in time at the beginning of our calculation during which multiple threads are competing for the same lock and CPU. Since all we care about is the final result of this calculation, it doesn't matter to us that some threads are temporarily starved for the lock: we still get the final answer in the same amount of time. We're concerned about lock starvation only if there's a period of time during which it matters whether the lock is allocated fairly.

All of the properties of lock starvation stem from the fact that a thread attempting to acquire a lock checks only to see if another thread is holding the lock—the thread knows nothing about other threads that are also waiting for the lock. This behavior in conjunction with properties of the program such as the number of threads, their priorities, and how they are scheduled manifests itself as a case of lock starvation.

Fortunately, this problem has already been solved by the ReentrantLock class. If we're in one of the rare situations where lock starvation can occur, we just need to construct a ReentrantLock object where the fairness flag is set to true. Since the ReentrantLock class with its fairness flag set grants the lock on very close to a first-come, first-served basis, it is not possible for any thread to be starved for a lock regardless of the number of threads or how they're written.

Unfortunately, the downside to using the ReentrantLock class in this manner is that we are affecting the scheduling. We discuss how threads are scheduled in Chapter 9, but in general, threads have a priority, and the higher-priority threads are given the CPU more often than low-priority threads. However, the ReentrantLock class does not take that into account when issuing locks: locks are issued first-come, first-served regardless of the thread's priority.

Programs that set thread priorities do so for a reason. The reason could be because the developer wanted to have the scheduler behave in a certain manner. While using the fair flag in the ReentrantLock class may prevent lock starvation, it may also change the desired scheduling behavior.

Lock starvation is a rare problem; it happens only under very distinct circumstances. While it can be easily fixed with the ReentrantLock class, it may also change some of these desired circumstances. On the other hand, if priorities and scheduling are not a concern, the ReentrantLock class provides a very simple and quick fix.

## Lock Starvation and Reader/Writer Locks

Generally, reader/writer locks are used when there are many more readers than writers; readers also tend to hold onto the lock for a longer period of time than they would a simple lock. This is why the reader/writer lock is needed—to share data access during the long periods of time when only reading is needed. Unfortunately, readers can't just grab the lock if the lock is held for reading by another thread. If many readers were holding the lock, it would be possible for many more readers to grab the lock before the first set of readers finished. Many more readers could then obtain the lock before the second set of readers finished. This would prevent the writer from ever obtaining the lock.

To solve this, the reader/writer lock does not grant the read lock to a new thread if there is a writer waiting for the lock. Instead it places the reader into a wait state until the first set of readers frees the lock. Once the first set of readers have completed, the first writer is given exclusive access to the lock. When that writer completes, the ReentrantReadWriteLock class consults its fairness flag to see what to do next. If the fairness flag is true, the thread waiting longest—whether a reader or a writer—is granted the lock (and multiple readers can get the lock in this case). If the fairness flag is false, locks are granted arbitrarily.

# Summary

The strong integration of locks into the Java language and API is very useful for programming with Java threads. Java also provides very strong tools to allow thread programming at a higher level. With these tools, Java provides a comprehensive library to use for your multithreaded programs.

Even with this library, threaded programming is not easy. The developer needs to understand the issues of deadlock and starvation, in order to design applications in a concurrent fashion. While it is not possible to have a program threaded automatically—with a combination of using the more advanced tools and development practices, it can be very easy to design and debug threaded programs.

## Example Classes

Here are the class names and Ant targets for the examples in this chapter:

| Description | Main Java class | Ant target |
| --- | --- | --- |
| Deadlock-detecting Lock | `javathreads.examples.ch06.example1.`<br>`DeadlockDetectingLock` | ch6-ex1 |
| Alternate Deadlock-detecting Lock | `javathreads.examples.ch06.example2.`<br>`AlternateDeadlockDetectingLock` | ch6-ex2 |

Three tests are available for each example. The first test uses two threads and two competing locks. The second test uses three threads and three competing locks. The third test uses condition variables to cause the deadlock. Test numbers are selected with this property:

```
<property name="DeadlockTestNumber" value="2"/>
```

# CHAPTER 7

# Threads and Swing

The Swing classes in Java are not threadsafe; if you access a Swing object from multiple threads, you run the chance of data corruption, hung GUIs, and other undesirable effects. To deal with this situation, you must make sure that you access Swing objects only from one particular thread. We saw some examples of this in previous chapters; this chapter explains the details of how threads interact with Swing. The general principles of this chapter apply to other thread-unsafe objects: you can handle any thread-unsafe class by accessing it in a single thread in much the same way as Swing objects must be accessed from a special thread.

We'll start with a general discussion of the threads that Swing creates automatically for you, and then we'll see how your own threads can interact with those threads safely. In doing so, we'll (finally) explain the last pieces of our typing program.

If you're interested in the general case of how to deal with a set of classes that are not threadsafe, you can read through the first section of this chapter for the theory of how this is handled, then review our example in Chapter 10 to see the theory put into practice.

## Swing Threading Restrictions

A GUI program has several threads. One of these threads is called the event-dispatching thread. This thread executes all the event-related callbacks of your program (e.g., the actionPerformed( ) and keyPressed( ) methods in our typing test program). Access to all Swing objects must occur from this thread.

The reason for this is that Swing objects have complex inner state that Swing itself does not synchronize access to. A JSlider object, for example, has a single value that indicates the position of the slider. If the user is in the middle of changing the position of the slider, that value may be in an intermediate or indeterminate state; all of that processing occurs on the event-dispatching thread. A second thread that attempts to read the value of the slider cannot read that value directly since by doing so the thread may read the value while the value is in its intermediate state. There-fore, the second thread must arrange for the event-dispatching thread to read the value and pass the value back to the thread.

Note that it's not enough for our second thread simply to synchronize access to the JSlider object. The internal Swing mechanisms aren't synchronizing access, so the two threads still simultaneously access the internal state of the slider. Remember that locks are cooperative: if all threads do not attempt to acquire the lock, race conditions can still occur.

It may seem like this restriction is overkill: the value of a JSlider is a single variable and could simply be made volatile. Actually, that's not the case. The value of things within Swing components can be very complex. Many Swing components follow a model-view-controller design pattern, and accessing those components from one thread while the model is being updated on the event-dispatching thread would be very dangerous. Even the simplest of Swing components contain complex state; it's never acceptable to call any of their methods from a thread other than the event-dispatching thread.

Consequently, all calls to Swing objects must be made on the event-dispatching thread. That's the thread that Swing uses internally to change the state of its objects; as long as you make calls to Swing objects from that thread, no race condition can occur. Four exceptions to this rule are:

- Swing objects that have not been displayed can be created and manipulated by any thread. That means you can create your GUI objects in any thread but once they've been displayed, they can be accessed only on the event-dispatching thread. A GUI object is displayed when the show( ) method of its parent frame is called.

- The repaint( ) method can be called from any thread.

- The invokeLater( ) method can be called from any thread.

- The invokeAndWait( ) method can be called from any thread other than the event-dispatching thread.

## Processing on the Event-Dispatching Thread

As we mentioned, all the event callbacks of your program occur on the event-dispatching thread. This is good news since it means that most of the code that needs to access Swing components is automatically called on the event-dispatching thread.

In our sample typing program, we access Swing components from these methods:

- CharacterDisplayCanvas( )

- CharacterDisplayCanvas.preferredSize( )

- CharacterDisplayCanvas.newCharacter( )

- `CharacterDisplayCanvas.paintComponent( )`
- `SwingTypeTester.initComponents( )`
- The `actionPerformed( )` methods of the `SwingTypeTester` button objects
- The `keyPressed( )` method of the `SwingTypeTester` canvas
- `ScoreLabel.setScore( )`
- `AnimatedCharacterDisplayCanvas( )`
- `AnimatedCharacterDisplayCanvas.newCharacter( )`
- `AnimatedCharacterDisplayCanvas.paintComponent( )`

To write a threadsafe Swing program, we must make sure that the methods listed above are accessed only from within the event-dispatching thread. Note that this list includes the constructor for the `AnimatedCharacterDisplayCanvas` class; remember that the constructor calls the constructor of its superclass.

The Swing classes have already made sure that all callbacks occur on the event-dispatching thread. The `preferredSize( )`, `paintComponent( )`, `keyPressed( )`, and `actionPerformed( )` methods are all callbacks, so we don't need to worry about those. The `initComponents( )` method is called from the main thread of the program, which is not the event-dispatching thread. The constructor for the display canvases is called from the same thread. However, the `initComponents( )` method and its constructors create the Swing objects; they have not yet been displayed. That falls into the first exception case that we listed earlier. The `newCharacter( )` method calls only the `repaint( )` method, so that falls into the second exception we listed above. Finally, the `setScore( )` method accesses Swing components only within the `invokeLater( )` method, so that falls into our third category. All access to Swing classes within our application is handled correctly.

The first two exceptions in our list are self-explanatory. In the next section, we explain the last two exceptions in our list.

## Using invokeLater( ) and invokeAndWait( )

In the `CharacterDisplayCanvas` class, we were able to work around Swing's threading restrictions because all the calls that manipulated Swing objects could go into an event callback method (the `paintComponent( )` method). That's not always convenient (or even possible). So Swing provides another mechanism that allows you to run code on the event-dispatching thread: the `invokeLater( )` and `invokeAndWait( )` methods.

The `invokeLater( )` and `invokeAndWait( )` methods allow you to define a task and ask the event-processing thread to perform that task. If you have a non-GUI thread that needs to read the value of a slider, for instance, you put the code to read the slider into a Runnable object and pass that Runnable object to the invokeAndWait( ) method, which returns the value the thread needs to read.

Let's look again at our score label class. The setScore( ) method of that class can be called when the user types a character (in which case it is running on the event-dispatching thread). It can also be called when the random character generator sends a new character. Therefore, the setScore( ) method must use the invokeLater( ) method to make that call:

```
package javathreads.examples.ch07.example1;
...
public class ScoreLabel extends JLabel implements CharacterListener {
    ...
    private void setScore() {
        SwingUtilities.invokeLater(new Runnable() {
            public void run() {
                setText(Integer.toString(score));
            }
        });
    }
}
```

The invokeLater( ) method takes a Runnable object as its parameter. It sends that object to the event-dispatching thread, which executes the run( ) method. This is why it's always safe for the run( ) method to execute Swing code.

Note that the run( ) method is in its own object. This is why we made the score variable volatile rather than protecting it by using synchronization. Synchronizing the run( ) method grabs the lock of the anonymous inner class object, not the lock of the ScoreLabel object. It's much easier to use a volatile variable.

For the most part, the invokeAndWait( ) method looks similar, but it has three important semantic differences. First, the invokeLater( ) method runs asynchronously at some time in the future. You don't know when it will actually run. On the other hand, the invokeAndWait( ) method is synchronous: it does not return until its target has completed execution. As a rule of thumb, then, you should use the invokeAndWait( ) method to read the value of Swing components or to ensure that something is displayed on the screen before you continue program execution. Otherwise, you can use the `invokeLater()` method.

The second difference is that the `invokeAndWait()` method cannot itself be called from the event-dispatching thread. The thread running the `invokeAndWait()` method must wait for the event-dispatching thread to execute some code. No thread, including the event-dispatching thread, can wait for itself to do something else. Consequently, if you execute the `invokeAndWait()` method from the event-dispatching thread, it throws a `java.lang.Error`. That causes the event-dispatching thread to exit (unless you've taken the unusual step of catching `Error` objects in your code); in turn, your entire program becomes disabled.

The third difference is that the `invokeAndWait()` method can throw an `InterruptedException` if the thread is interrupted before the event-dispatching thread runs the target, or an `InvocationTargetException` if the `Runnable` object throws a runtime exception or error.

If you have code that you want to take effect immediately and that might be called from the event-dispatching thread, you can use the `SwingUtilities.isEventDispatchThread()` method to check the thread your code is executing on. You can then either call `invokeAndWait()` (if you're not on the event-dispatching thread) or call the Swing methods directly.

We could use that method in our `ScoreLabel` class like this:

```
package javathreads.examples.ch07.example2;
...
public class ScoreLabel extends JLabel implements CharacterListener {
    ...
    private void setScore() {
        if (SwingUtilities.isEventDispatchThread())
            setText(Integer.toString(score));
        else try {
            SwingUtilities.invokeAndWait(new Runnable() {
                public void run() {
                    setText(Integer.toString(score));
                }
            });
        } catch (InterruptedException ie) {
        } catch (InvocationTargetException ite) {}
    }
}
```

# Long-Running Event Callbacks

There's another case when Swing programs and threads interact: a long-running event callback. While an event callback is executing, the rest of the GUI is unresponsive. If this happens for a long period of time, it can be very frustrating to users, who often assume that the program has hung. It's far better to execute the long-running task in a separate thread, providing GUI feedback as appropriate.

This task can be accomplished in a few ways. By now, you should be familiar enough with thread programming to spawn your own thread and execute the task, and that's often the simplest route to take. A utility class called the SwingWorker class, available on Sun's *java.sun.com* web site, can handle many of the threading details for you (but, in the end, it is not really any easier than spawning your own thread).

If you're going to have a lot of tasks like this, though, the easiest thing to do is use a thread pool or a task scheduler. If you have a lot of tasks to execute in parallel, you can use a thread pool (see Chapter 10). If you have only a single task to execute every now and then, you can use a task scheduler (see Chapter 11).

Here's an example of how to take the first path and set up a thread in a long-running callback. Suppose that in our type tester, the start method must log into a server in order to get the data it is to display. You want to perform that operation in a separate thread because it may take a long time, during which you don't want the GUI to be unresponsive. In fact, you want to give the user an option to cancel that operation in case communicating with the server takes too long.

Here's a class that simulates connecting to the server. While it's at it, the frame displays some progress messages:

```
package javathreads.examples.ch07.example3;

import java.lang.reflect.*;
import java.awt.*;
import java.awt.event.*;
import javax.swing.*;

public class FeedbackFrame extends JFrame implements Runnable {

    private SwingTypeTester stt;
    private Thread t;
    private JLabel label;
    private int state;

    static String[] stateMessages = {
        "Connecting to server...",
        "Logging into server...",
        "Waiting for data...",
        "Complete"
    };

    public FeedbackFrame(SwingTypeTester stt) {
        this.stt = stt;
        setupFrame();
        t = new Thread(this);
        t.start();
        pack();
        show();
    }
```

```java
private void setupFrame( ) {
    label = new JLabel( );
    label.setPreferredSize(new Dimension(200, 200));
    Container c = getContentPane( );
    JButton stopButton = new JButton("Stop");
    stopButton.addActionListener(new ActionListener( ) {
        public void actionPerformed(ActionEvent ae) {
            error( );
        }
    });
    c.add(label, BorderLayout.NORTH);
    c.add(stopButton, BorderLayout.SOUTH);
}

private void setText(final String s) {
    try {
        SwingUtilities.invokeAndWait(new Runnable( ) {
            public void run( ) {
                label.setText(s);
            }
        });
    } catch (InterruptedException ie) {
        error( );
    } catch (InvocationTargetException ite) {
        error( );
    }
}

private void error( ) {
    t.interrupt( );
    if (SwingUtilities.isEventDispatchThread( ))
        closeDown( );
    else SwingUtilities.invokeLater(new Runnable( ) {
        public void run( ) {
            closeDown( );
        }
    });
}

private void closeDown( ) {
    stt.setupCancelled( );
    hide( );
    dispose( );
}

public void run( ) {
    // Simulate connecting to server
    for (int i = 0; i < stateMessages.length; i++) {
        setText(stateMessages[i]);
        try {
            Thread.sleep(5 * 1000);
        } catch (InterruptedException ie) {}
        if (Thread.currentThread( ).isInterrupted( ))
            return;
    }
```

```
SwingUtilities.invokeLater(new Runnable() {
    public void run() {
        stt.setupDone();
        hide();
        dispose();
    }
});
    }
}
```

We've used all our Swing utilities and techniques in this example. The component itself is a frame, and it starts a new thread. Every few seconds, that thread displays a new status message in the frame by calling the setText( ) method. That method isn't executing on the event-dispatching thread, so it must use the invokeAndWait( ) method to pass the text to the label. When the thread has finished displaying status messages (meaning that in the real world, it has connected to the server), it informs the SwingTypeTester class that setup is complete—and since that class expects everything to run on the event-dispatching thread, the setupDone( ) method must be called from an invokeLater( ) method.

When the server gets an error or the user presses the Stop button, we need to tell the SwingTypeTester component that setup was cancelled. The code is the same, but the context is different: the actionPerformed( ) method runs on the event-dispatching thread while the exception in the run( ) method runs on a separate thread. So we must use the isEventDispatchThread( ) method to determine how to call the Swing components.

## Summary

The Swing classes comprise one of the largest set of classes in the Java API. While threads are an integral part of Java, the Swing classes themselves are not threadsafe. This places a responsibility on the developer, who must make sure that she follows the appropriate access patterns for Swing classes. Methods on Swing objects (with a few exceptions) can be invoked only on the event-dispatching thread.

Swing's use of the invokeLater( ) method gives us a hint about how we might handle thread-unsafe libraries in general: as long as access to those libraries occurs only on a single thread, we will not run into any threading problems. Passing a Runnable object to a thread pool that contains a single thread is precisely analogous to the technique used by the Swing classes.

## Example Classes

Here are the class names and Ant targets for the examples in this chapter:

| Description | Main Java class | Ant target |
| --- | --- | --- |
| Swing Type Tester (all components thread-safe) | javathreads.examples.ch07.example1. SwingTypeTester | ch7-ex1 |
| Swing Type Tester (uses invokeAndWait) | javathreads.examples.ch07.example2. SwingTypeTester | ch7-ex2 |
| Swing Type Tester with simulated server connection | javathreads.examples.ch07.example3. SwingTypeTester | ch7-ex3 |

# CHAPTER 8

# Threads and Collection Classes

In this chapter, we'll look at how threads interact with the collection classes provided by Java. We'll examine some synchronization issues and how they affect our choice and usage of collection classes.

The collection classes comprise many of the classes in the java.util package (and, in J2SE 5.0, some of the classes in the java.util.concurrent package). Collection classes are used to store objects in some data structure: a hashtable, an array, a queue, and so on. Collection classes interact with Java threads in a few areas:

- Collection classes may or may not be threadsafe, so threads that use those classes must understand their synchronization requirements.
- Not all collections have the same performance with regard to thread synchronization, so threads that use them must understand the conditions in which they can be used optimally.
- Newer collection classes automatically provide some threading semantics (such as using thread notification when their data changes).
- Threads commonly use collection classes to share data.

We begin this chapter with an overview of the collection classes; the overview addresses the thread-safety of the various classes. Next, we show how some of the newer collection classes interact with threads. And finally, we show a common design pattern in which multiple threads use the collections: the producer-consumer model.

## Overview of Collection Classes

In the beginning, Java provided only a few collection classes. In fact, in the first version of Java, these classes weren't even referred to as collection classes; they were simply utility classes that Java provided. For the most part, these classes were all threadsafe; the early collection classes were designed to prevent developers from inadvertently corrupting the data structures by using them in different threads without appropriate data synchronization.

JDK 1.2 introduced the formal idea of collection classes. The few existing data collection classes from JDK 1.0 and 1.1 were integrated into this framework, which was expanded to include new classes and new interfaces. Defining the collection classes in terms of interfaces made it possible to write programs that could use different collection implementations at runtime.

The controversial change introduced in JDK 1.2 is that most of the collection classes are now, by default, not threadsafe. Threadsafe versions of the classes exist, but the decision was made to allow the developer to manage the thread-safety of the classes. Two factors inform this decision: the performance of synchronization and the requirements of algorithms that use the collection. We'll have more to say on those issues in the next section. JDK 1.3 and 1.4 added some minor extensions to these collection classes.

J2SE 5.0 introduces a number of new collection classes. Some of these classes are simple extensions to the existing collections framework, but many of them have two distinguishing features. First, their internal implementation makes heavy use of the new J2SE 5.0 synchronization tools (in particular, atomic variables). Second, most of these classes are designed to be used by multiple threads and support the idea of thread notification when data in the collection becomes available.

## Collection Interfaces

As we mentioned, the collection classes are based around a set of interfaces introduced in JDK 1.2:

`java.util.List`
>    A list is an ordered set of data (e.g., an array). Unlike actual arrays, lists are not fixed in size; they can grow as more data is added. Lists provide methods to get and set data elements by index and also to insert or remove data at arbitrary points (expanding or shrinking the list as necessary). Therefore, they can also be thought of as linked lists.

`java.util.Map`
>    A map associates values with keys. Duplicate keys are not allowed; each key maps to at most one value. The `java.util.SortedMap` interface extends this to provide maps that are sorted based on a collection-specific definition. The `java.util.Dictionary` interface provides essentially the same interface as a map but is "obsolete" (unofficially deprecated).

`java.util.Set`

A set is a collection of elements that are stored in no particular order. Duplicate elements are not allowed. The `java.util.SortedSet` interface extends this to provide a sorted set of objects.

`java.util.Queue`

A queue is an ordered set of data that is operated on in either last-in-first-out (LIFO) or first-in-first-out (FIFO) order (although no implementations presently support a LIFO ordering). Previously, queues could be simulated by lists, but the new queue implementations are more efficient. This interface was introduced in J2SE 5.0.

## Threadsafe Collection Classes

Only a few collection classes are threadsafe. As we'll see later, being threadsafe does not necessarily mean that you can safely use them in *every* multithreaded program; programs must still be designed in a fashion that allows the collection to be used by multiple threads. Here are some of the more common threadsafe collection classes:

`java.util.Vector (a List)`

A simple array, allowing index-based operations and random insertion and deletion.

`java.util.Stack (a List)`

The `Stack` class extends the `Vector` class to provide the ability to treat the vector as a stack. Objects can be pushed onto the stack or popped from the stack, providing a LIFO ordering (however, this class does not implement the `Queue` interface).

`java.util.Hashtable (a Map)`

A simple, unordered map of keys to values.

`java.util.concurrent.ConcurrentHashMap (a Map)`

A class that implements an unordered map. It uses less synchronization than the `Hashtable` class.

`java.util.concurrent.CopyOnWriteArrayList (a List)`

A simple array list that provides safe semantics for unsynchronized iterator access.

`java.util.concurrent.CopyOnWriteArraySet (a Set)`

A simple set that provides safe semantics for unsynchronized iterator access.

`java.util.concurrent.ConcurrentLinkedQueue (a Queue)`

An unbounded FIFO queue. It is optimized for multiple threads inserting and removing items from the collection.

## Thread-Unsafe Collection Classes

The majority of collection classes are not threadsafe. When used in multithreaded programs, access to them must always be controlled by some synchronization. This synchronization can be accomplished either by using a "wrapper" class that synchronizes every access operation (using the Collections class, which we'll show later) or by using explicit synchronization:

java.util.BitSet
> A bit set stores an array of boolean (1-bit) values. The size of the array can grow at will. A BitSet saves space compared to an array of booleans since the bit set can store multiple values in one long variable. Despite its name, it does not implement the Set interface.

java.util.HashSet (a Set)
> A class that implements an unordered set collection.

java.util.TreeSet (a SortedSet)
> A class that implements a sorted (and ordered) set collection.

java.util.HashMap (a Map)
> A class that implements an unordered map collection.

java.util.WeakHashMap (a Map)
> This class is similar to the HashMap class. The difference is that the key is a weak reference—it is not counted as a reference by the garbage collector. The class therefore deletes key-value pair entries from the map when the key has been garbage collected.

java.util.TreeMap (a SortedMap)
> A class that implements a sorted (and ordered) map collection. This map is based on binary trees (so operations require log(n) time to perform).

java.util.ArrayList (a List)
> A class that implements a list collection. Internally, it is implemented using arrays.

java.util.LinkedList (a List and a Queue)
> A class that implements a list and a queue collection, providing a doubly linked list.

java.util.LinkedHashSet (a Set)
> A set collection that sorts its items based on the order in which they are added to the set.

java.util.LinkedHashMap (a Map)
> A map collection that sorts its items based on the order in which they are added to the map.

`java.util.IdentityHashMap (a Map)`
> A map collection. Unlike all other maps, this class uses == for key comparison instead of the equals( ) method.

`java.util.EnumSet (a Set)`
> A specialized set collection that holds only Enum values.

`java.util.EnumMap (a Map)`
> A specialized map collection that uses only Enum values as keys.

`java.util.PriorityQueue (a Queue)`
> An unbounded queue in which retrieval is not based on order (LIFO or FIFO); instead, objects are removed according to which is the smallest (as determined by the Comparable or Comparator interface).

## Thread-Notification Collection Classes

A number of classes in the java.util.concurrent package are designed to provide thread notification when their contents change. They are inherently threadsafe since they are expected to be used by multiple threads simultaneously. They simplify usage of collections by providing semantics to handle out-of-space and out-of-data conditions within the collection. We'll see examples of this later in the chapter.

`java.util.concurrent.ArrayBlockingQueue (a Queue)`
> A bounded FIFO queue. This collection supports the blocking interface, an interface that allows threads to wait either for space to be available (while storing data) or data to be available (while retrieving data).

`java.util.concurrent.LinkedBlockingQueue (a Queue)`
> A FIFO queue that can be either bounded or unbounded. This collection supports the blocking interface.

`java.util.concurrent.SynchronousQueue (a Queue)`
> A bounded FIFO queue. The bound on this queue is one (no elements are actually held in the collection), and multiple threads operate on it synchronously.

`java.util.concurrent.PriorityBlockingQueue (a Queue)`
> A threadsafe implementation of the PriorityQueue class. This class also supports the blocking interface.

`java.util.concurrent.DelayQueue (a Queue)`
> A class that implements an unbounded queue with a time-based order. Retrieval from the queue is based on the object whose getDelay( ) method has expired earliest: elements whose time expiration has not occurred can't be retrieved from the queue.

# Synchronization and Collection Classes

When writing a multithreaded program, the most important question when using a collection class is how to manage its synchronization. Synchronization can be managed by the collection class itself or managed explicitly in your program code. In the examples in this section, we'll explore both of these options.

## Simple Synchronization

Let's take the simple case first. In the simple case, you're going to use the collection class to store shared data. Other threads retrieve data from the collection, but there won't be much (if any) manipulation of the data.

In this case, the easiest object to use is a threadsafe collection (e.g., a Vector or Hashtable). That's what we've done all along in our CharacterEventHandler class:

```
package javathreads.examples.ch08.example1;

import java.util.*;

public class CharacterEventHandler {
    private Vector listeners = new Vector();

    public void addCharacterListener(CharacterListener cl) {
        listeners.add(cl);
    }

    public void removeCharacterListener(CharacterListener cl) {
        listeners.remove(cl);
    }

    public void fireNewCharacter(CharacterSource source, int c) {
        CharacterEvent ce = new CharacterEvent(source, c);
        CharacterListener[] cl = (CharacterListener[] )
                            listeners.toArray(new CharacterListener[0]);
        for (int i = 0; i < cl.length; i++)
            cl[i].newCharacter(ce);
    }
}
```

In this case, using a vector is sufficient for our purposes. If multiple threads call methods of this class at the same time, there is no conflict. Because the listeners collection is threadsafe, we can call its add( ), remove( ), and toArray( ) methods at the same time without corrupting the internal state of the Vector object. Strictly speaking, there is a race condition here in our use of the toArray( ) method; we'll talk about that a little more in the next section. But the point is that none of the methods on the vector see data in an inconsistent state because the Vector class itself is threadsafe.

A second option would be to use a thread-unsafe class (e.g., the ArrayList class) and manage the synchronization explicitly:

```
package javathreads.examples.ch08.example2;
...
public class CharacterEventHandler {
    private ArrayList listeners = new ArrayList();
    public synchronized void addCharacterListener(CharacterListener cl) {
        ...
    }
    public synchronized void removeCharacterListener(CharacterListener cl) {
        ...
    }
    public synchronized void fireNewCharacter(CharacterSource source, int c) {
        ...
    }
}
```

Or we could have synchronized the class like this:

```
package javathreads.examples.ch08.example3;
...
public class CharacterEventHandler {
    private ArrayList listeners = new ArrayList();

    public void addCharacterListener(CharacterListener cl) {
        synchronized(listeners) {
            listeners.add(cl);
        }
    }

    public void removeCharacterListener(CharacterListener cl) {
        synchronized(listeners) {
            listeners.add(cl);
        }
    }
    public void fireNewCharacter(CharacterSource source, int c) {
        CharacterEvent ce = new CharacterEvent(source, c);
        CharacterListener[] cl;
        synchronized(listeners) {
            cl = (CharacterListener[])
                            listeners.toArray(new CharacterListener[0]);
        }
        for (int i = 0; i < cl.length; i++)
            cl[i].newCharacter(ce);
    }
}
```

In this example, it doesn't matter whether we synchronize on the collection object or the event handler object (this); either one ensures that two threads are not simultaneously calling methods of the ArrayList class.

Our third option is to use a synchronized version of the thread-unsafe collection class. Most thread-unsafe collection classes have a synchronized counterpart that is threadsafe. The threadsafe collections are constructed by calling one of these static methods of the Collections class:

```
Set s = Collections.synchronizedSet(new HashSet(...));
Set s = Collections.synchronizedSet(new LinkedHashSet(...));
SortedSet s = Collections.synchronizedSortedSet(new TreeSet(...));
Set s = Collections.synchronizedSet(EnumSet.noneOf(obj.class));
Map m = Collections.synchronizedMap(new HashMap(...));
Map m = Collections.synchronizedMap(new LinkedHashMap(...));
SortedMap m = Collections.synchronizedSortedMap(new TreeMap(...));
Map m = Collections.synchronizedMap(new WeakHashMap(...));
Map m = Collections.synchronizedMap(new IdentityHashMap(...));
Map m = Collections.synchronizedMap(new EnumMap(...));
List list = Collections.synchronizedList(new ArrayList(...));
List list = Collections.synchronizedList(new LinkedList(...));
```

Any of these options protect access to the data held in the collection. This is accomplished by wrapping the collection in an object that synchronizes every method of the collection interface: it is not designed as an optimally synchronized class. Also note that the queue collection is not supported: the Collections class supplies only wrapper classes that support the Set, Map, and List interfaces. This is not a problem in most cases since the majority of the queue implementations are synchronized (and synchronized optimally).

## Complex Synchronization

A more complex case arises when you need to perform multiple operations atomically on the data held in the collection. In the previous section, we were able to use simple synchronization because the methods that needed to access the data in the collection performed only a single operation. The addCharacterListener( ) method has only a single statement that uses the listeners vector, so it doesn't matter if the data changes after the addCharacterListener( ) method calls the listeners.add( ) method. As a result, we could rely on the container to provide the synchronization.

We alluded to a race condition in the fireNewCharacter( ) method. After we call the listeners.toArray( ) method, we cycle through the listeners to call each of them. It's entirely possible that another thread will call the removeCharacterListener( ) method while we're looping through the array. That won't corrupt the array or the listeners vector, but in some algorithms, it could be a problem: we'd be operating on data that has been removed from the vector. In our program, that's okay: we have a benign race condition. In other programs, that may not necessarily be the case.

Suppose we want to keep track of all the characters that players typed correctly (or incorrectly). We could do that with the following:

```
package javathreads.examples.ch08.example4;

import java.util.*;
import javax.swing.*;
import javax.swing.table.*;
```

```java
public class CharCounter {
    public HashMap correctChars = new HashMap( );
    public HashMap incorrectChars = new HashMap( );
    private AbstractTableModel atm;

    public void correctChar(int c) {
        synchronized(correctChars) {
            Integer key = new Integer(c);
            Integer num = (Integer) correctChars.get(key);
            if (num == null)
                correctChars.put(key, new Integer(1));
            else correctChars.put(key, new Integer(num.intValue( ) +1));
            if (atm != null)
                atm.fireTableDataChanged( );
        }
    }

    public int getCorrectNum(int c) {
        synchronized(correctChars) {
            Integer key = new Integer(c);
            Integer num = (Integer) correctChars.get(key);
            if (num == null)
                return 0;
            return num.intValue( );
        }
    }

    public void incorrectChar(int c) {
        synchronized(incorrectChars) {
            Integer key = new Integer(c);
            Integer num = (Integer) incorrectChars.get(key);
            if (num == null)
                incorrectChars.put(key, new Integer(-1));
            else incorrectChars.put(key, new Integer(num.intValue( ) -1));
            if (atm != null)
                atm.fireTableDataChanged( );
        }
    }

    public int getIncorrectNum(int c) {
        synchronized(incorrectChars) {
            Integer key = new Integer(c);
            Integer num = (Integer) incorrectChars.get(key);
            if (num == null)
                return 0;
            return num.intValue( );
        }
    }

    public void addModel(AbstractTableModel atm) {
        this.atm = atm;
    }
}
```

Here we use thread-unsafe collections to hold the data and explicitly synchronize access around the code that uses the collections. It would be insufficient to use Hashtable collections in this code without also synchronizing as we did earlier. Although retrieving a value from a hashtable is threadsafe, and replacing an element in a hashtable is also threadsafe, the overall operation is not threadsafe: both collection operations must be atomic for the algorithm to succeed. Otherwise, two threads could simultaneously retrieve the stored value, increment it, and store it; the net result would be a score that is one less than it should be.

The moral of the story is that using a threadsafe collection does not guarantee the correctness of your program. Because of the explicit synchronization required in this example, we were able to use a thread-unsafe collection (although, as we'll see in Chapter 14, if you use a threadsafe collection, it's unlikely you'll see much difference.)

## Iterators and Enumerations

Many situations call for using each element of a collection. Such is the case in our example. We called the toArray( ) method, which returns an array containing every element in the vector. The Vector and Hashtable classes also have methods that return a java.util.Enumeration object that contains every element in the collection. More generally, all collection classes implement one or more methods that return a java.util.Iterator object. The iterator also contains every element in the collection.

Each of these techniques presents special synchronization concerns. We've already seen that looping through the array returned by the toArray( ) method can lead to a situation where we're accessing an element in the array that no longer appears in the collection. That may or may not be a problem for your program; if it is a problem, the solution is to synchronize access around the loop that uses the array.

Enumeration objects are difficult to use without explicit synchronization. The enumeration keeps state information about the collection; if the collection is modified while the enumeration is active, the enumeration may become confused. The enumeration fails in some random way, possibly through an unexpected runtime exception (e.g., a NullPointerException).

To use an enumeration of a collection that may also be used by multiple threads, you should synchronize on the collection object itself:

```
package javathreads.examples.ch08.example5;
...
    public void fireNewCharacter(CharacterSource source, int c) {
        CharacterEvent ce = new CharacterEvent(source, c);
        Enumeration e;
            synchronized(listeners) {
            e = listeners.elements();
```

```
        while (e.hasMoreElements()) {
                ((CharacterListener) e.nextElement()).newCharacter(ce);
        }
    }
  }
}
```

You could synchronize the method instead, as long as your collection is not used in any unsynchronized method. The point is that the enumeration and all uses of the collection must be locked by the same synchronization object.

Iterators behave somewhat differently. If the underlying collection of an iterator is modified while the iterator is active, the next access to the iterator throws a ConcurrentModificationException, which is also a runtime exception. Unlike enumerations, if the iterator fails, the underlying collection can still be used. The way in which iterators fail immediately after a modify operation is called "fail-fast."

The safest way to use an iterator is to make sure its use is synchronized by its underlying collection (just as we did with the enumeration)—or to make sure that it and the collection are protected by the same synchronization lock.

You can't rely upon the fail-fast nature of iterators. Iterators make a best effort at determining when the underlying collection has changed, but in the absence of synchronization, it's impossible to predict when the failure occurs. Once a failure has occurred, the iterator is not useful for further processing. Therefore, you're left with a situation where some elements of the collection have been processed and others have not.

Two classes—CopyOnWriteArrayList and CopyOnWriteArraySet—provide special iteration semantics. These classes are designed to copy the underlying collection when necessary so that iterators operate on a snapshot of the data from the time the iterator was created. Modifying the collection while the iterator is active creates a copy of the collection for the iterator.

This is an expensive operation, both in terms of time and memory usage. However, it ensures that iterators can be used from unsynchronized code because the iterators end up operating on old copies of the data. So, the iterators never throw a concurrent modification exception.

These classes are designed for cases where modifications to the collection are rare and the iterator of the collection is used frequently by multiple threads. This allows the iterators to be unsynchronized and still be threadsafe; as long as the updates are rare enough, this yields better overall performance. Note, however, that race conditions are still possible with this technique; it's essentially the same type of operation as we saw earlier with the toArray( ) method. The difference is when the copying occurs: when you call the toArray( ) method, a copy of the collection is made at that time. With the copy-on-write classes, the copy is made whenever the collection is modified.

## Thread-Aware Classes

Many collection classes are what we would term "thread-aware." They have many internal and subtle features that were designed specifically for threads:

- Some collections have an implementation that minimizes the need for synchronization by segmenting the collection. It is possible for threads to modify the collection simultaneously, without any synchronization, when they are operating on different segments.

- Some provide special services—such as iterator handling—that are specifically designed for multithreaded environments. The main reason for copy-on-write iterators is to balance the performance issues of many simultaneous threads iterating through the collection against a few updates to the collection.

- Interfaces have been enhanced to handle issues related to threads better. For example, the concurrent hashmap has the ability to add a key only if the key is not in the map; this simple enhancement removes the need for explicit synchronization for parallel writes of new elements.

# The Producer/Consumer Pattern

One of the more common patterns in threaded programming is the producer/consumer pattern. The idea is to process data asynchronously by partitioning requests among different groups of threads. The producer is a thread (or group of threads) that generates requests (or data) to be processed. The consumer is a thread (or group of threads) that takes those requests (or data) and acts upon them. This pattern provides a clean separation that allows for better thread design and makes development and debugging easier. This pattern is shown in Figure 8-1.

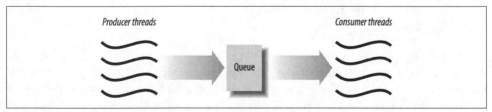

*Figure 8-1. The producer/consumer pattern*

The producer/consumer pattern is common for threaded programs because it is easy to make threadsafe. We just need to provide a safe way to pass data from the producer to the consumer. Data needs to be synchronized only during the small period of time when it is being passed between producer and consumer. We can use simple synchronization since the acts of inserting and removing from the collection are single operations. Therefore, any threadsafe vector, list, or queue can be used.

The queue-based collection classes added to J2SE 5.0 were specifically designed for this model. The queue data type is perfect to use for this pattern since it has the simple semantics of adding and removing a single element (with an optional ordering of the requests). Furthermore, blocking queues provide thread-control functionality: this allows you to focus on the functionality of your program while the queue takes care of thread and space management issues. Of course, if you need control over such issues, you can use a nonblocking queue and use your own explicit synchronization and notification.

Here's a simple producer that uses a blocking queue:

```
package javathreads.examples.ch08.example6;

import java.util.*;
import java.util.concurrent.*;

public class FibonacciProducer implements Runnable {
    private Thread thr;
    private BlockingQueue<Integer> queue;

    public FibonacciProducer(BlockingQueue<Integer> q) {
        queue = q;
        thr = new Thread(this);
        thr.start();
    }

    public void run() {
        try {
            for(int x=0;;x++) {
                Thread.sleep(1000);
                queue.put(new Integer(x));
                System.out.println("Produced request " + x);
            }
        } catch (InterruptedException ex) {
        }
    }
}
```

The producer is implemented to run in a separate thread; it uses the queue to store requests to be processed. We're using a blocking queue because we want the queue to handle the case where the producer gets too far ahead of the consumer. When that happens, we want the producer to block (so that it does not produce any more requests until the consumer catches up).

Here's the consumer:

```
package javathreads.examples.ch08.example6;

import java.util.concurrent.*;

public class FibonacciConsumer implements Runnable {
    private Fibonacci fib = new Fibonacci();
```

```
        private Thread thr;
        private BlockingQueue<Integer> queue;

        public FibonacciConsumer(BlockingQueue<Integer> q) {
            queue = q;
            thr = new Thread(this);
            thr.start();
        }

        public void run() {
            int request, result;
            try {
                while (true) {
                    request = queue.take().intValue();
                    result = fib.calculateWithCache(request);
                    System.out.println(
                            "Calculated result of " + result + " from " + request);
                }
            } catch (InterruptedException ex) {
            }
        }
    }
```

The consumer also runs in its own thread. It blocks until a request is in the queue, at which point it calculates a Fibonacci number based on the request. The actual calculation is performed by the Fibonacci class available in the online examples (along with a testing program).

Notice that the producer and consumer threads are decoupled: the producer never directly calls the consumer (and vice versa). This allows us to interchange different producers without affecting the consumer. It also allows us to have multiple producers serviced by a single consumer, or multiple consumers servicing a single producer. More generally, we can vary the number of either based on performance needs or user requirements.

The queue has also hidden all of the interesting thread code. When the queue is full, the producer blocks: it waits on a condition variable. Later, when the consumer takes an element from the queue, it notifies the waiting producer. A similar situation arises when the consumer calls the take( ) method on an empty queue. You could write all the condition variable code to handle this, but it's far easier to allow the queue to do it for you.

We chose to calculate a Fibonacci number in our test program because we used a recursive algorithm that takes an increasingly long time to compute. It's interesting to watch how the producer and consumer interact in this case. In the beginning, the consumer is blocked a lot of the time because it can calculate the Fibonacci number in less than one second (the time period between requests from the producer). Later, the producer spends most of its time blocked because it has overwhelmed the consumer and filled the queue.

If you have a multiprocessor machine, you can run the example with multiple consumer threads, but eventually the result is the same: the calculations take too long for the consumers to keep up.

## Using the Collection Classes

*So, which are the best collections to use?* Obviously, no single answer fits all cases. However, here are some general suggestions. By adhering to these suggestions, we can narrow the choice of which collection to use.

***When working with collection classes, work through interfaces.*** As with all Java programming, interfaces isolate implementation details. By using interfaces, the programmer can easily refactor a program to use a different collection implementation by changing only the initialization code.

***There is little performance benefit in using a nonsynchronized collection.*** This may be surprising to many developers—for an understanding of the performance issues around lock acquisition, see Chapter 14. In brief, performance issues with lock acquisitions occur only when there is contention for the lock. However, a nonsynchronized collection should have no contention for the lock. If there is contention, having race conditions is a more problematic issue than performance.

***For algorithms with a lot of contention, consider using the concurrent collections.***

The set, hashmap, and list collections that were added in J2SE 5.0 are highly optimized. If a program's algorithm fits into one of these interfaces, consider choosing a J2SE 5.0 collection over a synchronized version of a JDK 1.2 collection. The concurrent collections are much better optimized for multithreaded access.

***For producer/consumer-based programs, consider using a queue as the collection.***

Queues are best for the producer/consumer model for many reasons. First, queues provide an ordering of requests, preventing data starvation. Second, queues are highly optimized, having minimal synchronization, atomic accesses, and even safe parallel access in many cases. With these collections, a huge number of threads can work in parallel with little bottlenecking at the queue's access points.

***When possible, try to minimize the use of explicit synchronization.*** Iterators and other support methods that require tranversal of an entire collection may need more synchronization than the collection provides alone. This can be a problem when many threads are involved.

***Limit your use of iterators from the copy-on-write collections.*** First, use these classes only when the number of elements in the collection is small. This is because of the time and size requirements of the copy-on-write operation. Second, your program must not require that the collection have the most up-to-date information. The iterator contains only the information of the collection at the time that it is created.

*Consider using multiple collections.* While some of these collections have minimal synchronization, these synchronization periods can still be an issue when many threads are involved. Consider having an algorithm that uses segmented collections instead of a generic implementation in which all threads use the same collection.

*There is little difference between a set and a map.* Theoretically, a set and a map are different in a number of ways, but in terms of implementation, there is little difference. Many of the set collections are just implemented by using the map collection. This means that the choice is not actually a choice: an item stored in a set is merely stored as a key in a map.

# Summary

In this chapter, we have examined how threads interact with Java's collection classes. We've seen the synchronization requirements imposed by different classes and how to handle those requirements effectively. We've also examined how these classes can be used for the common design pattern known as the producer/consumer pattern.

## Example Classes

Here are the class names and Ant targets for the examples in this chapter. The online examples also include test code for the producer/consumer pattern.

| Description | Main Java class | Ant target |
| --- | --- | --- |
| Swing Type Tester | `javathreads.examples.ch08.example1.`<br>`SwingTypeTester` | ch8-ex1 |
| Swing Type Tester (uses array lists) | `javathreads.examples.ch08.example2.`<br>`SwingTypeTester` | ch8-ex2 |
| Swing Type Tester (uses synchronized blocks) | `javathreads.examples.ch08.example3.`<br>`SwingTypeTester` | ch8-ex3 |
| SwingTypeTester (counts character success/failures) | `javathreads.examples.ch08.example4.`<br>`SwingTypeTester` | ch8-ex4 |
| SwingTypeTester (uses enumeration) | `javathreads.examples.ch08.example5.`<br>`SwingTypeTester` | ch8-ex5 |
| Producer/Consumer Model | `javathreads.examples.ch08.example6.`<br>`FibonacciTest nConsumers` | ch8-ex6 |

In the Ant script, the number of consumer threads is defined by this property:

```
<property name="nConsumers" value="1"/>
```

# CHAPTER 9

# Thread Scheduling

The term "thread scheduling" covers a variety of topics. This chapter examines one of those topics, which is how a computer selects particular threads to run. The information in this chapter provides a basic understanding of when threads run and how computers handle multiple threads. There's little programming in this chapter, but the information we present is an important foundation for other topics of thread scheduling. In particular, the next few chapters discuss task scheduling and thread pools, which are the programmatic techniques you use to manage large numbers of threads and jobs.

The key to understanding Java thread scheduling is to realize that a CPU is a scarce resource. When two or more threads want to run on a single-processor machine, they end up competing for the CPU, and it's up to someone—either the programmer, the Java virtual machine, or the operating system—to make sure that the CPU is shared among these threads. The same is true whenever a program has more threads than the machine hosting the program has CPUs. The essence of this chapter is to understand how CPUs are shared among threads that want to access them.

In earlier examples, we didn't concern ourselves with this topic because, in those cases, the details of thread scheduling weren't important to us. This was because the threads we were concerned with didn't normally compete for a CPU: they had specific tasks to do, but the threads themselves were usually short-lived or only periodically needed a CPU in order to accomplish their task. Consider the event-processing thread in our typing program. Most of the time, this thread isn't using a CPU because it's waiting for the user to do something. When the user types a character or moves the mouse, the thread quickly processes the event and waits for the next event; since the thread doesn't need a CPU very often, we didn't need to concern ourselves with the thread's scheduling.

The topic of thread scheduling is a difficult one to address because the Java specification does not require implementations to schedule threads in a particular manner. It provides guidelines that threads should be scheduled based on a thread's priority, but they are not absolute, and different implementations of the Java virtual machine follow the guidelines differently. You cannot guarantee the order of execution of threads across all Java virtual machines.

## An Overview of Thread Scheduling

We'll start by looking at the basic principles of how threads are scheduled. Any particular virtual machine (and underlying operating system) may not follow these principles exactly, but the principles form the basis for our understanding of thread scheduling.

Let's start by looking at an example with some CPU-intensive threads. In this and subsequent chapters, we'll consume CPU resources with a recursive Fibonacci number generator, which has the advantage (for our purposes) of being an elegant and very slow program:

```java
package javathreads.examples.ch09;

import java.util.*;
import java.text.*;

public class Task implements Runnable {
    long n;
    String id;

    private long fib(long n) {
        if (n == 0)
            return 0L;
        if (n == 1)
            return 1L;
        return fib(n - 1) + fib(n - 2);
    }

    public Task(long n, String id) {
        this.n = n;
        this.id = id;
    }

    public void run() {
        Date d = new Date();
        DateFormat df = new SimpleDateFormat("HH:mm:ss:SSS");
        long startTime = System.currentTimeMillis();
        d.setTime(startTime);
        System.out.println("Starting task " + id + " at " + df.format(d));
        fib(n);
        long endTime = System.currentTimeMillis();
        d.setTime(endTime);
        System.out.println("Ending task " + id + " at " + df.format(d) +
                        " after " + (endTime - startTime) + " milliseconds");
    }
}
```

We've made this class a Runnable object so that we can run multiple instances of it in multiple threads:

```
package javathreads.examples.ch09.example1;

import javathreads.examples.ch09.*;

public class ThreadTest {

    public static void main(String[] args) {
        int nThreads = Integer.parseInt(args[0]);
        long n = Long.parseLong(args[1]);
        Thread t[] = new Thread[nThreads];

        for (int i = 0; i < t.length; i++) {
            t[i] = new Thread(new Task(n, "Task " + i));
            t[i].start();
        }
        for (int i = 0; i < t.length; i++) {
            try {
                t[i].join();
            } catch (InterruptedException ie) {}
        }
    }
}
```

Running this code with three threads produces this kind of output:

```
Starting task Task 2 at 00:04:30:324
Starting task Task 0 at 00:04:30:334
Starting task Task 1 at 00:04:30:345
Ending task Task 1 at 00:04:38:052 after 7707 milliseconds
Ending task Task 2 at 00:04:38:380 after 8056 milliseconds
Ending task Task 0 at 00:04:38:502 after 8168 milliseconds
```

Let's look at this output. Notice that the last thread we created and started (Task 2) was the first one that printed its first output. However, all threads started within 20 milliseconds of each other. The actual calculation took about eight seconds for each thread, and the threads ended in a different order than they started in. In particular, even though Task 2 started first, it took 349 milliseconds longer to perform the same calculation as Task 1 and finished after Task 1.

Generally, we'd expect to see similar output on almost any Java virtual machine running on almost any platform: the threads would start at almost the same time in some random order, and they would end in a (different) random order after having run for about the same amount of time.

Certain virtual machines and operating systems, however, would produce this output:

```
Starting task Task 0 at 00:04:30:324
Ending task Task 0 at 00:04:33:052 after 2728 milliseconds
Starting task Task 1 at 00:04:33:062
```

```
Ending task Task 1 at 00:04:35:919 after 2857 milliseconds
Starting task Task 2 at 00:04:35:929
Ending task Task 2 at 00:04:37:720 after 2791 milliseconds
```

The total here takes about the same amount of time, but now they have run sequentially: the second task did not begin to execute until the first task was finished. Another interesting fact about this output is that each individual task took less time than it did previously. That's a topic we'll cover in Chapter 10.

## Priority-Based Scheduling

In each of these examples, multiple threads compete for time on the CPU. When multiple threads want to execute, it is up to the underlying operating system to determine which of those threads are placed on a CPU. Java programs can influence that decision in some ways, but the decision is ultimately up to the operating system.

A Java virtual machine is required to implement a preemptive, priority-based scheduler among its various threads. This means that each thread in a Java program is assigned a certain priority, a positive integer that falls within a well-defined range. This priority can be changed by the developer. The Java virtual machine never changes the priority of a thread, even if the thread has been running for a certain period of time.

The priority value is important because the contract between the Java virtual machine and the underlying operating system is that the operating system must generally choose to run the Java thread with the highest priority. That's what we mean when we say that Java implements a priority-based scheduler. This scheduler is implemented in a preemptive fashion, meaning that when a higher-priority thread comes along, that thread interrupts (preempts) whatever lower-priority thread is running at the time. The contract with the operating system, however, is not absolute, which means that the operating system can sometimes choose to run a lower-priority thread.

Java's requirement for a priority-based, preemptive scheduling mechanism maps well to many operating systems. Solaris, the various Windows operating systems, Linux, and most other operating systems on desktop computers and servers all provide the support for that kind of thread scheduling. Certain operating systems, particularly those on specialized devices and on smaller, handheld devices, do not provide that level of scheduling support; Java virtual machine implementations for those operating systems must perform the necessary thread scheduling on their own.

Our first example, where the threads all complete at about the same time, is executed on a standard operating system (Solaris) where the thread scheduling is handled by the operating system. Our second example, where the threads run sequentially, is from a system where the Java virtual machine itself handles the thread scheduling. Both implementations are valid Java virtual machines.

# The Scheduling Process

Let's examine how the scheduling process works in a little more detail. At a conceptual level, every thread in the Java virtual machine can be in one of four states:

*Initial*

A thread object is in the initial state from the period when it is created (that is, when its constructor is called) until the start( ) method of the thread object is called.

*Runnable*

A thread is in the runnable state once its start( ) method has been called. A thread leaves the runnable state in various ways, but the runnable state can be thought of as a default state: if a thread isn't in any other state, it's in the runnable state.

A thread that is in the runnable state may not actually be running; it may be waiting for a CPU. A thread that is running on a CPU is called a currently running thread.

*Blocked*

A thread that is blocked is one that cannot be run because it is waiting for some specific event to occur. Threads block for many reasons: they attempt to read data (e.g., from a socket) when no data is available; they execute a thread-blocking method (e.g., the sleep( ), wait( ), or join( ) methods); or they attempt to acquire a synchronization lock that another thread already holds. We've seen APIs that also block, but internally those methods are all executing the wait( ) method.

*Exiting*

A thread is in the exiting state once its run( ) method returns (or its deprecated stop( ) method has been called).

The basic process of thread scheduling is essentially the same whether it's performed by the Java virtual machine or the underlying operating system. Our intent here is to provide an illustration of how thread scheduling works, not to provide a blueprint of how any particular thread scheduler is actually implemented.

We can conceive that a thread scheduler keeps track of all the threads on which it operates by using linked lists; every thread is on a list that represents the state of the thread. A Java thread can have one of 11 priorities, so we conceive of 14 linked lists: one for all threads in the initial state, one for all threads in the blocked state, one for all threads in the exiting state, and one for each priority level. The list of threads at a given priority level represents only those threads that are currently in the runnable state: a thread in the runnable state at priority 7 is placed on the priority 7 list, but when the thread blocks, it moves to the blocked linked list. We're speaking here of having 11 priorities, but that number is a Java abstraction: an operating system may have more or fewer priorities than that (but conceptually, each would still have its own linked list).

For simplicity, we conceive of these threads as being on an ordered list; in reality, they may be held in simple pools. Keeping the threads in a linked list implies that threads will be selected to run in a particular order. While that is a useful way of thinking about the process, it is not necessarily the way an implementation may work.

Let's see how this scheduling will occur with the example we show at the beginning of the chapter. That example has a total of four threads: the initial thread (which executes the main( ) method) and the three task threads we started. In fact, as we've mentioned, there are more threads because the virtual machine starts various background threads (like the garbage collection thread). But for our discussion, we'll consider only the four threads that are executing our code.

The threads that calculate a Fibonacci number never block: they move from the initial state to the runnable state to the executing state. The main thread is in the runnable state and then enters the blocking state when it executes the join( ) method to wait for the other threads.

The second time that we run the program, the state of the threads follows the transition path shown in Figure 9-1. The main thread is the currently running thread until it blocks at time T1. At that point, one of the task threads becomes the currently running thread; it remains the currently running thread until time T2 when it finishes and transitions to the exiting state. Another task thread becomes the currently running thread, and the cycle continues until all threads have completed.

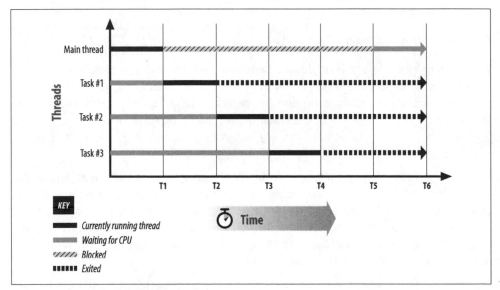

Figure 9-1. A simple thread-state diagram

That explains the output that we see when we run the program for a second time: everything (including the output) proceeds sequentially. So why is the output different the first time we run the example?

The first time we run the example, we do so on a typical operating system. The thread scheduler on that OS, in addition to being priority-based and preemptive, is also time-slicing. That means when threads are waiting for the CPU, the operating system allows one of them to run for a very short time. It then interrupts that thread and allows a second thread to run for a very short time, and so on. A portion of the thread transitions on such an operating system is shown in Figure 9-2.

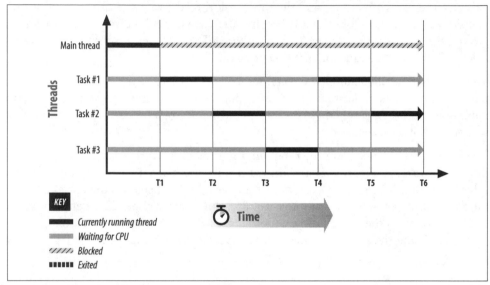

*Figure 9-2. Thread states with OS scheduling*

Java does not mandate that its threads be time-sliced, but most operating systems do so. There is often some confusion in terminology here: preemption is often confused with time-slicing. In fact, preemption means only that a higher-priority thread runs instead of a lower-priority one, but when threads have the same priority, they do not preempt each other. They are typically subject to time-slicing, but that is not a requirement of Java.

There's one other important point about these two figures. In our first figure, the time points (T1, T2, and so on) are relatively far apart. The time transitions in that case are determined when a particular thread changes state: when the main thread changes to the blocked state, a task thread changes to become the currently running thread. When that thread changes to the exiting state, a second task thread changes to become the currently running thread and so on.

In the second case, the time transitions occur at a much shorter interval, on the order of a few hundred milliseconds or so. In this case, the transitions of the threads between currently running and waiting for CPU are imposed by the operating system and not as a result of anything the thread itself has done. Of course, if a thread voluntarily changes to the exiting or waiting state, a transition occurs at that point as well.

## Priority Exceptions

When an operating system schedules Java threads, it may choose to run a lower-priority thread instead of a higher-priority thread in two instances, described next.

### Priority inversion

In a typical priority-based threading system, something unusual occurs when a thread attempts to acquire a lock that is held by a lower-priority thread: because the higher-priority thread becomes blocked, it temporarily runs with an effective priority of the lower-priority thread. Suppose that we have a thread with a priority of 8 that wants to acquire a lock that is held by a thread with a priority of 2. Because the priority 8 thread is waiting for the priority 2 thread to release the lock, it ends up running with an effective priority of 2. This is known as priority inversion.

Priority inversion is often solved by priority inheritance. With priority inheritance, a thread that holds a lock that is wanted by a thread with a higher priority has its priority temporarily and silently raised: its new priority becomes the same as the priority of the thread that it is causing to block. When the thread releases the lock, its priority is lowered to its original value.

The goal of priority inheritance is to allow the high-priority thread to run as soon as possible. It is a common feature of operating systems, and Java virtual machines running on those operating systems are subject to it. However, it is not a requirement of the Java specification.

### Complex priorities

The second case involves the priority assigned to threads by the operating system. We mentioned that Java has 11 priority levels (10 of which are available to developers), but this is an abstraction of the Java language. Operating systems usually have many more priorities. More important, though, is that the priority that the operating system assigns to a thread is a complex formula that takes many pieces of information into account.

A simple version of this formula might be this:

```
RealPriority = JavaPriority + SecondsWaitingForCPU
```

This type of formula accounts for the length of time that the thread has been waiting for a CPU. After a sufficient amount of time has passed, a thread with a Java priority of 3 has a real priority that is higher than a currently running Java thread with a priority of 5. This gives the priority 3 thread an opportunity to run, even though it has a lower priority than other unblocked threads.

Complex priorities are advantageous because they help to prevent thread starvation. Without such a model, a low-priority thread would have to wait for all other high-priority threads to block before it is given a chance to execute; it's likely that it might have to wait forever. With complex priorities, it can still run much less often than its higher-priority peers, but at least it will run sometimes.

On the other hand, complex priorities mean that you cannot guarantee thread scheduling. In particular, you cannot use thread priorities to try and prevent race conditions in data access: a lower-priority thread can interrupt a higher-priority thread while it is in the process of updating shared data. You also cannot use thread priorities to ensure a certain order of execution between tasks.

# Scheduling with Thread Priorities

The Thread class contains a number of methods and variables related to thread priorities:

```
package java.lang;
public class Thread implements Runnable {
    public static final int Thread.MAX_PRIORITY;
    public static final int Thread.MIN_PRIORITY;
    public static final int Thread.NORM_PRIORITY;
    public void setPriority(int priority);
    public int getPriority( );
}
```

The setPriority( ) method changes the priority of a particular thread. This method can be called at any time (subject to security restrictions, which we discuss in Chapter 13). As we'll see later in this chapter, using priorities to give preference to certain threads may or may not give you the effect you expect. In general, attempting to influence scheduling behavior using priorities offers limited benefit.

In the Java Thread class, three static final variables define the allowable range of thread priorities:

Thread.MIN_PRIORITY
> The minimum priority a thread can have (although the virtual machine is allowed to have lower-priority threads than this one)

Thread.MAX_PRIORITY
> The maximum priority a thread can have

Thread.NORM_PRIORITY
> The default priority for a thread

The symbolic definition of priority constants is not necessarily useful. Typically, we like to think of constant values like these in terms of symbolic names, which allows us to believe that the actual values are irrelevant. Using symbolic names also allows us to change the variables and have that change reflected throughout our code.

Unfortunately, that logic doesn't apply in the case of thread priorities: if we have to manipulate the individual priorities of threads, we sometimes have to know what the range of those values actually is. Because of the way in which these values map to thread priorities of operating systems, threads with different Java priorities may end up with the same operating system priority. When you write an applet, the thread that the applet runs in is given a priority of NORM_PRIORITY + 1. It's interesting to wonder how far you can take this: NORM_PRIORITY + 2, + 3, and so on until you get to MAX_PRIORITY. If you really want to work with Java's full range of priorities, the symbolic values don't help you: you have to know that the minimum priority available to developers is 1, the maximum is 10, and the default is 5. This yields 10 distinct priorities that you can assign to a a thread; the 11th priority (priority 0) is reserved for the virtual machine.

On the other hand, not all operating systems support 10 distinct levels of thread priorities, so NORM_PRIORITY − 2 and NORM_PRIORITY − 3 may be the same thing on your particular machine. Working with numeric values doesn't really provide a full range either. The best we can do for portable applications is to use the three symbolic priorities and realize that they're really just a hint to the virtual machine anyway.

Let's see what happens when we use these calls. We'll modify our Fibonacci calculator so that each of the task threads is started with a different priority:

```
for (int i = 0; i < t.length; i++) {
    t[i] = new Thread(new Task(n, "Task " + i));
    t[i].setPriority((i % 10) + 1);
    t[i].start();
}
```

What happens when we run this program is very dependent on the operating system hosting the program. We'll discuss that effect for several popular platforms in the next section.

## Other Thread-Scheduling Methods

Other methods in the Thread class also affect scheduling. For the most part, we do not recommend that you use these methods. The suspend( ) and resume( ) methods directly affect scheduling; a thread that is suspended is in the blocked state. However, as we discussed in Chapter 2, these methods are deprecated.

The Thread class also includes a yield( ) method, which asks the host operating system to select another thread to run. Its effect is very dependent on the operating system hosting the virtual machine; much of the time, the yield( ) method turns out to be a no-op. On the green thread model (see the next section), the yield( ) method can be very useful, but as the Java platform has evolved to support native threads of an operating system, the yield( ) method has lost its value.

# Popular Threading Implementations

We'll now look at how all of this plays out in the implementation of the Java virtual machine on several popular platforms. In many ways, this is a section that we'd rather not have to write: Java is a platform-independent language and to have to provide platform-specific details of its implementations certainly violates that precept. But we stress that these details actually matter in very few cases. This section is strictly for informational purposes.

## Green Threads

The first model that we'll look at is the simplest. In this model, the operating system doesn't know anything about Java threads at all; it is up to the virtual machine to handle all the details of the threading API. From the perspective of the operating system, there is a single process and a single thread.

Each thread in this model is an abstraction within the virtual machine: the virtual machine must hold within the thread object all information related to that thread. This includes the thread's stack, a program counter that indicates which Java instruction the thread is executing, and other bookkeeping information about the thread. The virtual machine is then responsible for switching thread contexts: that is, saving this information for one particular thread, loading it from another thread, and then executing the new thread. As far as the operating system is concerned, the virtual machine is just executing arbitrary code; the fact that the code is emulating many different threads is unknown outside of the virtual machine.

This model is known in Java as the green thread model. In other circles, these threads are often called user-level threads because they exist only within the user level of the application: no calls into the operating system are required to handle any thread details.

In the early days of Java, the green thread model was fairly common, particularly on most Unix platforms. Some specialized operating systems today use this model, but most computers use a native, system-level model.

The green thread model is completely deterministic with respect to scheduling. Running our priority calculation above, we see this output:

```
Starting task Task 5 at 07:23:12:074
Ending task Task 5 at 07:23:12:995 after 921 milliseconds
Starting task Task 4 at 07:23:13:111
Starting task Task 6 at 07:23:13:281
Ending task Task 6 at 07:23:14:256 after 975 milliseconds
Starting task Task 7 at 07:23:14:386
```

```
Ending task Task 7 at 07:23:15:398 after 1012 milliseconds
Starting task Task 8 at 07:23:15:504
Ending task Task 8 at 07:23:16:567 after 963 milliseconds
Starting task Task 9 at 07:23:16:624
Ending task Task 9 at 07:23:17:699 after 1075 milliseconds
Ending task Task 4 at 07:23:18:912 after 5801 milliseconds
Starting task Task 3 at 07:23:19:114
Ending task Task 3 at 07:23:20:177 after 1063 milliseconds
Starting task Task 2 at 07:23:20:301
Ending task Task 2 at 07:23:21:305 after 1004 milliseconds
Starting task Task 1 at 07:23:21:486
Ending task Task 1 at 07:23:22:449 after 963 milliseconds
```

As soon as the thread with priority 6 (task 5) becomes runnable, the green thread scheduler runs it, and all threads must wait. That includes the main thread, which cannot go on to create a higher-priority thread. This is why the priority 9 thread runs after the priority 6–8 threads have finished: the main thread cannot create the priority 9 thread because it runs at a priority of 5 and is blocked by the threads at priority 6–8. Task 4 gets to run occasionally when the main thread is blocked, and it eventually completes after very high-priority task 9.

# Windows Native Threads

In the native-threading model used on 32-bit Windows operating systems, the OS is fully cognizant of the multiple threads that the virtual machine uses, and there is a one-to-one mapping between Java threads and operating system threads. Therefore, the scheduling of Java threads is subject to the underlying scheduling of threads by the operating system.

This model is usually simple to understand because every thread can be thought of as a process. The OS scheduler makes no real distinction in this case between a process and a thread: it treats each thread like a process. Of course, there are still other differences in the OS between a thread and a process, but not as far as the scheduler is concerned.

Windows operating systems use a complex priority calculation to determine which thread should be the currently running thread. That calculation takes into account the Windows thread priority. This is very similar to the Java-level thread priority between 0 and 10, except that Windows provides only 7 priorities. Therefore, some overlap occurs as Java's 11 logical priorities are mapped to Windows 7 actual priorities. Different implementations of the virtual machine do this differently, but one common implementation performs the mapping listed in Table 9-1.

*Table 9-1. Mapping of Java thread priorities on Win32 platforms*

| Java priority | Win32 priority |
|---|---|
| 0 | THREAD_PRIORITY_IDLE |
| 1 (Thread.MIN_PRIORITY) | THREAD_PRIORITY_LOWEST |
| 2 | THREAD_PRIORITY_LOWEST |
| 3 | THREAD_PRIORITY_BELOW_NORMAL |
| 4 | THREAD_PRIORITY_BELOW_NORMAL |
| 5 (Thread.NORM_PRIORITY) | THREAD_PRIORITY_NORMAL |
| 6 | THREAD_PRIORITY_ABOVE_NORMAL |
| 7 | THREAD_PRIORITY_ABOVE_NORMAL |
| 8 | THREAD_PRIORITY_HIGHEST |
| 9 | THREAD_PRIORITY_HIGHEST |
| 10 (Thread.MAX_PRIORITY) | THREAD_PRIORITY_TIME_CRITICAL |

On this implementation, a thread with a Java priority of 3 and one with a Java priority of 4 have the same effective priority.

In addition to 7 priority levels, Windows operating systems also have 5 scheduling classes, and a thread is actually scheduled as a combination of its priority and its scheduling class. However, scheduling classes are not easy to change, so they do not factor into a discussion of Java threads.

Windows operating systems also use a complex priority calculation that includes the following:

- Threads are subject to priority inheritance.
- The actual priority of a thread is based on its programmed (or inverted) priority minus a value that indicates how recently the thread has actually run. This value is subject to continual adjustment: the more time passes, the closer to zero that

value becomes. This primarily distinguishes between threads of the same priority, and it leads to round-robin scheduling of threads of the same priority.

- On another level, a thread that has not run for a very long time is given a temporary priority boost. The value of this boost decays over time as the thread has a chance to run. This prevents threads from absolute starvation while still giving preference to higher-priority threads over lower-priority threads. The effect of this priority boost depends on the original priority of the thread.

- Threads running in a program that has keyboard and mouse focus are given a priority boost over threads in other programs.

The upshot of all this is that it's very difficult to guarantee explicitly ordered thread execution on Windows platforms, but the complex priority calculation ensures that threads do not starve.

On Windows operating systems, the output of our priority-based thread calculation looks something like this:

```
Starting task Task 9 at 21:19:23:590
Starting task Task 8 at 21:19:23:590
Starting task Task 7 at 21:19:23:590
Ending task Task 9 at 21:19:28:750 after 5160 milliseconds
Starting task Task 4 at 21:19:29:470
Ending task Task 8 at 21:19:30:180 after 6590 milliseconds
Starting task Task 2 at 21:19:30:180
Starting task Task 0 at 21:19:30:460
Ending task Task 7 at 21:19:32:050 after 8460 milliseconds
Starting task Task 6 at 21:19:23:590
Starting task Task 5 at 21:19:23:590
Starting task Task 3 at 21:19:30:180
Ending task Task 5 at 21:19:35:950 after 12360 milliseconds
Ending task Task 6 at 21:19:35:950 after 12360 milliseconds
Starting task Task 1 at 21:19:30:180
Ending task Task 4 at 21:19:37:820 after 8350 milliseconds
Ending task Task 2 at 21:19:41:610 after 11430 milliseconds
Ending task Task 3 at 21:19:41:720 after 11540 milliseconds
Ending task Task 0 at 21:19:45:120 after 14660 milliseconds
Ending task Task 1 at 21:19:45:120 after 14940 milliseconds
```

On this platform, the complex priority calculation places a great deal of emphasis on the Java priority level. In fact, the highest priority tasks finish before some of the lower-priority tasks even have a chance to start. Note also that several Java priority levels map to the same Windows priority level: priorities 6 and 7 (tasks 5 and 6) are given the same priority by the operating system, as are priorities 1 and 2 (tasks 0 and 1).

## Solaris Native Threads

Recent versions of the Solaris Operating Environment have had two different threading models. Solaris 7 featured a complex, two-level threading system, with user-level threads and system-level lightweight processes (LWPs). Java threads were equivalent to Solaris user-level threads, and there is an M-to-N mapping between the user-level threads and LWPs. Much of the flexibility of this model is lost on the Java developer, who can directly influence only the priority (and number) of the user-level threads but not the underlying LWPs.

In Solaris 9, a new one-to-one threading model is used. That makes it conceptually similar to the models on Windows operating systems, though its implementation details are quite different.

In Solaris 8, both models are available, and the user picks a model when the Java program (or any other program) is executed.

For Java programs, the one-to-one model is highly preferable, particularly when the machine has multiple CPUs and the Java threads are CPU-intensive. In other cases, the one-to-one threading model is still preferred, though the difference in threading models is not as significant. For this reason, many Java programs run better on Solaris 9 than on Solaris 7. On Solaris 8, you specify the new threading model by setting the environment variable LD_LIBRARY_PATH=/usr/lib/lwp in the shell (or script) in which the Java executable is started.

On Solaris 7, you can mimic some of the benefits of Solaris' new threading model by including these two flags in your Java command line: -Xboundthreads -XX:+UseLWPSynchronization.

The complex priority of a Solaris thread is determined by the following:

- Solaris native threads are subject to priority inheritance.

- The actual priority of a thread is a value from 0 to 59. That value is primarily determined by how long it's been since the thread has run. Though the calculation includes the Java-level priority, other factors dominate the calculation.

- Solaris also includes a variety of scheduling classes. All threads in a single program belong to the same scheduling class, so there is no variability in scheduling among them.

Running our priority-based calculator on Solaris produces this sort of output:

```
Starting task Task 7 at 21:26:33:040
Starting task Task 0 at 21:26:33:040
Starting task Task 6 at 21:26:33:039
Starting task Task 9 at 21:26:33:039
Starting task Task 4 at 21:26:33:039
Starting task Task 2 at 21:26:33:040
Starting task Task 5 at 21:26:33:039
Starting task Task 3 at 21:26:33:039
Starting task Task 8 at 21:26:33:039
Starting task Task 1 at 21:26:33:039
Ending task Task 6 at 21:27:02:580 after 29541 milliseconds
Ending task Task 1 at 21:27:02:802 after 29763 milliseconds
Ending task Task 4 at 21:27:03:618 after 30579 milliseconds
```

```
Ending task Task 7 at 21:27:04:173 after 31133 milliseconds
Ending task Task 0 at 21:27:04:259 after 31219 milliseconds
Ending task Task 9 at 21:27:04:375 after 31336 milliseconds
Ending task Task 3 at 21:27:04:457 after 31418 milliseconds
Ending task Task 5 at 21:27:05:050 after 32011 milliseconds
Ending task Task 8 at 21:27:05:159 after 32120 milliseconds
Ending task Task 2 at 21:27:05:287 after 32247 milliseconds
```

The lower-priority threads tend to start later than the higher-priority threads, but priority is no assurance of more CPU time: the thread at priority 8 finishes later than almost any other thread. The complex priority calculation being performed by the operating system ensures that all threads get adequate amounts of CPU time.

At an application level, threads on Solaris can have any of 128 priorities (though, as we mentioned, that priority is factored into a complex equation that yields 60 different runnable priorities). These priorities run from 0 to 127, and in C and C++ programs, the default priority for a thread is 127. In Java versions up to and including JDK 1.4, Java thread priorities were mapped to the full range of 128 priorities (0, 12, 24, and so on). This meant that the default priority for a Java thread was in the middle of this range and hence less than the default priority for a C or C++ thread. When a Solaris machine ran a CPU-intensive C program along with a CPU-intensive Java program, the Java program was at a disadvantage and received less than 50% of the available CPU time.

In J2SE 5.0, the mapping was changed and all Java threads with a priority of NORM_PRIORITY and higher are now mapped to a Solaris thread priority of 127. This allows Java and C programs to run at parity.

## Linux Native Threads

Until JDK 1.3, Linux-based virtual machines tended to use a green thread model. Some used Linux's native threads, but the kernel support for those threads did not support a large number of concurrent threads. JDK 1.3 added support for Linux native threads. However, the Linux kernel at the time was not optimal for threaded applications; in particular, the ps command listed all threads as if they were different processes.

New Linux kernels use the Native Posix Thread Library (NPTL), which provides the same one-to-one mapping of Java threads to kernel threads that we've seen in other operating systems. The complex priority calculation for those threads is similar to what we saw on Solaris, where the Java priority is only a small factor in the calculation. JDK 1.4.2 is the first version of Java to support this new kernel.

# Summary

Thread scheduling is a gray area of Java programming because actual scheduling models are not defined by the Java specification. As a result, scheduling behavior can (and does) vary on different machines.

In a general sense, threads have a priority, and threads with a higher-priority tend to run more often that threads with a lower priority. The degree to which this is true depends on the underlying operating system; Windows operating systems give more precedence to the thread priority while Unix-style operating systems give more precedence to letting all threads have a significant amount of CPU time.

For the most part, this thread scheduling doesn't matter: the information we've looked at in this chapter is important for understanding what's going on in your program, but there's not much you can do to change the way it works. In the next two chapters, we'll look at other kinds of thread scheduling and, using the information we've just learned, see how to make optimal use of multiple threads on multiple CPUs.

## Example Classes

Here is the class name and Ant target for the example in this chapter:

| Description | Main Java class | Ant target |
| --- | --- | --- |
| Recursive Fibonacci Calculator | javathreads.examples.ch09.example1.<br>ThreadTest nThreads FibCalcValue | ch9-ex1 |

The Fibonacci test requires command-line arguments that specify the number of threads to run simultaneously and the value to calculate. In the Ant script, those arguments are defined by these properties:

```
<property name="nThreads" value="10"/>
<property name="FibCalcValue" value="20"/>
```

# CHAPTER 10

# Thread Pools

For various reasons, thread pools are a very common tool in a multithreaded developer's toolkit. Most programs that use a lot of threads benefit in some way from using a thread pool.

J2SE 5.0 comes with its own thread pool implementation. Prior to this release, developers were left to write their own thread pool or use any number of commonly available implementations (including one we developed in earlier editions of this book and which is discussed in the Appendix). In this chapter, we discuss the thread pool implementation that comes with J2SE 5.0. If you can't use that implementation yet, the information in this chapter is still useful: you'll find out how and when using a thread pool can be advantageous. With that understanding, it's simple to use any thread pool implementation in your own program.

## Why Thread Pools?

The idea behind a thread pool is to set up a number of threads that sit idle, waiting for work that they can perform. As your program has tasks to execute, it encapsulates those tasks into some object (typically a Runnable object) and informs the thread pool that there is a new task. One of the idle threads in the pool takes the task and executes it; when it finishes the task, it goes back and waits for another task.

Thread pools have a maximum number of threads available to run these tasks. Consequently, when you add a task to a thread pool, it might have to wait for an available thread to run it. That may not sound encouraging, but it's at the core of why you would use a thread pool.

Reasons for using thread pools fall into three categories.

The first reason thread pools are often recommended is because it's felt that the overhead of creating a thread is very high; by using a pool, we can gain some performance when the threads are reused. The degree to which this is true depends a lot on your program and its requirements. It is true that creating a thread can take as much as a few hundred microseconds, which is a significant amount of time for some programs (but not others; see Chapter 14).

The second reason for using a thread pool is very important: it allows for better program design. If your program has a lot of tasks to execute, you can perform all the thread management for those tasks yourself, but, as we've started to see in our examples, this can quickly become tedious; the code to start a thread and manage its lifecycle isn't very interesting. A thread pool allows you to delegate all the thread management to the pool itself, letting you focus on the logic of your program. With a thread pool, you simply create a task and send the task to the pool to be executed; this leads to much more elegant programs (see Chapter 11).

The primary reason to use a thread pool is that they carry important performance benefits for applications that want to run many threads simultaneously. In fact, anytime you have more active threads than CPUs, a thread pool can play a crucial role in making your program seem to run faster and more efficiently.

If you read that last sentence carefully, in the back of your mind you're probably thinking that we're being awfully weasely: what does it mean that your program "seems" to run faster? What we mean is that the throughput of your CPU-bound program running multiple calculations will be faster, and that leads to the perception that your program is running faster. It's all a matter of throughput.

## Thread Pools and Throughput

In Chapter 9, we showed an example of what happens when a system has more threads than CPU resources. The way in which the threads perform the calculation has a big effect on the output. In particular, our first example produces this output:

```
Starting task Task 2 at 00:04:30:324
Starting task Task 0 at 00:04:30:334
Starting task Task 1 at 00:04:30:345
Ending task Task 1 at 00:04:38:052 after 7707 milliseconds
Ending task Task 2 at 00:04:38:380 after 8056 milliseconds
Ending task Task 0 at 00:04:38:502 after 8168 milliseconds
```

In this case, we have three threads and one CPU. The three threads run at the same time, are time-sliced by the operating system, and all completed execution in around eight seconds. Imagine that we have written this program as a server where each time a client connects, it is given a separate thread. When the three clients each request the service (that is, the calculation of the Fibonacci number), each will wait eight seconds for its answer.

In our second example, we run the threads sequentially and see this output:

```
Starting task Task 0 at 00:04:30:324
Ending task Task 0 at 00:04:33:052 after 2728 milliseconds
Starting task Task 1 at 00:04:33:062
Ending task Task 1 at 00:04:35:919 after 2857 milliseconds
```

```
Starting task Task 2 at 00:04:35:929
Ending task Task 2 at 00:04:38:720 after 2791 milliseconds
```

In this case, the total time to complete the calculation is still about 8 seconds, but each thread completes its execution in about 2.7 seconds. A server that runs the calculations sequentially will provide its first answer in 2.7 seconds, and the average waiting time for the clients will be 5.4 seconds.

This is what we mean by the throughput of the program. In both cases, we've done the same amount of work, but in the second case, users of the program are generally happier with the performance.

Now consider what happens if additional requests come in while the server is executing. If we create a new thread for every client, the server could quickly become overloaded: the more threads it starts, the slower it provides an answer for each request. With three simultaneous threads, our calculation takes eight seconds. If a new request arrives every 2.7 seconds or so, we never finish. The server starts more and more threads, each thread gets less and less CPU time, and none ever finish.

On the other hand, if we run the requests sequentially using only one thread, the server reaches a steady state. With three requests in the queue, each subsequent request arrives as another one finishes. We can supply an endless number of answers to the clients; each client waits about eight seconds for a response.

This reasoning applies to programs other than servers. For instance, an image processing application may nicely partition its image and be able to work on each partition in a separate thread. If a user is watching the image on screen, you might want to display the results of one partition while another one is being manipulated.

The similarity to programs like this and servers is that the results of each thread are interesting. The result of a single calculation is interesting to the client that requested it, the result of a partition of the image is interesting to the user viewing the screen, and so on. In these cases, throttling the number of threads provides a better experience for the users of the application.

Clearly, parts of this discussion are contrived; we've selected the numbers in the best way possible to make our point, and we've used a calculation that needs only CPU resources to complete. In the real world, requests arrive at the server in random bursts, and processing the request involves making database calls or something else that is likely to block. Those things complicate using a thread pool, but they do not eliminate its benefits.

The fact that threads may block means that we need to have more threads than CPUs in our pool. So far, we've considered cases where there is one CPU and have seen that one CPU-intensive thread gives us the best throughput. If the thread spends 50% of its time blocked, you want two threads per CPU; if the thread blocks 66% of the time, you want three threads per CPU, and so on.

Of course, you're unlikely to be able to model your program in such detail. And any model becomes far harder to calculate once you start to account for random bursts in traffic. In the end, you'll need to run some tests to determine an appropriate size for your thread pool. But if CPU resources are sometimes scarce, throttling the number of threads (while still keeping the CPUs utilized) increases the throughput of your application.

## Why Not Thread Pools?

If your program is doing batch processing, or simply providing a single answer or report, it doesn't really matter if you use as many threads as possible or a thread pool: if no one is interested in the results given by each thread, it doesn't matter if some of them finish before others. That doesn't mean that you can expect to create thousands of threads with impunity: threads take memory, and the more memory you use, the more impact you'll have on your system performance. Additionally, there is some slight overhead when the operating system manages thousands of threads instead of just a few. Still, if your program design nicely separates into multiple threads and you're interested only in the end result of all those threads, a thread pool isn't necessary.

Thread pools are also not necessary when available CPU resources are adequate to handle all the work the program needs to do. In fact, in this case a thread pool may do more harm than good. Obviously, if your system has eight CPUs and you have only four threads in your thread pool, tasks wait for a thread even though four CPUs are idle. With a thread pool, you want to throttle the total number of threads so that they don't overwhelm your system, but you never want to have fewer runnable threads than CPUs.

# Executors

Java's implementation of thread pools is based on an executor. An executor is a generic concept modelled by this interface:

```
package java.util.concurrent;
public interface Executor {
    public void execute(Runnable task);
}
```

Executors are a useful design pattern for multithreaded programs because they allow you to model your program as a series of tasks. You don't need to worry about the thread details associated with the task: you simply create the task and pass it to the execute( ) method of an appropriate executor.

J2SE 5.0 comes with two kinds of executors. It comes with a thread pool executor, which we'll show next. It also provides a task scheduling executor, which we examine in Chapter 11. Both of these executors are defined by this interface:

```
package java.util.concurrent;
public interface ExecutorService extends Executor {
    void shutdown( );
    List shutdownNow( );
    boolean isShutdown( );
    boolean isTerminated( );
    boolean awaitTermination(long timeout, TimeUnit unit)
            throws InterruptedException;
    <T> Future<T> submit(Callable<T> task);
    <T> Future<T> submit(Runnable task, T result);
    Future<?> submit(Runnable task);
    <T> List<Future<T>> invokeAll(Collection<Callable<T>> tasks)
            throws InterruptedException;
    <T> List<Future<T>> invokeAll(Collection<Callable<T>> tasks,
                                long timeout, TimeUnit unit)
            throws InterruptedException;
    <T> T invokeAny(Collection<Callable<T>> tasks)
            throws InterruptedException, ExecutionException;
    <T> T invokeAny(Collection<Callable<T>> tasks,  long timeout, TimeUnit unit)
            throws InterruptedException, ExecutionException, TimeoutException;
}
```

This interface provides a means for you to manage the executor and its tasks. The shutdown( ) method gracefully terminates the executor: any tasks that have already been sent to the executor are allowed to run, but no new tasks are accepted. When all tasks are completed, the executor stops its thread(s). The shutdownNow( ) method attempts to stop execution sooner: all tasks that have not yet started are not run and are instead returned in a list. Still, existing tasks continue to run: they are interrupted, but it's up to the runnable object to check its interrupt status and exit when convenient.

So there's a period of time between calling the shutdown( ) or shutdownNow( ) method and when tasks executing in the executor service are all complete. When all tasks are complete (including any waiting tasks), the executor service enters a terminated state. You can check to see if the executor service is in the terminated state by calling the isTerminated( ) method (or you can wait for it to finish the pending tasks by calling the awaitTerminated( ) method).

An executor service also allows you to handle many tasks in ways that the simple Executor interface does not accommodate. Tasks can be sent to an executor service via a submit( ) method, which returns a Future object that can be used to track the progress of the task. The invokeAll( ) methods execute all the tasks in the given collection. The invokeAny( ) methods execute the tasks in the given collection, but when one task has completed, the remaining tasks are subject to cancellation. We'll discuss Future objects and cancellation later in this chapter.

# Using a Thread Pool

To use a thread pool, you must do two things: you must create the tasks that the pool is to run, and you must create the pool itself. The tasks are simply Runnable objects, so that meshes well with a standard approach to threading (in fact, the task that we'll use for this example is the same Runnable task we use in Chapter 9 to calculate a Fibonacci number). You can also use Callable objects to represent your tasks (which we'll do later in this chapter), but for most simple uses, a Runnable object is easier to work with.

The pool is an instance of the ThreadPoolExecutor class. That class implements the ExecutorService interface, which tells us how to feed it tasks and how to shut it down. We'll look at the other aspects of that class in this section, beginning with how to construct it.

```
package java.util.concurrent;
public class ThreadPoolExecutor implements ExecutorService {
    public ThreadPoolExecutor(int corePoolSize,
                              int maximumPoolSize,
                              long keepAliveTime,
                              TimeUnit unit,
                              BlockingQueue<Runnable> workQueue);
    public ThreadPoolExecutor(int corePoolSize,
                              int maximumPoolSize,
                              long keepAliveTime,
                              TimeUnit unit,
                              BlockingQueue<Runnable> workQueue,
                              ThreadFactory threadFactory);
    public ThreadPoolExecutor(int corePoolSize,
                              int maximumPoolSize,
                              long keepAliveTime,
                              TimeUnit unit,
                              BlockingQueue<Runnable> workQueue,
                              RejectedExecutionHandler handler);
    public ThreadPoolExecutor(int corePoolSize,
                              int maximumPoolSize,
                              long keepAliveTime,
                              TimeUnit unit,
                              BlockingQueue<Runnable> workQueue,
                              ThreadFactory threadFactory,
                              RejectedExecutionHandler handler);
}
```

The core pool size, maximum pool size, keep alive times, and so on control how the threads within the pool are managed. We describe each of these concepts in our next section.

For now, we can use a constructor to create the tasks and put them in the thread pool:

```
package javathreads.examples.ch10.example1;

import java.util.concurrent.*;
import javathreads.examples.ch10.*;

public class ThreadPoolTest {

    public static void main(String[] args) {
        int nTasks = Integer.parseInt(args[0]);
        long n = Long.parseLong(args[1]);
        int tpSize = Integer.parseInt(args[2]);

        ThreadPoolExecutor tpe = new ThreadPoolExecutor(
            tpSize, tpSize, 50000L, TimeUnit.MILLISECONDS,
            new LinkedBlockingQueue<Runnable>());

        Task[] tasks = new Task[nTasks];
        for (int i = 0; i < nTasks; i++) {
            tasks[i] = new Task(n, "Task " + i);
            tpe.execute(tasks[i]);
        }
        tpe.shutdown();
    }
}
```

In this example, we're using the tasks to calculate Fibonacci numbers as we do in Chapter 9. Once the pool is constructed, we simply add the tasks to it (using the execute() method). When we're done, we gracefully shut down the pool; the existing tasks run to completion, and then all the existing threads exit. As you can see, using the thread pool is quite simple, but the behavior of the pool can be complex depending on the arguments used to construct it. We'll look into that in the next section.

## Queues and Sizes

The two fundamental things that affect a thread pool are its size and the queue used for the tasks. These are set in the constructor of the thread pool; the size can change dynamically while the queue must remain fixed. In addition to the constructor, these methods interact with the pool's size and queue:

```
package java.util.concurrent;
public class ThreadPoolExecutor implements ExecutionService {
    public boolean prestartCoreThread();
    public int prestartAllCoreThreads();
    public void setMaximumPoolSize(int maximumPoolSize);
    public int getMaximumPoolSize();
    public void setCorePoolSize(int corePoolSize);
    public int getCorePoolSize();
```

```
    public int getPoolSize();
    public int getLargestPoolSize();

    public int getActiveCount();
    public BlockingQueue<Runnable> getQueue();

    public long getTaskCount();
    public long getCompletedTaskCount();
}
```

The first set of methods deal with the thread pool's size, and the remaining methods deal with its queue.

*Size*

> The size of the thread pool varies between a given minimum (or core) and maximum number of threads. In our example, we use the same parameter for both values, making the thread pool a constant size.
>
> If you specify different numbers for the minimum and maximum number of threads, the thread pool dynamically alters the number of threads it uses to run its tasks. The current size (returned from the getPoolSize() method) falls between the core size and the maximum size.

*Queue*

> The queue is the data structure used to hold tasks that are awaiting execution. The choice of queue affects how certain tasks are scheduled. In this case, we've used a linked blocking queue, which places the least constraints on how tasks are added to the queue. Once you've passed this queue to the thread pool, you should not call any methods on it directly. In particular, do not add items directly to the queue; add them through the execute() method of the thread pool. The getQueue() method returns the queue, but you should use that for debugging purposes only; don't execute methods directly on the queue or the internal workings of the thread pool become confused.

These parameters allow considerable flexibility in the way the thread pool operates. The basic principle is that the thread pool tries to keep its minimum number of threads active. If it gets too busy (where busy is a property of the particular queue that the thread pool uses), it adds threads until the maximum number of threads is reached, at which point it does not allow any more tasks to be queued.

There are some nuances in this, particularly in how the queue interacts with the number of threads. Let's take it step by step:

1. The thread pool is constructed with $M$ core threads and $N$ maximum threads. At this point, no threads are actually created (though you can specify that the pool create the $M$ core threads by calling the thread pool's prestartAllCoreThreads() method or that it preallocate one core thread by calling the prestartCoreThread() method).

2. A task enters the pool (via the thread pool's execute( ) method). Now one of five things happens:

— If the pool has created fewer than $M$ threads, it starts a new thread and runs the new task immediately. Even if some of the existing threads are idle, a new thread is created in the pool's attempt to reach $M$ threads.

— If the pool has between $M$ and $N$ threads and one of those threads is idle, the task is run by an idle thread.

— If the pool has between $M$ and $N$ threads and all the threads are busy, the thread pool examines the existing work queue. If the task can be placed on the work queue without blocking, it's put on the queue and no new thread is started.

— If the pool has between $M$ and $N$ threads, all threads are busy, and the task cannot be added to the queue without blocking, the pool starts a new thread and runs the task on that thread.

— If the pool has $N$ threads and all threads are busy, the pool attempts to place the new task on the queue. If the queue has reached its maximum size, this attempt fails and the task is rejected. Otherwise, the task is accepted and run when a thread becomes idle (and all previously queued tasks have run).

3. A task completes execution. The thread running the task then runs the next task on the queue. If no tasks are on the queue, one of two things happens:

— If the pool has more than $M$ threads, the thread waits for a new task to be queued. If a new task is queued within the timeout period, the thread runs it. If not, the thread exits, reducing the total number of threads in the pool. The timeout period is a parameter used to construct the thread pool; in our example, we specified 50 seconds (50000L time units of TimeUnit.MILLISECONDS). Note that if the specified timeout is 0, the thread always exits, regardless of the requested minimum thread pool size.

— If the pool has $M$ or fewer threads, the thread blocks indefinitely waiting for a new task to be queued (unless the timeout was 0, in which case it exits). It runs the new task when available.

What are the implications of all this? It means that the choice of pool size and queue are important to getting the behavior you want. For a queue, you have three choices:

• A SynchronousQueue, which effectively has a size of 0. In this case, whenever the pool tries to queue a task, it fails. The implication of this is tasks are either run immediately (because the pool has an idle thread or is below its threshold and, therefore, creates a new thread) or are rejected immediately. Note that you can prevent rejection of a task if you specify an unlimited maximum number of threads, but this prevents the throttling benefit of using a thread pool in the first place.

- An unbounded queue, such as a LinkedBlockingQueue with an unlimited capacity. In this case, adding a task to the queue always succeeds, which means that the thread pool never creates more than $M$ threads and never rejects a task.

- A bounded queue, such as a LinkedBlockingQueue with a fixed capacity or an ArrayBlockingQueue. Let's suppose that the queue has a bounds of $P$. As tasks are added to the pool, it creates threads until it reaches $M$ threads. At that point, it starts queueing tasks until the number of waiting tasks reaches $P$. As more tasks are added, the pool starts adding threads until it reaches $N$ threads. If we reach a state where $N$ threads are active and $P$ tasks are queued, additional tasks are rejected.

In our example, we used a LinkedBlockingQueue with an unbounded capacity and a fixed pool size. This is perhaps the most common configuration of thread pools: it allows tasks to wait for an available thread, and a fixed number of threads is easier to monitor than a variable number of threads. A good alternative to this is to use a bounded queue with a fixed number of threads. In this model, if tasks start to arrive faster than they can be processed, they queue. Unlike the unbounded case, however, at some point the queue threshold is reached and your program must take appropriate action: if it's a server, it can reject future requests from clients, telling them that it's too busy right now and they should try again later.

If you use a thread pool, there is no magic formula that you can use to determine its optimal size and queuing strategy. When the operations are strictly CPU-bound, use only as many threads as there are CPUs. For more complex operations, choosing a thread pool size is a matter of testing different values to see which gives you the best program performance.

## Rejected Tasks

Depending on the type of queue you use in the thread pool, a task may be rejected by the execute( ) method. Tasks are rejected if the queue is full or if the shutdown( ) method has been called on the thread pool.

When a task is rejected, the thread pool calls the rejected execution handler associated with the thread pool. These APIs deal with the rejected execution handler:

```
package java.util.concurrent;
public interface RejectedExecutionHandler {
    public void rejectedExecution(Runnable r, ThreadPoolExecutor executor);
}

package java.util.concurrent;
public class ThreadPoolExecutor implements ExecutorService {
    public void setRejectedExecutionHandler(RejectedExecutionHandler handler);
    public RejectedExecutionHandler getRejectedExecutionHandler( );
    public static class AbortPolicy implements RejectedExecutionHandler;
    public static class CallerRunsPolicy implements RejectedExecutionHandler;
```

```
    public static class DiscardPolicy implements RejectedExecutionHandler;
    public static class DiscardOldestPolicy implements RejectedExecutionHandler;
}
```

There is one rejected execution handler for the entire pool; it applies to all potential tasks. You can write your own rejected execution handler, or you can use one of four predefined handlers. By choosing a predefined rejected execution handler—or by creating your own handler—your program can take appropriate action when a task is rejected.

Here are the predefined handlers:

AbortPolicy

> This handler does not allow the new task to be scheduled when the queue is full (or the pool has been shut down); in that case, the execute( ) method throws a RejectedExecutionException. That exception is a runtime exception, so when using this policy, it's up to the program to catch the exception. Otherwise, the exception is propagated up the stack.
>
> This is the default policy for rejected tasks.

CallerRunsPolicy

> This handler executes the new task independently of the thread pool if the queue is full. That is, rather than queuing the task and executing it in another thread, the task is immediately executed by calling its run( ) method, and the execute( ) method does not return until the task has completed. If the task is rejected because the pool has been shut down, the task is silently discarded.

DiscardPolicy

> This handler silently discards the task. No exception is thrown.

DiscardOldestPolicy

> This handler silently discards the oldest task in the queue and then queues the new task. When used with a LinkedBlockingQueue or ArrayBlockingQueue, the oldest task is the one that is first in line to execute when a thread becomes idle. When used with a SynchronousQueue, there are never waiting tasks and so the execute( ) method silently discards the submitted task.
>
> If the pool has been shut down, the task is silently discarded.

To create your own rejected task handler, create a class that implements the RejectedExecutionHandler interface. Your handler (just like a predefined handler) can then be set using the setRejectedExecutionHandler( ) method of the thread pool executor.

# Thread Creation

The thread pool dynamically creates threads according to the size policies in effect when a task is queued and terminates threads when they've been idle too long.

Those policies are set when the pool is constructed, and they can be altered with these methods:

```
package java.util.concurrent;
public interface ThreadFactory {
    public Thread newThread(Runnable r);
}

package java.util.concurrent;
public class ThreadPoolExecutor implements ExecutorService {
    public void setThreadFactory(ThreadFactory threadFactory);
    public ThreadFactory getThreadFactory();
    public void setKeepAliveTime(long time, TimeUnit unit);
    public long getKeepAliveTime(TimeUnit unit);
}
```

When the pool creates a thread, it uses the currently installed thread pool factory to do so. Creating and installing your own thread factory allows you to set up a custom scheme to create threads so that they are created with special names, priorities, daemon status, thread group, and so on.

The default thread factory creates a thread with the following characteristics:

- New threads belong to the same thread group as the thread that created the executor. However, the security manager policy can override this and place the new thread in its own thread group (see Chapter 13).

- The name of the thread reflects its pool number and its thread number within the pool. Within a pool, threads are numbered consecutively beginning with 1; thread pools are globally assigned a pool number consecutively beginning with 1.

- The daemon status of the thread is the same as the status of the thread that created the executor.

- The priority of the thread is Thread.NORM_PRIORITY.

## Callable Tasks and Future Results

Executors in general operate on tasks, which are objects that implement the Runnable interface. In order to provide more control over tasks, Java also defines a special runnable object known as a callable task:

```
package java.util.concurrent;
public interface Callable<V> {
    public <V> call() throws Execption;
}
```

Unlike a runnable object, a callable object can return a result or throw a checked exception. Callable objects are used only by executor services (not simple executors); the services operate on callable objects by invoking their call() method and keeping track of the results of those calls.

When you ask an executor service to run a callable object, the service returns a Future object that allows you to retrieve those results, monitor the status of the task, and cancel the task. The Future interface looks like this:

```
public interface Future<V> {
    V get() throws InterruptedException, ExecutionException;
    V get(long timeout, TimeUnit unit)
        throws InterruptedException, ExecutionException, TimeoutException;
    boolean isDone();
    boolean cancel(boolean mayInterruptIfRunning);
    boolean isCancelled();
}
```

Callable and future objects have a one-to-one correspondence: every callable object that is sent to an executor service returns a matching future object. The get() method of the future object returns the results of its corresponding call() method. The get() method blocks until the call() method has returned (or until the optional timeout has expired). If the call() method throws an exception, the get() method throws an ExecutionException with an embedded cause, which is the exception thrown by the call() method.

The future object keeps track of the state of an embedded Callable object. The state is set to cancelled when the cancel() method is called. When the call() method of a callable task is called, the call() method checks the state: if the state is cancelled, the call() method immediately returns.

When the cancel() method is called, the corresponding callable object may be in one of three states. It may be waiting for execution, in which case its state is set to cancelled and the call() method is never executed. It may have completed execution, in which case the cancel() method has no effect. The object may be in the process of running. In that case, if the mayInterruptIfRunning flag is false, the cancel() method again has no effect.

If the mayInterruptIfRunning flag is true, however, the thread running the callable object is interrupted. The callable object must still pay attention to this, periodically calling the Thread.interrupted() method to see if it should exit.

When an object in a thread pool is cancelled, there is no immediate effect: the object still remains queued for execution. When the thread pool is about to execute the object, it checks the object's internal state, sees that it has been cancelled, and skips execution of the object. So, cancelling an object on a thread pool queue does not immediately make space in the thread pool's queue. Future calls to the execute() method may still be rejected, even though cancelled objects are on the thread pool's queue: the execute() method does not check the queue for cancelled objects.

One way to deal with this situation is to call the purge() method on the thread pool. The purge() method looks over the entire queue and removes any cancelled objects. One caveat applies: if a second thread attempts to add something to the pool (using the execute() method) at the same time the first thread is attempting to purge the queue, the attempt to purge the queue fails and the canceled objects remain in the queue.

A better way to cancel objects with thread pools is to use the remove( ) method of the thread pool, which immediately removes the task from the thread pool queue. The remove( ) method can be used with standard runnable objects.

## The FutureTask Class

You can associate a Runnable object with a future result using the FutureTask class:

```
public class FutureTask<V> implements Future<V>, Runnable {}
```

This class is used internally by the executor service: the object returned from the submit( ) method of an executor service is an instance of this class. However, you can use this class directly in programs as well. This makes sense when you need to monitor the status of a runnable object within an executor: you can construct a future task with an embedded runnable object and send the future task to the execute( ) method of an executor (or an executor service). You can then use the methods of the Future interface to monitor the status of the run( ) method of the embedded runnable object.

A FutureTask object can hold either an embedded runnable or callable object, depending on which constructor is used to instantiate the object:

```
public FutureTask(Callable<V> task);
public FutureTask(Runnable task, V result);
```

The get( ) method of a future task that embeds a callable task returns whatever is returned by the call( ) method of that embedded object. The get( ) method of a future task that embeds a runnable object returns whatever object was used to construct the future task object itself.

We use this class in our next example and also in our examples in Chapter 15.

# Single-Threaded Access

In Chapter 7, we saw the threading restrictions placed on developers using the Swing library. Swing classes are not threadsafe, so they must always be called from a single thread. In the case of Swing, that means that they must be called from the event-dispatching thread, using the invokeLater( ) and invokeAndWait( ) methods of the SwingUtilities class.

What if you have a different library that isn't threadsafe and want to use the library in your multithreaded programs? As long as you access that library from a single thread, your program won't run into any problems with data synchronization.

Here's a class you can use to accomplish that:

```
package javathreads.examples.ch10;

import java.util.concurrent.*;
import java.io.*;

public class SingleThreadAccess {

    private ThreadPoolExecutor tpe;

    public SingleThreadAccess() {
        tpe = new ThreadPoolExecutor(
                1, 1, 50000L, TimeUnit.SECONDS,
                new LinkedBlockingQueue<Runnable>());
    }

    public void invokeLater(Runnable r) {
        tpe.execute(r);
    }

    public void invokeAndWait(Runnable r)
                    throws InterruptedException, ExecutionException {
        FutureTask task = new FutureTask(r, null);
        tpe.execute(task);
        task.get();
    }

    public void shutdown() {
        tpe.shutdown();
    }
}
```

The methods of this class function exactly like their counterparts in the SwingUtilities class: the invokeLater() method runs its task asynchronously and the invokeAndWait() method runs it synchronously. Because the thread pool has only a single thread, all tasks passed to the SingleThreadAccess object are executed by a single thread, regardless of how many threads use the access object: the tasks run by the SingleThreadAccess object can call thread-unsafe classes.

In Chapter 9, we show the effect of running our Fibonacci calculations when the threads are serialized; our online examples for this chapter show (as example 2) how to use the SingleThreadAccess class to achieve that same behavior.

## Summary

In this chapter, we began exploration of executors: utilities that process Runnable objects while hiding threading details from the developer. Executors are very useful because they allow programs to be written as a series of tasks; programmers can focus on the logic of their program without getting bogged down in details about how threads are created or used.

The thread pool executor is one of two key executors in Java. In addition to the programming benefits common to all executors, thread pools can also benefit programs that have lots of simultaneous tasks to execute. Using a thread pool throttles the number of threads. This reduces competition for the CPU and allows CPU-intensive programs to complete individual tasks more quickly.

The combination of individual tasks and a lack of CPU resources is key to when to use a thread pool. Thread pools are often considered important because reusing threads is more efficient than creating threads, but that turns out to be a red herring. From a performance perspective, you'll see a benefit from thread pools because when there is less competition for the CPU (because of fewer threads), the average time to complete an individual task is less than otherwise.

The key to effectively using Java's thread pool implementation is to select an appropriate size and queueing model for the pool. Selecting a queuing model is a factor of how you want to handle many requests: an unbounded queue allows the requests to accumulate while other models possibly result in rejected tasks that must be handled by the program. A little bit of work is required to get the most out of a thread pool. But the rewards—both in terms of the simplification of program logic and in terms of potential throughput—make thread pools very useful.

## Example Classes

Here are the class names and Ant targets for the examples in this chapter:

| Description | Main Java class | Ant target |
| --- | --- | --- |
| Fibonacci Calculator with Thread Pool | javathreads.examples.ch10.example1. ThreadPoolTest nRequests NumberToCalculate ThreadPoolSize | ch10-ex1 |
| Fibonacci Calculator using SingleThreadAccess | javathreads.examples.ch10.example2. SingleThreadTest nRequests NumberToCalculate | ch10-ex2 |

The properties for the Ant tasks are:

```
<property name="nThreads" value="10"/>
<property name="FibCalcValue" value="20"/>
<property name="ThreadPoolSize" value="5"/>
```

# CHAPTER 11

# Task Scheduling

In the previous chapter, we examined an interesting aspect of threads. Before we used a thread pool, we were concerned with creating, controlling, and communicating between threads. With a thread pool, we were concerned with the task that we wanted to execute. Using an executor allowed us to focus on our program's logic instead of writing a lot of thread-related code.

In this chapter, we examine this idea in another context. Task schedulers give us the opportunity to execute particular tasks at a fixed point in time in the future (or, more correctly, after a fixed point in time in the future). They also allow us to set up repeated execution of tasks. Once again, they free us from many of the low-level details of thread programming: we create a task, hand it off to a task scheduler, and don't worry about the rest.

Java provides different kinds of task schedulers. Timer classes execute tasks (perhaps repeatedly) at a point in the future. These classes provide a basic task scheduling feature. J2SE 5.0 has a new, more flexible task scheduler that can be used to handle many tasks more effectively than the timer classes. In this chapter, we'll look into all of these classes.

## Overview of Task Scheduling

Interestingly, this is not the first time that we have been concerned with when a task is to be executed. Previously, we've just considered the timing as part of the task. We've seen tools that allow threads to wait for specific periods of time. Here is a quick review:

*The* sleep( ) *method*

> In our discussion of the Thread class, we examined the concept of a thread waiting for a specific period of time. The purpose was either to allow other threads to accomplish related tasks, to allow external events to happen during the sleeping period, or to repeat a task periodically. The tasks that are listed after the sleep( )

method are executed at a later time period. In effect, the sleep( ) method controls when those tasks are executed.

*The* join( ) *method*

Our discussion of this method of the Thread class represents the first time that we examined alternate tasks to be executed at a later time. The goal of this method is to wait for a specific event—a thread termination. However, the expected thread termination event may not arrive, at least not within the desired time period, so the join( ) method provides a timeout. This allows the method to return—either by the termination of the thread or by the expiration of the timeout—thus allowing the program to execute an alternate task at a specific time and in a particular situation.

*The* wait( ) *method*

The wait( ) method of the Object class allows a thread to wait for any event. This method also provides the option to return if a specific time period passes. This allows the program to execute a task at a later time if the event occurs or to specify the exact time to execute an alternate task if the event does not occur. This functionality is also emulated with condition variables using the await( ) method.

*The* TimeUnit *class*

This class is used to define a time period, allowing methods to specify a time period in units other than milliseconds or nanoseconds. This class is used by many of the classes added in J2SE 5.0 to specify a time period for a timeout. This class also provides convenience methods to support certain periodic requests—specifically, it provides alternate implementations of the sleep( ), join( ), and wait( ) methods that use a TimeUnit object as their timeout argument.

*The* DelayQueue *class*

Our discussion of the DelayQueue class in Chapter 8 is the first time we encounter a class that allows data to be processed at a specific time. When a producer places data in a delay queue, it is not readable by consumers until after a specific period passes. In effect, the task to process the data is to be executed at a later time—a time period that is specified by the data itself.

As these examples show, in some cases, a program needs to execute code only after a specific event or after a period of time. Much of the time, the functionality is indirect in that the timeout is not expected to occur. Java also supports timeout functions directly by providing tools that allow the program to execute specific tasks at a specific time.

We've used these methods in our examples when a program needs to execute code only after a specific event or after a period of time. The timing in these cases has always been provided as a timeout value: after a certain period of time, the thread would regain control and be able to execute the appropriate task. However, in this case control always resides with the thread: execution of the appropriate task is synchronous with respect to the code being executed. Java also supports asynchronous task execution in alternate threads; it's that type of execution that we'll examine in the remainder of this chapter.

## The java.util.Timer Class

The `java.util.Timer` class was added to JDK 1.3 specifically to provide a convenient way for tasks to be executed asynchronously. This class allows an object (of a specific class we'll look at) to be executed at a later time. The time can be specified either relative to the current time or as an absolute time. This class also supports the repeated execution of the task.

The `Timer` class executes tasks with a specific interface:

```
public abstract class TimerTask implements Runnable {
    protected TimerTask();
    public abstract void run();
    public boolean cancel();
    public long scheduledExecutionTime();
}
```

Tasks to be executed by the `Timer` class must inherit from the `TimerTask` class. As in the `Thread` class, the task to be executed is the `run()` method. In fact, the `TimerTask` class actually implements the `Runnable` interface. The `Timer` class requires a `TimerTask` object so that two methods can be attached to the task; these methods can be used to maintain the task. These methods do not have to be implemented; the `TimerTask` class provides a default implementation for them. A class that inherits from the `TimerTask` class need only implement the `run()` method.

The downside of this technique is that the task can't inherit from other classes. Since the `TimerTask` class is not an interface, it means that tasks have to either be created from classes that don't already inherit from other classes, or wrapper classes have to be created to forward the request.

The `cancel()` method is used to stop the class from being executed. A task that is already executing is unaffected when this method is called. However, if the task is repeating, calling the `cancel()` method prevents further execution of the class. For tasks that are executed only once, the `cancel()` method returns whether the task has been cancelled: if the task is currently running, has already run, or has been previously cancelled, it returns a boolean value of `false`. For repeating tasks, this method always returns a boolean value of `true`.

The `scheduledExecutionTime()` method is used to return the time at which the previous invocation of a repeating task occurred. If the task is currently running, it is the time at which the task began. If the task is not running, it is the time at which the previous execution of the task began. Its purpose is a bit obscure but it will make more sense after we discuss the `Timer` class.

Here is the interface of the Timer class:

```
public class Timer {
    public Timer();
    public Timer(boolean isDaemon);
    public Timer(String name);
    public Timer(String name, boolean isDaemon);

    public void schedule(TimerTask task, long delay);
    public void schedule(TimerTask task, Date time);
    public void schedule(TimerTask task, long delay, long period);
    public void schedule(TimerTask task, Date firstTime, long period);

    public void scheduleAtFixedRate(TimerTask task, long delay, long period);
    public void scheduleAtFixedRate(TimerTask task, Date firstTime, long period);

    public void cancel();
    public int purge();
}
```

The Timer class provides the means to execute tasks at a later time. The tasks that are scheduled are placed in an ordered queue and are executed sequentially by a single thread.

Four constructors are provided to create different versions of the Timer class. The most important parameter of these constructors allows the definition of whether the created thread is a daemon thread (see Chapter 13). This is useful for tasks which are needed only if the user is still interacting with the program. If the timer thread is a daemon thread, the program can exit when all the user threads terminate. The other parameter is used to name the thread; this is important if the threads are to be monitored by a debugger.

The first two overloaded versions of the schedule() method are used to schedule one-time tasks. The first allows for the specification of a delay: a time period in milliseconds relative to the current time. The second allows for the specification of an absolute time.

The last two overloaded versions of the schedule() method are used to schedule repeating tasks. The third parameter is used to specify the period in milliseconds between invocations of the repeated tasks.

There are a few important issues in the timer implementation, particularly for repeated tasks. First, only a single thread executes the tasks. While it is recommended that the tasks executed by the Timer class be short-lived, no check ensures that this is so. This means that if the Timer object is overwhelmed, a task may be executed at a time much later than the specified time. For repeated tasks, the schedule() method does not take this into account. The schedule time is allowed to drift, meaning that the next iteration of the task is based on the previous iteration. This is not very useful if the task is used to maintain a clock or other time-critical task.

Two mechanisms can be used to resolve this. The first mechanism is the two over-loaded scheduleAtFixedRate( ) methods. The schedule( ) method schedules the next execution of the task based on when the previous execution actually occurred. The next iteration of the task scheduled by the scheduleAtFixedRate( ) method is calcu-lated from when the previous iteration was *supposed* to execute—not when the previous iteration actually executes.

The second mechanism is the scheduledExecutionTime( ) method of the TimerTask class. This method can be used by the task itself to determine when the task is sup-posed to run. Based on the comparison to the current time, the task can adjust its behavior. This is even more important when the scheduleAtFixedRate( ) method is used to schedule the task. Since the tasks are not allowed to drift, more than one iter-ation of the repeated task may be waiting to execute. As a result, a timer task may want to skip a particular execution if it knows that another execution is pending in the queue. For example, a task that runs every five seconds can tell if it has missed an execution by using this code:

```java
public class MyTimerTask extends TimerTask {
    public void run() {
        if (System.currentTimeMillis() - scheduledExecutionTime() > 5000) {
            // We're more than five seconds off; skip this because another task
            // will already have been scheduled.
            return;
        }
        ...
    }
}
```

Table 11-1 shows when tasks would be executed under different scheduling models of the Timer class. In this example, we're assuming that the task is to be run every second, executes for .1 seconds, and the system becomes bogged down for .5 sec-onds between the second and third iteration. The schedule( ) method drifts by .5 seconds on subsequent executions. The scheduleAtFixedRate( ) method runs the delayed iteration .5 seconds late but still executes the remaining iterations according to the original schedule. Neither takes into account the time required to execute the task.

*Table 11-1. Execution time of java.util.Timer tasks*

| | Execution start time | | | | |
|---|---|---|---|---|---|
| **Method** | **Iteration 1** | **Iteration 2** | **Iteration 3** | **Iteration 4** | **Iteration 5** |
| schedule() | 1 seconds | 2 seconds | 3.5 seconds | 4.5 seconds | 5.5 seconds |
| scheduleAtFixedRate() | 1 seconds | 2 seconds | 3.5 seconds | 4 seconds | 5 seconds |

The cancel( ) method is provided by the Timer class to destroy the timer. All the tasks in the timer are simply cancelled, and no new tasks are allowed to be sched-uled. The Timer object can no longer be used to schedule any more tasks. If a task is currently executing, it is allowed to finish; currently executing tasks are not interrupted.

The purge( ) method is used for maintenance. The task's cancel( ) method does not actually delete the task from the task queue; the task is simply marked as cancelled. The task is deleted from the queue by the timer when it is time for the task to execute: because the task is marked as cancelled, the task is skipped and deleted from the queue at that time. The purge( ) method is important only when a large number of tasks are being cancelled (or the tasks themselves consume a lot of memory). By purging the timer, the task objects are removed from the queue, allowing them to be garbage collected.

## Using the Timer

Here's an example that uses the Timer class. The example program allows you to monitor the reachability of one or more web sites: it periodically attempts to retrieve a URL from each web site. Web sites that are reachable are displayed in green; web sites that are down are displayed in red.

We start with the timer task that contacts the web site:

```
package javathreads.examples.ch11.example1;

import java.util.*;
import java.net.*;

public class URLPingTask extends TimerTask {

    public interface URLUpdate {
        public void isAlive(boolean b);
    }

    URL url;
    URLUpdate updater;

    public URLPingTask(URL url) {
        this(url, null);
    }

    public URLPingTask(URL url, URLUpdate uu) {
        this.url = url;
        updater = uu;
    }

    public void run( ) {
        if (System.currentTimeMillis() - scheduledExecutionTime() > 5000) {
            // Let the next task do it
            return;
        }
        try {
            HttpURLConnection huc = (HttpURLConnection) url.openConnection( );
```

```
            huc.setConnectTimeout(1000);
            huc.setReadTimeout(1000);
            int code = huc.getResponseCode();
            if (updater != null)
                updater.isAlive(true);
        } catch (Exception e) {
            if (updater != null)
                updater.isAlive(false);
        }
    }
}
```

The run( ) method periodically contacts the given URL and then updates the status watcher depending on whether or not reading the URL was successful. Note that if more than five seconds have elapsed since the last time the task runs, the task skips itself.

The program that sets up the task looks like this:

```
package javathreads.examples.ch11.example1;

import java.awt.*;
import java.awt.event.*;
import java.net.*;
import javax.swing.*;
import java.util.Timer;

public class URLMonitorPanel extends JPanel implements URLPingTask.URLUpdate {

    Timer timer;
    URL url;
    URLPingTask task;
    JPanel status;
    JButton startButton, stopButton;

    public URLMonitorPanel(String url, Timer t) throws MalformedURLException {
        setLayout(new BorderLayout());
        timer = t;
        this.url = new URL(url);
        add(new JLabel(url), BorderLayout.CENTER);
        JPanel temp = new JPanel();
        status = new JPanel();
        status.setSize(20, 20);
        temp.add(status);
        startButton = new JButton("Start");
        startButton.setEnabled(false);
        startButton.addActionListener(new ActionListener() {
            public void actionPerformed(ActionEvent ae) {
                makeTask();
                startButton.setEnabled(false);
                stopButton.setEnabled(true);
            }
        });
        stopButton = new JButton("Stop");
```

```
                stopButton.setEnabled(true);
                stopButton.addActionListener(new ActionListener() {
                    public void actionPerformed(ActionEvent ae) {
                        task.cancel();
                        startButton.setEnabled(true);
                        stopButton.setEnabled(false);
                    }
                });
                temp.add(startButton);
                temp.add(stopButton);
                add(temp, BorderLayout.EAST);
                makeTask();
            }

            private void makeTask() {
                task = new URLPingTask(url, this);
                timer.schedule(task, 0L, 5000L);
            }

            public void isAlive(final boolean b) {
                SwingUtilities.invokeLater(new Runnable() {
                    public void run() {
                        status.setBackground(b ? Color.GREEN : Color.RED);
                        status.repaint();
                    }
                });
            }

            public static void main(String[] args) throws Exception {
                JFrame frame = new JFrame("URL Monitor");
                Container c = frame.getContentPane();
                c.setLayout(new BoxLayout(c, BoxLayout.Y_AXIS));
                Timer t = new Timer();
                for (int i = 0; i < args.length; i++) {
                    c.add(new URLMonitorPanel(args[i], t));
                }
                frame.addWindowListener(new WindowAdapter() {
                    public void windowClosing(WindowEvent evt) {
                        System.exit(0);
                    }
                });
                frame.pack();
                frame.show();
            }
        }
```

Each individual panel monitors a single URL. Note that the isAlive( ) method runs from the timer thread, so its invocation of Swing methods is placed within a call to the invokeLater( ) method. Also note that since a task cannot be reused, the actionPerformed( ) method associated with the Start button must set up a new task.

This application points out the basic shortcomings of the Timer class. We've set it up so that all the panels share a single instance of the timer, which means a single thread. Although our task uses timeouts to talk to the web server, it's conceivable that a single execution of the run( ) method of the task could take almost two seconds (though it's more likely to take only one second if the site is down). If you monitor 10 sites and your ISP goes down, the single timer thread ends up with a backlog of tasks. That's the reason we put logic into the run( ) method of the task to check to see whether it missed its scheduled execution time.

The alternative is to create a new timer for each panel. In that case, we don't have to worry about a backlog of tasks. The downside is that we now have one thread for every site we're monitoring. That's not a big deal unless we're monitoring thousands of sites, but it's not optimal either. We'll revisit this later in this chapter.

## The javax.swing.Timer Class

As we've discussed, Swing objects cannot be accessed from arbitrary threads—which includes the threads from the Timer class (and the threads in the thread pool of the ScheduledThreadPoolExecutor class that we discuss later in this chapter). We know that we can use the invokeLater( ) and invokeAndWait( ) methods of the SwingUtilities class to overcome this, but Java also provides a Timer class just for Swing objects. The javax.swing.Timer class provides the ability to execute actions at a particular time, and those actions are invoked on the event-dispatching thread.

Here is the interface to the javax.swing.Timer class:

```
public class Timer {
    public Timer(int delay, ActionListener listener);

    public void addActionListener(ActionListener listener);
    public void removeActionListener(ActionListener listener);
    public ActionListener[] getActionListeners();
    public EventListener[] getListeners(Class listenerType);

    public static void setLogTimers(boolean flag);
    public static boolean getLogTimers();

    public void setDelay(int delay);
    public int getDelay()
    public void setInitialDelay(int initialDelay);
    public int getInitialDelay();

    public void setRepeats(boolean flag);
    public boolean isRepeats();

    public void setCoalesce(boolean flag);
    public boolean isCoalesce();

    public void start();
    public boolean isRunning();
    public void stop();
    public void restart();
}
```

This class is not really a generic scheduler. In fact, even though multiple callbacks (event listeners) can be attached to the timer, it has only one schedule: all the listeners use the schedule defined by the Timer class itself (rather than the schedule defined by particular tasks). Tasks that require a different schedule need a different instance of the Swing timer. Most of the methods provided by this class are used to configure the schedule and control the timer.

Unlike the java.util.Timer class, this Timer class uses the ActionListener interface. This provides an interface that Swing developers are accustomed to: all Swing objects use event listeners to execute callbacks. When a scheduled time is reached, it is treated as any other event (such as a button press): the registered action listeners are called.

The constructor to the class takes two parameters. The first is the delay in milliseconds. This value is used by the timer as both the initial time to wait to fire the first action listener and the time to wait between repeated firings of the action listeners. The second parameter is an action listener to fire. Both of these parameters can be modified at a later time.

The addActionListener() and removeActionListener() methods are used to add listeners to and remove listeners from the timer. The getActionListeners() method is used to retrieve the listeners that have been registered to the timer. The getListeners() method provides the added qualification of the event listener type. This allows the developer to get specific types of listeners that are registered to the timer. In most cases, this is probably not very useful, as the limitation of the timer as a generic scheduler also limits the number of action listeners registered to each timer.

The getDelay() and setDelay() methods are used to retrieve and modify the time between repeated events (which by default is set in the constructor). This allows it to be different from the initial delay time. That delay time is handled by the getInitialDelay() and setInitialDelay() methods.

The isRepeats() and setRepeats() methods are used to control whether events are repeated. By default, the timer repeats events, as this Timer class was originally designed for tasks such as a blinking cursor. The isCoalesce() and setCoalesce() methods are used to handle repeated methods that are backlogged. For example, if a method is to be called once every second, and three seconds have elapsed, then the listener may have to be called three times. If the coalesce flag is set, the listener is called only once. This is important for tasks such as blinking the cursor. If the timer has already missed two blinks, blinking three times very fast does not fix the problem; it is better to just skip the missed blinks.

The getLogTimers() and setLogTimers() methods are used to control debugging of the timer. If debugging is activated, messages are sent to standard output to report the actions of the timer.

Finally, the timer must be activated upon completion of the registration of the listeners (and, possibly, adjusting the initial delay and repeat times). This is accomplished by the start( ) method. The timer can later be terminated by calling the stop( ) method. The restart( ) method resets the timer: the timer then waits until its initial delay time period has elapsed, at which point it starts calling its listeners. The isRunning( ) method is used to determine whether the timer has been started.

## Using the javax.swing.Timer Class

We can use the javax.swing.Timer class in our typing program. Previously, our animated canvas set up a thread to handle the animation; this thread periodically told the animation canvas to repaint itself. Now, we'll use a timer.

```
package javathreads.examples.ch11.example2;

import javax.swing.*;
import java.awt.*;
import java.awt.event.*;
import java.util.concurrent.*;
import java.util.concurrent.locks.*;
import javathreads.examples.ch11.*;

public class AnimatedCharacterDisplayCanvas extends CharacterDisplayCanvas
            implements ActionListener, CharacterListener {

    private int curX;
    private Timer timer;

    public AnimatedCharacterDisplayCanvas(CharacterSource cs) {
        super(cs);
        timer = new Timer(100, this);
    }

    public synchronized void newCharacter(CharacterEvent ce) {
        curX = 0;
        tmpChar[0] = (char) ce.character;
        repaint( );
    }

    public synchronized void paintComponent(Graphics gc) {
        if (tmpChar[0] == 0)
            return;
        Dimension d = getSize( );
        int charWidth = fm.charWidth(tmpChar[0]);
        gc.clearRect(0, 0, d.width, d.height);
        gc.drawChars(tmpChar, 0, 1, curX++, fontHeight);
        if (curX > d.width - charWidth)
            curX = 0;
    }
```

```
    public void actionPerformed(ActionEvent ae) {
        repaint();
    }

    public void setDone(boolean b) {
        if (!b)
            timer.start();
        else timer.stop();
    }
}
```

Note that this implementation is much simpler than our previous implementations. Previously, we set up a thread in the setDone() method; now, we simply call the timer start() method.

Using the timer has also allowed us to simplify the locking around the calls to the repaint() method. Knowing when the animation should run used to require a wait-and-notify mechanism (or condition variable). Now we just defer that to the timer. The Timer class itself has the waiting logic within it: operationally, we haven't saved anything. But in terms of development, using a timer has saved us some effort. This is a clear example of why using higher-level thread constructs makes things simpler for the developer.

## The ScheduledThreadPoolExecutor Class

J2SE 5.0 introduced the ScheduledThreadPoolExecutor class, which solves many problems of the Timer class. In many regards, the Timer class can be considered obsolete because of the ScheduledThreadPoolExecutor class. Why is this class needed? Let's examine some of the problems with the Timer class.

First, the Timer class starts only one thread. While it is more efficient than creating a thread per task, it is not an optimal solution. The optimal solution may be to use a number of threads between one thread for all tasks and one thread per task. In effect, the best solution is to place the tasks in a pool of threads. The number of threads in the pool should be assignable during construction to allow the program to determine the optimal number of threads in the pool.

Second, the TimerTask class is not necessary. It is used to attach methods to the task itself, providing the ability to cancel the task and to determine the last scheduled time. This is not necessary: it is possible for the timer itself to maintain this information. It also restricts what can be considered a task. Classes used with the Timer class must extend the TimerTask class; this is not possible if the class already inherits from another class. It is much more flexible to allow any Runnable object to be used as the task to be executed.

Finally, relying upon the run() method is too restrictive for tasks. While it is possible to pass parameters to the task—by using parameters in the constructor of the task—there is no way to get any results or exceptions. The run() method has no return variable, nor can it throw any type of exceptions other than runtime exceptions (and even if it could, the timer thread wouldn't know how to deal with it).

The ScheduledThreadPoolExecutor class solves all three of these problems. It uses a thread pool (actually, it inherits from the thread pool class) and allows the developer to specify the size of the pool. It stores tasks as Runnable objects, allowing any task that can be used by the thread object to be used by the executor. Because it can work with objects that implement the Callable interface, it eliminates the restrictive behavior of relying solely on the Runnable interface.

Here's the interface of the ScheduledThreadPoolExecutor class itself:

```
public class ScheduledThreadPoolExecutor extends ThreadPoolExecutor {
    public ScheduledThreadPoolExecutor(int corePoolSize);
    public ScheduledThreadPoolExecutor(int corePoolSize,
                            ThreadFactory threadFactory);
    public ScheduledThreadPoolExecutor(int corePoolSize,
                            RejectedExecutionHandler handler);
    public ScheduledThreadPoolExecutor(int corePoolSize,
                            ThreadFactory threadFactory,
                            RejectedExecutionHandler handler);
    public <V> ScheduledFuture<V> schedule(Callable<V> callable,
                    long delay, TimeUnit unit);

    public ScheduledFuture<V> scheduleAtFixedRate(Runnable command,
                    long initialDelay, long period, TimeUnit unit);
    public ScheduledFuture<V> scheduleWithFixedDelay(
                    Runnable command, long initialDelay,
                    long delay, TimeUnit unit);

    public void execute(Runnable command);

    public void shutdown( );
    public List shutdownNow( );

    public void setContinueExistingPeriodicTasksAfterShutdownPolicy(
                            boolean value);
    public boolean getContinueExistingPeriodicTasksAfterShutdownPolicy( );
    public void setExecuteExistingDelayedTasksAfterShutdownPolicy(
                            boolean value);
    public boolean getExecuteExistingDelayedTasksAfterShutdownPolicy( );
}
```

The ScheduledThreadPoolExecutor class provides four constructors to create an object. These parameters are basically the same parameters as the thread pool constructors since this executor inherits from the thread pool executor. Therefore, this class is also a thread pool, meaning that some of the parameters assigned by these constructors can also be retrieved and modified by the methods of the ThreadPoolExecutor class.

Note, however, that the constructors have no parameter to specify the maximum number of threads or the type of queue the thread pool should use. The scheduled executor always uses an unbounded queue for its tasks, and the size of its thread pool is always fixed to the number of core threads. The number of core threads, however, can still be modified by calling the setCorePoolSize( ) method.

The schedule( ) method is used to schedule a one-time task. You can use the ScheduledFuture object returned by this method to perform the usual tasks on the callable object: you can retrieve its result (using the get( ) method), cancel it (using the cancel( ) method), or see if it has completed execution (using the isDone( ) method).

The scheduleAtFixedRate( ) method is used to schedule a repeated task that is not allowed to drift. This is basically the same scheduling model as the scheduleAtFixedRate( ) method of the Timer class.

The scheduleWithFixedDelay( ) method is used to schedule a repeated task where the period between the tasks remains constant; this is useful when the delay between iterations is to be fixed. For instance, this model is better for animation since there is no reason to have animation cycles accumulate if the start times drift. If one cycle of the animation runs late, there is no advantage to running the next cycle earlier.

Table 11-2 shows when tasks would be executed under different scheduling models of the ScheduledThreadPoolExecutor class. In this example, we're again assuming that the task is to be run every second, executes for .1 seconds, and the system becomes bogged down for .5 seconds between the second and third iteration. The scheduleAtFixedRate( ) method runs the delayed iteration .5 seconds late but still executes the remaining iterations according to the original schedule (exactly the same as the java.util.Timer class). The scheduleWithFixedDelay( ) method takes into account the execution time of the task; this is why each iteration drifts by .1 seconds. It does not compensate for the .5-second delay, so it drifts over time.

*Table 11-2. Execution time of java.util.Timer tasks*

| | Execution start time | | | | |
|---|---|---|---|---|---|
| **Method** | **Iteration 1** | **Iteration 2** | **Iteration 3** | **Iteration 4** | **Iteration 5** |
| scheduleAtFixedRate( ) | 1 seconds | 2 seconds | 3.5 seconds | 4 seconds | 5 seconds |
| scheduleWithFixedDelay( ) | 1 seconds | 2.1 seconds | 3.7 seconds | 4.8 seconds | 5.9 seconds |

The execute( ) and submit( ) methods are used to schedule a task to run immediately. These methods are present mainly because the Executor interface requires them. Still, it may be useful for one task to add other tasks to be run in the pool rather than execute them directly, because then the primary task doesn't own the thread in the pool for a huge period of time. It also allows the thread pool to assign the subtasks to other threads in the pool if the pool is not busy.

The shutdown( ) and shutdownNow( ) methods are also part of the thread pool class. The shutdown( ) method is used to shut down the executor but allows all pending tasks to complete. The shutdownNow( ) method is used to try to cancel the tasks in the pool in addition to shutting down the thread pool. However, this works differently from a thread pool because of repeating tasks. Since certain tasks repeat, tasks could technically run forever during a graceful shutdown.

To solve this, the task executor provides two policies. The ExecuteExistingDelayedTasksAfterShutdownPolicy is used to determine whether the tasks in the queue should be cancelled upon graceful shutdown. The ContinueExistingPeriodicTasksAfterShutdownPolicy is used to determine whether the repeating tasks in the queue should be cancelled upon graceful shutdown. Therefore, setting both to false empties the queue but allows currently running tasks to complete. This is similar to how the Timer class is shut down. The shutdownNow( ) method cancels all the tasks and also interrupts any task that is already executing.

With the support of thread pools, callable tasks, and fixed delay support, you might conclude that the Timer class is obsolete. However, the Timer class has some advantages. First, it provides the option to specify an absolute time. Second, the Timer class is simpler to use: it may be preferable if only a few tasks or repeated tasks are needed.

## Using the ScheduledThreadPoolExecutor Class

Here's a modification of our URL monitor that uses a scheduled executor. Modification of the task itself means a simple change to the interface it implements:

```
package javathreads.examples.ch11.example3;
...
public class URLPingTask implements Runnable {
    ...
}
```

Our Swing component has just a few changes:

```
package javathreads.examples.ch11.example3;
...
import java.util.concurrent.*;

public class URLMonitorPanel extends JPanel implements URLPingTask.URLUpdate {
    ScheduledThreadPoolExecutor executor;
    ScheduledFuture future;
    ...
    public URLMonitorPanel(String url, ScheduledThreadPoolExecutor se)
                        throws MalformedURLException {
        executor = se;
        ...
        stopButton.addActionListener(new ActionListener( ) {
            public void actionPerformed(ActionEvent ae) {
                future.cancel(true);
                startButton.setEnabled(true);
                stopButton.setEnabled(false);
```

```
            }
        });
        ...
    }

    private void makeTask() {
        task = new URLPingTask(url, this);
        future = executor.scheduleAtFixedRate(
                            task, OL, 5L, TimeUnit.SECONDS);
    }

    public static void main(String[] args) throws Exception {
        ...
        ScheduledThreadPoolExecutor se = new ScheduledThreadPoolExecutor(
                (args.length + 1) / 2);
        for (int i = 0; i < args.length; i++) {
            c.add(new URLMonitorPanel(args[0], se));
        }
        ...
    }
}
```

The main enhancement that this change has bought us is the ability to specify a number of threads for the executor. We've chosen half as many threads as the machines we're monitoring: in between the number of suboptimal choices we had previously. In this case, it would have been even more ideal for the task executor to be more flexible in its thread use.

## Using the Future Interface

The other case when using a scheduled executor makes sense is when you want to use the callable interface so that you can later check the status of the task. This is logical equivalent to using the join() method to tell if a thread is done.

We'll extend our example slightly to see how this works. Let's suppose we want our URL monitor to have a license; without a license, it runs in a demo mode for two minutes. In the absence of a valid license, we can set up a callable task that runs after a delay of two minutes. After that task has run, we know that the license period has expired.

We'll have to poll the license task periodically to see whether it has finished. Normally, we don't like polling because of its inefficiencies, but in this case, we have a perfect time to do it: because the status thread runs every five seconds, it can poll the license task without wasting much CPU time at all. Since in this case we don't have to unnecessarily wake up a polling thread, we can afford the simple method call to handle the poll.

First, we need a simple task.

```
package javathreads.examples.ch11.example4;

class TimeoutTask implements Callable {
    public Integer call( ) throws IOException {
        return new Integer(0);
    }
}
```

As required, we've implemented the Callable interface. In this simple example, we don't actually care about the return value: if the task has run, the license has expired. In a more complicated case, the license task might check with a license server and return a more interesting result. Checking with the license server might create an IOException, which is why we've declared that this task throws that exception.

Now we must add this to our monitor:

```
package javathreads.examples.ch11.example4;

public class URLMonitorPanel extends JPanel implements URLPingTask.URLUpdate {

    static Future<Integer> futureTaskResult;
    static volatile boolean done = false;
    ...

    private void checkLicense( ) {
        if (done) return;
        try {
            Integer I = futureTaskResult.get(0L, TimeUnit.MILLISECONDS);
            // If we got a result, we know that the license has expired
            JOptionPane.showMessageDialog(null,
                        "Evaluation time period has expired", "Expired",
                    JOptionPane.INFORMATION_MESSAGE);
            done = true;
        } catch (TimeoutException te) {
            // Task hasn't run; just coninue
        } catch (InterruptedException ie) {
            // Task was externally interrupted
        } catch (ExecutionException ee) {
            // Task threw IOException, which can be obtained like
            IOException ioe = (IOException) ee.getCause( );
            // Clean up after the exception
        }
    }

    public void isAlive(final boolean b) {
        try {
            SwingUtilities.invokeAndWait(new Runnable( ) {
                public void run( ) {
                    checkLicense( );
                    if (done) {
                        future.cancel(true);
                        startButton.setEnabled(false);
```

```
                        stopButton.setEnabled(false);
                        return;
                    }
                    status.setBackground(b ? Color.GREEN : Color.RED);
                    status.repaint();
                }
            });
        } catch (Exception e) {}
    }

    public static void main(String[] args) throws Exception {
        ...
        TimeoutTask tt = new TimeoutTask();
        futureTaskResult = se.schedule(tt, 120, TimeUnit.SECONDS);
        ...
    }
}
```

The checkLicense() method is called every time status is reported; it polls the time-out task. When the poll succeeds, the checkLicense() method sets a done flag so that other panels know that the license has expired (the done flag is static and shared among all panels). Alternately, we could let each panel poll the futureTaskResult object itself.

If you look carefully, you'll notice that there's no synchronization for the checkLicense() method and that it appears that the option pane might get displayed twice if two panels invoke that method at the same time. However, that's not possible because the checkLicense() method is called via the invokeAndWait() method. That blocks the event-dispatching thread so we are already assured that only one thread at a time is executing the checkLicense() method.

# Summary

In this chapter, we've looked at various ways in which tasks may be scheduled in the future. The simplest way to do this is to use the java.util.Timer class, which can run instances of a special class (the TimerTask class) at a point in the future, repeating the task if necessary. Each instance of a timer is a single thread; that thread can handle multiple tasks but long-running tasks may need their own thread (and consequently their own timer).

The javax.swing.Timer class is functionally similar, except that it ensures that tasks are run on the event-dispatching thread so that they may safely access Swing components. However, the javax.swing.Timer class has a fixed time schedule for all the tasks it runs; tasks that have different scheduling needs require different instances of the timer.

Finally, the ScheduledThreadPoolExecutor class provides a more flexible (but more complex) interface to task scheduling. Because it uses a thread pool, it can be more efficient when running a lot of tasks simultaneously. It also allows you to poll for task status or to use generic Runnable objects as your task.

The key benefit of task executors and timers is that they free you from having to worry about thread-related programming for your tasks: you simply feed the task to the timer or executor and let it worry about the necessary thread controls. This makes the code that you write that much simpler.

## Example Classes

Here are the class names and Ant targets for the examples in this chapter:

| Description | Main Java class | Ant target |
|---|---|---|
| URL Monitor with java.util.Timer class | javathreads.examples.ch11.example1. URLMonitor URL1 URL2 ... | ch11-ex1 |
| Type Tester with Timer animation | javathreads.examples.ch11.example2. SwingTypeTester | ch11-ex2 |
| URL Monitor with scheduled executor | javathreads.examples.ch11.example3. URLMonitor URL1 URL2 ... | ch11-ex3 |
| URL Monitor with timeout | javathreads.examples.ch11.example4. URLMonitor URL1 URL2 ... | ch11-ex4 |

The ant property to specify the URL is:

```
<property name="hostlist" value="http://www.ora.com/"/>
```

Unfortunately, Ant offers no way to specify multiple hostnames. If you want to try a URL monitor with more than one URL, you must execute the class directly.

# CHAPTER 12

# Threads and I/O

If you're not interested in parallel processing, the area where you're most likely to encounter threads in Java is in dealing with I/O—and particularly in dealing with network I/O. That's the topic we explore in this chapter.

In early versions of Java, all I/O was blocking. If your program attempted to read data from a socket and no data was present, the read( ) method would block until at least some data was available. That situation is also true of reading a file. For the most part, delays in reading files aren't noticeable; you may have to wait a few cycles for the disk to rotate to the correct location and the operating system to transfer data from the disk. In most programs, blocking for that amount of time makes little difference, but in those programs where it does make a difference, the concepts that apply to network I/O are just as relevant to file I/O.

For network I/O, the delay can be quite significant. Networks are subject to delays at various points (particularly if the network involves long distances or slow links). Even if there's no physical delay on the network lines, network I/O is done in the context of a conversation between two peers, and a peer may not be ready to furnish its output when its partner wants it. A database server reads commands from a user, but the user may take a few minutes to type in the SQL to be executed. Once the SQL has been sent to the database, the user is ready to read back the response, but it may take the database a few minutes to obtain the results of the query.

Because early versions of Java did not have a way to handle nonblocking I/O, Java servers would typically start a new thread for every client that connected to them. Java clients would typically start a new thread to send requests to the server so that the rest of the program would remain active while the client was waiting for a response.

In JDK 1.4, this situation changed: Java introduced the NIO package, which allowed developers to utilize nonblocking I/O in their programs. This changed the rule for the way in which Java servers (and other I/O-intensive programs) are threaded, though it does not eliminate all threading considerations from those programs.

In this chapter, we look at servers that employ each type of I/O and show common techniques for handling the server's threads.

# A Traditional I/O Server

Let's start with the simplest case, which is based on Java's original (blocking) I/O model. In this model, a network server must start a new thread for every client that attaches to the server. We already know that by reading data from a socket in a separate thread, we solve the problem of blocking while we're waiting for data. Threading on the server side has an additional benefit: by having a thread associated with each client, we no longer need to worry about other clients within any single thread. This simplifies our server-side programming: we can code our classes as if we were handling a single client at a time.

Before we show the code for the server, let's review some networking basics. Figure 12-1 shows the data connections between several clients and a server. The server-side socket setup is implemented in two steps. First, an instance of the ServerSocket class is used to listen on a port known to the client. The client connects to this port as a means to negotiate a private connection with the server.

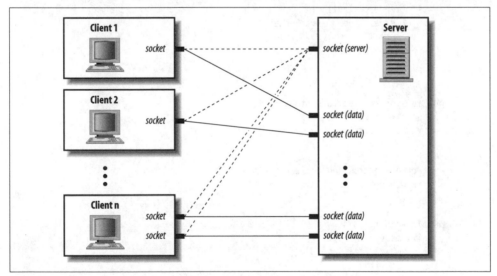

Figure 12-1. Network connections between clients and a server

Once a data connection has been negotiated, the server and client communicate through the private connection. In general, this process is generic: most developers are concerned with the data sockets (the private connection). Furthermore, the data sockets on the server side are usually self-contained to a particular client. While it's possible to have different mechanisms that deal with many data sockets at the same time, generally the same code is used to deal with each of the data sockets independently.

Since the setup is generic, we can develop a generic TCPServer class that handles the setup and defers the data processing to its subclasses. This TCPServer class creates the server socket and accepts connections. For each connection, it spawns a new thread (a clone of itself, so that the new thread has a copy of all the interesting data that the server holds). Here's the implementation of this class, which serves as the superclass for many of the examples in this chapter:

```java
package javathreads.examples.ch12;

import java.net.*;
import java.io.*;

public class TCPServer implements Cloneable, Runnable {
    Thread runner = null;
    ServerSocket server = null;
    Socket data = null;

    private boolean done = false;

    public synchronized void startServer(int port) throws IOException {
        if (runner == null) {
            server = new ServerSocket(port);
            runner = new Thread(this);
            runner.start();
        }
    }

    public synchronized void stopServer() {
        done = true;
        runner.interrupt();
    }

    protected synchronized boolean getDone() {
        return done;
    }

    public void run() {
        if (server != null) {
            while (!getDone()) {
                try {
                    Socket datasocket = server.accept();
                    TCPServer newSocket = (TCPServer) clone();

                    newSocket.server = null;
                    newSocket.data = datasocket;
                    newSocket.runner =
                        new Thread(newSocket);
                    newSocket.runner.start();
                } catch (Exception e) {}
            }
        }
```

```
            } else {
                run(data);
            }
        }

        public void run(Socket data) {
        }
    }
```

The TCPServer class implements the Runnable interface; it creates multiple threads and copies of itself to run in each of those threads. Creating the copies requires that the server implement the Cloneable interface as well. Since the first TCPServer object operates on the server socket (while the clones operate on the data sockets), the TCPServer class must be written to service both kinds of sockets.

The logic to handle the clients is contained within the run() method. The conditional at the beginning of the run() method is what distinguishes between the type of socket to be handled. When we first enter the run() method, the server variable is set to the server socket, so we continue into the inner loop that accepts new connections. When a new connection has been accepted, we clone the TCPServer object and set the server variable in the cloned object to null. The cloned object is then executed in a new thread. When the cloned object executes the run() method, its server variable is null and so it calls the run(Socket data) method. In the base class, that method does nothing; to have a useful TCPServer, you must extend it (which we'll do next).

To start the server, you must call the startServer() method. That method creates a thread that runs the server. By handling the server socket in this thread, the startServer() method can return immediately, and the same program can instantiate multiple servers. The stopServer() method is used to stop the server: it follows our traditional pattern of setting a done flag and interrupting the target thread (the runner thread). Note that the stopServer() method stops the server thread, which prevents the server from accepting new client connections but all existing client connections and threads remain running. This allows for a graceful shutdown. It's a simple extension to the class to keep track of all client threads and interrupt them if you want them to shut down as well.

One more point about this implementation: you'll notice that the startServer() and stopServer() methods are synchronized because they operate on shared data, but that data appears to be accessed from the unsynchronized run() method. Appearances here are deceiving. In every client thread, the client has a separate clone of the object, so each thread is operating on its own private data. As a result, that data need not be synchronized. If the client threads need to share data, they are responsible for making sure that the data is properly synchronized.

# An Example Multithreaded Server

For our first example, we'll subclass the TCPServer class to perform I/O within the run(Socket data) method. For a complete example, we must provide the TCPServer implementation and a client that can connect to that server. In this section, we'll develop the server; the client will be developed in the next section. We'll develop a server that can serve as the beginning of a multiplayer typing game: multiple clients connect to the server, which sends the same string to each client and keeps track of all their scores. We'll develop only the first part of that server, the part that sends a string to each client. The remaining logic contains no new information about threading, so we'll leave it as an exercise for the reader.

Developing a server like this depends on establishing a protocol between the client and server. For our example, we use a simple protocol where messages are a single byte (the message type), optionally followed by data specific to the message type. We define three types of messages:

```
package javathreads.examples.ch12;

public class TypeServerConstants {
    public final static byte WELCOME = 0;
    public final static byte GET_STRING_REQUEST = 1;
    public final static byte GET_STRING_RESPONSE = 2;
}
```

The WELCOME message must be sent by the server when it accepts a new client into the game; it has no optional data. The GET_STRING_REQUEST message is sent by the client when it wants a new string; it too has no optional data. Finally, the GET_STRING_RESPONSE message is sent by the server when it has processed a GET_STRING_REQUEST; it must be followed by a UTF-8–encoded string that the client is expected to type.

Here's the implementation of our server:

```
package javathreads.examples.ch12.example1;

import java.io.*;
import java.net.*;
import javathreads.examples.ch12.*;

public class TypeServer extends TCPServer {
    public void run(Socket data) {
        try {
            DataOutputStream dos =
                    new DataOutputStream(data.getOutputStream());
            dos.writeByte(TypeServerConstants.WELCOME);
            DataInputStream dis =
                    new DataInputStream(data.getInputStream());
            while (true) {
                byte b = dis.readByte();
                if (b != TypeServerConstants.GET_STRING_REQUEST) {
                    System.out.println("Client sent unknown request " + b);
```

```
                continue;
            }
            dos.writeByte(TypeServerConstants.GET_STRING_RESPONSE);
            dos.writeUTF("Thisisateststring");
            dos.flush( );
        }
    } catch (Exception e) {
        System.out.println("Client terminating: " + e);
        return;
    }
}

public static void main(String[] args) throws IOException {
    TypeServer ts = new TypeServer();
    ts.startServer(Integer.parseInt(args[0]));
    System.out.println("Server ready and waiting...");
}
}
```

Remember that the run( ) method in this class is called after a new connection has been made (and within a new thread). It writes out the welcome message and then simply loops. Each time it executes the readByte( ) method, it blocks until the client sends the actual request for a string. That's the reason why we're running the client in a separate thread; other clients execute the readByte( ) method on completely separate sockets in separate threads. When a message is received, the string to type is sent back in the proper UTF-8 encoded format. The string here is always the same, but you could generate random strings in your server.

This class is also responsible for starting the server, which is a simple case of instantiating the server object and calling its startServer( ) method. Note that the main thread then exits, depending on the thread started by the startServer( ) method to continue all the work. We've not provided any way to stop the server other than killing the entire process, although we'll explore some ways to do that in later examples.

## Using the multithreaded server

Now we must develop the client side of our first example. We use our standard typing program as the client and change its random-character generator to connect to our server and send characters retrieved from that server. Here's the random-character generator that accomplishes that:

```
package javathreads.examples.ch12.example1;

import java.net.*;
import java.io.*;
import java.util.*;
import java.util.concurrent.*;
import java.util.concurrent.locks.*;
import javathreads.examples.ch12.*;

public class RandomCharacterGenerator extends Thread implements CharacterSource {
    private char[] chars;
```

```
    private int curChar;
    private Random random = new Random( );
    private CharacterEventHandler handler;
    private boolean done = true;
    private Lock lock = new ReentrantLock( );
    private Condition cv = lock.newCondition( );
    private Socket sock;
    private DataInputStream reader;
    private DataOutputStream writer;

    public RandomCharacterGenerator(String host, int port) throws IOException {
        handler = new CharacterEventHandler( );
        sock = new Socket(host, port);
        reader = new DataInputStream(sock.getInputStream( ));
        reader.read( );        // Welcome
        writer = new DataOutputStream(sock.getOutputStream( ));
        getString( );
    }

    private synchronized void getString( ) throws IOException {
        byte b = TypeServerConstants.GET_STRING_REQUEST;
        writer.write(b);
        writer.flush( );
        b = (byte) reader.readByte( );
        if (b != TypeServerConstants.GET_STRING_RESPONSE)
            throw new IllegalStateException("Bad recv state " + b);
        String s = reader.readUTF( );
        chars = s.toCharArray( );
        curChar = 0;
    }

    public int getPauseTime(int minTime, int maxTime) {
        return (int) (minTime + ((maxTime-minTime)*random.nextDouble( )));
    }

    public int getPauseTime( ) {
        return getPauseTime(2000, 5500);
    }

    public void addCharacterListener(CharacterListener cl) {
        handler.addCharacterListener(cl);
    }

    public void removeCharacterListener(CharacterListener cl) {
        handler.removeCharacterListener(cl);
    }

    public void nextCharacter( ) {
        handler.fireNewCharacter(this,
                                 (int) chars[curChar++]);
        if (curChar == chars.length) {
            try {
                getString( );
```

```
            } catch (IOException ioe) {
                // Put up a dialog box to alert user of error
            }
        }
    }

    public void run() {
        try {
            lock.lock();
            while (true) {
                try {
                    if (done) {
                        cv.await();
                    } else {
                        nextCharacter();
                        cv.await(getPauseTime(), TimeUnit.MILLISECONDS);
                    }
                } catch (InterruptedException ie) {
                    return;
                }
            }
        } finally {
            lock.unlock();
        }
    }

    public void setDone(boolean b) {
        try {
            lock.lock();
            done = b;

            if (!done) cv.signal();
        } finally {
            lock.unlock();
        }
    }
}
```

The only thread here is the one we've always had, which sends out the next character from the string retrieved from the server. A simple extension for your own practice would be to use the approach from Chapter 7 and show connection progress in the main Swing application.

## Scaling Using Traditional I/O

The primary issue when using the server we've just implemented is that it can handle only a finite number of clients. Two factors limit the number of clients the server can handle. First, the server can start only a certain number of threads. That number depends on the operating system hosting the server, the amount of memory available to the server, and so on, but the number of threads that a typical server can handle is far less than the number of sockets it could otherwise handle. The second limit has to do with the throughput of the server; as we saw in Chapter 10, with too many active threads, the total throughput of the program suffers. Even if you have enough memory to handle thousands of threads, you don't want them all to use the CPU at the same time, or all requests take a very long time.

To address these concerns, let's look at how to limit the number of threads that handle I/O in the server. Using traditional I/O, we can set up a pool of threads to handle requests; this places an upper limit on the number of simulataneous client requests that we can handle. Our second example shows the server and client code to use when you want to throttle the number of threads.

This approach works only for applications in which the client connections are short-lived. It depends on the fact that the threads in the server do not block because they do not read data from the client (other than the initial request, which is typically available as soon as the client has made a connection). This approach can also work if you don't care whether new clients are not always able to connect. If you set an upper limit of, say, 200 clients and don't mind that client number 201 has to wait an indeterminate amount of time for a previous client to exit, you can use the example in this section. Otherwise, if the scaling issues of traditional I/O are a problem for your application, look at the new I/O techniques described in the next section of this chapter.

The design pattern of this example is known as the leader-follower pattern. It relies on the fact that only one thread can execute the accept( ) method; that is, the internal implementation of the accept( ) method is synchronized. The thread that obtains that lock can establish the connection with a client and obtain that client's data socket. It can then release the lock, and the next thread in line then obtains the lock and processes the next client.

To use this pattern, we must extend our TCPServer class:

```java
package javathreads.examples.ch12;

import java.net.*;
import java.io.*;

public abstract class TCPThrottledServer implements Runnable {
    ServerSocket server = null;
    Thread[] serverThreads;
    volatile boolean done = false;

    public synchronized void startServer(int port, int nThreads)
                                        throws IOException {
        server = new ServerSocket(port);

        serverThreads = new Thread[nThreads];
        for (int i = 0; i < nThreads; i++) {
            serverThreads[i] = new Thread(this);
            serverThreads[i].start( );
        }
    }
}
```

```
        public synchronized void setDone( ) {
            done = true;
        }

        public void run( ) {
            while (!done) {
                try {
                    Socket data;
                    data = server.accept( );
                    run(data);
                } catch (IOException ioe) {
                    System.out.println("Accept error " + ioe);
                }
            }
        }

        public void run(Socket data) {
        }
    }
```

Notice that our implementation is now much simpler because we no longer need to create threads on the fly. We establish a fixed number of threads in the startServer( ) method. Each thread executes the run( ) method, where each in turn gets a client data socket. Because the thread itself operates on the socket, the server object no longer needs to clone itself; it can simply call the run(Socket data) method. The only other significant change is that the startServer( ) method must now keep track of all the threads so that the stopServer( ) method can interrupt the threads.

Our actual TypeServer implementation is very similar to its previous incarnation, except that it now can read only a single client request:

```
package javathreads.examples.ch12.example2;

import java.io.*;
import java.net.*;
import javathreads.examples.ch12.*;

public class TypeServer extends TCPThrottledServer {
    public void run(Socket data) {
        try {
            DataOutputStream dos =
                    new DataOutputStream(data.getOutputStream( ));
            dos.writeByte(TypeServerConstants.WELCOME);
            DataInputStream dis =
                    new DataInputStream(data.getInputStream( ));
            byte b = dis.readByte( );
            if (b != TypeServerConstants.GET_STRING_REQUEST) {
                System.out.println("Client sent unknown request " + b);
                return;
            }
            dos.writeByte(TypeServerConstants.GET_STRING_RESPONSE);
            dos.writeUTF("Thisisateststring");
            dos.flush( );
```

```
        } catch (Exception e) {
            System.out.println("Client terminating: " + e);
            return;
        } finally {
            try {
                data.close();
            } catch (IOException ioe) {
            }
        }
    }
}

public static void main(String[] args) throws IOException {
    TypeServer ts = new TypeServer();
    ts.startServer(Integer.parseInt(args[0]), Integer.parseInt(args[1]));
    System.out.println("Server ready and waiting...");
}
}
```

Handling only a single request has simplified this implementation as well. There is no free lunch however: the RandomCharacterGenerator class is now more complicated because it can no longer keep its connection to the server open. Instead, each time it wants a new string, it must make a new connection to the server:

```
package javathreads.examples.ch12.example2;
...
public class RandomCharacterGenerator extends Thread implements CharacterSource {
    ...
    public RandomCharacterGenerator(String host, int port) {
        handler = new CharacterEventHandler();
        this.host = host;
        this.port = port;
    }

    private synchronized void getString() throws IOException {
        Socket sock = new Socket(host, port);
        DataInputStream reader = new DataInputStream(sock.getInputStream());
        reader.read();          // Welcome
        DataOutputStream writer = new DataOutputStream(sock.getOutputStream());
        byte b = TypeServerConstants.GET_STRING_REQUEST;
        writer.write(b);
        writer.flush();
        b = (byte) reader.readByte();
        if (b != TypeServerConstants.GET_STRING_RESPONSE)
            throw new IllegalStateException("Bad recv state " + b);
        String s = reader.readUTF();
        chars = s.toCharArray();
        curChar = 0;
        sock.close();
    }
    ...
}
```

Continually making new connections to the server can be a nuisance, as well as having performance implications: it takes a significant amount of time to set up a socket

---

connection. If the protocol of your application is such that messages flow frequently between client and server, this implementation is inefficient. For applications that handle a large number of clients making single requests, however, this is a good way to scale your server using traditional I/O.

# A New I/O Server

When you need to handle a large number of clients making an arbitrary number of requests, the examples we've seen so far are impractical. The traditional I/O server cannot scale up to thousands of clients, and the traditional throttled I/O server is suitable only for short-lived requests.

Because of this situation, Java introduced a new I/O package (java.nio) in JDK 1.4. The I/O classes in this package allow you to use nonblocking I/O. This obviates the need for a single thread for every I/O socket (or file); instead, you can have a single thread that processes all client sockets. That thread can check to see which sockets have data available, process that data, and then check again for data on all sockets. Depending on the operations the server has to perform, it may need (or want) to spawn some additional threads to assist with this processing, but the new I/O classes allow you to handle thousands of clients in a single thread.

Given this efficiency, why would you ever use the traditional I/O patterns we looked at earlier? As you'll see, the answer lies in the complexity of the code. Dealing with nonblocking I/O is much harder than dealing with blocking I/O. In those situations where you have a known small number of clients, the ease of development with the traditional I/O classes makes the job of developing and maintaining your code much simpler. In other cases, however, the runtime efficiencies of the new I/O classes make up for its initial programming complexity.

## Nonblocking I/O

To understand the complexities we're facing, let's compare blocking and nonblocking I/O. Our program reads a UTF-encoded string. That string is represented as a series of bytes. The first four bytes make up an integer that indicates how much data the string contains. The remaining data is character data, the representation of which depends on the locale in which the data is produced. The data representation for the string "Thisisateststring" appears in Figure 12-2. The first four bytes tell us that the string has 17 characters, and the next 17 bytes are the ASCII representation of that string.

An application that wants to read this string first requests 2 bytes, calculates the length, and then requests 17 bytes.

As this data travels over the network, it may become fragmented. Data on a network is sent in packets, and each packet has a maximum size that it can accomodate. It's

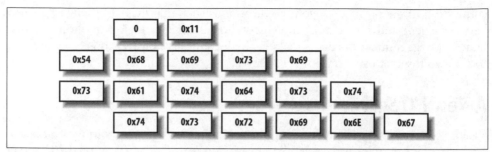

*Figure 12-2. Byte representation of a UTF-encoded string*

possible, then, for the first part of the data to arrive much sooner than the second part of the data. In the case of a network failure (or an extremely ill-timed computer failure on the sending machine), the second part of the data may never arrive. Therefore, when the application requests the 17 bytes, it may get back only the few bytes that have already arrived (the same is true when it requests the 2 bytes). The application must then request more data to complete reading the string.

The difference between blocking and nonblocking I/O is in how this situation is handled. With blocking I/O, the readUTF( ) method can just request the additional data. Requesting that data blocks until the data finally makes its way to the machine, at which point the readUTF( ) method can complete its construction of the string and return that string to the user.

With nonblocking I/O, that solution doesn't work. When a method attempts to read data and none is available, the method immediately returns with an indication that no data was present. You can't immediately retry reading the data because it still may not be available, and you'd end up continually wasting CPU cycles as you attempt to read the nonexistent data. Worse, you'd lose any benefit of nonblocking I/O: if you're going to read data until everything is ready, you may as well use traditional, blocking I/O.

When you use nonblocking I/O, then, it's your responsibility to be prepared for this situation and cope with the fact that all the data you need to process may not be immediately available. It's this programming that makes nonblocking I/O more difficult to use.

This situation isn't limited to reading data from sockets. When you write data to sockets, the data you're writing is buffered in the operating system until the OS can put the data on the network. If the network is very busy, the OS buffer may fill up, and you won't be able to write any data to it. Worse, you may attempt to write 100 bytes, but the OS buffers may have only 64 bytes available: you'll end up writing the first 64 bytes, but then you must go back later and write the remaining 36 bytes.

File I/O can have a similar problem. When you're reading data from the disk, the operating system may have to retrieve the actual data from many different locations on the disk. As a result, some of the data may be available immediately while the remaining data may not be available until the disk completes its rotation to the correct spot for the operating system to read it. In writing data, you may face the same problem: you may write faster than the operating system can flush its buffers to disk, in which case, you'll have a partial write of your data.

The situations we've described here are very similar to a race condition; they depend on a certain sequence of events occurring in a particular order. It turns out that they are just as rare. It's possible to write a server or other program using nonblocking I/O and always assume when you read data that you'll read everything you need and when you write data that it will all get written correctly. Such a program will work almost all the time. Almost.

## A Single-Threaded NIO Server

Now we'll develop our third example: a single-threaded network server that uses the NIO classes. As before, we'll develop a generic NIO server and the example server that completes the implementation of the server. We do not need to develop a new client to use this server, however. The TCP protocol is the same whether we use traditional I/O or NIO. As a result, we can use the client from example 1 to connect to this server.

We'll start with the generic NIO server:

```
package javathreads.examples.ch12;

import java.net.*;
import java.io.*;
import java.nio.channels.*;
import java.util.*;

public abstract class TCPNIOServer implements Runnable {
    protected ServerSocketChannel channel = null;
    private boolean done = false;
    protected Selector selector;
    protected int port = 8000;

    public void startServer() throws IOException {
        channel = ServerSocketChannel.open();
        channel.configureBlocking(false);
        ServerSocket server = channel.socket();
        server.bind(new InetSocketAddress(port));
        selector = Selector.open();
        channel.register(selector, SelectionKey.OP_ACCEPT);
    }

    public synchronized void stopServer() throws IOException {
        done = true;
        channel.close();
    }
```

```
protected synchronized boolean getDone( ) {
    return done;
}

public void run( ) {
    try {
        startServer( );
    } catch (IOException ioe) {
        System.out.println("Can't start server:  " + ioe);
        return;
    }
    while (!getDone( )) {
        try {
            selector.select( );
        } catch (IOException ioe) {
            System.err.println("Server error: " + ioe);
            return;
        }
        Iterator it = selector.selectedKeys().iterator( );
        while (it.hasNext( )) {
            SelectionKey key = (SelectionKey) it.next( );
            if (key.isReadable( ) || key.isWritable( )) {
                // Key represents a socket client
                try {
                    handleClient(key);
                } catch (IOException ioe) {
                    // Client disconnected
                    key.cancel( );
                }
            } else if (key.isAcceptable( )) {
                try {
                    handleServer(key);
                } catch (IOException ioe) {
                    // Accept error; treat as fatal
                    throw new IllegalStateException(ioe);
                }
            } else System.out.println("unknown key state");
            it.remove( );
        }
    }
}

protected void handleServer(SelectionKey key) throws IOException {
    SocketChannel sc = channel.accept( );
    sc.configureBlocking(false);
    sc.register(selector, SelectionKey.OP_READ);
    registeredClient(sc);
}

protected abstract void handleClient(SelectionKey key) throws IOException;
protected abstract void registeredClient(SocketChannel sc) throws IOException;
}
```

Our intent here is not to explain in great detail the NIO classes themselves; for a good reference, see *Java NIO* (O'Reilly). From a threading perspective, this is the classic approach to a single-threaded server than handles multiple clients. The selector keeps track of two things: the rendezvous socket and all open client sockets. When any of those sockets have data available, the selector is notified, and the set of sockets with pending data is returned via the selectedKeys( ) method. Our server iterates over each socket in that set. If the socket is the rendezvous socket, the handleServer( ) method is called, a new client connection is made, and the client socket is registered with the selector. Otherwise, the socket is a client data socket, and the handleClient( ) method is called.

The reason we can do this all in a single thread is that the I/O that occurs in the handleClient( ) and handleServer( ) methods never blocks. Consequently, our single thread never blocks; even with thousands of client sockets with pending I/O, each is handled in turn.

As before, we need to provide a subclass of this framework that handles the actual client data. Here's how we'd write a subclass based on our typing server protocol:

```
package javathreads.examples.chio.example3;

import java.io.*;
import java.nio.*;
import java.nio.channels.*;
import java.nio.charset.*;
import java.net.*;
import java.util.*;
import javathreads.examples.chio.*;

public class TypeServer extends TCPNIOServer {
    static String testString = "Thisisateststring";
    static class ClientInfo {
        ByteBuffer inBuf = ByteBuffer.allocateDirect(512);
        ByteBuffer outBuf = ByteBuffer.allocateDirect(512);
        boolean outputPending = false;
        SocketChannel channel;
    }
    Map allClients = new HashMap( );
    Charset encoder = Charset.forName("UTF-8");

    protected void handleClient(SelectionKey key) throws IOException {
        SocketChannel sc = (SocketChannel) key.channel( );
        ClientInfo ci = (ClientInfo) allClients.get(sc);
        if (ci == null)
            throw new IllegalStateException("Unknown client");
        if (key.isWritable( ))
            send(sc, ci);
        if (key.isReadable( ))
            recv(sc, ci);
    }
```

```
private void recv(SocketChannel sc, ClientInfo ci) throws IOException {
    ci.channel.read(ci.inBuf);
    ByteBuffer tmpBuf = ci.inBuf.duplicate();
    tmpBuf.flip();
    int bytesProcessed = 0;
    boolean doneLoop = false;
    while (!doneLoop) {
        byte b;
        try {
            b = tmpBuf.get();
        } catch (BufferUnderflowException bue) {
            // Processed all data in buffer
            ci.inBuf.clear();
            doneLoop = true;
            break;
        }
        switch(b) {
            case TypeServerConstants.WELCOME:
                bytesProcessed++;
                break;
            case TypeServerConstants.GET_STRING_REQUEST:
                bytesProcessed++;
                if (ci.outputPending) {
                    // Client is backed up. We can't append to
                    // the byte buffer because it's in the wrong
                    // state. We could allocate another buffer
                    // here and change our send method to know
                    // about multiple buffers, but we'll just
                    // assume that the client is dead
                    break;
                }
                ci.outBuf.put(TypeServerConstants.GET_STRING_RESPONSE);
                ByteBuffer strBuf = encoder.encode(testString);
                ci.outBuf.putShort((short) strBuf.remaining());
                ci.outBuf.put(strBuf);
                ci.outBuf.flip();
                send(sc, ci);
                break;
            case TypeServerConstants.GET_STRING_RESPONSE:
                int startPos = tmpBuf.position();
                try {
                    int nBytes = tmpBuf.getInt();
                    byte[] buf = new byte[nBytes];
                    tmpBuf.get(buf);
                    bytesProcessed += buf.length + 5;
                    String s = new String(buf);
                    // Send the string to the GUI
                    break;
                } catch (BufferUnderflowException bue) {
                    // Processed all available data
                    ci.inBuf.position(ci.inBuf.position() + bytesProcessed);
                    doneLoop = true;
```

```
                }
                break;
            }
        }
    }

    private void send(SocketChannel sc, ClientInfo ci) throws IOException {
        int len = ci.outBuf.remaining();
        int nBytes = sc.write(ci.outBuf);
        if (nBytes != len) {
            // Client not ready to receive data
            ci.outputPending = true;
            ci.channel.register(selector,
                    SelectionKey.OP_READ|SelectionKey.OP_WRITE);
        }
        else {
            ci.outBuf.clear();
            if (ci.outputPending) {
                ci.outputPending = false;
                ci.channel.register(selector, SelectionKey.OP_READ);
            }
        }
    }

    protected void registeredClient(SocketChannel sc) throws IOException {
        ClientInfo ci = new ClientInfo();
        ci.channel = sc;
        ci.outBuf.clear();
        ci.outBuf.put(TypeServer.WELCOME);
        ci.outBuf.flip();
        allClients.put(sc, ci);
        send(sc, ci);
    }

    public static void main(String[] args) throws Exception {
        TypeServer ts = new TypeServer();
        ts.port = Integer.parseInt(args[0]);
        Thread t = new Thread(ts);
        t.start();
        System.out.println("Type server ready...Type CTRL-D to exit");
        while (System.in.read() > 0)
            ;
        ts.stopServer();
        t.join();
    }
}
```

Note the greatly increased complexity in this example from our multithreaded blocking I/O example: that's the price we have to pay to handle all the additional clients. In the recv( ) method, we're reading all the data available from a client. That is usually just a single request, but, in fact, nothing prevents the client from sending multiple requests at the same time. Therefore, we must be ready to process all the available data, which is why we set up the outer loop that attempts to read a series of requests.

Our requests are a single byte long, so when I/O is available, we know that there's at least one request. However, some messages have additional data. The GET_STRING_RESPONSE message consists of the single byte indicating the message type and the UTF-encoded string. Notice how we read this from a temporary buffer in case all the data isn't present: if in processing the data we find that it isn't all there, we can just discard the temporary buffer. The next time the recv( ) method is called (which happens when we've received at least some of the remaining data), that data is appended to the buffer and we try to process it again.

In the send( ) method, we also check to make sure that we've written all the data. If not, we have to change our selection criteria. We're not interesting in knowing whether the socket can accept data unless we actually have pending data to send to it, so that's the only time we ask to be signaled for OP_WRITE.

## A Multithreaded New I/O Server

Our new I/O server is very efficient at handling a large number of clients, but it may not be making the best use of machine resources. If our server has multiple CPUs, we use only one of them. In other cases, we might have a handleClient( ) method that makes a database call, in which case the handleClient( ) method itself may need to wait for a response (we could of course use nonblocking I/O to handle the database call, but that would make our programming even more difficult). So occasionally you want to use nonblocking I/O to handle a large number of clients but still multi-thread your program for ease of development and optimal use of machine resources.

This situation is handled with a thread pool: as requests come into the server, the handleClient( ) method places the requests on the thread pool queue. Threads in the pool take the requests in order and execute them in parallel.

For our fourth example, we adapt our code from Chapter 10 and turn it into a server that can satisfy a large number of client requests.

```
package javathreads.examples.ch12.example4;

import java.util.concurrent.*;
import java.io.*;
import java.nio.*;
import java.nio.channels.*;
import javathreads.examples.ch12.*;

public class CalcServer extends TCPNIOServer {

    static ThreadPoolExecutor pool;

    class FibClass implements Runnable {
        long n;
```

```
        SocketChannel clientChannel;
        ByteBuffer buffer = ByteBuffer.allocateDirect(8);

        FibClass(long n, SocketChannel sc) {
            this.n = n;
            clientChannel = sc;
        }

        private long fib(long n) {
        if (n == 0)
            return 0L;
        if (n == 1)
            return 1L;
        return fib(n - 1) + fib(n - 2);
        }

        public void run( ) {
            try {
                long answer = fib(n);
                buffer.putLong(answer);
                buffer.flip( );
                clientChannel.write(buffer);
                if (buffer.remaining( ) > 0) {
                    Selector s = Selector.open( );
                    clientChannel.register(s, SelectionKey.OP_WRITE);
                    while (buffer.remaining( ) > 0) {
                        s.select( );
                        clientChannel.write(buffer);
                    }
                    s.close( );
                }
            } catch (IOException ioe) {
                System.out.println("Client error " + ioe);
            }
        }
    }

    protected void handleClient(SelectionKey key) throws IOException {
        SocketChannel sc = (SocketChannel) key.channel( );
        ByteBuffer buffer = ByteBuffer.allocateDirect(8);
        sc.read(buffer);
        buffer.flip( );
        long n = buffer.getLong( );
        FibClass fc = new FibClass(n, sc);
        pool.execute(fc);
    }

    protected void registeredClient(SocketChannel sc) {
    }

    public static void main(String[] args) throws Exception {
        CalcServer cs = new CalcServer( );
        cs.port = Integer.parseInt(args[0]);
        int tpSize = Integer.parseInt(args[1]);
```

```
        pool = new ThreadPoolExecutor(
                        tpSize, tpSize, 50000L, TimeUnit.MILLISECONDS,
                        new LinkedBlockingQueue<Runnable>());
        cs.run();
        System.out.println("Calc server waiting for requests...");
    }
}
```

From a threading perspective, the interesting thing to note here is that the handling of nonblocking I/O is somewhat easier. Because there are now multiple threads, we can afford to wait if one particular client is delayed in reading or writing data. One of our threads might periodically block now (but only for 60 seconds), but that won't greatly affect the overall throughput of our server.

One point about using multiple threads and the new I/O classes: the buffers and channels of these classes are typically not threadsafe. That's not usually a problem because the point of the exercise is to handle each channel in a separate thread (or everything in a single thread).

# Interrupted I/O

In Chapter 2, we introduced the interrupt( ) method, which interrupts a thread that is blocked in a sleep( ), wait( ), join( ), or similar method. The interrupt( ) method also sets a flag in the thread that is frequently used as a signal to the thread that it should terminate.

Traditional I/O methods in Java can also block: we've seen how reading from a socket is a blocking method. The accept( ) method of the ServerSocket class is inherently blocking; socket constructors may block while the connection is established, and, under some circumstances, writing to a socket may block. File I/O can also block, though much more rarely (although if the file is from a network file server, blocking becomes more likely).

What is the effect of calling interrupt( ) on a thread that is blocked in I/O? The answer to that is platform-dependent. On Unix operating systems such as Solaris and Linux, the interrupt( ) method causes the blocked I/O method to throw an InterruptedIOException. Unfortunately, Windows operating systems do not support interruptible I/O, so on those platforms a thread blocked on an I/O method remains blocked after it has been interrupted.

So what's a programmer to do? The safest answer is not to rely on the interrupt( ) method to unblock a thread that is waiting for I/O to complete: if you need to unblock such a thread, you should close the input or output stream on which the thread is blocked. If interruptible I/O as a generic feature is added to Java in the future, it will likely have a different interface than the method throwing an InterruptedIOException.

If you do rely on interruptible I/O, be aware that the I/O in question is not restartable: it's impossible to determine the state of the I/O and know at which point it should start again. The difficulty of dealing with the issue of restarting I/O that has been interrupted is a prime reason why its implementation is inconsistent between operating systems.

Under certain circumstances, you can still use the interrupt( ) method to close down an I/O thread on all platforms. This can work if, when you call the interrupt( ) method, you intend to close the input stream in question since closing the input stream unblocks the thread on all platforms.

This abstract class demonstrates this principle:

```
package javathreads.examples.ch12;

import java.net.*;
import java.io.*;

public abstract class InterruptibleReader extends Thread {
    private Object lock = new Object();
    private InputStream is;
    private boolean done;
    private int buflen;

    protected void processData(byte[] b, int n) { }

    class ReaderClass extends Thread {
        public void run() {
            byte[] b = new byte[buflen];
            while (!done) {
                try {
                    int n = is.read(b, 0, buflen);
                    processData(b, n);
                } catch (IOException ioe) {
                    done = true;
                }
            }
            synchronized(lock) {
                lock.notify();
            }
        }
    }

    public InterruptibleReader(InputStream is) {
        this(is, 512);
    }

    public InterruptibleReader(InputStream is, int len) {
        this.is = is;
        buflen = len;
    }
```

```java
public void run( ) {
    ReaderClass rc = new ReaderClass( );
    synchronized(lock) {
        rc.start( );
        while (!done) {
            try {
                lock.wait( );
            } catch (InterruptedException ie) {
                done = true;
                rc.interrupt( );
                try {
                    is.close( );
                } catch (IOException ioe) {}
            }
        }
    }
}
```

What we've done in this class is to start two threads: one that is reading the data and one that is waiting for an interrupt to occur. When the waiting thread is interrupted, it closes the input stream that the reading thread is blocked on, and both threads then exit. This allows us to shut down the thread (and close the input stream associated with the thread) by interrupting the waiting thread:

```java
InterruptibleReader ir = ...some concrete subclass of interruptible reader...;
... Do other things until we need to shut down the reader ...
ir.interrupt( );
```

A concrete implementation of the interruptible reader might look like this:

```java
package javathreads.examples.ch12.example5;

import java.net.*;
import java.io.*;
import javathreads.examples.ch12.*;

public class InterruptibleClient extends InterruptibleReader {

    public void processData(byte[] b, int n) {
        System.out.println("Got data " + new String(b, 0, n));
    }

    public InterruptibleClient(InputStream is) {
        super(is);
    }

    public static void main(String[] args) throws Exception {
        Socket s = new Socket(args[0], Integer.parseInt(args[1]));
        InputStream is = s.getInputStream( );
        InterruptibleClient c = new InterruptibleClient(is);
        c.start( );
```

```
        System.out.println("Main thread sleeping");
        Thread.sleep(10000);
        System.out.println("Main thread woke up");
        c.interrupt();
        System.out.println("Main thread called interrupt");
    }
}
```

Rather than going to all this effort, we might simply have closed the input stream directly. Similarly, we might have written a shutdown() method in the InterruptibleReader class that closed the input stream (which would have saved us a thread). The reason you might select this approach is that it keeps things consistent among all threads: you can use the interrupt() method to stop all of them. Chapter 13 describes how you can arrange to interrupt a group of threads at once, which is another advantage to this approach.

## Summary

Using multiple threads well is very important in any Java program that performs a lot of I/O. In the simplest case, I/O (and particularly socket I/O) may block at any point in time; if you want to make sure that your program remains responsive while performing I/O, you must perform the I/O in another thread. For simple cases, this means having a single thread for every I/O source you're interested in.

That model does not scale completely as the number of I/O sources grows. At this point, you must begin to look at other threading solutions. One solution is to continue to use blocking I/O but to limit the number of threads active at any time. Although that solution has limited applicability, it's a simple extension to a basic idea.

In most other cases, you'll need to use the nonblocking features of Java's NIO classes. Although these classes increase the complexity of your applications, they allow you to handle many I/O sources with a single thread. The complexity of using nonblocking I/O can be mitigated somewhat by using multiple threads with nonblocking I/O; that solution is also appropriate when you have multiple CPUs available to process requests or when the requests themselves need to block for other reasons.

Used judiciously, Java's threading and I/O models allow you great flexibility in developing complex programs.

## Example Classes

Here are the class names and Ant targets for the examples in this chapter:

| Description | Main Java class | Ant target |
|---|---|---|
| Single-Threaded Server | javathreads.examples.ch12.example1. TypeServer portNumber | ch12-ex1-server |
| Single-Threaded Client | javathreads.examples.ch12.example1. SwingTypeTester hostname portNumber | ch12-ex1-client |
| Throttled Server | javathreads.examples.ch12.example2. TypeServer portNumber | ch12-ex2-server |
| Throttled Client | javathreads.examples.ch12.example2. SwingTypeTester hostname portnumber | ch12-ex2-client |
| NIO Single-Threaded Server | javathreads.examples.ch12.example3. TypeServer portNumber | ch12-ex3-server |
| Multithreaded Calc Server | javathreads.examples.ch12.example4. CalcServer portNumber nServerThreads | ch12-ex4-server |
| Calc Client | javathreads.examples.ch12.example4. CalcServer nClientRequests FibNumber hostname portNumber | ch12-ex4-client |
| Interruptible Client | javathreads.examples.ch12.example5. InterruptibleClient hostname port | ch12-ex5-client |

The single-threaded client (example 1) can be used with either single-threaded server (examples 1 and 3). The interruptible client can be used with any type of server. To change ports and hostnames for the Ant targets, use these properties:

```
<property name="TypeServerHost" value="localhost"/>
<property name="TypeServerPort" value="8003"/>
<property name="TypeServerNThreads" value="10"/>
<property name="CalcServerNThreads" value="5"/>
<property name="CalcClientNThreads" value="10"/>
<property name="CalcServerFibNumber" value="20"/>
<property name="CalcServerHost" value="localhost"/>
<property name="CalcServerPort" value="8003"/>
```

# CHAPTER 13

# Miscellaneous Thread Topics

Threads are a basic feature of the Java platform. As a result, threads interact with several of Java's other programming and runtime features. In this chapter, we'll briefly touch on some of these features (and issues), including thread groups, Java security, daemon threads, class loading, exception handling, and memory usage. Some of these topics are interrelated: in particular, the thread group class is used by the security manager as the basis for its decisions. In general, the topics here will complete your understanding of how threads permeate the Java platform.

## Thread Groups

All threads belong to a thread group, which, as its name implies, is a group of threads. Thread groups are defined by the java.lang.ThreadGroup class. Although we haven't yet mentioned them, thread groups have been around all along. Every thread you create automatically belongs to a default thread group that the Java virtual machine sets up on your behalf. Every thread we've looked at so far belongs to this existing thread group, which is known as the "main" thread group.

The virtual machine also has a "system" thread group. This thread group contains the threads that handle finalization and weak references. This group does not contain all threads of the virtual machine: some system-level threads (such as the garbage collection thread(s)) have no corresponding Java thread object and do not exist in any Java thread group.

Thread groups are more than just arbitrary groupings of threads; they are related to each other. Every thread group has a parent thread group, so thread groups exist in a tree hierarchy. The obvious exception to this, of course, is the root of the tree, which is known as the root thread group or the system thread group. Every Java program has by default two thread groups: the system thread group contains the threads of some system-level tasks.* The system thread group has one child, the main thread group, which contains the thread that starts your program, the AWT event-dispatching thread, any default thread you create, and any threads started by the Java API. Figure 13-1 shows a sample thread hierarchy from a system running the Java Plug-in. In this figure, each applet is given its own thread which is started in its own thread group. Some of the applets have created additional thread groups to complete the hierarchy shown.

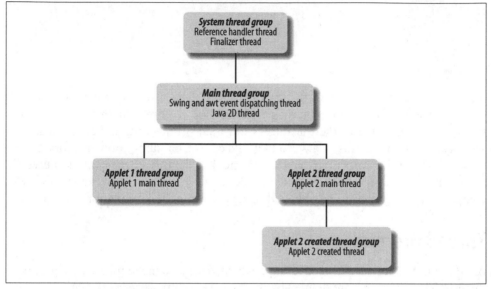

*Figure 13-1. An (incomplete) thread group hierarchy*

You can create your own thread groups as well and make this hierarchy arbitrarily complex. Thread groups are created just like any Java object; when you instantiate a thread group object, you specify its parent thread group in the hierarchy (by default, the parent thread group is the current thread group). When you instantiate a Thread object, you may optionally specify the thread group to which it should belong. If you don't specify a thread group, one of two things happens:

- If a security manager has been installed, the getThreadGroup( ) method of the security manager is called and the thread joins the group returned by that method.

- Otherwise, the thread joins the current thread group (the thread group of the instantiating thread).

---

* Not all virtual machine–level threads have a corresponding Java thread object, so the system group does not contain all possible threads.

Thread groups have two advantages. First, convenience methods of the thread group class allow you to operate on all threads in the group. If, for example, you wanted to interrupt all threads in a particular group, you could call the interrupt( ) method on the thread group object, and it would call the interrupt( ) method of each of its threads. The interrupt( ) method is really the only method of the ThreadGroup class that can affect all the threads in the group; stop( ), suspend( ), and resume( ) methods operate in the same way, but they are, of course, deprecated.

The second advantage of thread groups relates to thread security. If you write custom security code for your application, decisions about whether one thread can access and/or modify the state of another thread take into account the thread group to which the threads belong. The Java Plug-in and appletviewer provide such customization so that threads in one applet are prevented from modifying the threads in another applet. To make security decisions in this way, however, requires that you write a custom security manager.

# Threads and Java Security

One of Java's hallmarks is that it is designed from the ground up with security in mind. It's no surprise, then, that threads have a number of interesting security-related properties.

In its default configuration, security in a Java program is enforced by the security manager, an instance of the java.lang.SecurityManager class. When certain operations are attempted on threads or thread groups, the Thread and ThreadGroup classes consult the security manager to determine if those operations are permitted.

There is one method in the SecurityManager class that handles security policies for the Thread class and one that handles security policies for the ThreadGroup class. These methods have the same name but different signatures:

void checkAccess(Thread t)
> Checks if the current thread is allowed to modify the state of the thread t

void checkAccess(ThreadGroup tg)
> Checks if the current thread is allowed to modify the state of the thread group tg

Like all methods in the SecurityManager class, these methods throw a SecurityException if they determine that performing the operation would violate the security policy. As an example, here's a conflation of the code that the interrupt( ) method of the Thread class implements:

```
public void interrupt( ) {
    SecurityManager sm = System.getSecurityManager( );
    if (sm != null)
        sm.checkAccess(this);
    interrupt0( );
}
```

This is canonical behavior for thread security: the checkAccess( ) method is called, which generates a runtime exception if thread policy is violated by the operation. Assuming that no exception is thrown, an internal method is called that actually performs the logic of the method.

---

### Security and the checkAccess( ) Method

Both the Thread and ThreadGroup classes have an internal method called checkAccess( ); this method, by default, calls the security manager's checkAccess( ) method, passing the appropriate thread or thread group object.

The checkAccess( ) method within the Thread and ThreadGroup classes is public, so you can call it directly from any thread or thread group object if you want to check what security policy is in place.

The checkAccess( ) method within the ThreadGroup class is final; it may not be overridden. The checkAccess( ) method of the Thread class, however, is not final, meaning that you could override it and effectively change the security model for your particular Thread subclass. Remember, however, that this would affect only your class and not other threads within the system.

---

Because only one method in the SecurityManager class is used to check for security information, thread security policy is an all-or-nothing proposition. If the security manager determines that a particular thread is prevented from interrupting other threads, that thread is also prevented from setting the priority of other threads.

The checkAccess( ) method itself looks to see which thread group the target thread belongs to. If the thread is not a member of the root thread group, the checkAccess( ) method immediately returns; all threads are allowed to modify the state of all other threads that are not members of the root thread group. Otherwise, the security manager consults the policy for the program.

Java security is normally determined via a series of policy files, including the files *$JAVAHOME/lib/security/java.policy* and *$HOME/.java.policy*. The policy files used by a program contain a mapping between the URLs where the application code was loaded from and the permission granted to code loaded from those particular locations. When the checkAccess( ) method (or any other method of the security manager) is called, the security manager looks at the stack of the current thread: every class on the stack must have permission to execute the given method.

For thread access, code must be granted one of these two permissions:

```
permission java.security.AllPermission;
permission java.security.RuntimePermission "thread";
```

When the checkAccess( ) method is called and each method presently on the stack has one of these permissions, no security exception is thrown. The security manager is consulted whenever a program calls any of the methods listed in Table 13-1.

*Table 13-1. Thread and ThreadGroup methods affected by the security manager*

| Thread methods | ThreadGroup methods |
| --- | --- |
| Thread( ) (calls checkAccess( ) on its thread group) | ThreadGroup( ) |
| stop( ) | stop( ) |
| suspend( ) | suspend( ) |
| resume( ) | resume( ) |
| interrupt( ) | interrupt( ) |
| setPriority( ) | setMaxPriority( ) |
| setDaemon( ) | setDaemon( ) |
| setName( ) | destroy( ) |

The stop( ) method is handled somewhat differently. In addition to calling the checkAccess( ) method of the security manager, the stop( ) method also checks to see if the classes on the stack have this permission:

```
permission java.lang.RuntimePermission "stopThread";
```

By default, this permission is granted to all code, and the other thread permissions are not granted to any code. Users and system administrators may change their policy files at will to allow or disallow any of the thread access.

By default, then, threads can modify the state of any other thread (including itself) unless the target thread belongs to the root thread group. Threads that are in the root thread group cannot be modified unless the user has set up specific permissions to allow that.

However, the security policy of the Java virtual machine is quite flexible and can be overriden by applications at several levels. As we've mentioned, the Java Plug-in and appletviewer provide their own implementation of the security manager. When the checkAccess( ) method of that security manager is called, the security manager consults the thread group of the calling thread: it is allowed to access or modify its own threads and threads in any descendent thread groups, but nothing else.

For more details on how Java security works, including how you can override the security manager, see *Java Security* (O'Reilly).

# Daemon Threads

Java has two types of threads: daemon and user. The threads that we've looked at so far have all been user threads. The implication of these names is that daemon threads are threads created internally by the virtual machine and that user threads are those that you create yourself, but this is not the case. Any thread can be a daemon thread or a user thread.

A daemon thread is identical to a user thread in almost every way. The one exception occurs in determining when the virtual machine exits. The virtual machine automatically exits when all of its nondaemon threads have exited. Daemon threads only live to serve user threads; if there are no more user threads, there is nothing to serve and no reason to continue.

The canonical daemon thread in Java is the garbage collection thread (and, in recent virtual machines, multiple garbage collection threads). The garbage collector runs from time to time and frees those Java objects that no longer have valid references. If we don't have any other threads running, however, there's nothing for the garbage collector to do: after all, garbage is not spontaneously created (at least not inside a Java program). So if the garbage collector is the only thread left running in the Java virtual machine, clearly there's no more work for it to do, and the Java virtual machine can exit.

The daemon mode of a thread is set by calling the setDaemon( ) method with either true (set to daemon mode) or false (set to user mode). The setDaemon( ) method can be called only before the thread has been started. While the thread is running, you cannot cause a user thread to become a daemon thread (or vice versa); attempting to do so generates an exception. To be completely correct, an exception is generated any time the thread is alive and the setDaemon( ) method is called.

By default, a thread is a user thread if it is created by a user thread; it is a daemon thread if it is created by a daemon thread.

# Threads and Class Loading

Classes in Java are loaded by a classloader object, which consults the directories and jar files in your classpath to find the class definitions. Applications can construct their own classloaders to find class files in locations other than the classpath. For example, the Java Plug-in constructs a classloader for each applet based on the codebase specified in the applet's tag; J2EE application servers construct a classloader for each J2EE application they run.

Classloaders form a hierarchy. The root of the hierarchy is the bootstrap classloader, which loads classes from *rt.jar* and other system jar files. Its immediate child is the application classloader which loads classes from the classpath. From that point, the class loading tree can become arbitrarily complicated. Figure 13-2 shows the class loading hierarchy of a program that has started two different classloaders. Note that two classes in this hierarchy have the same name: it's an interesting property of the virtual machine that classes loaded by different classloaders are considered completely different classes.

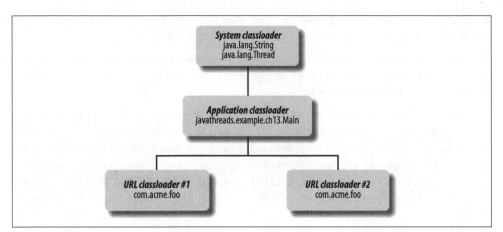

*Figure 13-2. A classloader hierarchy*

Despite the similarity of this hierarchy to the thread group hierarchy, the two are unrelated. Threads can freely share classes that are loaded in other threads, no matter what classloader is used to load them.

Threads interact with the classloader in one particular case. Each thread is assigned a specific classloader known as the context classloader. This classloader is retrieved with the getContextClassLoader( ) method and set with the setContextClassLoader( ) method.

The context classloader is used to load classes (and resources) only in certain specific cases. Developers often assume that the context classloader can be used to affect where a thread loads things from in a general case, but that is not true. In the general case, when a thread runs the code of class A and comes across a reference for class B, it attempts to load the code for class B from the same classloader that loaded class A (or one of that classloader's ancestors in the classloading hierarchy). This approach is taken irrespective of which threads or classloaders were originally involved in loading class A. A classloader knows only about its ancestors, not its descendants.

The context classloader only comes into play with certain internal classes in the virtual machine. For example, when you pass serialized objects over IIOP, the ORB classes consult the thread's context classloader when it tries to retrieve the class definition for the classes it attempts to deserialize. Application servers typically take the same approach when attempting to load resources specific to a J2EE application.

The reason a context classloader is needed in these circumstances is that the ORB classes were loaded by the system classloader; they don't know about any other classloaders that exist in the class-loading hierarchy. When an ORB class dereferences an object and needs to load a new class, it can consult only the system classloader. Clearly, the application classes it needs to deserialize the object won't be defined in the system classloader; it must have a hook to get to the special class-loader that the application wants to use to define its classes.

This hook is unrelated to threading issues: the context classloader can be set and reset as often as you want in your application. The Thread class simply provides a convenient location to put this hook.

The default context classloader for a thread is the classloader that loaded the class defining the thread. For application threads, this is typically the application class-loader (unless you've defined your own classloader within the application). So in the vast majority of cases, you don't need to worry about setting the context classloader. If you've defined and used multiple classloaders in your application, however, you need to set the context classloader of a thread before it calls into the ORB (or certain other system resources).

## Threads and Exception Handling

In Chapter 2, we examine how to create a thread and we mention that the start( ) method performs some internal housekeeping and then calls the run( ) method. Let's examine that in a little more detail. The start( ) method does start another thread of control, but the run( ) method is not really the "main" method of the new thread. The run( ) method is executed inside a context that allows the virtual machine to handle runtime exceptions thrown from the run( ) method. This process is shown in Figure 13-3.

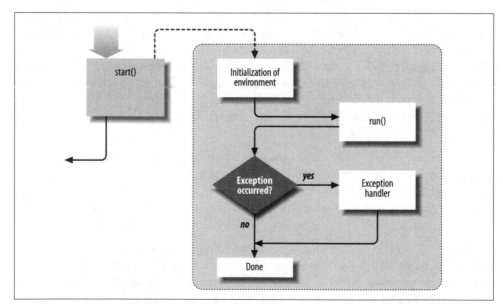

Figure 13-3. Flowchart of the main thread

All uncaught exceptions are handled by code outside of the run( ) method before the thread terminates. The default exception handler is a Java method; it can be overridden. This means that it is possible for a program to write a new default exception handler.

The default exception handler is the uncaughtException( ) method of the ThreadGroup class. It is called only when an exception is thrown from the run( ) method. The thread is technically completed when the run( ) method returns, even though the exception handler is still running the thread.

The default implementation of the uncaughtException( ) method is to print out the stack trace of the Throwable object thrown by the run( ) method (unless that object is an instance of the ThreadDeath class, discussed next). In most cases, this is sufficient: the only exceptions that the run( ) method can throw are runtime exceptions or errors. By the time the run( ) method has returned, it's too late to recover from these errors.

One case in which it's useful to override the uncaughtException( ) method is to send a priority notification to an administrator that an unusual, fatal error has occurred. Here's an example that does that when its thread eventually encounters an out-of-memory error:

```
package javathreads.examples.ch13;

import java.util.*;

public class TestOverride implements Runnable {

    static class OverrideThreadGroup extends ThreadGroup {
        public OverrideThreadGroup( ) {
            super("Administrator Alert Group");
        }
        public void uncaughtException(Thread t, Throwable e) {
            alertAdministrator(e);
        }
    }

    public static void alertAdministrator(Throwable e) {
        // Use Java Mail to send the administrator's pager an email
        System.out.println("Adminstrator alert!");
        e.printStackTrace( );
    }

    public static void main(String[] args) {
        ThreadGroup tg = new OverrideThreadGroup( );

        Thread t = new Thread(tg, new TestOverride( ));
        t.start( );
    }
```

```
    public void run( ) {
        ArrayList al = new ArrayList( );
        while (true) {
            al.add(new byte[1024]);
        }
    }
}
```

When the out of memory error occurs, the application prints a message alerting the system administrator of this fact. In J2SE 5.0, this idea has been expanded, and it is now possible to set an uncaught exception handler for each thread.

```
package java.lang;
public class Thread implements Runnable {
    public interface UncaughtExceptionHandler {
        void uncaughtException(Thread t, Throwable e);
    }
    public static setDefaultExceptionHandler(Thread.UncaughtExceptionHandler ueh);
    public static Thread.UncaughtExceptionHandler getDefaultExceptionHandler( );
    public setExceptionHandler(Thread.UncaughtExceptionHandler ueh);
    public Thread.UncaughtExceptionHandler getExceptionHandler( );
}
```

The static methods of the Thread class set or retrieve a default thread handler used by all new threads. When a thread is constructed, its exception handler is set to the default, so calling the setDefaultExceptionHandler( ) method does not affect any threads that have already been constructed. The exception handler for a particular thread can be set at any time.

By default, the exception handler for a thread is its thread group: the ThreadGroup class implements the Thread.UncaughtExceptionHandler interface and calls the uncaughtException( ) method, as we've already explained. Therefore, the changes to J2SE 5.0 are fully backward-compatible with existing exception handling.

## The ThreadDeath Class

The ThreadDeath class is a special Throwable class that was formerly used to stop a thread. When the stop( ) method is called on a thread, that thread immediately throws a ThreadDeath error. The ThreadDeath class extends the Error class and so is not usually caught by application programming. It is possible, of course, to catch any Throwable object, but it is not advisable to use this technique to prevent the death of the thread. After all, if we didn't want the thread to die, why was the stop( ) method called? And if we prevent the thread from exiting, another thread executing the join( ) method never completes.

The ThreadDeath class is what caused the stop( ) method to become deprecated. Because it's thrown immediately upon receipt of the stop( ) method, it has the potential to leave shared data in an inconsistent state. And because it releases any locks on synchronized blocks or data that it holds, it has the potential to allow other threads to access the inconsistent data, even if that data is correctly synchronized.

The uncaughtException( ) method handles the ThreadDeath class differently: while it prints out a stack trace for all other errors and exceptions, the thread death errors are silently swallowed.

This leads us to one limited circumstance in which the ThreadDeath class is useful as a replacement for the stop( ) method. Suppose that a thread encounters an error and wants to terminate itself, but the error is not egregious enough that it wants the user to see the error. The normal way to do this is to return from the run( ) method, but it may be difficult for the thread to unwind all of its methods in order to do that. A second way is for the thread to call the stop( ) method on itself. The third and final way is for the thread to throw a ThreadDeath error.

Even so, a thread that wants to terminate itself cannot simply throw a ThreadDeath error willy-nilly: the thread must throw this object only when it is sure that it has not left any data in a possibly inconsistent state. If you've programmed your thread very carefully and are sure that the thread has left all data in a consistent state, it's safe to throw the ThreadDeath object to make your thread exit immediately. The only difference between this and the thread calling the stop( ) method on itself is that the compiler warns you about the deprecated method in the latter case (even if a thread knows it's safe to call stop( ) on itself). The compiler does not complain if you throw a ThreadDeath object. Still, you have to be very careful only to do this when it's absolutely safe to do so.

## Threads, Stacks, and Memory Usage

In Chapter 2, we mention that when you construct a thread, you can specify its stack size. Using this particular constructor can lead to unportable Java programs because the stack details of threads vary from platform to platform. We'll explain the details in this section.

The stack is where a thread keeps track of information about the methods it's currently executing. Let's look again at our class that calculates Fibonacci numbers:

```
package javathreads.examples.ch10;

import java.util.*;
import java.text.*;

public class Task implements Runnable {
    long n;
    String id;

    private long fib(long n) {
        if (n == 0)
            return 0L;
```

```
        if (n == 1)
            return 1L;
        return fib(n - 1) + fib(n - 2);
    }

    public Task(long n, String id) {
        this.n = n;
        this.id = id;
    }

    public void run() {
        Date d = new Date();
        DateFormat df = new SimpleDateFormat("HH:mm:ss:SSS");
        long startTime = System.currentTimeMillis();
        d.setTime(startTime);
        System.out.println("Starting task " + id + " at " + df.format(d));
        fib(n);
        long endTime = System.currentTimeMillis();
        d.setTime(endTime);
        System.out.println("Ending task " + id + " at " +
                        df.format(d) + " after " + (endTime - startTime) +
                        " milliseconds");
    }
}
```

When a thread executes the run() method of this class, it creates a stack frame. The stack frame has information specific to this execution of the run() method. That means it has a place to store the local variables (d, df, startTime, and endTime) that the method execution uses. When the run() method calls the fib() method, a new stack frame representing the fib() method is placed on the stack. That stack frame has storage for the local variable (n) of the fib() method. Successive calls to the fib() method place a new frame on the stack, each with its own local copy of the variable n. At some point, then, the stack resembles Figure 13-4: the run() method has called the fib() method with a value of 2, and the fib() method has recursively called itself. At this point, as the fib() method returns, frames are popped off the stack, freeing memory for later use.

Stack frames contain more information than the local variables of a method: they contain program counters that indicate which statement in the method the thread is executing and other bookkeeping information for the thread. The size of the local variables plus the size of this bookkeeping information determines the size of the stack frame.

That size is platform dependent. Although the local variables must have the same size (since Java defines the size of all variables), the space needed to store the local variables may differ across platform. For example, certain CPUs work better if variables are aligned on an even-word boundary or an 8-byte boundary. Therefore, a stack frame that defines four separate variables of type byte may be able to store those variables in 4 bytes on some CPUs but require 16 or more bytes on other

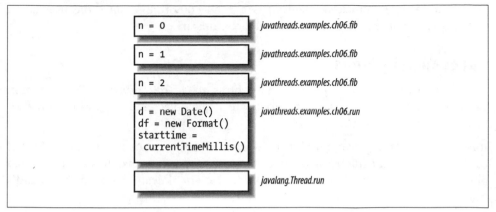

*Figure 13-4. A Java thread's stack*

CPUs. In addition, the bookkeeping information for a stack is dependent on the Java implementation; it may vary between different Java releases on the same platform (as well as differing between platforms).

The size of the stack (and the frames it holds) impacts Java's memory usage in two ways: stack overflows occur when a stack is not big enough, and out-of-memory conditions can occur when stacks are too big.

## Stack Overflow Errors

Java stacks have a fixed size, say 1024 KB. Suppose that the size of a stack frame for the fib( ) method is 16 bytes: 4 bytes for the variable n, and 12 bytes for other information. If we attempt to calculate fib(65536), we'll get a stack overflow error: all the stack frames needed for the recursive calls to the fib( ) method won't fit in the available memory.

This is one case where you might want to use the stack-size argument to the constructor of the thread object to allocate more space for the thread. If you specify a stack size larger than 1024 KB, you'll be able to calculate a larger Fibonacci number without getting a stack overflow error. Note that the constructor that allows you to specify the thread's stack size is available only beginning with J2SE 5.0 and that the number specified is only a hint to the virtual machine. The operating system picks a size for the stack that meets any OS-level requirements (e.g., stack sizes often must be a multiple of 128 KB).

The problem here is what value to pick for the stack size. The optimal value is dependent on two things: the maximum number of frames you'll need to store and the size of each frame. You may be able to figure out the first value in advance, but the second value is different on different platforms and with different Java implementations. Allowing the user to specify the stack size for the thread through a command-line argument (or some other mechanism) is a good compromise since the user could change that number based on her particular circumstances.

## Out of Memory Errors

In a number of cases, Java programs may throw an OutOfMemoryError. The common case, of course, is when you attempt to create a new object and the Java heap has no room to store that object.

It is also possible to get an out of memory error when you construct a thread. In that case, the error might still be caused because your heap is too small to store the thread object. But it's far more likely that the system cannot allocate space for the thread's stack.

Java stacks are not stored in the Java heap; they are stored in the general memory of the virtual machine. This effectively limits the number of threads that an application can create.

Suppose again that a default Java stack is 1024 KB. On a Linux or Windows platform, the maximum memory size of a program is 2 GB, but that size includes the Java heap and all the shared libraries (DLLs) that the virtual machine uses. If we specify a max heap size of 768 KB and assume that the shared libraries and executable code take up 256 KB, that leaves us 1 GB in which to store thread stacks. In this scenario, we'll be able to create about 1024 threads with a 1024 KB stack size before we get an out-of-memory error.

On SPARC systems running Solaris, the maximum size of a process is 4 GB, leaving us that much more memory available for stacks (and/or a bigger heap). Most SPARC systems, and some AMD and Intel systems, can run a 64-bit virtual machine, effectively making this issue irrelevant.

So depending on the number of threads you need to create and the platform you're running on, you might need to specify a smaller stack size for at least some of the threads in order to fit in the available memory.

## Specifying Stack Sizes

We've already mentioned that the stack size for a thread can be specified when the thread is constructed. That argument, available only in J2SE 5.0, allows you to have a different stack size for different threads.

On many Java implementations, you can also specify the stack size for *all* threads using a command-line argument—typically, the -Xss argument. For example, the following command would make all Java threads use a stack of 128 KB:

```
% java -Xss128k MyClass
```

This is a good technique to use when your application throws an out of memory error when creating a new thread, since it doesn't require changing your program code. However, this argument is nonstandard, so it is not available in all Java implementations.

## Stack APIs

The Thread class has four miscellaneous methods that provide information about a Java stack:

```
package java.lang;
public class Thread implements Runnable {
    public int countStackFrames();  // deprecated
    public static void dumpStack();
    public StackTraceElement[] getStackTrace();
    public static Map getAllStackTraces();
}
```

The countStackFrames() method can only be called on a thread that is suspended; its use is deprecated since the suspend() method is deprecated. In J2SE 5.0, you can use the getStackTrace() method instead, which returns all the methods on the stack of the target thread. The getAllStackTraces() method calls the getStackTrace() method for every thread in the virtual machine and returns a map containing the stack traces for all the threads. The dumpStack() method is a utility method to dump the current thread's stack to System.err.

# Summary

In this chapter, we've filled in a lot of the details about how threads work. Threads belong to a thread group, and thread groups exist in a hierarchical format. Thread groups serve a few purposes: they allow you to interrupt a group of threads with one method call, and they allow a custom security manager to make sure that unrelated threads cannot interfere with each other.

We've also looked at how threads handle uncaught exceptions: though they normally just print out the uncaught exception to System.err and exit, you can arrange for the exiting thread to perform one final act. Finally, we've seen how threads interact with the Java heap and memory systems and how you may need to adjust memory parameters in a program that handles a lot of threads.

## Example Classes

Here are the class names and Ant targets for the examples in this chapter:

| Description | Main Java class | Ant target |
| --- | --- | --- |
| Uncaught Exception handler test | javathreads.examples.ch13.TestOverride | ch13-ex1 |

# CHAPTER 14
# Thread Performance

In a few places in this book, we've referred to performance characteristics of thread-related programming. We've glossed over a lot of that information; in this chapter, we'll look at these performance issues in more depth. In particular, we'll look at thread creation performance, the performance advantages of using a thread pool, and the real costs of synchronization. However, we'll start with an overview of factors that affect Java performance.

## Overview of Performance

Most developers are concerned about the performance of their program. Even though there are many programs for which performance doesn't really matter, no one wants to write a badly performing program. And there are many more programs for which performance is crucial.

Performance, however, is not the most important aspect in developing good programs. We've frequently met developers who allow their concerns about performance to complicate their program development: for example, believing that synchronization is inherently expensive, they may spend days attempting to write a class that doesn't need synchronization. The resulting code is complex, difficult to maintain, and more prone to bugs than a simpler (in this case, synchronized) version.

Without any prior knowledge of a program's behavior, this is counterproductive. Developer time is wasted, and support costs are increased. This observation leads us to our first rule of performance: premature optimization is the root of much evil.[*]

Performance bottlenecks can be assessed only through actual observation. The risk in doing otherwise is that you may spend a lot of time trying to make code run faster with no measurable effect on your program while in the meantime ignoring the

---

[*] Tony Hoare is credited with originating the quote "Premature optimization is the root of all evil," and Donald Knuth has widely popularized that saying. We're not prepared to go quite *that* far.

program's actual performance bottlenecks. Consequently, our second rule of performance:

> Make performance testing a regular part of the development cycle.

In an ideal situation, coding would go through a cycle shown in Figure 14-1. Regular profiling of the application isolates those areas of the code that need optimization, increasing the productivity of developers.

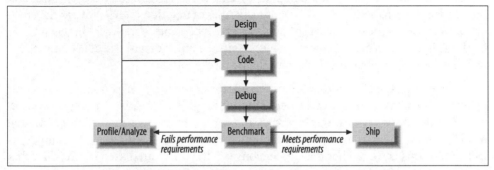

*Figure 14-1. The performance-aware development cycle*

## Measuring Java Performance

Measuring performance of a Java program presents certain difficulties, particularly when attempting to measure isolated tasks (as we do in this chapter). If you're interested in how quickly a program can perform a fixed set of tasks, measurement is easy since the elapsed time to run the program is an adequate answer.

If you're interested in measuring the performance of a long-running Java program (and in particular, a Java server application), there are certain things you must account for. Java virtual machines perform just-in-time compilation of the Java bytecodes that make up an application. This means that the longer an application runs, the more efficient the code becomes: more of it becomes compiled, more methods become inlined, more loops become unrolled, and so on.

Measuring performance in this situation requires a ramp-up time that allows the compiler a chance to perform a significant part of its optimizations. In truth, the optimizations performed by the compiler are never completely over; performance of a Java program continually improves. However, the bulk of the optimizations are performed during the first few minutes of the program, so waiting just a short time before timing performance is usually sufficient.

If you're writing a benchmark to test performance of a particular operation, you must take this into account. Your synthetic benchmark should run through the major loops of your application a few thousand times to make sure that the code is well-optimized before timing it.

A second complication is introduced by Java's garbage collector. Once again, if you're timing an actual task, the effect of the garbage collector doesn't matter: the garbage collector takes whatever time it takes as the task runs. But if you're trying to write a microbenchmark and time discrete operations, any time the garbage collector runs, it will throw off your timing.

In our tests (available in the online source), we execute certain methods a large number of times. We warm up the compiler by executing the method 10,000 times and then time executing the method for a large number of iterations. This reduces the effect of compilation on the test. We also call the System.gc( ) and System.runFinalization( ) methods in between measurements, which limits the effect of garbage collection to that which is directly attributable to the method being executed.

Many platform-specific factors affect the performance of Java programs. Different operating systems show different performance for thread creation and synchronization. Optimizations within the Java virtual machine itself mean that different virtual machine implementations show different behavior. Faster chips affect timings as well. All of this is to say that the conclusions we draw here are based on the data that we produced on the given platforms, but your mileage may vary. This is yet another reason why performing your own measurements is so important.

The tests reported in this chapter were run with the beta version of J2SE 5.0 on machines with the following CPUs and memory:

| CPUs | Java virtual machine arguments | Operating system |
|---|---|---|
| Sun Microsystems UltraSPARC III Four CPUs, 750 MHz | -server -Xms3500m -Xmx3500m | Solaris 9 Operating Environment |
| Intel Xeon Two CPUs, 1400 MHz | -server -Xmn1800m -Xms1800m | Red Hat Linux Advanced Server 3.0 |
| Intel Xeon Two CPUs, 3060 MHz | -server -Xmn1600m -Xms1600m | Microsoft Windows Server 2003 |

Differences in heap size reflect the underlying support of the operating system for the largest heap possible (which helps with the garbage collection issue). While we quote numbers for specific tests, it's best to consider them in terms of order-of-magnitude approximations (rather than, for example, concluding that it takes exactly 184.5 nanoseconds to perform a synchronization operation on an UltraSPARC III CPU).

# Synchronized Collections

Let's look into some synchronization issues, starting with a question. When should you use an unsynchronized collection class? We're going to argue that the times when you need to do that are very rare indeed.

To reach this conclusion, we looked at the performance of adding objects to four kinds of lists: vectors, array lists, synchronized array lists, and a modified vector class from which we removed synchronization. Specifically, we're testing this method:

```java
public void doTest(List l) {
    Integer n = new Integer(0);
    for (int i = 0; i < nLoops; i++)
        l.add(n);
}
```

For a sufficiently large value of nLoops, taking the time to execute this method when the list is synchronized, subtracting the time required to execute the method when the list is unsynchronized, and dividing by nLoops gives us a fair approximation of the time required to synchronized the add( ) method (and in general, to obtain an uncontended synchronization lock).

Although the Vector and ArrayList classes are conceptually similar, their implementation differs enough that they are not comparable for this test. Therefore, we compare the Vector class to a modified version of that class, and we compare the ArrayList class to the class returned from the Collections.synchronizedCollection( ) method when given an array class. In both cases, the average time difference is about the same and is shown in Table 14-1.

*Table 14-1. Time difference of synchronized versus unsynchronized method invocations*

| Test platform | Synchronized versus unsynchronized methods: time difference per method invocation |
| --- | --- |
| SPARC/Solaris | 185 nanoseconds |
| Intel/Linux | 65 nanoseconds |
| Intel/Windows | 92 nanoseconds |

This is a single-threaded test, of course, since access to an array list (or our modified vector class) is not threadsafe. So access to the synchronized methods of the Vector class is always uncontended. Modern virtual machines (starting with Sun's HotSpot implementation for JDK 1.2, and improving after that) are written so that uncontended lock acquisition is very fast indeed: depending on the speed of the underlying CPU, as little as 65 nanoseconds.

The performance of contended locks is much different (as we'll see in the next section). But if you're planning to use an unsynchronized collection class, access to the synchronization lock is necessarily uncontended.

If you really know that a particular data structure won't be accessed by more than one thread, you can save a few nanoseconds and use an unsynchronized one. But in general, there's no real penalty for using a synchronized collection class, and doing so can often prevent inadvertent race conditions from plaguing your program. For

## Atomic Variables and Contended Synchronization

Next, let's look at the difference between using classes in the java.util.concurrent. atomic package versus regular synchronization. We mentioned in Chapter 5 that using an atomic variable is one way in which synchronization can be avoided. We'll see the benefits of doing that in this section. Unlike our last test, we'll look at contended locks (since we already know that uncontended locks suffer little performance penalty).

Atomic variables offer advantages other than performance: they neatly encapsulate operations, and they prevent inadvertent access to data from unsynchronized code. So quite apart from any performance benefit that they may or may not offer, their use offers important contributions from a developer's point of view.

For this test, we gauge the performance of incrementing an integer variable. In one case, we write a synchronized method that increments the integer; in the second case, we call the AtomicInteger.getAndIncreent() method. We test access to these methods from a single thread and from multiple threads simultaneously, obtaining the results in Table 14-2.

*Table 14-2. Time difference between using atomic variables versus synchronized methods*

| | Time difference between atomic variables and synchronized methods | | |
| --- | --- | --- | --- |
| **Test platform** | **One thread** | **Two threads** | **Eight threads** |
| SPARC/Solaris | 92 nanoseconds | 1400 nanoseconds | 650 nanoseconds |
| Intel/Linux | 20 nanoseconds | 700 nanoseconds | 400 nanoseconds |
| Intel/Windows | 60 nanoseconds | 3200 nanoseconds | 5800 nanoseconds |

When there is only one thread running, the locks are uncontended, and we get similar results as our last example: there is a very, very slight benefit to using an atomic variable. When there are two threads, contention for the lock is introduced. Now the difference becomes much greater: as much as three microseconds. That's a significant difference for many programs.

Much more interesting is what happens when many threads are contending for the lock (or the atomic variable). Now the difference has been cut in half on Unix systems. This is because the atomic variable methods loop until they achieve the desired result (as we saw in our examples in Chapter 5).

It's also interesting to note that this behavior is not observed on Windows Server 2003. That's more a reflection of the greatly increased cost of the contention for the synchronized lock on this platform. With eight threads contending for the single lock, the increase in the operating system time to service the lock contention is much greater than the increase in time spent within the loops within the class using atomic variables. In both tests, the Windows Server 2003 platform spends a great deal more time dealing with eight threads than two threads, but the proportion of time favors using atomic variables.

If profiles of your program show a great deal of time spent waiting for particular locks, refactoring the code to use atomic variables is, if possible, a good solution for removing that bottleneck. But as we saw in Chapter 5, writing a class to use multiple atomic variables can be complex; it may not be worth the effort unless you know that you're facing a performance bottleneck.

## The ConcurrentHashMap Class

An interesting case arises with the ConcurrentHashMap class, which allows threads to access a hashtable concurrently yet still provides thread-safety. Comparing operations that insert and retrieve values from a hashtable and a concurrent hashmap, we see the differences in Table 14-3.

*Table 14-3. Time difference between ConcurrentHashMap and Hashtable*

| | Time difference between ConcurrentHashMap and Hashtable | | |
| Test platform | One thread | Two threads | Eight threads |
| --- | --- | --- | --- |
| SPARC/Solaris | 100 nanoseconds | 3500 nanoseconds | 2000 nanoseconds |
| Intel/Linux | −200 nanoseconds | 1500 nanoseconds | 1100 nanoseconds |
| Intel/Windows | −25 nanoseconds | 6000 nanoseconds | 13,000 nanoseconds |

In the uncontended case (where you could use a HashMap rather than a Hashtable, though we test only the latter case), there is little to no difference between implementations. In fact, as CPUs get faster, the simpler implementation of the Hashtable class allows it to perform slightly better.

As we add contention, the Hashtable class pays the predictable penalty, and now the concurrent hashmap is at least 1.5 microseconds faster (and more on other platforms). Because of the "optimistic" nature of the concurrent hashmap, the advantage is mitigated somewhat as we add more contention (except on Windows Server 2003 again, where the added lock contention in the operating system overwhelms the added code executed by the concurrent hashmap).

# Thread Creation and Thread Pools

The final performance aspect we'll discuss is thread creation and the use of thread pools. A common assumption is that creating a thread is an expensive operation and that this should be avoided by using a thread pool whenever possible. Is that actually a good idea?

To reiterate one of the points we make in Chapter 10: one of the determining factors in using a thread pool is the design of your program. If the design of your program more easily lends itself to starting new threads, you should do that; if it more easily lends itself to creating tasks and feeding them to an executor, you should do that. And the perceived performance of a program can often be improved by using a thread pool to throttle the number of active threads on a machine.

That said, is it really more efficient to use a thread pool than to spawn a new thread? The answer is yes, but not always to an extent that it affects your program. To reach this conclusion, we have written a method that increments the value of an atomic integer. We run this method three different ways: in a simple loop, in a `Runnable` object feeding to a thread pool, and in a `Runnable` object being used to create a new thread. Subtracting the time required to execute the method in a loop from the time required to execute the method in a thread pool (or a new thread) allows us to obtain the values shown in Table 14-4.

*Table 14-4. Time difference between thread creation and thread pool*

| Test platform | Time difference between thread creation and thread pool |
| --- | --- |
| SPARC/Solaris | 400 microseconds |
| Intel/Linux | 175 microseconds |
| Intel/Windows | 190 microseconds |

A few hundred microseconds is nothing to sneeze at in computer time. In an application server, you might reasonably expect a quick answer from the server: maybe something in a few microseconds. Starting a thread for those requests would indeed cause a profound difference in the application response time.

In many programs this additional overhead does not make a big difference. On our Solaris platform, this test took 38.5 seconds to run and created 100,000 threads compared to .1 seconds to run with a thread pool: almost 400 times longer.

On the other hand, our program doesn't do anything interesting at all. If the logic of our target method took 20 milliseconds, creating threads for the tasks would take only 2% longer. At some point, the added time to create the threads becomes lost in the actual calculation time.

The moral of the story is if you need to spawn a few threads, don't sweat it. If you create a lot of threads, look at your program profiles and response times to see if a thread pool makes sense. But overall, use what makes sense for your program design.

# Summary

Performance is an overriding concern for many developers, and performance of thread-related constructs occupies a prominent position in the mind of the performance-oriented Java developer. In this chapter, we examined the basic performance of simple thread constructs: thread creation and synchronization. We found that thread creation is cheap enough so that it doesn't matter in many cases, that there's no reason to use an unsynchronized collection instead of a synchronized one, and that contended locks can become very expensive. The latter case can sometimes be avoided by using atomic variables for data access.

It's important to measure your particular program to see if these issues affect it. A development cycle that includes frequent performance measurements can help you narrow down the performance bottlenecks of your program and focus your efforts on the more important spots of the program.

## Example Classes

The online examples have our test code and can be run with the following classes or Ant targets:

| Description | Main Java class | Ant target |
| --- | --- | --- |
| Synchronized Collection Test | javathreads.examples.ch14.CollectionTest nLoops | ch14-ex1 |
| Atomic Test | javathreads.examples.ch14.AtomicTest nLoops nThreads | ch14-ex2 |
| Hashtable Test | javathreads.examples.ch14.HashTest nLoops nThreads | ch14-ex3 |
| Thread Creation Test | javathreads.examples.ch14.CreateTest nLoops | ch14-ex4 |

The Ant targets accept the following properties:

```
<property name="nLoops" value="100000"/>
<property name="nThreads" value="10"/>
```

# CHAPTER 15

# Parallelizing Loops for Multiprocessor Machines

In previous chapters, we examined threading as a technique that allows us to simplify programming: we used threading to achieve asynchronous behavior and perform independent tasks. Although we discussed how threads are scheduled on machines with multiple processors, by and large the techniques that we've shown so far are not affected by a machine with multiple processors nor do they exploit the number of processors on a machine to make the program run faster.

Multithreaded programs have a special bond with multiprocessor systems. The separation of threads provides a clear and simple separation for the multiprocessor machine. Since the operating system can place different threads on different processors, the program runs faster.

In this chapter, we'll look at how to parallelize Java programs so that they run faster on a machine with multiple CPUs. The processes that we examine are beneficial not only to newly developed Java programs but also to existing Java programs that have a CPU-intensive loop, allowing us to improve the performance of those programs on a multiprocessor system.

*How does the Java threading system behave in a multiprocessor system?* There are no conceptual differences between a program running on a machine with one processor and a machine with two or more processors; threads behave exactly the same in either case. The real difference is that the threads actually do execute simultaneously. In Chapter 2, we discussed how the operating system switches between the list of instructions for certain threads and how that switching gave the illusion of simultaneity. On a multiprocessor system, the simultaneity is real.

For Java developers, threaded code running on multiple processors means that race conditions that happen very infrequently on a single-processor system are much more likely to occur. Hopefully, you have by now learned to write threadsafe programs. Testing those programs on a multiprocessor machine is one good way to be more confident in the results.

# Parallelizing a Single-Threaded Program

Without redesigning a program, the best area to parallelize—that is, the area in which to introduce multiple threads to increase the program's performance—is where the program is CPU-bound. After all, it doesn't make sense to bring in more processors if the first processor cannot stay busy. In many of the cases where the process is CPU-bound—that is, the process is using all of the computer processors' cycles while not using the disks or the network at full capacity—the program's speed increases with the addition of more processors. The process could be involved in a long mathematical calculation or, more likely, in large iterations of shorter mathematical calculations. Furthermore, these calculations probably involve a large control loop or even a large number of loops inside loops. These are the types of common algorithms that we examine here. Consider the following calculation:

```
package javathreads.examples.ch15.example1;

public class SinTable {
    private float lookupValues[] = null;

    public synchronized float[] getValues() {
        if (lookupValues == null) {
            lookupValues = new float [360 * 100];
            for (int i = 0; i < (360 * 100); i++) {
                float sinValue = (float)Math.sin(
                                    (i % 360)*Math.PI/180.0);
                lookupValues[i] = sinValue * (float)i / 180.0f;
            }
        }
        return lookupValues;
    }
}
```

This code is the basis of our examples in the rest of this chapter. A single thread, and therefore a single processor, executes the loop as specified in the code and stores the results in the lookupValues array. Assuming that the calculation of the sinValue variable is time-consuming, the whole loop may take a long time to execute. In some cases, this is acceptable. However, on a 12-processor computer without any other programs running, only one CPU is working while the other 11 are sitting idle. Considering the cost of a 12-processor machine, this is not acceptable.

Before we get started, let's define some terminology. The variable sinValue has a few special properties. Obviously, it exists only for the duration of the loop. It is a temporary variable used to aid the calculation of the lookup table. It does not carry a value in one iteration of the loop that is used in another iteration of the loop, and the value of the variable is reassigned in the next iteration. We define sinValue as a *loop-private variable*, that is, a variable that is initialized, calculated, and used entirely in a single iteration of the loop.

Furthermore, we can state that the index variable i is also a loop-private variable: it is also used completely in an iteration of the loop. It can be considered a special type of loop-private variable. Since it is never changed during an iteration and is directly tied to the iteration index, we can actually treat it as a constant during the iteration of a loop. However, for now, simply considering it as a loop-private variable is good enough.

We may try to break the parts of this loop among many threads as follows:

```
package javathreads.examples.ch15.example2;

public class SinTable implements Runnable {
    private class SinTableRange {
        public int start, end;
    }

    private float lookupValues[];
    private Thread lookupThreads[];
    private int startLoop, endLoop, curLoop, numThreads;

    public SinTable() {
        lookupValues = new float [360 * 100];
        lookupThreads = new Thread[12];
        startLoop = curLoop = 0;
        endLoop = (360 * 100);
        numThreads = 12;
    }

    private synchronized SinTableRange loopGetRange() {
        if (curLoop >= endLoop)
            return null;
```

```
        SinTableRange ret = new SinTableRange();
        ret.start = curLoop;
        curLoop += (endLoop-startLoop)/numThreads+1;
        ret.end = (curLoop<endLoop)?curLoop:endLoop;
        return ret;
    }

    private void loopDoRange(int start, int end) {
        for (int i = start; i < end; i += 1) {
            float sinValue = (float)Math.sin((i % 360)*Math.PI/180.0);
            lookupValues[i] = sinValue * (float)i / 180.0f;
        }
    }

    public void run() {
        SinTableRange str;
        while ((str = loopGetRange()) != null) {
            loopDoRange(str.start, str.end);
        }
    }

    public float[] getValues() {
        for (int i = 0; i < numThreads; i++) {
            lookupThreads[i] = new Thread(this);
            lookupThreads[i].start();
        }
        for (int i = 0; i < numThreads; i++) {
            try {
                lookupThreads[i].join();
            } catch (InterruptedException iex) {}
        }
        return lookupValues;
    }
}
```

The code in this new version is functionally the same as the previous version, albeit
with many modifications to its logic. First, instead of a loop that does the calculation, we now have a loop that starts off 12 (numThreads) different worker threads and
provides each worker thread with different parts of the mathematical loop to calculate. The original mathematical calculation is moved to a new method, loopDoRange().
In this method, the loop has been modified to work on only part of the lookup table
instead of the whole table. Each different thread is responsible for calculating only its
portion of the table. Each thread must call the loopGetRange() method to determine
which portion it must calculate. The thread that started the 12 worker threads then
simply waits for all 12 worker threads to finish. Since the long calculation is now
accomplished by 12 threads instead of by a single thread, it is now possible for a
multiprocessor-based operating system to place the different threads on different
processors.

The calculation works for a number of reasons. First, the loop index variable i and
the sinValue variable, which were originally classified as loop private, are now stack

variables in each worker thread. The loopDoRange( ) method uses different copies of these two variables in each thread executing the loop. This means that each of the 12 worker threads has its own copy of these variables while completing its portion of the calculation.

Second, although the lookupTable array is not loop private, the individual members of the array can be considered loop private. Each individual member of the array is accessed only in a particular iteration. There is no race condition because each iteration affects one and only one member of the array, and although the different worker threads handle many iterations of the loop, no single iteration is handled by more than one thread.

The only synchronization we need is in the assignment of the different ranges. To prevent the worker threads from stepping on each other during this assignment, the loopGetRange( ) method is synchronized. In this example, since the loop is partitioned into only 12 ranges, there is little contention for this lock.

The code for this new version is more complicated than our first version. This new code now has to start and track 12 separate threads. The worker threads had to be modified to handle parts of the loop whose ranges they have to determine. Although very little synchronization is needed in this case, we could easily have had a complicated requirement for synchronization depending on the algorithm used in the mathematical calculation.

Given the complexity we introduced to handle this simple loop, it may become too hard to handle more complex loops. To help with this complexity, we'll move all the logic related to loop management into a separate class. We can then implement the loop by simply using the services provided by this class:

```
package javathreads.examples.ch15;

public class LoopHandler implements Runnable {
    protected class LoopRange {
        public int start, end;
    }
    protected Thread lookupThreads[];
    protected int startLoop, endLoop, curLoop, numThreads;

    public LoopHandler(int start, int end, int threads) {
        startLoop = curLoop = start;
        endLoop = end;
        numThreads = threads;
        lookupThreads = new Thread[numThreads];
    }

    protected synchronized LoopRange loopGetRange() {
        if (curLoop >= endLoop)
            return null;
        LoopRange ret = new LoopRange();
        ret.start = curLoop;
```

```
                curLoop += (endLoop-startLoop)/numThreads+1;
                ret.end = (curLoop<endLoop) ? curLoop : endLoop;
                return ret;
            }

            public void loopDoRange(int start, int end) {
            }

            public void loopProcess() {
                for (int i = 0; i < numThreads; i++) {
                    lookupThreads[i] = new Thread(this);
                    lookupThreads[i].start();
                }
                for (int i = 0; i < numThreads; i++) {
                    try {
                        lookupThreads[i].join();
                        lookupThreads[i] = null;
                    } catch (InterruptedException iex) {}
                }
            }

            public void run() {
                LoopRange str;
                while ((str = loopGetRange()) != null) {
                    loopDoRange(str.start, str.end);
                }
            }
        }
```

In our new `LoopHandler` class, we have implemented the logic that we applied in our `SinTable` class. The logic of creating, tracking, and joining back with the original thread has been moved to the newly created `loopProcess()` method. The logic of determining the ranges and processing the loop—originally coded in the `run()` and `loopGetRange()` methods of the `SinTable` class—remains nearly unchanged. The loop handler has also been modified to handle more generic loops and has a constructor that assigns the start of the loop, the end of the loop, and the number of threads. Just as in our earlier example, the algorithm calls the `loopDoRange()` method to handle the processing. However, in this case, the `LoopHandler` class has an empty implementation for this method.

Now our implementation of the `SinTable` class is much simpler:

```
package javathreads.examples.ch15.example3;

import javathreads.examples.ch15.*;

public class SinTable extends LoopHandler {
    private float lookupValues[];

    public SinTable() {
        super(0, 360*100, 12);
        lookupValues = new float [360 * 100];
    }
```

```
public void loopDoRange(int start, int end) {
    for (int i = start; i < end; i++) {
        float sinValue = (float)Math.sin((i % 360)*Math.PI/180.0);
        lookupValues[i] = sinValue * (float)i / 180.0f;
    }
}

public float[] getValues() {
    loopProcess();
    return lookupValues;
}
}
```

In this case, we simply configure the ranges needed by the loop handler, provide the logic of the loop in the loopDoRange( ) method, and call the loopProcess( ) method to process the loop in a multithreaded fashion. While this is still more complicated than the first SinTable class implementation, it is now much more manageable and less complex than the previous implementation.

## Loop Scheduling and Load Balancing

We define the process of distributing the iterations of the loop to the individual threads as loop scheduling. In our LoopHandler class, this is handled by the loopGetRange( ) method. To maximize processor usage, we should distribute the work to the threads as evenly as possible, with the least amount of overhead in determining this distribution. This is defined as load balancing.

The basic loop-scheduling types at our disposal include static or chunk scheduling, self-scheduling, guided self-scheduling, and user-defined scheduling.

### Static or chunk scheduling

Under static scheduling, each thread is assigned an equal number of iterations that depends on the number of threads available. If 1000 loop iterations are to be distributed and 10 threads are assigned to the task, each thread is assigned 100 iterations of the loop. This is the algorithm that is used by the LoopHandler class. The algorithm also adds 1 to the size to make sure that the distribution is rounded up. Otherwise, there might be an iteration left over and a worker thread would have to perform that single iteration after already performing the original chunk.

The problem with this algorithm is that it assumes that each iteration of the loop takes the same amount of time. If this is not true, one of the threads takes more time than the other threads to complete. Since all the work is divided up at the beginning of the loop, the other threads are idle while the final iterations are completed by the last remaining thread.

## Self-scheduling

In self-scheduling, each worker thread grabs a small chunk of the iterations to execute. After completion of its assigned range, it grabs another small chunk. If 1000 loop iterations are to be distributed and 10 threads are assigned to the task, each worker thread works on a small chunk—e.g., 20—until all 1000 iterations are completed.

As with static scheduling, the different worker threads may not complete at the same time. However, since the chunks are small in the self-scheduling model, the idle time of the threads at the end of the process is also small. To make this idle time even smaller, we can make the individual chunks smaller. However, there is an overhead in obtaining the ranges to execute; this overhead increases as the chunks get smaller.

Here's an implementation of this model:

```
package javathreads.examples.ch15;

public class SelfLoopHandler extends PoolLoopHandler {
    protected int groupSize;

    public SelfLoopHandler(int start, int end, int size, int threads) {
        super(start, end, threads);
        groupSize = size;
    }

    protected synchronized LoopRange loopGetRange() {
        if (curLoop >= endLoop)
            return null;
        LoopRange ret = new LoopRange();
        ret.start = curLoop;
        curLoop += groupSize;
        ret.end = (curLoop<endLoop)?curLoop:endLoop;
        return ret;
    }
}
```

Implementation of a self-scheduling loop handler is straightforward. Our current LoopHandler class already has the logic of working until the loop completes. We simply need to modify the constructor to handle the chunk size requested and modify the loopGetRange() method to return this fixed chunk size. In our implementation of the self-scheduler, we simply subclass from the original loop handler and implement only the changes.*

---

* Note that we've started extending the PoolLoopHandler class, which is functionally equivalent to the LoopHandler class. We'll discuss this change later in the chapter.

## Guided self-scheduling

Guided self-scheduling is a compromise between the static scheduler and the self-scheduler. In the beginning, the guided scheduler grabs a large number of iterations of the loop, which becomes progressively smaller near the end of the loop. The guided self-scheduler also uses a minimum chunk size. Thus, it basically behaves like a static scheduler that slowly becomes a self-scheduler.

If 1000 iterations in the loop are to be distributed and 10 threads are assigned to the task, the first worker thread gets one-tenth of the work—100 iterations. The second thread gets one-tenth of the remaining work—90 iterations. This slowly gets smaller and smaller until the minimum—e.g., 10—is assigned; the minimum is assigned until all 1000 iterations are completed.

This algorithm seems to have the fewest problems. Unlike the self-scheduler, the extra overhead appears only at the end of the loop. And unless the individual iterations have drastically different execution periods from the longer-term iterations at the beginning, it doesn't have the problems that the static scheduler has.

Here's how to implement guided self-scheduling:

```
package javathreads.examples.ch15;

public class GuidedLoopHandler extends PoolLoopHandler {
    protected int minSize;

    public GuidedLoopHandler(int start, int end, int min, int threads){
        super(start, end, threads);
        minSize = min;
    }

    protected synchronized LoopRange loopGetRange() {
        if (curLoop >= endLoop)
            return null;
        LoopRange ret = new LoopRange();
        ret.start = curLoop;
        int sizeLoop = (endLoop-curLoop)/numThreads;
        curLoop += (sizeLoop>minSize)?sizeLoop:minSize;
        ret.end = (curLoop<endLoop)?curLoop:endLoop;
        return ret;
    }
}
```

Implementation of a guided self-scheduling loop handler is also straightforward. We simply need to modify the constructor to handle the minimum size required, and modify the loopGetRange( ) method to return a portion of the remaining loop. In our implementation of the guided self-scheduler, we also subclass the original loop handler and implement only the changes.

### User-defined scheduling

The implementation of the self-scheduler and the guided self-scheduler is simple for a reason: it was designed to be so. The original loop handler was designed to be subclassed so that the scheduler algorithm could be modified. As good as the implementation of the guided self-scheduler may be, it is still designed for a generic loop. In some cases, one scheduler works better than another. However, if enough information concerning the loop is known and the effort is large enough, it may justify the implementation of yet another scheduler. This entails figuring out the appropriate logic and coding a new loopGetRange( ) method.

To use any of these other algorithms in our SinTable class, we simply subclass from the appropriate handler class and modify our constructor to pass the minimum chunk size.

## Variable Classifications

In the implementation of the SinTable class, we classify the variables used in the original unthreaded loop as loop-private variables, but other variable classifications exist. The reason for classifying variables at all is that different types of variables require different types of handling within and between threads. Many loops have a data dependency that occurs between iterations. By classifying the variables, we are able to correctly update and modify them without any race conditions. Different types of variable classifications can be determined by their usage, and these classifications determine how they are to be implemented or treated in the multithreaded loop handler.

### Loop-private variables

A loop-private variable is a variable that does not pass its value from one iteration of the loop to another. It can actually be a variable that is declared in the loop itself, and it can also be an instance or publicly accessed variable that is accessed by only one iteration of the loop. This is the case with the lookupValues array variable, where each member of the array is accessed only by one iteration of the loop. Although the whole array is not loop private to any iteration, specific members are loop private to specific iterations.

As shown with the SinTable class, loop-private variables are often handled with a local copy of the variable in each thread. Since each thread has a copy, no interference between the threads is possible. In the case of the lookupValues array, the threads will respect the privacy of the other threads by accessing only the loop-private portions of the array.

### Read-only variables

Read-only variables are variables where values do not change during the execution of the loop. They can be true constants or simply variables that are initialized and do not change until after the loop is processed.

Read-only variables require no special treatment. The worker threads do not need to have their own copies of the variables, and access to them does not require synchronization of any type.

### Storeback variables

Storeback variables are basically loop-private variables that are needed after the loop has been completed. For example, suppose that the `lookupValues` array requires some extra processing after the loop is finished:

```
public float[] getValues( ) {
    if (lookupValues == null) {
        float sinValue = 0;
        lookupValues = new float [360 * 100];
        for (int i = 0; i < (360*100); i++) {
            sinValue = (float)Math.sin((i % 360)*Math.PI/180.0);
            lookupValues[i] = sinValue * (float)i / 180.0f;
        }
        lookupValues[0] += sinValue;
    }
    return lookupValues;
}
```

In this slightly modified version of the `SinTable` loop, both the `sinValue` variable and the individual members of the `lookupValues` array are still loop-private variables. These two variables have no data dependency in different iterations of the loop. However, in this case the `sinValue` variable is also a storeback variable. Since the variable is important after the loop has completed, it must be set to the value it would have had if the loop had run in the correct order. The members of the `lookupValues` array were always considered as storeback variables, but since no individual copies were kept, there was little need to make this extra distinction.

Here's how we can handle the storeback variable:

```
package javathreads.examples.ch15.example4;

import javathreads.examples.ch15.*;

public class SinTable extends GuidedLoopHandler {
    private float lookupValues[];
    private float sinValue;

    public SinTable( ) {
        super(0, 360*100, 100, 12);
        lookupValues = new float [360 * 100];
    }
```

```
public void loopDoRange(int start, int end) {
    float sinValue = 0;
    for (int i = start; i < end; i++) {
        sinValue = (float)Math.sin((i % 360)*Math.PI/180.0);
        lookupValues[i] = sinValue * (float)i / 180.0f;
    }
    if (end == endLoop)
        this.sinValue = sinValue;
}

public float[] getValues() {
    loopProcess();
    lookupValues[0] += sinValue;
    return lookupValues;
}
}
```

The sinValue variable is still treated as a loop-private variable. However, since this variable is really a storeback variable, we need to store the "last" value of this variable. Since the algorithm is now executed in a multithreaded manner, the last iteration is not necessarily the last value assigned to the variable by a thread.

A thread must check that it has executed the last chunk of the loop before copying the value of its loop-private copy to the global copy. Also note that no synchronization is necessary. Since only the last iteration is copied, only one thread is executing the code, and no race condition is possible.

### Reduction variables

Obviously, it is not possible to make every variable a loop-private variable since there are cases where real data dependencies exist between different iterations of the loop. Because of these data dependencies, different threads executing different iterations might interfere with each other during execution. We call these types of variables *shared variables* since they are shared between iterations of the loop.

Shared variables have many problems. The first is the race conditions that exist when different threads access the variable simultaneously. The second is that the value of a variable may depend on the order in which it is processed. In the first case, we can simply use synchronization techniques to prevent the race conditions from existing. The second case poses a much greater problem.

*However, what if the order does not matter?* We will be able to process the loop in any order and will simply have to synchronize access to the shared variable. For example, assume that we also need to calculate the sum of our SinTable:

```
public float[] getValues() {
    for (int i = 0; i < (360*100); i++) {
        sinValue = (float)Math.sin((i % 360)*Math.PI/180.0);
        lookupValues[i] = sinValue * (float)i / 180.0f;
```

```
        sumValue += lookupValues[i];
    }
    return lookupValues;
}
```

In this case, the sumValue variable is clearly not a loop-private variable. The value of sumValue is passed from one iteration to another, and the correct result requires this dependency to exist. However, the sumValue variable is useful only after the loop completes. The iterations simply add to the running total—subtotals or other order-based requirements are not necessary. Furthermore, addition itself is order-independent: it is possible to add a bunch of numbers in any order, and the final result is the same.

---

### Sometimes Order Does Matter

In the examples of this section, we assume that we can perform the addition in any order that we like. Since addition is associative, this is supposed to work.

On a computer, however, addition is not necessarily associative. Because of the internal mechanism that the computer uses to store numbers of infinite precision in a fixed number of bits, some rounding error occurs in every mathematical calculation. Normally, these errors are small enough that we don't need to worry about them, and they often cancel each other out. But in many cases the propagation of this error leads to vastly different results when the order of the operations is changed.

If you're performing sensitive numerical analysis, be aware that the tricks of this section may lead to unacceptable error propagation and incorrect answers.

---

The sumValue variable is a reduction variable. It must still be shared among the threads, but since order does not matter, this sharing only requires synchronization to prevent race conditions:

```
package javathreads.examples.ch15.example5;

import javathreads.examples.ch15.*;

public class SinTable extends GuidedLoopHandler {
    private float lookupValues[];
    public float sumValue;

    public SinTable() {
        super(0, 360*100, 100, 12);
        lookupValues = new float [360 * 100];
    }

    public void loopDoRange(int start, int end) {
        float sinValue = 0;
        for (int i = start; i < end; i++) {
```

```
            sinValue = (float)Math.sin((i % 360)*Math.PI/180.0);
            lookupValues[i] = sinValue * (float)i / 180.0f;
            synchronized (this) {
                sumValue += lookupValues[i];
            }
        }
    }

    public float[] getValues() {
        loopProcess();
        return lookupValues;
    }
}
```

Race conditions in this example are prevented by using the synchronization lock of the SinTable instance. If we have many reduction variables that are not dependent on each other and we cannot store them all at the same time, it might be a better idea to have separate synchronization locks—or explicit instances of Lock interfaces—for each reduction variable.

Furthermore, we are synchronizing with each iteration of the loop. This is not very efficient. It is better to assign the value to loop-private variables and only synchronize the final summed value of the range to the reduction variable. By doing this, we are removing most of the need for synchronization, which can drastically add to the parallelization of the threads:

```
package javathreads.examples.ch15.example6;

import javathreads.examples.ch15.*;

public class SinTable extends GuidedLoopHandler {
    private float lookupValues[];
    public float sumValue;

    public SinTable() {
        super(0, 360*100, 100, 12);
        lookupValues = new float [360 * 100];
    }

    public void loopDoRange(int start, int end) {
        float sinValue = 0.0f;
        float sumValue = 0.0f;
        for (int i = start; i < end; i++) {
            sinValue = (float)Math.sin((i % 360)*Math.PI/180.0);
            lookupValues[i] = sinValue * (float)i / 180.0f;
            sumValue += lookupValues[i];
        }
        synchronized (this) {
            this.sumValue += sumValue;
        }
    }
```

```
public float[] getValues() {
    loopProcess();
    System.out.println(sumValue);
    return lookupValues;
}
}
```

In this new example, we are doing a two-stage reduction of the values. We are reducing the value of each iteration to the local copy of the sumValue variable, and then we are reducing this local copy to the actual reduction variable. Since the local copy of the sumValue variable is loop private, synchronization is not necessary. Synchronization is still necessary when adding to the reduction variable. However, this is now done once per range instead of once per iteration.

A reduction variable is a good candidate for an atomic variable. You could use the AtomicDouble class from Chapter 5 to store the sumValue variable in this example. We'll test this later in the chapter, and you can consult the online source code to see exactly how that works.

All reduction variables are storeback variables. There is no need to have special storeback handling logic for reduction variables.

## Shared variables

Originally, all variables in the loop are shared variables since all variables can be accessed by all the threads that are executing the loop. As we parallelize the loop, we can quickly classify the shared variables that are also read-only variables. We can also reclassify those variables that are loop-private variables. Of the remaining shared variables, it may be possible either to convert them to loop-private variables or to classify them as reduction variables.

Unfortunately, in some cases a shared variable cannot be classified as anything but a shared variable, and this is where our technique fails to work. As much as we would like to convert any loop to run in a multithreaded environment, not all algorithms can be redesigned to run in a parallel environment.

The other problem with shared variables is the side effect. For example, if we need to save each of the subtotals of the sumValue variable, it cannot be treated as a reduction variable since the changes in the variable are also important. If we have to print the subtotals during the loop, not only will the intermediate results be out of order, but the intermediate results will be different.

When variable classification is not enough for parallelization, we have other techniques that can help. They may not solve every case, but with experience, more and more loops can be converted to run in a multithreaded environment.

# Loop Analysis and Transformations

To assist our parallelizing techniques, we can analyze the algorithms of the loop itself instead of just analyzing the variables in the loop. In the majority of the cases, there is little we can do without redesigning the algorithm, but in a few situations we can quickly modify the code without a complete redesign. By implementing simple transformations on the original code, we may be able to use the techniques discussed so far to thread the loop.

## Loop distribution

In many cases, only a small portion of a large complex loop contains code that must be executed sequentially. It may be possible to separate the large complex loop into two separate loops. Once the complex loop is separated into two loops—one loop containing the code that can be parallelized, the other containing the sequential code—we can then parallelize a portion of the original loop. We may even be able to run the sequential loop in parallel with the loop that can be threaded.

Returning to our SinTable example, let's assume that we need to generate a running subtotal in addition to a total:

```
public float[] getValues( ) {
    for (int i = 0; i < (360*100); i++) {
        sinValue = (float)Math.sin((i % 360)*Math.PI/180.0);
        lookupValues[i] = sinValue * (float)i / 180.0f;
        if (i == 0) {
            sumValues[0] = lookupValues[0];
        } else {
            sumValues[i] = lookupValues[i] + lookupValues[i-1];
        }
    }
    return lookupValues;
}
```

The sumValues array variable is definitely a shared variable. The members of the sumValues variable are also shared in that some of them are accessed by two different threads. Furthermore, the order matters. It is not possible for one thread to start a chunk before the thread that is working on the previous chunk is finished.

We can solve that problem like this:

```
package javathreads.examples.ch15.example7;

import javathreads.examples.ch15.*;

public class SinTable extends GuidedLoopHandler {
    private float lookupValues[];
    public float sumValues[];

    public SinTable( ) {
        super(0, 360*100, 100, 12);
```

```
        lookupValues = new float [360 * 100];
        sumValues = new float [360 * 100];
    }

    public void loopDoRange(int start, int end) {
        float sinValue = 0.0f;
        for (int i = start; i < end; i++) {
            sinValue = (float)Math.sin((i % 360)*Math.PI/180.0);
            lookupValues[i] = sinValue * (float)i / 180.0f;
        }
    }

    public float[] getValues() {
        loopProcess();
        sumValues[0] = lookupValues[0];
        for (int i = 1; i < (360*100); i++) {
            sumValues[i] = lookupValues[i] + lookupValues[i-1];
        }
        return lookupValues;
    }
}
```

While it is not possible to parallelize the running subtotal without drastically changing the algorithm, we can quickly convert the loop into two separate loops. The first loop contains the threadable code, and the second processes the subtotal. Once this is accomplished, we can then thread the first loop without changing the second. In the new SinTable class, we have moved the running subtotal code to a separate loop. This separate loop runs on a single thread, only after the first loop is processed.

Consider the potential benefit before applying this technique. Since a large portion of the loop may be running in a single thread, the performance gain may not justify the effort involved. In most cases, calculations of the subtotal are small considering the effort of the main calculation, and the performance penalty may be small in comparison.

### Loop isolation

Many programs do not contain a single large loop. Even if a particular loop is determined to be unparallelizable, there may be other loops in the program. Even if these other loops cannot be parallelized, we may be able to run each separate loop in a different thread.

Although the many loops may be very complex, with large data dependencies between iterations, there may be few data dependencies between the different loops. It may be possible to isolate the individual loops themselves and run them each in a separate thread. With this technique, load balancing is no longer possible. After all, if the program contains four major loops and you were able to isolate them all, it is still impossible to distribute these four loops among twelve processors.

## Loop interchange

Multilayered loops are a prime cause of CPU-bound applications that run for a long period of time. This could be loops that are directly inside of other loops or, more likely, loops that call methods that contain loops. This scenario is so common that we examine inner-loop threading later in this chapter. For now, here is a simple case to look for:

```
public float[][] getValues( ) {
    for (int i = 0; i < 360; i++) {
        lookupValues[0][i] = 0;
    }
    for (int j = 1; j < 1000; j++) {
        for (int i = 0; i < 360; i++) {
            float sinValue = (float)Math.sin((i % 360)*Math.PI/180.0);
            lookupValues[j][i] = sinValue * (float)i / 180.0f;
            lookupValues[j][i] += lookupValues[j-1][i]*(float)j/180.0f;
        }
    }
    return lookupValues;
}
```

For multilayered loops, it is generally more profitable to thread the outer loop instead of the inner one. It is not necessary to thread both the inner and outer loop because threading either one should use all the processors. If the outer loop is threaded, threading the inner loop does not provide any further speedup since there are no more processors to run the extra threads (and vice versa). The reason we prefer to thread the outer loop is that there is an overhead in creating, destroying, and synchronizing among the many threads. By threading the outer loop, we create and destroy the threads once and synchronize only at a coarse level—consequently, less synchronization should be necessary.

In this new version of the table calculation, we are now working on a two-dimensional table. Three loops are used during this calculation. However, the first loop is merely setting the first row of values to zero. The next two loops are actually a pair of multilayered loops. The algorithm is looping the processing from row to row, executing the inner loop that is processing the values to be stored in the different columns.

The problem in this case is a data dependency between the rows themselves. Because the calculation at any row is dependent on the calculation of the previous row, the members of any column in the lookupValues array cannot be considered—or made— loop private. The inner loop can be parallelized with no problem since there are no data dependencies between the iterations. The only requirement is that the inner loop must assume that the outer loop ran in the correct order; this requirement is fine since we are not threading the outer loop.

However, we could also rewrite our original code as follows:

```
public float[][] getValues() {
    for (int i = 0; i < 360; i++) {
        lookupValues[0][i] = 0;
    }
    for (int i = 0; i < 360; i++) {
        for (int j = 1; j < 1000; j++) {
            float sinValue = (float)Math.sin((i % 360)*Math.PI/180.0);
            lookupValues[j][i] = sinValue * (float)i / 180.0f;
            lookupValues[j][i] += lookupValues[j-1][i]*(float)j/180.0f;
        }
    }
    return lookupValues;
}
```

In this example, the loops are interchanged. Instead of working from row to row, we can work from column to column. The inner loop can then process the data from row to row. By interchanging the loops, the inner loop is no longer threadable because of the data dependency between the members of the columns in the lookupValues array. However, the outer loop is now threadable. Once the outer loop has been threaded, there is no longer a reason to thread the inner loop. Since it is more profitable to thread an outer loop than an inner loop, this simple change prior to multithreading gives us a better return on our development time investment.

Unfortunately, although loops within loops are common, this example may not be. There is generally setup code for an inner loop, and there may be multiple loops that are run sequentially within the outer loop, or the inner loop may be inside another method that is called from the outer loop. The data dependencies may be such that a loop interchange does not solve the problem.

Having an inner loop that is threadable in an outer loop that is not threadable is common. We examine inner-loop threading in more detail later in this chapter.

## Loop reimplementation

As you may have noticed, the loop handler that we have developed is fairly restrictive. It applies only to for loops, the range of the loop must be known prior to execution, it works only with integers as its index, and it has an interval of only one between iterations. While some of these restrictions are because we have not implemented support for certain features in the loop handler, the main cause is that it is difficult, if not impossible, to implement an algorithm that can handle all generic loops.

If all else fails during loop transformation, programming experience is still very useful. A while or a do loop may be converted to a for loop. The start and end iterations may be calculated prior to loop execution. Code may be moved from, into, or between loops, to allow other loop transformations to occur. Code changes can also cause variable classifications to change. A shared variable may be reclassified as loop private or as a reduction variable because of how it is used in a loop.

Unfortunately, success is never guaranteed. The goal is to balance the effort of development with the acceleration that may be gained. It may take days to implement a change that achieves only one or two percent acceleration. After all, if unlimited effort were allowed, we would redesign the whole program from scratch.

## Inner-Loop Threading

The issues that we have discussed so far do not change when the loops are nested: if you apply the techniques only to the inner loop, they work. However, some other, very subtle issues may apply to inner loops. Let's return to our two-dimensional SinTable. As mentioned, a loop interchange should allow the outer loop to be threaded. However, instead of the loop transformation, let's try to thread the inner loop:

```
public float[][] getValues( ) {
    for (int i = 0; i < 360; i++) {
        lookupValues[0][i] = 0;
    }
    for (int j = 1; j < 1000; j++) {
        for (int i = 0; i < 360; i++) {
            float sinValue = (float)Math.sin((i % 360)*Math.PI/180.0);
            lookupValues[j][i] = sinValue * (float)i / 180.0f;
            lookupValues[j][i] += lookupValues[j-1][i]*(float)j/180.0f;
        }
    }
    return lookupValues;
}
```

The first variable to classify is the outer-loop-index variable, j. We must classify this variable since it is used inside the inner loop. In this case, j is classified as a read-only variable. At first glance, this does not make sense: how could an index variable be read-only? We must only look at the scope that we are attempting to thread. During the execution of the inner loop, the variable has a single value that does not change throughout the entire execution of the loop.

While the lookupValues array variable is a shared variable, the elements can be classified as loop private. Since each iteration of the loop accesses a different member of the array based on the loop index and the read-only variable j, its members may be considered loop private. The members of the lookupValues array are also considered storeback variables. Since we are not creating a local copy of these variables, there is no need to store the variables back.

The last two variables—sinValue and i—are simply classified as loop-private variables, and separate copies are created for each thread. Neither of these variables is used after the loop has completed, so storeback handling is not necessary.

The loop scheduler is chosen by examining the algorithm inside the inner loop itself. In this case, there is nothing that should cause any iteration to execute longer than any other iteration. Choosing the default—static or chunk—scheduler is probably best. However, there should be no harm in choosing either the self- or guided self-scheduler.

Once these tasks are completed, the loop is threaded by using the loop handler as usual. However, a slight complication arises: compared with the outer loop, the inner loop is executed many more times. This means many more times the thread creation and destruction overhead. Furthermore, the loop handler is designed as a "one use" object. A new loop handler must be created for each iteration of the outer loop. Although using the loop handler works without any problems, the overhead may be more significant than for threading a higher-level loop.

We can partially overcome this complication as follows:

```
package javathreads.examples.ch15;

import java.util.concurrent.*;

public class PoolLoopHandler implements Runnable {
    protected static class LoopRange {
        public int start, end;
    }

    protected static class PoolHandlerFactory implements ThreadFactory {
        public Thread newThread(Runnable r) {
            Thread t = new Thread(r);
            t.setDaemon(true);
            return t;
        }
    }

    static protected ThreadPoolExecutor threadpool;
    static protected int maxThreads = 1;
    protected int startLoop, endLoop, curLoop, numThreads;

    synchronized static void getThreadPool(int threads) {
        if (threadpool == null)
            threadpool = new ThreadPoolExecutor(
                            1, 1,
                            50000L, TimeUnit.MILLISECONDS,
                            new LinkedBlockingQueue<Runnable>(),
                            new PoolHandlerFactory());
        if (threads > maxThreads) {
            maxThreads = threads;
            threadpool.setMaximumPoolSize(maxThreads);
            threadpool.setCorePoolSize(maxThreads);
        }
    }
```

```
public PoolLoopHandler(int start, int end, int threads) {
    numThreads = threads;
    getThreadPool(numThreads);
    setRange(start, end);
}

public synchronized void setRange(int start, int end) {
    startLoop = start;
    endLoop = end;
    reset();
}

public synchronized void reset() {
    curLoop = startLoop;
}

protected synchronized LoopRange loopGetRange() {
    if (curLoop >= endLoop)
        return null;
    LoopRange ret = new LoopRange();
    ret.start = curLoop;
    curLoop += (endLoop-startLoop)/numThreads+1;
    ret.end = (curLoop<endLoop)?curLoop:endLoop;
    return ret;
}

public void loopDoRange(int start, int end) {
}

public void loopProcess() {
    reset();
    FutureTask t[] = new FutureTask[numThreads];
    for (int i = 0; i < numThreads; i++) {
        t[i] = new FutureTask(this, null);
        threadpool.execute(t[i]);
    }
    for (int i = 0; i < numThreads; i++) {
        try {
            t[i].get();
        } catch (ExecutionException ee) {
            throw new RuntimeException(ee.toString());
        } catch (InterruptedException ie) {
            throw new InterruptedException(ie.toString());
        }
    }
}

public void run() {
    LoopRange str;
    while ((str = loopGetRange()) != null) {
        loopDoRange(str.start, str.end);
    }
}
}
```

The fact that our original LoopHandler class can be used only once is merely a design flaw. The loop index can never be set back to the start of the loop nor can the range of the loop be changed. To fix this, we simply add two new methods, reset( ) and setRange( ), that reset the index back to the start of the loop and specify new ranges for the loop. To avoid creating a lot of threads, we use the thread pool executor we looked at in Chapter 10. Instead of creating threads in the loopProcess( ) method, this method now assigns the tasks to the threads in a thread pool. We can then simply wait for all the threads in the pool to complete their assigned tasks. This all helps somewhat, but the synchronization that we have introduced into the calculation will have an effect on the ultimate acceleration of our program.

---

## A Warning About Inner Loops

Prior to threading any loop, we should always examine that loop. We should not thread the loop if it executes in a very short period of time. For these cases, the overhead in the setup and teardown of the threaded loop may be greater than any speed gained from threading the loop.

When moving from the outer loop to the inner loop, we must examine the inner loop. Just because the outer loop is a candidate for threading does not mean the inner loop is a candidate for threading. If the number of iterations in the outer loop is many times higher than the inner loop, the inner loop may execute only for a short period of time. There could also be method calls in the outer loop, and not in the inner loop, that are taking a long period of time to execute.

---

We can implement other scheduling models in the pool handler quite easily:

```
package javathreads.examples.ch15;

public class PoolSelfLoopHandler extends PoolLoopHandler {
    private int groupSize;

    public PoolSelfLoopHandler(int start, int end,
                                    int size, int threads) {
        super(start, end, threads);
        setSize(size);
    }

    public synchronized void setSize(int size) {
        groupSize = size;
        reset();
    }

    protected synchronized LoopRange loopGetRange() {
        if (curLoop >= endLoop)
            return null;
        LoopRange ret = new LoopRange();
```

```
            ret.start = curLoop;
            curLoop += groupSize;
            ret.end = (curLoop<endLoop)?curLoop:endLoop;
            return ret;
        }
    }
```

What's interesting here is the similarity to our original SelfLoopHandler class. However, to be more configurable, we have modified the handler to allow the extra parameters, such as the chunk size, to be changed.

Here's how we use our new handler:

```
package javathreads.examples.ch15.example8;

import javathreads.examples.ch15.*;

public class SinTable extends PoolLoopHandler {
    private float lookupValues[][];
    private int j;

    public SinTable() {
        super(0, 360, 12);
        lookupValues = new float[1000][];
        for (int j = 0; j < 1000; j++) {
            lookupValues[j] = new float[360];
        }
    }

    public void loopDoRange(int start, int end) {
        float sinValue = 0.0f;
        for (int i = start; i < end; i++) {
            sinValue = (float)Math.sin((i % 360)*Math.PI/180.0);
            lookupValues[j][i] = sinValue * (float)i / 180.0f;
            lookupValues[j][i] += lookupValues[j-1][i]*(float)j/180.0f;
        }
    }

    public float[][] getValues() {
        for (int i = 0; i < 360; i++) {
            lookupValues[0][i] = 0;
        }
        for (j = 1; j < 1000; j++) {
            loopProcess();
        }
        return lookupValues;
    }
}
```

To implement the SinTable class, we place the code from the inner loop in the loopDoRange() method and then call the loopProcess() method to process the inner loop. Since the j index variable is a read-only shared variable, it is now an instance variable of the SinTable class.

Having a loop handler that can be used more than once is also very important. If we use the earlier version of the loop handler, we will have to create a new instance of the loop handler for each inner loop that we execute. This means that the code for the outer loop and the inner loop cannot be in the same class. Furthermore, we will need to pass a reference to the j variable and lookupValues array to each instance since these are shared between the different inner loop handlers.

## Loop Printing

The task of sending a string to a file or the display is an I/O-bound task. Using multi-threaded techniques on a loop of output does not make sense. Since the operation is I/O-bound, the threads spend most of their time waiting, and there is little difference in having 1 or 12 processors available to run waiting threads. Furthermore, the order of the output is important. Data that is written to a file or the display is eventually read by a person or another program. The output must look the same whether the calculation is done as a single- or multithreaded program.

However, what if the printing portion of the loop is small when compared with the mathematical calculation? If enough of the loop is CPU-intensive, it might be silly to abandon an attempt at parallelizing the loop just because it contains a println( ) method call. The only problem that needs to be solved is the ordering of the output. This can be done by a two-step printing process. Instead of printing directly to the display or file, the program can print to a virtual, memory-based display along with an index used to order the output. When the processing of the loop has completed, the output can then be sent to the display or file, using the index information to ensure that the data is sent in the correct order.

Let's reexamine our SinTable loop:

```
public synchronized float[] getValues() {
    if (lookupValues == null) {
        for (int i = 0; i < (360*100); i++) {
            float sinValue = (float)Math.sin((i % 360)*Math.PI/180.0);
            lookupValues[i] = sinValue * (float)i / 180.0f;
            System.out.println(" " + i + "     " + lookupValues[i]);
        }
    }
    return lookupValues;
}
```

In this new version of the getValues( ) method, we are also printing the table to standard output. Obviously, this simple example can be transformed with a loop distribution to two separate loops, but let's assume that the printing process is highly integrated into the algorithm and the loop transformation is not possible.

To solve this problem, we'll use this class:

```java
package javathreads.examples.ch15;

import java.util.*;
import java.io.*;

public class LoopPrinter {
    private Vector pStorage[];
    private int growSize;

    public LoopPrinter(int initSize, int growSize) {
        pStorage = new Vector[initSize];
        this.growSize = growSize;
    }

    public LoopPrinter() {
        this(100, 0);
    }

    private synchronized void enlargeStorage(int minSize) {
        int oldSize = pStorage.length;
        if (oldSize < minSize) {
            int newSize = (growSize > 0) ?
                oldSize + growSize : 2 * oldSize;
            if (newSize < minSize) {
                newSize = minSize;
            }
            Vector newVec[] = new Vector[newSize];
            System.arraycopy(pStorage, 0, newVec, 0, oldSize);
            pStorage = newVec;
        }
    }

    public synchronized void print(int index, Object obj) {
        if (index >= pStorage.length) {
            enlargeStorage(index+1);
        }
        if (pStorage[index] == null) {
            pStorage[index] = new Vector();
        }
        pStorage[index].addElement(obj.toString());
    }

    public synchronized void println(int index, Object obj) {
        print(index, obj);
        print(index, "\n");
    }

    public synchronized void send2stream(PrintStream ps) {
        for (int i = 0; i < pStorage.length; i++) {
            if (pStorage[i] != null) {
                Enumeration e = pStorage[i].elements();
```

```
            while (e.hasMoreElements()) {
                ps.print(e.nextElement());
            }
        }
    }
  }
}
```

The loop printer is implemented using a two-dimensional vector. The first dimension is used to separate the output. This output index could be related to the index of the actual loop, or to a chunk of the loop, or it could even be a combination of multiple loop indices. In any case, an output index should not be assigned to more than one thread since the ordering inside an indexed vector is based on it. The second dimension holds the strings that are sent to the output. Since the indices have already ordered the strings to be printed, this dimension is just used to store the many strings that are sent to this index.*

Printing an object to the virtual display is done with the print() and println() methods. Along with the object to be printed, the program must supply an index as a reference of the printing order. These methods simply store a reference to the strings so that they may be printed at a later time. The second phase of the printing process is done by the send2stream() method. Once the loop has completed, a call to this method prints the result to the output specified.

Here's how to use the LoopPrinter class:

```
package javathreads.examples.ch15.example9;

import javathreads.examples.ch15.*;

public class SinTable extends GuidedLoopHandler {
    private float lookupValues[];
    private LoopPrinter lp;

    public SinTable() {
        super(0, 360*100, 100, 12);
        lookupValues = new float [360 * 100];
        lp = new LoopPrinter(360*100, 0);
    }

    public void loopDoRange(int start, int end) {
        for (int i = start; i < end; i++) {
            float sinValue = (float)Math.sin((i % 360)*Math.PI/180.0);
            lookupValues[i] = sinValue * (float)i / 180.0f;
            lp.println(i, " " + i + " " + lookupValues[i]);
        }
    }
}
```

---

* Technically, we could have done the same thing with a single-dimensional array of string buffers.

```
    public float[] getValues() {
        loopProcess();
        lp.send2stream(System.out);
        return lookupValues;
    }
}
```

The loop printer is created prior to the loop, all printing that was previously sent to a file or the display is sent to the loop printer, and the send2stream( ) method is called upon completion of the loop. Since the loop printer sends all the information to one target, multiple loop printers must be created if the loop prints to different streams.

Also note that we constructed the loop printer with the index size as its initial size. The loop printer is written to expand to any size, so this extra definition is not necessary. We want to avoid expanding the size because this operation not only requires the method to be synchronized, but also, depending on the size, takes some time to execute. The print( ) and println( ) methods must also be synchronized. This serves two purposes: First, it allows the array size to be increased without a race condition. Second, it allows the methods to work—although the print order is no longer guaranteed—if an index is assigned to two threads. If the loop printer is modified so as not to allow the array to be enlarged, and if it is assumed that developers will not assign two threads to the same index, synchronization at this level will no longer be necessary.

## Multiprocessor Scaling

Scaling is a term that is sometimes overused. It can apply to how many programs a computer can execute simultaneously, how many disks can be written to simultaneously, or how many cream cheese bagel orders can be processed by the local bagel shop's crew. When the output cannot be increased no matter how many resources are added, this limit is generally the value used to specify what something scales to. If the oven cannot produce more bagels per hour, it does not matter how many people are added to the assembly line: the rate of bagels cannot exceed the rate produced by the oven. The scaling limit can also be controlled by many other factors, such as the rate that the cream cheese can be produced, the size of the refrigerators, or even by the suppliers for the bagel shop.

In this chapter, when we refer to the scalability of a multithreaded program, we are referring to the limit on the number of processors we can add and still obtain an acceleration. Adding more than this limit does not make the program run faster. Obviously, how a program scales depends on many factors: the operating system, the Java virtual machine implementation, the browser or application server, and the Java program itself. The best a program can scale is based on the scalability limits of all of these factors.

For perfect CPU-bound programs in a perfect world, we could expect perfect scaling: adding a second CPU would halve the amount of time that it takes the program to run, adding another CPU would reduce the time by another third, and so on. Even for the loop-based programs we've examined in this chapter, however, the amount of scaling is also limited by these important constraints:

*Setup time*

A certain amount of time is required to execute the code outside of the loop that is being parallelized. This amount of time is independent of the number of threads and processors that are available because only a single thread executes that code.

*New synchronization requirements*

In parallelizing the loops of this chapter, we've introduced some additional bookkeeping code, some of which is synchronized. Because some of these are contended locks, this increases the time required to execute the code.

*Serialization of methods*

Some methods in our parallelized code must run sequentially because they are synchronized. Contention for the lock associated with these methods also affects the scalability of our parallelized programs.

---

## The Effect of the Virtual Machine

One of the factors that can affect the scalability of a particular program is the implementation of the virtual machine itself. Obtaining a synchronization lock, for instance, takes a certain amount of time, and the code in the virtual machine that actually implements the synchronization is often synchronized itself. Two threads attempting to obtain different synchronization locks may still compete for a resource within the virtual machine. And there are other examples where the virtual machine or operating system affects the scalability of a program.

The results that we present in this chapter are based on the J2SE 5.0 Beta 1 release by Sun Microsystems. They are drastically different (and better) than results we've presented in previous editions of this book. Most notably, in the first and second edition of this book, results were based on the 1.1.6 production release of the Java virtual machine from Sun Microsystems. In those results, the amount of scaling observed was far less due to two factors: the overall slower execution of the code and the much longer time required to obtain a synchronization lock (even in the uncontended case).

---

If we view the setup time, synchronization time, and time required to execute the serialized methods as a percentage of the total running time, the remaining time is the amount of code that is parallelized. The maximum amount of scaling that we'll see is given by Amdahl's Law:

$$S = (1 - F) + \frac{F}{N}$$

Here, $S$ is the scaling we'll see, assuming that $F$% of code is parallelized over $N$ processors. If 95% of the code is parallelized and we have eight processors available, the code runs in 16.8% of the original time required (.05 +.95/8). However, when we introduce code to calculate loop ranges (or any other code), we've actually increased the amount of serialized code, so $F$ could potentially be a negative number. In that case, our parallelized code takes longer to run than our original code.

What sort of scaling can we expect from the techniques of this chapter? To answer this question, we test several implementations of our sample double loop:

```java
public float[][] getValues() {
    for (int i = 0; i < 360; i++) {
        lookupValues[0][i] = 0;
    }
    for (int j = 1; j < 1000; j++) {
        for (int i = 0; i < 360; i++) {
            float sinValue = (float)Math.sin((i % 360)*Math.PI/180.0);
            lookupValues[j][i] = sinValue * (float)i / 180.0f;
            lookupValues[j][i] += lookupValues[j-1][i]*(float)j/180.0f;
        }
    }
    return lookupValues;
}
```

To make testing easier, we use the following class and interface to build a system by which we may test various loop handlers.

```java
package javathreads.examples.ch15;

import java.util.*;
import java.text.*;
import java.io.*;

public class ScaleTest {
    private int nIter = 200;
    private int nRows = 2000;
    private int nCols = 200;
    private int nThreads = 8;
    Class target;

    ScaleTest(int nIter, int nRows, int nCols, int nThreads,
                String className) {
        this.nIter = nIter;
        this.nRows = nRows;
        this.nCols = nCols;
        this.nThreads = nThreads;
        try {
```

```
            target = Class.forName(className);
        } catch (ClassNotFoundException cnfe) {
            System.out.println(cnfe);
            System.exit(-1);
        }
    }

    void chart() {
        long sumTime = 0;
        long startLoop = System.currentTimeMillis();
        try {
            ScaleTester st = (ScaleTester) target.newInstance();
            for (int i = 0; i < nIter; i++) {
                st.init(nRows, nCols, nThreads);
                System.gc();
                long then = System.currentTimeMillis();
                float ans[][] = st.doCalc();
                long now = System.currentTimeMillis();
                sumTime += (now - then);
            }
        } catch (Exception e) {
            e.printStackTrace();
            System.exit(-1);
        }
        long endLoop = System.currentTimeMillis();
        long calcTime = endLoop - startLoop;
        System.err.println("Loop time " + sumTime +
                        " (" + ((sumTime * 100) / calcTime) + "%)");
        System.err.println("Calculation time  " + calcTime);
    }

    public static void main(String args[]) {
        if (args.length != 5) {
            System.out.println(
    "Usage: java ScaleTester nIter nRows nCols nThreads className");
            System.exit(-1);
        }
        ScaleTest sc = new ScaleTest(Integer.parseInt(args[0]),
                                    Integer.parseInt(args[1]),
                                    Integer.parseInt(args[2]),
                                    Integer.parseInt(args[3]),
                                    args[4]);
        sc.chart();
    }
}
```

When we use the ScaleTest class, we get two numbers: the number of milliseconds required to run the entire program (including initialization, which is single-threaded) and the number of milliseconds required to run just the loop calculation. We then compare these numbers to determine the scalability of various implementations of our loop-handling classes.

In the remainder of this section, we'll develop examples that use this class to see the effect of parallelization of our loop given the constraints we've discussed in this chapter.

## A Simple Loop Test

In this example, we'll explore how various loop handlers affect parallelization. As a baseline, we take the measurement of this class:

```
package javathreads.examples.ch15.example10;

import javathreads.examples.ch15.*;

public class Basic implements ScaleTester {
    private float lookupValues[][];
    int nCols, nRows;

    public void init(int nRows, int nCols, int nThreads) {
        this.nCols = nCols;
        this.nRows = nRows;
        lookupValues = new float[nRows][];
        for (int j = 0; j < nRows; j++) {
            lookupValues[j] = new float[nCols];
        }
    }

    public float[][] doCalc() {
        for (int i = 0; i < nCols; i++) {
            lookupValues[0][i] = 0;
        }
        for (int j = 1; j < nRows; j++) {
            for (int i = 0; i < nCols; i++) {
                float sinValue =
                        (float)Math.sin((i % 360)*Math.PI/180.0);
                lookupValues[j][i] = sinValue * (float)i / 180.0f;
                lookupValues[j][i] +=
                        lookupValues[j-1][i]*(float)j/180.0f;
            }
        }
        return lookupValues;
    }
}
```

This class contains no threading; it is the way that we would normally implement the basic calculation we're interested in testing. We compare this class with the following loop handler class:

```
package javathreads.examples.ch15.example10;

import javathreads.examples.ch15.*;

public class GuidedLoopInterchanged implements ScaleTester {
    private float lookupValues[][];
    private int nRows, nCols, nThreads;
```

```
private class GuidedLoopInterchangedHandler
                         extends GuidedLoopHandler {
    GuidedLoopInterchangedHandler(int nc, int nt) {
        super(0, nc, 10, nt);
    }

    public void loopDoRange(int start, int end) {
        for (int i = start; i < end; i++) {
            lookupValues[0][i] = 0;
        }
        for (int i = start; i < end; i++) {
            for (int j = 1; j < nRows; j++) {
                float sinValue =
                            (float)Math.sin((i % 360)*Math.PI/180.0);
                lookupValues[j][i] = sinValue * (float)i / 180.0f;
                lookupValues[j][i] +=
                            lookupValues[j-1][i]*(float)j/180.0f;
            }
        }
    }
}

public void init(int nRows, int nCols, int nThreads) {
    this.nRows = nRows;
    this.nCols = nCols;
    this.nThreads = nThreads;
    lookupValues = new float[nRows][];
    for (int j = 0; j < nRows; j++) {
        lookupValues[j] = new float[nCols];
    }
}

public float[][] doCalc() {
    GuidedLoopInterchangedHandler loop =
                new GuidedLoopInterchangedHandler(nCols, nThreads);
    loop.loopProcess();
    return lookupValues;
}
}
```

This class uses our simple loop handler to process the loop; notice, however, that
we've interchanged the loops in order to make the outer loop threadable. The online
examples have similar handlers that perform a simple loop interchange and a self-
guided loop interchange.

Table 15-1 lists the results of the ScaleTest program when run with different implementations of the interchanged loop: we've used chunk, self-scheduled, and guided
self-scheduling loop handlers in conjunction with the code we showed earlier. These
tests were run on a machine with eight CPUs, using an iteration count of 200, a row
count of 1500, and a column count of 3000. We've normalized the running time for
the baseline run to be 100 so that other numbers can be viewed as a percentage: the
best that we do is run in 20% of the time required for the original run.

---

Table 15-1. *Scalability of simple loop handlers*

|  | Number of threads | Total time | Loop time |
|---|---|---|---|
| **Basic**<br>javathreads.examples.ch15.example10.Basic | 1 | 100%<br>(baseline) | 94.0% |
| **Chunk scheduling**<br>javathreads.examples.ch15.example10.<br>LoopInterchanged | 1 | 108.0% | 101.8% |
|  | 2 | 57.5% | 51.4% |
|  | 4 | 32.7% | 26.7% |
|  | 8 | 20.7% | 14.6% |
|  | 12 | 23.3% | 17.0% |
|  | 16 | 21.2% | 14.9% |
| **Self-scheduling**<br>javathreads.examples.ch15.example10.<br>SelfLoopInterchanged | 1 | 111.2% | 105.0% |
|  | 2 | 74.3% | 68.2% |
|  | 4 | 42.1% | 35.9% |
|  | 8 | 25.3% | 19.1% |
|  | 12 | 25.2% | 19.0% |
|  | 16 | 25.1% | 18.9% |
| **Guided self-scheduling**<br>javathreads.examples.ch15.example10.<br>GuidedLoopInterchanged | 1 | 108.0% | 101.9% |
|  | 2 | 58.7% | 52.6% |
|  | 4 | 32.7% | 26.6% |
|  | 8 | 20.0% | 13.8% |
|  | 12 | 21.9% | 15.8% |
|  | 16 | 21.3% | 15.0% |

We can draw a few conclusions from this table:

- The overhead of setting up the thread and loop handling class itself is significant: it requires 8% to 11% more time to execute that code when only a single thread is available. We would not want to use this technique on a machine with only one CPU.

- The scaling of the loop calculation itself is good. Since the original loop accounted for 94% of the code, with eight CPUs the best that we can hope for (using Amdahl's law) is 17.8%. We've achieved 20%, which implies that 88.5% of the code is now parallelized: the 5% difference is accounted for by the serialized calls to the loopGetRange( ) method and the fact that each thread is probably not doing the same amount of work.

- Going past eight threads—that is, the number of CPUs available—yields a penalty. This is partially because we now have threads competing for a CPU, but it is also because of the synchronization around the additional calls to the loopGetRange( ) method: there's now a greater chance that the synchronization is contended. However, note that while there is a penalty for 12 threads, the penalty for 16 threads is less. With 12 threads, at some points in time only 4 threads have work left to do, which leaves 4 CPUs idle.

- The guided self-scheduler is the best choice in this example. This is not surprising: calculations based on sin values do not always require the same amount of time, so the chunk scheduler can be penalized by having one particular thread that requires too much time. That contributes to a loss of scaling since the threads do not end up performing equal amounts of work.

All in all, though, we've achieved very good scalability.

## A Reduction Variable Test

What effect does a reduction variable have in our testing? In our next series of tests (example 11 in the online archive), we rewrite our tests so that every time we calculate a lookup value, we add that value to a sumValue instance variable. Using the reduction technique we showed earlier, the modified test generates the numbers given in Table 15-2.

Table 15-2. Scalability of loop handlers with reduction variables

| | Number of threads | Total time | Loop time |
|---|---|---|---|
| **Basic** <br> javathreads.examples.ch15.example11.Basic | 1 | 100% (baseline) | 93.8% |
| **Chunk scheduling** <br> javathreads.examples.ch15.example11. LoopInterchanged | 1 | 111.8% | 105.5% |
| | 2 | 59.2% | 52.9% |
| | 4 | 33.6% | 27.3% |
| | 8 | 20.9% | 14.6% |
| | 12 | 23.7% | 17.3% |
| | 16 | 21.5% | 15.0% |
| **Guided self-scheduling** <br> javathreads.examples.ch15.example11. GuidedLoopInterchanged | 1 | 110.0% | 103.6% |
| | 2 | 58.0% | 51.7% |
| | 4 | 32.7% | 26.4% |
| | 8 | 20.1% | 13.8% |
| | 12 | 22.1% | 15.8% |
| | 16 | 21.5% | 15.1% |
| **Guided atomic self-scheduling** <br> javathreads.examples.ch15.example11. GuidedAtomicLoopnterchanged | 1 | 114.2% | 107.8% |
| | 2 | 60.4% | 54.0% |
| | 4 | 33.8% | 27.4% |
| | 8 | 21.2% | 14.9% |
| | 12 | 24.0% | 17.5% |
| | 16 | 21.8% | 15.3% |

Because there's only one reduction variable, the effect on scaling is minor. In fact, in some cases we did slightly better because the baseline now takes longer to execute. However, the effect of many reduction variables could potentially aggregate into something more noticeable.

We did no better—in fact, slightly worse—by replacing the synchronized call to the sumValue with a call to our AtomicDouble class from Chapter 5. In this test, the overhead comes almost entirely from the loop handling rather than the synchronization after every loop completion.

## A Small Inner-Loop Test

What if we had threaded only the inner loop? This question is interesting since it demonstrates the effect of synchronization overhead versus the amount of savings we obtain if the inner loop is small. As shown in example 12 in the online archive, we rewrite our first test (with no reduction variable) so that no loop interchange is performed and the inner loop is threaded instead, which produces the results in Table 15-3.

*Table 15-3. Scalability of inner loop handlers*

| | Number of threads | Total time | Loop time |
| --- | --- | --- | --- |
| **Basic**<br>javathreads.examples.ch15.example12.Basic | 1 | 100%<br>(baseline) | 94.7% |
| **Guided self-scheduling**<br>javathreads.examples.ch15.example12.<br>GuidedLoopInterchanged | 1 | 100% | 94.6% |
| | 2 | 57.7% | 52.0% |
| | 4 | 38.4% | 32.4% |
| | 8 | 41.5% | 35.5% |
| | 12 | 53.2% | 47.1% |
| | 16 | 58.2% | 52.0% |

In this test, we start out with some scaling, through about four CPUs. Even at four CPUs, however, we're not seeing the same scaling as in our previous tests. By the time we get to eight CPUs, the inner loop has only 375 calculations, and the additional overhead of repeatedly calling the loopGetRange( ) method has overcome any advantage we received by running the small loops in parallel. Things get worse as we add more threads.

This effect becomes even more pronounced if we run with a smaller inner loop size. With only 1000 columns, running with 4 threads requires 72.3% of the original time, and running with 16 threads now requires 123.8% of the original time. The loop itself runs so fast that the calls to loopGetRange( ) (and the contention for its lock) make our program actually run slower.

As we mentioned, threading of small loops—and particularly of small inner loops—is not necessarily worthwhile.

## A Printing Test

What if we add code to the loop that prints out the result of some calculations? We can still thread such a case using the LoopPrinter class that we developed earlier. However, remember that we ended our section on the LoopPrinter class with a discussion that would enable us to remove its synchronization. Because in this particular test we always know the size of the output array and we can ensure that the same index is not used by two different threads, we can rewrite the LoopPrinter class like this:

```
package javathreads.examples.ch15;

import java.util.*;
import java.io.*;

// Non-thread-safe version of a loop printer
public class LoopPrinterUnsafe {
    private Vector pStorage[];

    public LoopPrinterUnsafe(int size) {
        pStorage = new Vector[size];
    }

    public void print(int index, Object obj) {
        if (pStorage[index] == null) {
            pStorage[index] = new Vector();
        }
        pStorage[index].addElement(obj.toString());
    }

    public void println(int index, Object obj) {
        print(index, obj);
        print(index, "\n");
    }

    public void send2stream(PrintStream ps) {
        for (int i = 0; i < pStorage.length; i++) {
            if (pStorage[i] != null) {
                Enumeration e = pStorage[i].elements();
                while (e.hasMoreElements()) {
                    ps.print(e.nextElement());
                }
            }
        }
    }
}
```

This version of the loop printer eliminates the synchronization of our first implementation. There is still some synchronization when adding the string to the vector, but if we set up the thread indices correctly, this is all uncontended synchronization and has little effect on our time. It still takes longer to add strings to these vectors and then dump them out than to simply call the ps.println( ) method. However, the difference between our threadsafe and thread-unsafe versions of this class is important. Table 15-4 lists the results that we obtained for both cases cases (using the classes from example 13 in the online archive).

*Table 15-4. Scalability of loop printer handlers*

|  | Number of threads | Total time | Loop time |
|---|---|---|---|
| **Basic**<br>javathreads.examples.ch15.example13.Basic | 1 | 100%<br>(baseline) | 96.3% |
| **Threadsafe loop printer**<br>javathreads.examples.ch15.example13.<br>GuidedLoopInterchanged | 1 | 106.7% | 99.2% |
|  | 2 | 90.2% | 82.7% |
|  | 4 | 83.9% | 76.4% |
|  | 8 | 86.0% | 78.5% |
|  | 12 | 89.3% | 81.8% |
|  | 16 | 86.5% | 78% |
| **Thread-unsafe loop printer**<br>javathreads.examples.ch15.example13.<br>UnsafePrinterInterchanged | 1 | 109.2% | 101.7% |
|  | 2 | 85.1% | 77.6% |
|  | 4 | 75.4% | 67.9% |
|  | 8 | 65.2% | 57.7% |
|  | 12 | 67.7% | 60.2% |
|  | 16 | 66.4% | 58.9% |

The numbers in this table are obtained from printing out the result of every 20th calculation. Even when the loop printer class is not synchronized, the extra overhead of all the object manipulation within the printer class adds a lot of time to the overall execution; printing the strings in the stored vectors (which is still a single-threaded operation) takes over 40% of the execution time. In the synchronized case, contention for the locks prevents us from getting much scaling benefit at all. This is one case where a careful design that allows you to avoid synchronization can have a benefit.

It's interesting to compare these results to a case in which we print out only every 1000th calculation. Now the printing time no longer dominates the calculation (see Table 15-5).

Table 15-5. Scalability of loop printer handlers

| | Number of threads | Total time | Loop time |
|---|---|---|---|
| **Basic**<br>javathreads.examples.ch15.example13.Basic1000 | 1 | 100%<br>(baseline) | 96.3% |
| **Threadsafe loop printer**<br>javathreads.examples.ch15.example13.<br>GuidedLoopInterchanged1000 | 1 | 131.5% | 112.8% |
| | 4 | 54.7% | 35.9% |
| | 8 | 42.3% | 23.5% |
| **Thread-unsafe loop printer**<br>javathreads.examples.ch15.example13.<br>UnsafePrinterInterchanged1000 | 1 | 134.4% | 115.7% |
| | 4 | 54.2% | 35.4% |
| | 8 | 41.8% | 23.0% |

We get better scalability here, though still clearly worse than when we had no printing at all. The lesson here is clear: when you want to get the most benefit out of running code in parallel, reducing the amount of serial code makes a big difference in the benefits you'll see.

# Summary

In this chapter, we examined techniques that allow us to utilize multiprocessor machines so that our Java programs run faster on those machines. We examined loops—the most common source of CPU-intensive code—and developed classes that allow these loops to run in a multithreaded fashion. Along the way, we have classified variables, used various scheduling algorithms, and applied simple loop transformations to achieve this parallelization.

The goals here are to write fast programs from the start, to increase the performance of old algorithms without redesigning them from scratch, and to provide a rich set of options that can be used for cases where high performance is required.

## Example Classes

The first nine SinTable classes we showed should mainly be used as a reference. They contain testing code, but the printed output isn't as interesting as the code itself.

Examples 10–13 are somewhat different from the examples from earlier chapters. These examples are used for the tests that produced the tables in this chapter. These tests are all run via the same class: the ScaleTest class. One of the arguments required to run the scale test is the name of the target class to test. The classes that are executed in those tests are listed in the tables shown earlier in this chapter.

| Description | Main Java class | Ant target |
|---|---|---|
| Table Generator (Single-threaded) | javathreads.examples.ch15.example1.SinTable | ch15-ex1 |
| Table Generator (Multithreaded) | javathreads.examples.ch15.example2.SinTable | ch15-ex2 |

| Description | Main Java class | Ant target |
|---|---|---|
| Table Generator (Using loop handler) | javathreads.examples.ch15.example3.SinTable | ch15-ex3 |
| Table Generator (Handling reduction variables) | javathreads.examples.ch15.example4.SinTable | ch15-ex4 |
| Table Generator (Handling reduction variables) | javathreads.examples.ch15.example5.SinTable | ch15-ex5 |
| Table Generator (Two-stage reduction) | javathreads.examples.ch15.example6.SinTable | ch15-ex6 |
| Table Generator (Handling shared variables) | javathreads.examples.ch15.example7.SinTable | ch15-ex7 |
| Table Generator (Threading inner loops) | javathreads.examples.ch15.example8.SinTable | ch15-ex8 |
| Table Generator (Printing) | javathreads.examples.ch15.example9.SinTable | ch15-ex9 |
| Scale Tester | javathreads.examples.ch15.ScaleTest scaleLoops nRows nColumns nThreads classname | ch15-scale |

For the ScaleTest class, the class name argument appears in table listings earlier in this chapter (e.g., the first test in Table 15-1 is the class javathreads.examples.ch15.example10.Basic). In the ant target, the properties to use for the different parameters are as follows:

```
<property name="nThreads" value="10"/>
<property name="scaleLoops" value="200"/>
<property name="nRows" value="1500"/>
<property name="nCols" value="2000"/>
<property name="classname" value="javathreads.examples.ch15.example10.Basic"/>
```

# Superseded Threading Utilities

Readers of previous editions of this book will have noticed that many of the classes we developed for those editions have been replaced. The reason has to do with the many new classes provided by J2SE 5.0. Prior to J2SE 5.0, developers were left to create or purchase a library that provided the high-level threading support needed by more complex programs. While these libraries can still be used, it is recommended that programs migrate to the core J2SE 5.0 classes since that leaves one less library to maintain, test, and download during execution.

While the examples in the previous edition of this book are now obsolete, there are a few advantages to including them in this appendix (and in the online source). The examples were designed to teach the subject of threading. They were designed to be simplistic, not loaded with features, and specifically target a particular subject. Most of those subjects are now discussed in relation to the new classes in J2SE 5.0, and the rest of them are no longer necessary since we are no longer maintaining our own library. Still, for research purposes, there is advantage in examining them.

As this book goes to press, J2SE 5.0 is only a beta release, so many developers cannot yet use the new classes in J2SE 5.0. Those developers will also find these classes useful.

So for those who may be interested, here is a quick review of our obsolete classes. Obviously, learning the examples in this appendix is optional. Using these tools should be considered only if you must use a virtual machine earlier than J2SE 5.0.

## The BusyFlag Class

We'll start with a BusyFlag class:

```
package javathreads.examples.appa;

public class BusyFlag {
    protected Thread busyflag = null;
    protected int busycount = 0;
```

```
public synchronized void getBusyFlag() {
    while (tryGetBusyFlag() == false) {
        try {
            wait();
        } catch (Exception e) {}
    }
}

public synchronized boolean tryGetBusyFlag() {
    if (busyflag == null) {
        busyflag = Thread.currentThread();
        busycount = 1;
        return true;
    }
    if (busyflag == Thread.currentThread()) {
        busycount++;
        return true;
    }
    return false;
}

public synchronized void freeBusyFlag() {
    if (getBusyFlagOwner() == Thread.currentThread()) {
        busycount--;
        if (busycount == 0) {
            busyflag = null;
            notify();
        }
    }
}

public synchronized Thread getBusyFlagOwner() {
    return busyflag;
}
}
```

The BusyFlag class implements a basic, no-frills, mutually exclusive lock. It also allows the locks to be nested—the owner thread can lock the busy flag multiple times. It is much simpler than the ReentrantLock class. There is no internal support for condition variables. There is no support for timeouts. There is no concept of fairness in granting the busy flag. And our implementation does not attempt to minimize synchronization.

Simplistically, the purpose of this class is to use Java's basic synchronization mechanism to achieve, well, synchronization. This allows the program to lock at any scope or for any purpose.

The BusyFlag class contains four methods. The tryGetBusyFlag() class is used to obtain a lock (a.k.a. the busyflag). It grabs the busy flag if it is available while returning false if the flag is already owned by another thread. It also allows nested locks by incrementing a counter if the current thread already owns the flag. The synchronized keyword is used to protect against race conditions while grabbing this flag.

---

The getBusyFlag( ) method uses the tryGetBusyFlag( ) method to repeatedly try grabbing the flag until it is successful. If the flag is not available, it uses the wait-and-notify mechanism to wait for the flag to be returned. The freeBusyFlag( ) method decrements the counter. And if the counter is zero, this method declares that the flag has no owner and notifies any threads that are waiting to grab the flag.

The getBusyFlagOwner( ) method is merely an administration method that allows a thread to determine who is the owner of the busy flag. Also note that due to a race condition, the result that is returned is only guaranteed not to change if the current thread is returned as the owner of the busy flag.

# The CondVar Class

Here is an implementation of the CondVar class:

```
package javathreads.examples.appa;

public class CondVar {
        private BusyFlag SyncVar;

        public CondVar( ) {
                this(new BusyFlag( ));
        }

        public CondVar(BusyFlag sv) {
                SyncVar = sv;
        }

        public void cvWait( ) throws InterruptedException {
                cvTimedWait(SyncVar, 0);
        }

        public void cvWait(BusyFlag sv) throws InterruptedException {
                cvTimedWait(sv, 0);
        }

        public void cvTimedWait(int millis) throws InterruptedException {
                cvTimedWait(SyncVar, millis);
        }

        public void cvTimedWait(BusyFlag sv, int millis)
                                throws InterruptedException {
                int i = 0;
                InterruptedException errex = null;

                synchronized (this) {
                        // You must own the lock in order to use this method
                        if (sv.getBusyFlagOwner( ) != Thread.currentThread( )) {
                                throw new IllegalMonitorStateException(
                                                        "current thread not owner");
                        }
```

```
                        // Release the lock (Completely)
                        while (sv.getBusyFlagOwner() == Thread.currentThread()) {
                                i++;
                                sv.freeBusyFlag();
                        }

                        // Use wait() method
                        try {
                                if (millis == 0) {
                                        wait();
                                } else {
                                        wait(millis);
                                }
                        } catch (InterruptedException iex) {
                                errex = iex;
                        }
                }

                // Obtain the lock (Return to original state)
                for (; i>0; i--) {
                        sv.getBusyFlag();
                }

                if (errex != null) throw errex;
                return;
        }

        public void cvSignal() {
                cvSignal(SyncVar);
        }

        public synchronized void cvSignal(BusyFlag sv) {
                // You must own the lock in order to use this method
                if (sv.getBusyFlagOwner() != Thread.currentThread()) {
                        throw new IllegalMonitorStateException(
                                                "current thread not owner");
                }
                notify();
        }

        public void cvBroadcast() {
                cvBroadcast(SyncVar);
        }

        public synchronized void cvBroadcast(BusyFlag sv) {
                // You must own the lock in order to use this method
                if (sv.getBusyFlagOwner() != Thread.currentThread()) {
                        throw new IllegalMonitorStateException(
                                                "current thread not owner");
                }
                notifyAll();
        }
}
```

The CondVar class implements a basic condition variable for use with the BusyFlag class. There is no concept of fairness in notification. It is constructed separately from the BusyFlag class—as compared to Condition objects, which are generated from the Lock class via the newCondition( ) method. And like the BusyFlag class, the implementation doesn't attempt to minimize synchronization.

The purpose of this class is to allow Java's wait-and-notify mechanism to work with explicit locking (locks at any scope). This allows the program to have condition variable support for the BusyFlag class. It also allows a single lock to have more than one condition variable, where the wait-and-notify mechanism needs a separate object for every type of notification.

The CondVar class provides four methods for waiting for notification; three of these methods can be considered convenience methods. The primary method is the cvTimedWait( ) method. This method frees the ownership of the busy flag completely and then uses the standard wait( ) method to perform the wait. If the time to wait is zero, this method waits indefinitely for the notification. Otherwise, it uses the timeout specified. Upon returning, it grabs the lock (note that it must do that as many times as the lock was released to support the nesting semantics of our BusyFlag class). Also note that it may still wait upon receiving notification as it can still block while reacquiring the flag. In fact, that's the case with all notification-based techniques (the Condition class, the wait-and-notify mechanism); it's just in this code that you see the effect explicitly.

Two of the convenience methods allow the program to specify a timeout or wait indefinitely. The last one allows you to specify an alternate busy flag class—a flag that is different from the one specified during construction. Specifying an alternate busy flag is not a feature supported by the Condition class—a Condition instance is tightly bound to the Lock instance from which it was obtained. This feature allows notification between two groups of threads that are operating on different locks. In terms of functionality, this is a minor enhancement for a very rare need. Using the Condition class, a common Lock object could be created just for notification between the two groups of threads to achieve the same thing.

The cvSignal( ) method is used to send a single notification—using the notify( ) method. As with the wait methods, it is overloaded to allow the program to specify an alternate busy flag. The cvBroadcast( ) method is used to send notifications to all the waiting threads—using the notifyAll( ) method. It, too, is overloaded to allow the program to specify an alternate busy flag.

# The Barrier Class

Here is an implementation of the Barrier class:

```
package javathreads.examples.appa;

public class Barrier {
        private int threads2Wait4;
        private InterruptedException iex;

        public Barrier (int nThreads) {
                threads2Wait4 = nThreads;
        }

        public synchronized int waitForRest()
                        throws InterruptedException {
                        int threadNum = --threads2Wait4;

                if (iex != null) throw iex;
                if (threads2Wait4 <= 0) {
                        notifyAll();
                        return threadNum;
                }
                while (threads2Wait4 > 0) {
                        if (iex != null) throw iex;
                        try {
                                wait();
                        } catch (InterruptedException ex) {
                                iex = ex;
                                notifyAll();
                        }
                }
                return threadNum;
        }

        public synchronized void freeAll() {
                iex = new InterruptedException("Barrier Released by freeAll");
                notifyAll();
        }
}
```

The Barrier class is a basic, no-frills implementation of a barrier. Implementation of the Barrier class with the basic synchronization techniques is straightforward. We simply have each thread that arrives at the barrier (i.e., that calls the waitForRest() method) call the wait() method while the last thread to arrive at the barrier has the task of notifying all of the waiting threads. If any of the threads receives an interruption, all of the threads receive the same interruption. Another method, freeAll(), is also provided to generate an interrupt on all of the threads. As an added benefit, a thread number is assigned to the threads to help distinguish the waiting threads. The last thread to reach the barrier is assigned the value of zero, and any thread that reaches the barrier after the barrier has been released is assigned a negative value. This indicates an error condition for the thread.

This implementation of the barrier is a single-use implementation. Once the barrier reaches the thread limit as specified by the constructor, or an error is generated, the barrier no longer blocks any threads.

## The RWLock Class

Here is an implementation of the RWLock (reader/writer lock) class:

```java
package javathreads.examples.appa;

import java.util.*;

class RWNode {
        static final int READER = 0;
        static final int WRITER = 1;
        Thread t;
        int state;
        int nAcquires;
        RWNode(Thread t, int state) {
                this.t = t;
                this.state = state;
                nAcquires = 0;
        }
}

public class RWLock {
        private Vector waiters;

        private int firstWriter() {
                Enumeration e;
                int index;
                for (index = 0, e = waiters.elements();
                        e.hasMoreElements(); index++) {
                        RWNode node = (RWNode) e.nextElement();
                        if (node.state == RWNode.WRITER)
                                return index;
                }
                return Integer.MAX_VALUE;
        }

        private int getIndex(Thread t) {
                Enumeration e;
                int index;
                for (index = 0, e = waiters.elements();
                        e.hasMoreElements(); index++) {
                        RWNode node = (RWNode) e.nextElement();
                        if (node.t == t)
```

```
                    return index;
            }
            return -1;
    }

    public RWLock( ) {
            waiters = new Vector( );
    }

    public synchronized void lockRead( ) {
            RWNode node;
            Thread me = Thread.currentThread( );
            int index = getIndex(me);
            if (index == -1) {
                    node = new RWNode(me, RWNode.READER);
                    waiters.addElement(node);
            }
            else node = (RWNode) waiters.elementAt(index);
            while (getIndex(me) > firstWriter( )) {
                    try {
                            wait( );
                    } catch (Exception e) {}
            }
            node.nAcquires++;
    }
    public synchronized void lockWrite( ) {
            RWNode node;
            Thread me = Thread.currentThread( );
            int index = getIndex(me);
            if (index == -1) {
                    node = new RWNode(me, RWNode.WRITER);
                    waiters.addElement(node);
            }
            else {
                    node = (RWNode) waiters.elementAt(index);
                    if (node.state == RWNode.READER)
                            throw new IllegalArgumentException("Upgrade lock");
                    node.state = RWNode.WRITER;
            }
            while (getIndex(me) != 0) {
                    try {
                            wait( );
                    } catch (Exception e) {}
            }
            node.nAcquires++;
    }

    public synchronized void unlock( ) {
            RWNode node;
            Thread me = Thread.currentThread( );
            int index;
            index = getIndex(me);
            if (index  > firstWriter( ))
                    throw new IllegalArgumentException("Lock not held");
```

```
                    node = (RWNode) waiters.elementAt(index);
                    node.nAcquires--;
                    if (node.nAcquires == 0) {
                            waiters.removeElementAt(index);
                            notifyAll( );
                    }
            }
    }
```

The RWLock class implements a basic reader-writer lock. As with Java's ReentrantReadWriteLock class, this class is implemented in a way to prevent lock starvation.

The interface to the reader-writer lock is very simple: there's a lockRead( ) method to acquire the read lock, a lockWrite( ) method to acquire the write lock, and an unlock( ) method to release the lock. (only a single unlock( ) method is required, for reasons we'll explore in a moment). Threads that are attempting to acquire the lock are held in a waiters vector. This is to allow the RWLock class to order the requests for the purpose of preventing lock starvation. Furthermore, the Vector class is used, instead of the more recent container classes, in order to allow the reader-writer lock to be used with older versions of Java.

Because we need to keep track of how each thread wants to acquire the lock—whether it wants to acquire the read lock or the write lock—we need to create a class to encapsulate the information of the thread that made the request and the type of request it made. This is the RWNode class; our waiters vector holds elements of type RWNode.

Acquisition of the read lock is done in an orderly manner—the RWLock class doesn't just grant the read lock because another thread is also holding the read lock. In order to obtain the read lock, a thread that wants the write lock must not already be in the queue. If the nodes that are ahead of the current thread in the waiters queue want only to acquire the read lock, we can go ahead and acquire the lock. Otherwise, we must wait until all of the nodes that want to acquire the write lock—and are ahead in the waiter vector—acquire and ultimately free the lock.

Acquisition of the write lock is stricter: we must be in position zero in the vector. Only one thread may hold the write lock at a time.

This class also supports nested locks. This is accomplished by keeping track of the number of acquisitions requested. Since the read lock can be granted to multiple threads simultaneously, we can no longer use a simple instance variable (as we did in the BusyFlag class); we must associate the nAcquires count with each particular thread. Both acquisition methods must check to see if there is already a node associated with the calling thread.

This reader-writer lock class does not have the notion of "upgrading" the lock; that is, if you hold the reader lock, you can't acquire the writer lock. You must explicitly release the reader lock before you attempt to acquire the writer lock, or you receive an IllegalArgumentException. If an upgrade feature were provided, the class itself would also have to release the reader lock before acquiring the writer lock. A true upgrade is not possible due to writer lock requests or possible upgrades requests from threads that are also holding reader locks.

Finally, the reader-writer lock class contains some methods to search the waiters vector for the first node in the queue that represents a thread attempting to acquire the write lock (the firstWriter( ) method) and to find the index in the vector of the node associated with the calling thread (the getIndex( ) method). We can't use the indexOf( ) method of the Vector class for this purpose because we'd have to pass the indexOf( ) method an object of type RWNode, but all we have is a Thread object.*

## The ThreadPool Class

Here is an implementation of the ThreadPool class:

```
package javathreads.examples.appa;

import java.util.*;

public class ThreadPool {

    class ThreadPoolRequest {
        Runnable target;
        Object lock;

        ThreadPoolRequest(Runnable t, Object l) {
            target = t;
            lock = l;
        }
    }

    class ThreadPoolThread extends Thread {
        ThreadPool parent;
        boolean shouldRun = true;

        ThreadPoolThread(ThreadPool parent, int i) {
            super("ThreadPoolThread " + i);
            this.parent = parent;
        }

        public void run( ) {
            ThreadPoolRequest obj = null;
            while (shouldRun) {
                try {
                    parent.cvFlag.getBusyFlag( );
```

---

* In J2SE 5.0, that's no longer a problem, since the Vector class supports intrinsics. But in J2SE 5.0, you'll be using the ReadWriteLock class anyway.

```
                        while (obj == null && shouldRun) {
                            try {
                                obj = (ThreadPoolRequest)
                                        parent.objects.elementAt(0);
                                parent.objects.removeElementAt(0);
                            } catch (ArrayIndexOutOfBoundsException aiobe) {
                                obj = null;
                            } catch (ClassCastException cce) {
                                System.err.println("Unexpected data");
                                obj = null;
                            }
                            if (obj == null) {
                                try {
                                    parent.cvAvailable.cvWait();
                                } catch (InterruptedException ie) {
                                    return;
                                }
                            }
                        }
                    } finally {
                        parent.cvFlag.freeBusyFlag();
                    }
                    if (!shouldRun)
                        return;
                    obj.target.run();
                    try {
                        parent.cvFlag.getBusyFlag();
                        nObjects--;
                        if (nObjects == 0)
                            parent.cvEmpty.cvSignal();
                    } finally {
                        parent.cvFlag.freeBusyFlag();
                    }
                    if (obj.lock != null) {
                        synchronized(obj.lock) {
                            obj.lock.notify();
                        }
                    }
                    obj = null;
                }
            }
        }

    Vector objects;
    int nObjects = 0;
    CondVar cvAvailable, cvEmpty;
    BusyFlag cvFlag;
    ThreadPoolThread poolThreads[];
    boolean terminated = false;

    public ThreadPool(int n) {
        cvFlag = new BusyFlag();
        cvAvailable = new CondVar(cvFlag);
        cvEmpty = new CondVar(cvFlag);
```

```
        objects = new Vector( );
        poolThreads = new ThreadPoolThread[n];
        for (int i = 0; i < n; i++) {
            poolThreads[i] = new ThreadPoolThread(this, i);
            poolThreads[i].start( );
        }
    }

    private void add(Runnable target, Object lock) {
        try {
            cvFlag.getBusyFlag( );
            if (terminated)
                throw new IllegalStateException("Thread pool has shutdown");
            objects.addElement(new ThreadPoolRequest(target, lock));
            nObjects++;
            cvAvailable.cvSignal( );
        } finally {
            cvFlag.freeBusyFlag( );
        }
    }

    public void addRequest(Runnable target) {
        add(target, null);
    }

    public void addRequestAndWait(Runnable target)
                                throws InterruptedException {
        Object lock = new Object( );
        synchronized(lock) {
            add(target, lock);
            lock.wait( );
        }
    }

    public void waitForAll(boolean terminate) throws InterruptedException {
        try {
            cvFlag.getBusyFlag( );
            while (nObjects != 0)
                cvEmpty.cvWait( );
            if (terminate) {
                for (int i = 0; i < poolThreads.length; i++)
                    poolThreads[i].shouldRun = false;
                cvAvailable.cvBroadcast( );
                terminated = true;
            }
        } finally {
            cvFlag.freeBusyFlag( );
        }
    }

    public void waitForAll( ) throws InterruptedException {
        waitForAll(false);
    }
}
```

The ThreadPool class implements a thread pool—similar to the thread pool executor discussed in Chapter 10. The inner class in this example performs most of the work. Each thread waits for work; when it is signaled, it simply pulls the first object from the vector and executes the object. When execution of that object is finished, the thread must notify the lock associated with the object (if any) so that the addRequestAndWait( ) method knows when to return; the thread must also notify the thread pool itself so that the waitForAll( ) method checks to see if it is time for it to return.

As a result, this code has three waiting points :

- Some request objects have an associated lock object (the Object created in the addRequestAndWait( ) method). The addRequestAndWait( ) method uses the standard wait and notify technique to wait on this object; it receives notification after the run( ) method has been executed by one of the ThreadPoolThread objects.

- A CondVar object (i.e., a condition variable), cvAvailable, is associated with the cvBusyFlag. This condition is used to signal that work is available to be performed. Whenever the nObjects variable is incremented, work is available, so the add( ) method signals a thread that a new object is available. Similarly, when there are no objects in the vector to be processed, the ThreadPoolThread objects wait on that condition variable.

- A CondVar object, cvEmpty, is also associated with the same cvBusyFlag. This condition is used to signal that all pending work has been completed—that is, that the nObjects variable has reached zero. The waitForAll( ) method waits for this condition, which is signaled by a ThreadPoolThread when it sets nObjects to zero.

We use condition variables for the last two cases because they share the same lock (the cvBusyFlag, which protects access to nObjects) even though they have different values for their condition. If we had used the standard wait-and-notify mechanism to signal the threads that are interested in the value of nObjects, we could not have controlled notification as well: whenever nObjects was set to zero, we'd have to notify all ThreadPoolThreads as well as notifying the thread that is executing the waitForAll( ) method.

Note that objects that are to be run by the thread pool are expected to implement the Runnable interface. This is similar to the thread pool executor. This doesn't mean that a new thread is created for each task. This interface allows us to take existing code that uses threads and run those tasks via a thread pool instead.

Interestingly enough, there is no way to shut down a thread pool automatically. If the thread pool object were to go out of scope, it would never be garbage collected. The thread pool thread objects (like all thread objects) are held in an internal data structure within the virtual machine, so they are not garbage collected until they exit. And because they have a reference to the thread pool itself, the thread pool cannot be garbage collected until the thread pool threads are garbage collected. So we have to have some way of signaling the thread pool to exit: we do that by passing a true parameter to the waitForAll( ) method. Then, when the thread pool has run all of its jobs, the waitForAll( ) method arranges for the thread pool threads to terminate and marks the thread pool so that no more jobs can be added to it. The thread pool threads then exit, and the thread pool can be garbage collected.

# The JobScheduler Class

Here is an implementation of the JobScheduler class to execute a task:

```
package javathreads.examples.appa;

import java.util.*;

public class JobScheduler implements Runnable {
    final public static int ONCE = 1;
    final public static int FOREVER = -1;
    final public static long HOURLY = (long)60*60*1000;
    final public static long DAILY = 24*HOURLY;
    final public static long WEEKLY = 7*DAILY;
    final public static long MONTHLY = -1;
    final public static long YEARLY = -2;

    private class JobNode {
        public Runnable job;
        public Date executeAt;
        public long interval;
        public int count;
    }
    private ThreadPool tp;
    private DaemonLock dlock = new DaemonLock( );
    private Vector jobs = new Vector(100);

    public JobScheduler(int poolSize) {
        tp = (poolSize > 0) ? new ThreadPool(poolSize) : null;
        Thread js = new Thread(this);
        js.setDaemon(true);
        js.start( );
    }

    private synchronized void addJob(JobNode job) {
        dlock.acquire( );
        jobs.addElement(job);
        notify( );
    }

    private synchronized void deleteJob(Runnable job) {
        for (int i=0; i < jobs.size( ); i++) {
            if (((JobNode) jobs.elementAt(i)).job == job) {
                jobs.removeElementAt(i);
```

```
                    dlock.release();
                    break;
            }
        }
    }

    private JobNode updateJobNode(JobNode jn) {
        Calendar cal = Calendar.getInstance();
        cal.setTime(jn.executeAt);
        if (jn.interval == MONTHLY) {
                // There is a minor bug. (see java.util.calendar)
                cal.add(Calendar.MONTH, 1);
                jn.executeAt = cal.getTime();
        } else if (jn.interval == YEARLY) {
                cal.add(Calendar.YEAR, 1);
                jn.executeAt = cal.getTime();
        } else {
                jn.executeAt = new Date(jn.executeAt.getTime() + jn.interval);
        }
        jn.count = (jn.count == FOREVER) ? FOREVER : jn.count -1;
        return (jn.count != 0) ? jn : null;
    }

    private synchronized long runJobs() {
        long minDiff = Long.MAX_VALUE;
        long now = System.currentTimeMillis();

        for (int i=0; i < jobs.size();) {
            JobNode jn = (JobNode) jobs.elementAt(i);
            if (jn.executeAt.getTime() <= now) {
                if (tp != null) {
                    tp.addRequest(jn.job);
                } else {
                    Thread jt = new Thread(jn.job);
                    jt.setDaemon(false);
                    jt.start();
                }
                if (updateJobNode(jn) == null) {
                    jobs.removeElementAt(i);
                    dlock.release();
                }
            } else {
                long diff = jn.executeAt.getTime() - now;
                minDiff = Math.min(diff, minDiff);
                i++;
            }
        }
        return minDiff;
    }

    public synchronized void run() {
        while (true) {
            long waitTime = runJobs();
            try {
```

```
            wait(waitTime);
        } catch (Exception e) {};
    }
}

public void execute(Runnable job) {
    executeIn(job, (long)0);
}

public void executeIn(Runnable job, long millis) {
    executeInAndRepeat(job, millis, 1000, ONCE);
}

public void executeInAndRepeat(Runnable job, long millis, long repeat) {
    executeInAndRepeat(job, millis, repeat, FOREVER);
}

public void executeInAndRepeat(Runnable job, long millis,
                               long repeat, int count) {
    Date when = new Date(System.currentTimeMillis() + millis);
    executeAtAndRepeat(job, when, repeat, count);
}

public void executeAt(Runnable job, Date when) {
    executeAtAndRepeat(job, when, 1000, ONCE);
}

public void executeAtAndRepeat(Runnable job, Date when, long repeat) {
    executeAtAndRepeat(job, when, repeat, FOREVER);
}

public void executeAtAndRepeat(Runnable job, Date when,
                               long repeat, int count) {
    JobNode jn = new JobNode();
    jn.job = job;
    jn.executeAt = when;
    jn.interval = repeat;
    jn.count = count;
    addJob(jn);
}

public void cancel(Runnable job) {
    deleteJob(job);
}
}
```

The JobScheduler class implements a time-based execution system—similar to the scheduled executor discussed in Chapter 11. Like the ScheduledThreadPoolExecutor class, this class also uses a thread pool internally, allowing the tasks to execute in the separate threads within the pool. However, this class also provides the option not to use a thread pool, meaning that separate threads are started for every job. This option is useful if the job is a long-term task or for a job that runs in the background indefinitely. Assuming that the threading system doesn't get overloaded, this also allows the jobs to be executed as close to the requested time as possible.

The class is designed to be as simple—and as basic—as possible: the class just iterates over the requested jobs (the elements in the jobs vector) and either adds the jobs that need to be executed to a thread pool for processing or starts a new thread to execute the job. In addition, we need to find the time for the job that is due to run next, and wait for this time to occur. The entire process is then repeated.

For completeness, we've added a little complexity in our JobScheduler class. In addition to accepting a runnable object that can be executed and a time at which to perform the job, we also accept a count of the number of times the job is to be performed and the time to wait between executions of the job. Consequently, after a job is executed, we need to calculate whether another iteration is necessary and when to perform this iteration.

In our JobScheduler class, this is all handled by a single thread that calls the runJobs() method. The task of deciding whether the job needs to be executed again is done by the updateJobNode() method; adding jobs to and deleting jobs from the requested jobs vector is accomplished by the addJob() and deleteJob() methods, respectively. Most of the logic for the JobScheduler class is actually the implementation of the many options and methods in the interface provided for the developer.

Our JobScheduler class provides eight methods:

public void execute(Runnable job)
   Used for a job that is to be executed once; simply runs the job.

public void executeIn(Runnable job, long millis)
   Used for a job that is to be executed once; runs the job after the specified number of milliseconds has elapsed.

public void executeAt(Runnable job, Date when)
   Used for a job that is to be executed once; runs the job at the time specified.

public void executeInAndRepeat(Runnable job, long millis, long repeat)
public void executeInAndRepeat(Runnable job, long millis, long repeat, int count)
public void executeAtAndRepeat(Runnable job, Date when, long repeat)
public void executeAtAndRepeat(Runnable job, Date when, long repeat, int count)
   Used for repeating jobs. These methods run the job after the number of milliseconds specified by the millis parameter has elapsed (or at the time specified by the when parameter). They run the job again after the number of milliseconds specified by the repeat parameter has elapsed. This process is repeated as specified by the count parameter. If no count is specified, the job is repeated forever.

   The constants HOURLY, DAILY, WEEKLY, MONTHLY, and YEARLY may also be passed as the repeat parameter. The HOURLY, DAILY, and WEEKLY parameters are provided for convenience. However, the MONTHLY and YEARLY parameters are processed differently by the job scheduler since the scheduler has to take into account the different number of days in the month and the leap year.

public void cancel(Runnable job)

Cancels the specified job. No error is generated if the job is not in the requested jobs vector since it is possible that the job has executed and been removed from the vector before the cancel( ) method is called. If the same job is placed on the list more than once, this method removes the first job that it finds on the list.

As rich as the set of methods provided by this class, it can be considered weak in features by those who have used job schedulers provided by some operating systems. In those systems, developers can specify criteria such as day of the week, day of the month, week of the year, and so on. Compared to the ScheduledThreadPoolExecutor class, it is also missing some of the control features for repeating jobs.

## The DaemonLock Class

Our job scheduler class depends on the DaemonLock class. The purpose of the DaemonLock class is to allow the job scheduler to shut down gracefully. The main thread should exit without shutting down the job scheduler abruptly: if there are scheduled tasks, we want them to complete. When the job scheduler has finished all its tasks, we want the program to exit.

We accomplish this by making the threads in the job scheduler daemon threads; that way they exit when no more user threads are active. The DaemonLock class protects against premature exit: it makes sure that one user thread is active as long as the job scheduler has tasks to run.

Note that the ScheduledThreadPoolExecutor class doesn't need to use something like this class since its shutdown( ) method accomplishes a graceful shutdown.

The DaemonLock class looks like this:

```
package javathreads.examples.appa;

public class DaemonLock implements Runnable {
    private int lockCount = 0;

    public synchronized void acquire() {
        if (lockCount++ == 0) {
            Thread t = new Thread(this);
            t.setDaemon(false);
            t.start();
        }
    }
}
```

```
public synchronized void release( ) {
    if (--lockCount == 0) {
        notify( );
    }
}

public synchronized void run( ) {
    while (lockCount != 0) {
        try {
            wait( );
        } catch (InterruptedException ex) {};
    }
}
}
```

# Summary

In a way, this appendix is like a history lesson: we have just reviewed the major classes developed in the previous editions of this book. These classes have been superceded by the additions in J2SE 5.0. While the enhancements in J2SE 5.0 provide production quality support, they also make it more difficult for readers. The new classes are designed to be used, not to be educational tools—therefore, their code is written optimally rather than simply.

By reviewing these superceded classes, we accomplish two tasks. We provide edification by showing classes that are simpler to understand. We also provide tools that can be used by developers who have not yet upgraded to J2SE 5.0. For those developers, these classes, available in the online source for this book, could be used in the interim.

# Index

We'd like to hear your suggestions for improving our indexes. Send email to *index@oreilly.com*.

getStackTrace( ) method, 259
GET_STRING_REQUEST message, 224
GET_STRING_RESPONSE message, 224,
238
getter/setter pattern, 107
getThreadGroup( ) method, 246
green threads, 178
groups, 18, 245–247
guided self-scheduling, 276

## H

handleClient( ) method, 235
handleServer( ) method, 235
hard waiting lists, 130
Hashtable class, 161
hashtables, 265
heaps, 14
helper classes, 16
hierarchies, 246

## I

implementations
    scheduling, 178–183
    TCPServer class, 224
independent tasks, 9
InheritableThreadLocal class, 108
initial state, scheduling, 172
initialization of barriers, 115
initialValue( ) method, 107
inner loops, 287, 290
    testing, 303
interaction, 35–36
interchanges, loops, 285
interfaces
    ActionListener, 210
    barriers, 114
    collection classes, 153–157
    Condition, 79
    countdown latches, 115
    exchangers, 116
    executors, 188–189
    Future, 197, 216
    javax.swing.Timer class, 209
    Lock, 50–52, 122
    lock, 56
    locks, 117
    RejectedExecutionHandler, 195
    Runnable, 14, 31–35
    semaphores, 112
    stacks, 259
    Timer class, 203

Internet Explorer, 2
interpreters, 2
interrupt( ) method, 240, 247
interrupted I/O servers, 240–243
interruptible locking requests, deadlock
        detection, 135
interrupting threads, 29
inversion, 175
invokeAll( ) methods, 189
invokeAndWait( ) method, 145–147
invokeAny( ) methods, 189
invokeLater( ) method, 145–147
I/O
    asynchronous behavior, 7
    multiplexing, 8
    nonblocking, 7
    servers, 221–231
        interrupted, 240–243
        JDK 1.4, 231–240
isAlive( ) method, 25
isCoalesce( ) method, 210
isEventDispatchThread( ) method, 150
isolation, loops, 284
isRepeats( ) method, 210
isRunning( ) method, 211
isTerminated( ) method, 189
iteration, loops, 270
iterators, 161

## J

J2EE (Java 2 Enterprise Edition), 3
J2SE 5.0, 3–4, 56, 90, 183
    categories of features added to, x
    classes, 112–118
Java, 2
Java 2 Enterprise Edition (J2EE), 3
Java Specification Request (JSR), x
Java Thread class, 176
java.lang.SecurityManager class, 247–249
java.lang.ThreadGroup class, 245–247
java.lang.ThreadLocal class, 107
java.util.ArrayList (a List), 155
java.util.BitSet, 155
java.util.concurrent.ArrayBlockingQueue (a
        Queue), 156
java.util.concurrent.ConcurrentHashMap (a
        Map), 154
java.util.concurrent.ConcurrentLinkedQueue
        (a Queue), 154
java.util.concurrent.CopyOnWriteArrayList
        (a List), 154

## W

wait( ) method, 71, 202
wait trees, 126
wait-and-notify mechanism, 69
  synchronization, 71–76
waiting areas, 68–71

weakCompareAndSet( ) method, 88
webs sites, Timer class, 206
WELCOME message, 224
Windows, native threads, 179
writer locks, 111, 116
  starvation, 141

## About the Authors

**Scott Oaks** is a senior software engineer for the Java Performance Engineering group at Sun Microsystems. He has worked for Sun since 1987, specializing in many disparate technologies, from the SunOS™ software kernel to network programming and RPCs to the X Window System to threading.

He is the author of four books in the O'Reilly Java Series: *Java Security*, *Java Threads*, *Jini in a Nutshell* (also with Henry Wong), and *JXTA in a Nutshell*. Around the Internet, Mr. Oaks is best known as the author of olvwm, the OPEN LOOK window manager. He holds a B.S. in mathematics and computer science from the University of Denver and an M.S. in computer science from Brown University. Prior to joining Sun, he worked in the research division of Bear, Stearns.

In his other life, Scott enjoys music (he plays flute and piccolo with community bands in New York), cooking, theatre, and traveling with his husband, James.

**Henry Wong** is an independent consultant involved in various Java-related projects. He previously worked as a computer engineer at Sun Microsystems from 1989 to 2003. Originally hired as a consultant to help customers with special device drivers, kernel modifications, and DOS interoperability products, Henry has also worked on Solaris ports, performance-tuning projects, and multithreaded design and implementations for benchmarks and demos. Since early 1995, Henry has been involved in developing Java prototypes and supporting customers who are using Java.

In 1986, Henry joined a small software company working on SCSI device drivers, image and audio data compression, and graphics tools used for a medical information system. He earned a B.S. in chemical engineering from The Cooper Union in 1987.

When not in front of a computer, Henry is an instrument-rated private pilot who also enjoys archery, cooking, scuba diving, and traveling to different places with his wife, Nini.

## Colophon

Our look is the result of reader comments, our own experimentation, and feedback from distribution channels. Distinctive covers complement our distinctive approach to technical topics, breathing personality and life into potentially dry subjects.

The animal on the cover of *Java Threads*, Third Edition is a marine invertebrate. Invertebrates, or animals without backbones, make up over 97 percent of all animal species on the planet. Marine invertebrates are abundant in every ocean, and include such diverse species as crabs, sea cucumbers, jellyfish, starfish, urchins, anemones, and shrimps. One of the most intelligent animals in the sea, the octopus, is also an invertebrate.

Many invertebrates have protective shells to shield them from hungry, razor-toothed predators. You may think that invertebrates without shells would be particularly vulnerable, but many have developed some effective defenses. Sea anemones brandish tentacles that sting their enemies, urchins have sharp spikes that cover their entire bodies, and sea slugs just don't taste very good.

Though you may not realize it, marine invertebrates are quite beneficial to humans. For one, they constitute a huge food source. Shrimps, crabs, octopuses, clams, oysters, squids, lobsters, scallops, and crayfish are all tasty delicacies. Invertebrates are also nature's vacuum cleaners, taking in dead and discarded material and recycling it through the food chain. And after millions of years, the bodies of invertebrates settle on the sea floor and form oil deposits, a major source of the world's energy.

Matt Hutchinson was the production editor for *Java Threads*, Third Edition. Octal Publishing, Inc. provided production services. Sarah Sherman, Marlowe Shaeffer, and Claire Cloutier provided quality control.

Emma Colby designed the cover of this book, based on a series design by Edie Freedman. The cover image is a 19th-century engraving from the Dover Pictorial Archive. Emma Colby produced the cover layout with QuarkXPress 4.1 using Adobe's ITC Garamond font.

David Futato designed the interior layout. This book was converted by Joe Wizda to FrameMaker 5.5.6 with a format conversion tool created by Erik Ray, Jason McIntosh, Neil Walls, and Mike Sierra that uses Perl and XML technologies. The text font is Linotype Birka; the heading font is Adobe Myriad Condensed; and the code font is LucasFont's TheSans Mono Condensed. The illustrations that appear in the book were produced by Robert Romano and Jessamyn Read using Macromedia FreeHand 9 and Adobe Photoshop 6. This colophon was written by Matt Hutchinson.